RAF Bomber Command Squadron Profiles

138 Squadron

Other Bomber Command books from Mention the War

Striking Through Clouds – The War Diary of 514 Squadron RAF
(Simon Hepworth and Andrew Porrelli)
Nothing Can Stop Us – The Definitive History of 514 Squadron RAF
(Simon Hepworth, Andrew Porrelli and Harry Dison)
Lancasters at Waterbeach – Some of the Story of 514 Squadron
(Harry Dison)

A Short War – The History of 623 Squadron RAF
(Steve Smith)
A Stirling Effort – Short Stirling Operations at RAF Downham Market 1942-1944
(Steve Smith)

RAF Bomber Command Profiles by Chris Ward:
83 Squadron
103 Squadron (with David Fell)
106 Squadron (with Herman Bijlard)
300 (Masovian) Squadron (with Grzegorz Korcz)
617 Squadron

'…and in the morning…' Bomber Command Compendiums by Barry Hope:
57 Squadron RAF
630 Squadron RAF
514 Squadron RAF

Trusty to the End: The History of 148 (Special Duties) Squadron, 1918 – 1945
(Oliver Clutton-Brock)
A Special Duty – A Crew's Secret War with 148 (SD) Squadron
(Jennifer Elkin)
Wig's Secret War – The Biography of an SOE Air Operations Expert
(Gavin Wigginton)
Skid Row to Buckingham Palace
(Ed Greenburgh)
The Boy and the Bomber
(Francois Ydier)
The Pendulum and the Scythe
(Ken Marshall)

The above books are available through Amazon worldwide, as well as from the publisher. For further details or to purchase a signed and dedicated copy, please contact bombercommandbooks@gmail.com or visit www.bombercommandbooks.com

RAF Bomber Command Squadron Profiles

138 Squadron

by Chris Ward
with Piotr Hodyra

Bomber Command Books

From

This edition first published 2017 by Mention the War Ltd., 32 Croft Street, Farsley, Yorkshire, LS28 5HA.

Copyright 2016 © Chris Ward.

The right of Chris Ward to be identified as Author of this work is asserted by him in accordance with the Copyright, Designs and Patents Act 1988.

The original Operational Record Book of 138 Squadron and the Bomber Command Night Raid Reports are Crown Copyright and stored in microfiche and digital format by the National Archives.

All rights reserved. No part of this publication may be reproduced, stored in a retrieval system, transmitted in any form or by any means, electronic, mechanical or photocopied, recorded or otherwise, without the written permission of the copyright owners.

This squadron profile has been researched, compiled and written by its author, who has made every effort to ensure the accuracy of the information contained in it. The author will not be liable for any damages caused, or alleged to be caused, by any information contained in this book. E. & O.E.

Photographs are sourced from identified contributors wherever possible, and attributed accordingly. Some photographs are disseminated on more than one site across the internet and it has not been possible to identify the copyright owner. Where it has been deemed that there is a significant historical interest in including such photographs, and it has not been possible to attribute the original copyright owner, this has been done in good faith. Copyright owners of the original image are invited to contact the publishers in such cases. Please email mtwpublications@gmail.com.

Cover design: Topics - The Creative Partnership www.topicsdesign.co.uk

A CIP catalogue reference for this book is available from the British Library.

ISBN 978-1-911255-20-8

Contents

Introduction 7
Acknowledgements 9
Section One 11
Narrative WWII History 11
First Quarter 1941 14
July 1941 19
August 1941 21
September 1941 23
October 1941 27
November 1941 31
December 1941 39
January 1942 44
February 1942 48
March 1942 52
April 1942 63
May 1942 72
June 1942 78
July 1942 85
August 1942 89
September 1942 93
October 1942 99
November 1942 108
January 1943 116
February 1943 121
March 1943 129
May 1943 149
June 1943 158
July 1943 166
August 1943 173
September 1943 183
October 1943 191
November 1943 198
December 1943 205

January 1944	210
February 1944	216
March 1944	222
April 1944	232
May 1944	240
June 1944	248
July 1944	256
August 1944	264
September 1944	269
October 1944	275
November 1944	278
December 1944	284
January 1945	287
February 1945	289
March 1945	295
April 1945	298
Section Two	301
Stations	301
Aircraft	301
Commanding Officers	302
Operational Record	303
419 and 1419 Flights	303
138 Squadron	303
Section Three: Aircraft Histories	304
419 Flight	304
1419 Flight	304
138 Squadron	305
Glossary	311

Introduction

RAF Bomber Command Squadron Profiles first appeared in the late nineties, and proved to be very popular with enthusiasts of RAF Bomber Command during the Second World War. They became a useful research tool, particularly for those whose family members had served and were no longer around. The original purpose was to provide a point of reference for all of the gallant men and women who had fought the war, either in the air, or on the ground in a support capacity, and for whom no written history of their unit or station existed. I wanted to provide them with something they could hold up, point to and say, "this was my unit, this is what I did in the war". Many veterans were reticent to talk about their time on bombers, partly because of modesty, but perhaps mostly because the majority of those with whom they came into contact had no notion of what it was to be a "Bomber Boy", to face the prospect of death every time they took to the air, whether during training or on operations. Only those who shared the experience really understood what it was to go to war in bombers, which is why reunions were so important. As they approached the end of their lives, many veterans began to speak openly for the first time about their life in wartime Bomber Command, and most were hurt by the callous treatment they received at the hands of successive governments with regard to the lack of recognition of their contribution to victory. It is sad that this recognition in the form of a national memorial and the granting of a campaign medal came too late for the majority. Now this inspirational, noble generation, the like of which will probably never grace this earth again, has all but departed from us, and the world will be a poorer place as a result.

RAF Bomber Command Squadron Profiles are back, the basic format remaining, but, where needed, additional information has been provided. Squadron Profiles do not claim to be comprehensive histories, but rather detailed overviews of the activities of the squadron. There is insufficient space to mention as many names as one would like, but all aircraft losses are accompanied by the name of the pilot. Fundamentally, the narrative section is an account of Bomber Command's war from the perspective of the bomber group under which the individual squadron served, and the deeds of the squadron are interwoven into this story. Information has been drawn from official records, such as group, squadron and station ORBs, and from the many, like myself, amateur enthusiasts, who dedicate much of their time to researching individual units, and become unrivalled authorities on them. I am grateful for their generous contributions, and their names will appear in the appropriate Profiles. The statistics quoted in this series are taken from The Bomber Command War Diaries, that indispensable tome written by Martin Middlebrook and Chris Everitt, and I am indebted to Martin for his kind permission to use them.

Finally, let me apologise in advance for the inevitable errors, for no matter how hard I and other authors try to write "nothing but the truth", there is no such thing as a definitive account of history, and there will always be room for disagreement and debate. Official records are notoriously unreliable tools, and yet we have little choice but to put our faith in them. It is not my intention to misrepresent any person or RAF unit, and I ask my readers to understand the enormity of the task I have undertaken. It is relatively easy to become an authority on single units or even a bomber group, but I chose to write about them all, idiot that I am, which means 128 squadrons serving operationally in Bomber Command at some time between the 3rd of September 1939 and the 8th of May 1945. I am dealing with eight bomber groups, in which some 120,000 airmen served, and I am juggling around 28,000 aircraft serial numbers, code letters and details of provenance and fate. I ask not for your sympathy, it was, after all, my choice, but rather your understanding, if you should find something with which you disagree. My thanks to you, my readers, for making the original series of RAF Bomber Command Squadron Profiles so popular, and I hope you receive this new incarnation equally enthusiastically. My thanks also to Simon Hepworth of Mention The War Publications, for seeing the potential of bringing them back.

Chris Ward. Lutterworth. April 2017.

Acknowledgements

Most of the deeds of Bomber Command's war are well documented. In the main, the wartime record of each squadron's service, written with reasonable accuracy at the time, is available for scrutiny. As a result, many heroes have emerged since the end of the war, and the full extent of the various roles performed by Bomber Command's squadrons is a matter of history. There is just one exception. Such was the secrecy surrounding the activities of the moon squadrons at Gibraltar Farm, which became RAF Tempsford, that records, initially at least, were a luxury only occasionally indulged in. Brief hand-written entries allow a glimpse into this end of the Special Operations Executive, an organization, which at the highest level, was known to government departments as a set of initials with obscure accommodation addresses, and dispensed information on the strictest need-to-know basis. It was not unusual in the early days for a pilot to arrive at Tempsford on posting, only to kick his heels for days and even weeks, before being given an insight into the station's activities and his part in the grand plan.

Later on, the demand to service resistance organizations saw crews pressed into service with much greater alacrity, but the level of security never wavered. The greater one's insight into SOE and SIS matters, the more insistent becomes the question, how did they do it? In 1943 and 1944, with all the latest electronic gadgetry to hand, giant armadas of bombers were failing to find the centre of huge urban areas like Berlin, Stuttgart, Hanover, Leipzig and Nuremberg. How then, did Whitley crews in 1940 and 1941 manage to navigate to Poland, southern Germany and Austria, and find a tiny pinpoint deep in the countryside? How were Lysander pilots able to locate a specific meadow in France to deliver an agent into the hands of the waiting reception committee? Of course, such comparisons are unfair, and an over simplification of the case, but even that does not make the question go away.

When writing my first 138 Squadron Profile, in the late nineties, I referred to the works of Freddie Clark and Hugh Verity. They, having served with 138 and 161 Squadrons respectively, took the trouble to write superb books about them, which are excellent points of reference in the face of economically written official records. Freddie Clark flew from Tempsford between late January and early April 1944, and is the F/O Clark referred to in this Profile. With his unique personal insight, and contact with people "in the know", his book, Agents by Moonlight, has to stand as a definitive account of operations from Tempsford, if ever a written work of history can be described as definitive. Faced with far too many gaps in my research when writing, I approached Freddie for permission to use information from his book, and he generously agreed to help where-ever he could. Ken Merrick also wrote extensively on the subject of SOE/SIS operations, providing an excellent insight into the political manoeuvres behind the scenes. Much of the information not arising from the squadron and station ORBs, that relates to statistics, names of pilots/agents, destinations, number of sorties per night, fate of agents etc., are included through reference to these other works, for which I am very grateful.

138 Squadron has presented unique problems, as each sortie was an operation in its own right, and had to be dealt with individually. This meant that from mid 1943, as many as 170 or more sorties in some single months had to be itemised, demanding that they be reduced to short statements of detail. This does not make for enjoyable reading, but provides the necessary facts, which, to me, is more important, and, in keeping with this series generally, it is best

treated as a reference work to delve into for information relating to a specific day/night or operation.

My thanks are also due to Betty Clements, who has researched deeply into the magnificent part played in the wartime RAF by Polish airmen, and with whom I corresponded in the late nineties. For my original Profile, she kindly provided me with information from her research material about the Polish contingent in 138 Squadron, and mentioned the valuable contribution to knowledge made by Mr Kajetan Bieniecki. He has written two books on the subject, the English titles of which are; Polish Crews over Europe 1942-1945, and Poles in Special Duties Operations and Aerial support for the Polish Home Army. Kelvin Youngs, of the magnificent website *Aircrew Remembered (www.aircrewremembered.com),* has helped greatly by allowing me to reproduce a number of crew photos of those commemorated from 138 Squadron. Through Kelvin, Peter Green has kindly shared a number of photographs of the Freeland and MacFarlane crews. The writing of a wartime squadron history is something of a team effort, and, as always, I am also hugely indebted to my gang of conspirators, Andreas Wachtel, Steve Smith and Greg Korcz for their contributions. I am pleased to add a new Polish contact, Piotr Hodyra, a fellow historian, who has provided additional information on the Polish involvement with the squadron, and contributed many photographs for publication.

Section One
Narrative WWII History

The reformation of what would become 138 Squadron began in August 1941, but what might properly be viewed as its conception took place in the dark days of 1940, as Britain stood alone against the might of all-conquering Germany. The battle for air supremacy over Britain, between RAF Fighter Command and Goering's legions, was reaching a crescendo, and invasion fever gripped the nation like a vice. Prime Minister Churchill already knew, that a long war lay ahead, and that every advantage must be found, no matter how small, to thwart the enemy, until Britain and her allies had grown strong enough to take an offensive stance. Intelligence and armed resistance are vital constituents to a protracted war, and to these ends, a small group of people came together in a sparsely furnished block of offices in Baker Street, London.

The existence of the Special Operations Executive (SOE) was known only to those involved in its work, and other than to its directors, information was dispensed on a need to know basis only. Even the other services were kept in the dark, and knew it only as a set of initials at various addresses. To those who would carry out its orders, the organisation became known as the Firm. Its main objectives were as follows; to inspire in all of the occupied countries a belief in Britain and faith in victory, to organise sabotage of industrial plants and communications, to establish routes in and out of Fortress Europe, to encourage the afflicted, to harness the passion of zealots, to arm and train resistance groups, and to prepare a mighty army of patriots to rise up against the Nazis at the appointed hour. As a tiny but indispensable component of this enormous project, 419 Flight was officially formed on the 21st of August 1940 on the fighter station at North Weald, situated a few miles to the north-east of London in the Epping region of Essex. From here it would operate on behalf of the Special Operations Executive in support of resistance organisations in the occupied countries, and the Special Intelligence Service (SIS), which was otherwise known as MI6, delivering and collecting agents to and from fields in France. Operating under 11 Group Fighter Command, the new unit was commanded by F/L Farley, an experienced Hurricane pilot, who would find it difficult to restrict himself to his new role.

The very first clandestine sortie to deliver and pick up passengers in France had actually taken place with disastrous results on the night of the 17/18th of June, when an attempt had been made to rescue the family of General de Gaulle from possible capture by the advancing German army. They were waiting in the town of Carantec, situated on the northern coast of the Brest peninsular, and an amphibious Walrus, L2312, flown by a crew from 10 Squadron RAAF of Coastal Command, was sent to collect them. In the event, a navigation error, after a long flight over water on a night of poor visibility, brought the aircraft to the village of Ploudaniel, some twenty miles west-south-west of the planned destination, where an attempt was made to land in a field. The pilot, F/L Bell, had no way of knowing, that the apparently level field featured a small embankment, which caused the aircraft to nose over, break up and burst into flames, killing all on board, including a British Secret Service agent, who was to have remained in

France. The fate of the Walrus was not discovered until forty years later, and had simply been posted as missing, after it failed to return.

419 Flight's initial equipment amounted to two Lysanders, R2625 and R2626, with a further two in reserve, and these were joined within days by two Whitleys. The plan was to deliver by Whitley and collect by Lysander, but the limited range of the latter, which was ideally suited to the task of landing and taking off from an unprepared grass field, restricted the radius of pick-up operations. The first of the Whitleys to be taken on charge was P5029, a brand new aircraft minus guns and a radio, and, on the night of its arrival, F/O Jackie Oettle, who was something of a character, and had just been posted in as the official Whitley pilot, took it on the unit's maiden sortie. Some guns had been found and installed, but there was still no radio as they collected an agent from Tangmere, and dropped him by parachute into the French countryside near Paris. The NCO members of the unit referred to Agents as Joes or Joe Soaps, which was slang for someone who had been handed a rotten job, and, while having great respect and admiration for them, they did their best to remain detached.

On the night of the 28/29th of August, Oettle, who always flew in his great coat, delivered a Dutch naval officer to Holland without the services of a reception committee, but this man soon fell into enemy hands and was executed in the following summer. The Luftwaffe's assault on Fighter Command airfields led to a number of attacks on North Weald, and 419 Flight was consequently relocated on the 3rd of September to Stapleford Tawney, a satellite field five miles to the south, where accommodation was initially of the canvas variety. Some people spent their days-off playing golf or generally relaxing, F/L Farley, on the other hand, reputedly spent his flying Hurricanes in the Battle of Britain on behalf of 46 and 151 Squadrons, the airfield's other resident units. F/L Keast was posted in from Hendon with 3,500 hours in his log book, and was to train as the Flight's second Whitley pilot. Just two further Whitley sorties would be carried out from the new home before a further move took place. P/O Oettle took P5025 to Tangmere on the evening of the 13th of September, where he collected two agents and delivered them to the Brest region of France. The reserve Lysanders, R9025 and T1508, arrived on the 18th and 25th respectively, before the final operation from Stapleford Tawney took place on the 9th of October, the day on which the Flight began moving to Stradishall, a bomber station in the county of Suffolk, a dozen miles or so south of Newmarket and Bury St Edmunds. From this point until the end of the war, 138 Squadron and its antecedents would remain under the control of 3 Group Bomber Command. At 10.00 that morning, P/O Oettle flew P5029 to Abingdon, to collect agent Philip Schneidau, and delivered him that night, along with two pigeons, to the Fontainebleau region of France, south of Paris.

P/O Greenhill was posted in as a Lysander pilot, apparently with no experience on Whitleys, and, at 18.43 on the evening of the 11th, while the new arrivals were still in process of settling in to their new home, he wrote off P5025 in a landing crash on the edge of the airfield to register the unit's first casualty. Forgetting that he was not in a Lysander, he overshot the approach and stalled, but, fortunately, cuts and bruises were the only injuries reported, and P/O Greenhill departed the Flight shortly afterwards. F/L Keast undertook his first sortie on the night of the 12/13th, when flying to Belgium as second pilot to P/O Oettle. The first Lysander operation, to pick up the agent Philip Schneidau, was delayed by bad weather conditions until the night of the 20/21st. It had been scheduled for Saturday the 19th, and F/L Farley flew down to Tangmere in R9027 to make ready. The rear cockpit of the Lysander had been removed to facilitate a speedy embarkation, and the Fairfield Aviation Company had fitted a small ladder to the fuselage. Schneidau released his pigeons on the Sunday morning, and they arrived safely in London with their messages. The weather was still appallingly bad as F/L Farley departed Tangmere for the rescheduled pick-up, and rain entering the open rear fuselage shorted out the radio. The weather had cleared by the time he reached the target area, and the L-shaped light formation was clearly identified, allowing all, initially, to proceed according to plan. However, shortly after departing the French field, he sensed that something was interfering with free movement of the elevator. As he was attempting to clear the problem, a rifle bullet smashed the compass between his legs, and this problem was compounded by a fresh wave of bad weather, which closed in on them on the way home. Farley was forced to fly above it at 16,000 feet, and, without compass or radio, set a rough course towards Tangmere, hoping for a break in the cloud to enable him to pinpoint his whereabouts. This was not forthcoming, and, in the face of a gale from the south-west, there was a danger of being pushed northwards. By 06.30 the fuel tank gauge registered empty, but they remained airborne for a further twenty minutes, until cliffs were spotted and the fuel finally became exhausted. Farley put down in a field festooned with pine posts, wrecking the Lysander, but without injury to himself or his passenger. They had actually come down in Scotland, and had the fuel lasted much longer, they would almost certainly have been lost in the Atlantic.

The threat of invasion had, meanwhile, diminished, following the Luftwaffe's heavy defeat on the 15th of September, but Bomber Command maintained its offensive against the occupied ports, where the fleets of marine invasion craft had been assembled. Whitley, T4264, was taken on charge on the 5th of November as a replacement for the wrecked P5025. P/O Oettle and F/L Keast tried to deliver a Gaullist agent to the Morlaix region of unoccupied France on the night of the 14/15th, but he refused to jump, and was brought home. An operation to Holland took place on the 19/20th, and Belgium was the destination for another on the night of the 21/22nd. F/O Hockey was posted to 419 Flight during the final week of November, and, like F/L Keast, he came from 24 Communications Squadron at Hendon, where he had spent much of the war to date transporting VIPs. Shortly after his arrival he was hospitalized with exhaustion, and would play no further part in the Flight's activities until the following March. From then on, his contribution to SOE and SIS operations would be enormous, but for the time being, all Whitley sorties were conducted with F/O Oettle as captain and F/L Keast as second pilot. The manpower situation was further compromised during December by the loss of F/L Farley, who was shot down in a Hurricane while on leave, and broke a leg. He, too, would return in time. The Oettle/Keast combination was active again on the night of the 10/11th of December and again twenty-four hours later, suggesting, perhaps, that the first occasion had been unsuccessful. The planned delivery of an agent to Poland on the 20th was cancelled, possibly because of the prevailing weather conditions, which were most unfavourable. By year's end, 419 Flight had successfully completed ten Whitley operations to France, Belgium and Holland, delivering an agent on all but a couple of occasions, and there had been just the one Lysander operation previously mentioned.

First Quarter 1941

A second successive harsh winter provided inhospitable weather conditions at the start of the year, and F/O Oettle was forced to abandon a sortie to France in P5029 on the night of the 4/5th of January. Five nights later, he reached his briefed destination of Brussels, but was diverted to Honington on return because of the weather conditions. On the night of the 10/11th, a nine-hour trip to the south of France also ended with a diversion, this time to Digby, and, two nights later, an attempt was made to deliver an agent to Belgium. Oettle flew to Marham on the 13th in preparation for the next sortie, but this was cancelled. Further operations to France were carried out on the nights of the 16/17th and 18/19th, the latter with F/L Keast acting as captain for the first time.

Meanwhile, back at Bomber Command HQ, the recently installed C-in-C, AM Sir Richard Peirse, received a new Air Ministry directive on the 15th, which alluded to a critical period for the enemy's oil situation over the next six months. A list of seventeen synthetic oil production sites was drawn up, the top nine of which represented 80% of Germany's domestic output, and Peirse was to concentrate the bulk of his resources against them. It would be February before he could implement his orders, and as he was to discover, frequently changing priorities would make it difficult to fulfil the often unrealistic expectations of his masters. Whitley Z6473 was taken on charge on the 10th, and F/L Keast flew a further sortie to France that night, and another on the night of the 13/14th, before undertaking the unit's longest flight yet, to deliver three Polish agents to their homeland on the night of the 15/16th. Operation ADOLPHUS was carried out in Z6473, which was fitted with additional fuel tanks inside the fuselage. The three agents, Messrs Krzymowski, Zabielski and Raczkowski, were to be delivered to the Krakow region of southern Poland, close to the Czech border, which represented an 1,800-mile round trip from Stradishall. In the event, and due to a navigational error, they parachuted sixty miles inside German-occupied territory, where they were fortunate to meet up with fellow Poles, who helped them to reach their intended destination, but without their containers, which could not be retrieved. The Whitley landed back at base after a trip lasting eleven hours and twenty minutes, and Keast's passengers would later exonerate the crew from any blame for the navigational error in the most difficult of weather conditions.

Although probably somewhat weary, F/L Keast was called into action again on the night of the 17/18th, to transport an SIS agent to Namur in Belgium. On the way home at 200 feet, having just dropped the agent and released leaflets as a cover, T4264 was hit by flak and lost an engine. The other engine failed shortly afterwards through a coolant leak, and the Whitley was put down on its belly on the edge of a wood without serious injury to the occupants. Keast and his crew were soon in enemy hands, however, having been given away by locals, and were interrogated for five days, before spending the rest of the war behind barbed wire, ultimately in a Russian prison camp. They were the first to fail to return from an SOE/SIS operation.

With a heavy schedule of sixteen sorties planned for March, the manpower situation was now critical, with Farley and Hockey in hospital, and Keast and crew on extended leave in Germany. Fortunately, the cavalry, in the form of S/L Knowles, rode over the crest of the hill to save the day. He was appointed as the new commanding officer, and would be joined over the ensuing weeks by an experienced new Lysander pilot, F/O Scotter, who was still only twenty-one years old. South African F/L Jackson was also added to the strength, while two replacement Whitleys, T4166 and T4165 were acquired from 4 Group's 78 Squadron on the 1st and 15th respectively. T4166 had been modified for the first ever operation by X Troop, an organisation which would ultimately evolve into the SAS. Six Whitleys had been employed to deliver them to the Tragino aqueduct in Italy on the night of the 10/11th of February, for Operation Colossus, while two others carried out a diversionary raid on Foggia. Not all of the men and equipment was dropped into the correct location, and the raid was only partially successful. All of the soldiers were captured, but the Whitleys made it home, providing 1419 Flight with the unexpected bonus. Gordon Scotter had been a Lysander pilot since joining 2 Army Co-operation Squadron back in January 1939, and he would prove to be a very valuable acquisition. He was to remain with 1419 Flight and its successor, 138 Squadron, until being posted briefly to the sister "Moon" Squadron, 161, in May 1942. The nature of clandestine operations called for special characteristics among the pilots, and it seems that this was taken into consideration when selecting new recruits from the RAF generally. Another arrival in March was F/O Alan "Sticky" Murphy, an outstanding athlete, who represented the RAF in both track and field events before the war, and set a long-standing long jump record. He had spent most of the war to date training others, and he too would serve with both "Moon" Squadrons.

On the 9th of March, Peirse received a new Air Ministry directive, which was issued in response to the mounting losses of shipping to U-Boats in the Atlantic. For the next four months, the main focus of attention was to be upon the shipyards of northern Germany, the French ports being used as U-Boat bases, and the factories engaged in producing components and assemblies for U-Boats and their partner in crime, the long-range maritime reconnaissance bomber, the Focke-Wulf Kondor. As a distraction to this, although in keeping with the maritime theme, the German cruisers Scharnhorst and Gneisenau would take up residence at Brest at the end of March, and remain there almost without break until the following February. Throughout this time, Bomber Command would expend much energy and effort in trying to destroy them, and sacrifice many crews in the process.

The French agent, Philip Schneidau, who had been Farley's passenger during the incident-packed single Lysander sortie to date, parachuted back into the Fontainebleau region of France on the night of the 10/11th from a Whitley captained by F/O Oettle. On the following night, F/O Oettle set off for Czechoslovakia in T4166, but decided to turn back three hours after take-off, when it became clear, that daylight would return before he did. S/L Knowles took off in Z6473 on the evening of the 12th, to undertake his first operation since joining the unit. F/O Oettle continued to carry the burden of fulfilling the Flight's obligations with further sorties on the 13/14th and 14/15th, on the latter occasion delivering a parachute company of five men to France. Their brief was to assassinate crews belonging to the Luftwaffe Pathfinder unit, Kampfgeschwader 100, which guided the enemy bomber force to its targets in Britain from its station at Meucon, near Vannes on the southern edge of the Brest peninsular. They travelled by bus during off-duty jaunts, which left them vulnerable to attack, and their removal would require the Germans to train up new crews to "fly the beams" of the Knickebein guidance system, which would take time. The drop was covered by an RAF attack on the airfield, but, unfortunately, the assassins and their two containers of arms and specially designed road trap to disable the bus, landed five miles from the intended drop zone, and it was learned on the following day, that the crews were now using cars for their trips out anyway, which rendered the operation impractical.

During the course of the month, 419 Flight became 1419 Flight, to prevent confusion arising out of the numbering of Commonwealth units in the 400 series. F/O Hockey returned to duty on the 13th. This was the day after the Command delivered the first of two effective attacks on Hamburg in line with the recent directive, inflicting damage on the Blohm & Voss shipyard, while a second force landed some high explosive bombs on the Focke-Wulf factory at Bremen. F/O Hockey had experience on a vast range of aircraft types, and to him was entrusted the task of evaluating the Martin Maryland's suitability for SOE/SIS operations. There had been talk for some time of the Flight being given one, and AR718, which had been part of an order by the French, but had not reached them before the signing of the armistice, duly arrived at Stradishall, where Hockey took it for the first of forty-three trials flights on the 31st. The British had taken over the French contract, and the type had been in use for photo-reconnaissance, in which role, its speed was useful. Hockey would fly the aircraft on extensive tests until the 23rd of October, which demonstrated it to be totally unsuitable for special duties operations. Among its faults for the role were too long a nose, which masked the ground ahead during landing, static lines fouling flying controls, crew positions physically inaccessible to each other, with communication only by R/T, propellers prone to snapping into fine pitch, and instruments reflecting onto the windscreen at night.

Second Quarter 1941

F/O Hockey participated in his first sortie since joining the unit, when flying to Belgium as second pilot to F/L Jackson in P5029 on the night of the 8/9th of April. On the following day, he took two French agents up for parachute practice over the airfield, and one was killed after his canopy failed to deploy. On the following night, the 10/11th, F/O Oettle loaded his crew and six Polish soldiers into T4165 and set off from Tangmere for Bordeaux on Operation JOSEPHINE. Their brief was to destroy the Pessac power station, south-west of the city, but while crossing the Loire outbound, and still some 150 miles short of the target area, a fault in the electrical circuitry caused two containers of arms and explosives to be prematurely released, and the sortie had to be abandoned. During the landing attempt at Tangmere, and as a result of a shift in the centre of gravity, which was caused by too much weight towards the rear, the Whitley stalled in a nose-up attitude and crashed, before catching fire. The rear gunner and observer were killed, while F/O Oettle, second pilot, P/O Wilson and the wireless operator sustained injuries, which put them in hospital. It seems, however, that the passengers emerged shaken, but more or less unscathed.

F/O Scotter flew only the unit's second Lysander sortie on the night of the 11/12th, to pick up a Lieutenant "Cartwright" from a field in France, between Levroux and Brion, a few miles to the north of Chateauroux. After a testing time, during which he became lost, was shadowed by enemy night fighters carrying searchlights, landed on a horribly rutted field, and got away again just as a Gestapo car was bearing down on the location, he and his passenger returned safely to Tangmere, to find it under attack. He was forced to stooge around for a time, before landing without lights, and was rewarded for his tenacity with an immediate DFC. The final operation of April's moon period took F/L Jackson and his crew to Belgium in mid month, from where they returned safely, despite the attentions of flak and searchlights.

Two new Whitleys, Z6727 and Z6728, arrived on the 3rd of May, in time for the new moon period, which began with two sorties by the type on the night of the 5/6th. F/L Jackson set out in T4166 to return to Belgium with F/O Hockey as second pilot, but they were defeated by icing conditions, and had to abandon their sortie. Meanwhile, S/L Knowles took off on Operation BOMBPROOF, to deliver the very first F Section (French Section) SOE operative into his homeland. Georges Bégué, also known as George Noble, was dropped without a reception committee twenty miles north of Chateauroux with a wireless set, which he used to make contact with SIS by the 9th. Jackson and Hockey suffered further frustration when attempting their drop again on the following night, before eventually succeeding on the night of the 9/10th, despite experiencing engine trouble. S/L Knowles delivered two more agents to France on the night of the 10/11th, during the course of which sortie, they were intercepted by a ME110 north of le Mans. The rear gunner poured a five-second burst into it, and watched it explode and crash. F/O Scotter picked up Phillip Schneidau in the Lysander on the night of the 11/12th, under cover of a Hurricane night intruder operation against local Luftwaffe airfields. That, and a light bombing raid in the general area, stirred up some night fighter activity, and they were followed by an enemy aircraft for a time, without an attack ensuing. A new Whitley, Z6727, arrived early in May, and this was used by Hockey and Jackson, also on the 11/12th, to drop three French saboteurs, including Roger Cottin, west of Bordeaux to join Georges Bégué.

F/O Hockey undertook the unit's final sortie of the moon period, with a trip to Vannes on the night of the 13/14th. A new Lysander, T1770 was taken on charge on the 15th.

On the 22nd, 1419 Flight completed its move to the well-known racecourse site at Newmarket, ten miles north-west of Stradishall, which had been turned into a satellite airfield. Its layout provided it with the longest grass runways in the RAF, while the jockeys' weighing room and the cellars beneath the grandstand served as the Flight's HQ and offices. The stables were also pressed into service to provide accommodation. It was around this time, that another of the war's great characters joined the unit as a Whitley/Lysander pilot. F/L "Whippy" Nesbitt-Dufort would become something of a legend, if, indeed, he had not already achieved that status. He acquired the "Whippy" appellation pre-war, while returning from the Hendon Air Pageant, where he and others had thrilled the crowds with their aerobatic skill and daring. Sudden engine failure over Bedfordshire had him scouring the terrain below for a suitable landing ground, and an unbelievably flat and inviting area of green presented itself. He pulled off a perfect landing, and while congratulating himself on his deliverance, noticed a rhinoceros moving in his direction, head lowered. It was at this point, that a number of lions reputedly came to his attention, but he managed to beat all-comers to the fence. Here, he learned that he had landed in the grounds of Whipsnade Zoo, with which he would forever, thereafter, be associated. Posted in at the same time as "Whippy" was another new Whitley pilot, Sgt Austin.

June's operations were condensed into three consecutive nights from the 11/12th to the 13/14th. S/L Knowles, Sgt Austin and F/O Hockey were the pilots on the first occasion, the last named flying his first sortie as captain, with F/L Jackson alongside. Not one of the three sorties to France was concluded successfully, but Knowles and Austin tried again on the night of the 13/14th, and carried out their assigned tasks. In between, on the 12/13th, and after three previous failed attempts, Sgt Austin delivered two containers to a location ten miles east of Limoges, in what was the first of almost sixty thousand drops to SOE circuits in France over the ensuing three and a half years. The operation, on behalf of the Ventriloquist circuit of Philippe de Vomecourt, was not without its difficulties, after an electrical fault delayed the drop of the second container for an hour, and attracted the attention of the local police, who were eventually persuaded that all was in order.

July 1941

July brought a small increase in activity, and an improvement in the sortie success ratio. On the night of the 4/5th, F/O Hockey and F/L Jackson repeated the operation to France aborted through bad weather in June, and this time achieved success. Sgt Austin was also aloft on this night over Holland, while Hockey and Jackson went in vain to Belgium on the following night, with an additional crew member in the form of F/L Romanoff, a member of the Russian royal dynasty, and cousin of the assassinated Tsar Nikolas. There is some confusion as to which crew was carrying the two-man team of Labit and Cartigny to Normandy on Operation TORTURE, a reconnaissance for a future operation, but it is believed that S/L Knowles was the pilot. Cartigny was captured and eventually executed, while Labit escaped, and was successful in setting up his own circuit. It was Sgt Austin's turn to operate over Belgium on the night of the 6/7th, and Hockey and Jackson took the unit's new Whitley, Z6727, to France on the night of the 7/8th. Engine trouble eventually forced the abandonment of the sortie, and would soon cause the demise of the aircraft. On the night of the 7/8th, Sgt Austin completed the operation to Belgium attempted by Hockey and Jackson two nights earlier, and S/L Knowles returned from a successful drop in the Limoges area.

When F/O Hockey took off from Tangmere for France on the night of the 9/10th, F/L Romanoff was again beside him as an unofficial second pilot. It was the second time he had flown with Hockey, but, sadly, he was destined to lose his life serving with the unit in the following March. It seems that the operation was unsuccessful, but as a small consolation, Sgt Austin was at least able to deliver two parachutists into France on the same night. F/L Jackson had just been cleared to operate as crew captain, and did so for the first time twenty-four hours later, when re-flying the Hockey/Romanoff sortie. Z6473 suffered the failure of an engine during take-off for France on the evening of the 12th, but F/O Hockey was able to maintain control and land safely. It had been a successful moon period, with ten completed sorties out of twelve attempted. Whatever the engine problem afflicting Z6727, it struck again on the 25th, during the testing of secret equipment. F/L Jackson was unable to maintain height, and the Whitley collided with a telegraph pole before crashing at 15.25 close to the airfield. The crew of four and four technicians emerged more or less unscathed from the wreckage, but the Whitley was a write-off.

Bomber Command's performance, taken as a whole at this time, was showing less promise, and the small-scale goings-on in SOE/SIS matters represented a bright spot known only to those involved. June and July were significant months for the Command, which had now come under the close scrutiny of civil servant Mr D M Butt. He had been commissioned to analyse the effectiveness of night operations over Germany by studying thousands of bombing photographs, and in due course he would deliver his report to the War Cabinet. Meanwhile, a new Air Ministry directive issued to C-in-C Peirse on the 9th of July signalled an end to the maritime diversion, and a full return to targets in Germany. It was now considered that the enemy's transportation system and the morale of its civilian population were weak points, and Peirse was ordered to concentrate his main thrust in these directions. A new list of targets was drawn up, which featured the major railway centres ringing the industrial Ruhr. Their destruction would inhibit the import of raw materials and components, and reduce the export of finished war related products. They were, however, precision targets, and would require attacks to be carried out in conditions of moonlight. On moonless nights, the Rhine cities of Cologne, Duisburg and Düsseldorf would be easier to locate, while, in generally unfavourable weather, the more distant cities in northern, eastern and southern Germany would provide the objectives.

August 1941

August began for 1419 Flight with trips to Belgium on the night of the 3/4th for F/O Hockey and Sgt Austin, with F/L Nesbitt-Dufort acting as second pilot to the former. Both operations failed, and would be re-attempted later in the month. On the night of the 5/6th, F/O Hockey went to France, and blooded another new Whitley pilot, Sgt Reimer, while on the following night, Sgt Austin dropped a pair of agents into Vichy France. Hockey had "Sticky" Murphy alongside him on night of the 12/13th, when they completed the operation to France, that had been aborted through engine trouble on the 7/8th of July. Meanwhile, on the same night, Sgt Austin re-flew the month's earlier Belgium trips, and this time succeeded in delivering his cargoes. The moon period ended with Sgt Reimer flying a complicated operation to France and Belgium involving four dropping zones, and S/L Knowles carrying out two sorties over Belgium. "Sticky" Murphy operated over France without the aid of the moon on the night of the 20/21st, and this proved to be the final sortie conducted by the unit under its 1419 Flight title.

A few days earlier, on the 18th, the Butt Report was released, and its revelations sent shock waves reverberating around the Cabinet Room and the Air Ministry. Having studied around four thousand photographs taken on a hundred night raids over the previous two months, the author concluded that only a tiny fraction of bombs were falling within five miles of their intended targets. This swept away at a stroke any notion, that Bomber Command was having a materiel effect on Germany's capacity to wage war, and showed its claims of success to be little more than propaganda. Not only did this provide the Command's critics with ample ammunition in their calls for the dissolution of an independent bomber force, and the distribution of its aircraft to other theatres of operation, it also forever unjustly blighted the period of tenure as C-in-C of Sir Richard Peirse.

There had been discussions in senior circles for some time about raising the Flight to full squadron status, and, on the 25th, 1419 Flight became 138 Squadron, the number it would carry proudly until the end of the war. It was assigned the code letters NF for its complement of six Whitleys and four Lysanders. S/L Knowles remained in command, but was promoted to wing commander, with F/L Jackson and S/L Nesbitt-Dufort as A Flight (Whitleys) and B Flight (Lysanders) commanders respectively. The newly commissioned P/O Austin had earlier been officially re-posted to the squadron along with P/O Smith, but the hand written entries in the ORB suggest that these movements predate the formation of the squadron. P/O Widdup arrived from 10 O.T.U. on the 31st, by which time 138 Squadron had carried out its first operation. At 20.35 on the 29th, Z6473 took off at 20.33 on Operation TROMBONE, with F/O Hockey at the controls, and S/L "Pick" Pickard as second pilot. Pickard was already a legend, and, indeed, a film star, having acted as the pilot of F-Freddie in the 1941 morale-boosting feature film, Target for Tonight. His reputation within Bomber Command did not, of course, rely on his acting ability, but rather on his outstanding record of operational service, which began with 99 Squadron at Newmarket at the outbreak of war. He moved on to command a newly formed Czechoslovakian unit, 311 Squadron, and it was during this period that he worked on the film. Afterwards, he was appointed as a flight commander with 9 Squadron, and it was at the conclusion of this tour in early August, that "Pick" was posted to 3 Group HQ at Exning with sixty-five sorties to his credit. Apparently taking advantage of a spot of leave, he called in at Newmarket to visit his friend F/O Hockey, and quickly accepted the offer of a job.

The pair successfully delivered their cargo at 23.52 from 500 feet to a location near Châteauroux, and returned safely after almost eight hours in the air. On the last night of the month, "Pick" flew as second pilot to New Zealander, F/L McGilivary, on a most unusual operation, which is not recorded in the ORB. The aircraft was a Wellington borrowed from 214 Squadron based at Stradishall, presumably because of a shortage of serviceable Whitleys, and its cargo was six 250lb bombs and half a million cigarettes, the latter for the benefit of the unfortunate Dutch people under occupation. This concluded Pickard's involvement with special duties for the time being, but he would return in October 1942 to command 138's sister squadron, 161, which would be formed early in the coming year. In the meantime, he was posted to the command of 4 Group's 51 Squadron, and would lead the famous Bruneval operation, in which commandos were successfully parachuted onto an enemy radar station on the French coast. They dismantled the equipment, captured an operator, and returned safely home, enabling British scientists to examine a working example of German radar technology. Sadly, the larger-than-life Pickard was not destined to survive the war, losing his life in a Mosquito during the 2 TAF's famous and audacious attack on the walls of Amien prison in February 1944.

September 1941

A number of sorties were carried out on the night of the 2/3rd of September, beginning with F/L Jackson taking off at 20.00 on Operation ADJUDICATE, to be followed twenty-seven minutes later by W/C Knowles on Operation GLASSHOUSE, and, finally, by P/O Austin on Operation PORTER at 20.45. W/C Knowles set course for Terschelling in the Dutch Frisians, but ten-tenths cloud persuaded him to abandon his sortie and return home. F/L Jackson headed for the Normandy coast, in an attempt to complete an operation that had been aborted three times before. He crossed the French coast at 21.44 at 5,000 feet over Grandcamp, in the vicinity of what would become the Omaha and Utah landing grounds on D-Day, picked up the River Loire, and followed it to Limoges in west-central France, which he reached shortly after midnight. It would take a further ninety minutes to find the drop zone in poor visibility, and deliver Count Dziergowski as the first Polish agent to attempt to set up a sabotage organization in the country, utilizing some of the four thousand former Polish troops living there. Sadly, the count fell into trees and was badly injured, a detail unknown to F/L Jackson, who made a safe return after more than eight hours aloft. Ultimately, Dziergowski would recover, and recruit eighty-seven operatives to form small sabotage cells. Meanwhile, P/O Austin watched his agents drop away at 00.05, observing their parachutes to open, but nothing was seen of them on the ground. Course was then set for Bruges to release pigeons, but the weather was unsuitable, and they were brought home to land at 02.50. It was the same again for P/O Austin on the following night, when Operation CONJUGAL took him once more to Belgium, flying all the way over ten-tenths cloud, until reaching Courtrai, where the skies cleared, and the agents were delivered shortly afterwards at 22.35 in fine conditions. Thereafter, the weather closed in again, and the pigeons were brought home.

It was on the night of the 4/5th of September, that 138 Squadron mounted its first Lysander operation. The honour fell upon S/L Nesbitt-Dufort, who spent the afternoon at Tangmere, where the Lysander Flight was based, studying maps and meteorological reports. Agents, or "Joes", were accommodated at Tangmere Cottage prior to departure, the length of their stay dictated by the weather. On this night all seemed well, and Whippy's passenger, a Monsieur Morel, actually Major Morel, was driven to the rendezvous with the already run-up aircraft at its dispersal. After brief introductions he climbed aboard, and immersed himself in his private thoughts, while Whippy set about the exacting task of getting him to the appointed field in France, where he was to collect a returning agent, Major de Geulis. They took off at 20.52, and crossed the French coast at 21.35 at 9,000 feet, blissfully unaware that matters were going horribly awry outside of a hotel in a town about ten miles from the pick-up point. Having settled their bill, the agent and his colleague walked out onto the street, to be immediately confronted by a policeman, who asked to see their identification papers. Not entirely satisfied, the policeman invited them to accompany him to the police station, where the duty sergeant took an interminably long time to examine the documents, before pronouncing them to be in order. This delay had not been built into the schedule, and not only had the men to reach the landing field, they had also to place three flares in the inverted "L" configuration before the pilot would risk landing. They raced back to the hotel to collect their bicycles, and pedalled for all their worth towards the landing field.

Whippy pinpointed on the River Loire, and continued on in fine visibility, until reaching the landing zone, where no lights were visible. He began circling at 23.15, as down below, the cyclists were covering the final stretch, and could hear Whippy's Lysander circling above the field. Whippy and Major Morel were straining their eyes for the glimmer of light confirming that the reception committee was in place. It wasn't, but the panting and sweating cyclists leapt off their bikes and scrambled into the nearest field to lay their torches, desperately hoping that the pilot had not abandoned them, and that the unexamined field held no hidden obstacles. A few minutes later, the Lysander reappeared, and dropped in over the boundary hedge for a successful if uncomfortable landing on the bumpy surface. Whippy taxied back, disgorged his passenger, gaining a new one almost in the same instant, and was immediately into his take-off run. As the Lysander climbed over the hedge, it snagged high-tension cables and telephone wires, causing a sudden, violent jolt, which almost arrested its flight, but Whippy maintained control, setting course for England with a few metres of telephone wire trailing behind him.

A number of sorties were launched on the night of the 6/7th, beginning at 20.05 with the departures of F/L Jackson on Operation STUDENT, and F/L Murphy on Operation FELIX/DASTARD, which were both subsequently abandoned through unfavourable weather conditions. "Sticky" Murphy, who was in a Lysander, reported ten-tenths cloud with a base at 1,000 feet, which forced him to climb to 7,000 feet over the Channel. Pinpointing over France proved to be impossible, although, he did find a formation of lights, which he circled, before feeling a bump at the rear of the aircraft. He decided to turn back, and, on landing, discovered damage to the tail-wheel spat. Meanwhile, Sgt Reimer had taken off at 20.15 in Whitley Z6728 with six agents on board, to deliver to a location near Tours in France under Operations DRAFTSMAN/AUTOGYRO/DOWNSTAIRS/VESTIGE, combined with Operations TROPICAL and UKULELE. He crossed the English coast south of Tangmere at 21.22, but was unable to pinpoint on the French coast because of the cloud cover. He assumed that he made landfall over France close to Caen some fifty minutes later, and continued on over ten-tenths cloud until reaching the Tours area, where breaks allowed glimpses of the ground. He found a reception committee awaiting his arrival, and watched the parachutes of all six agents open, establishing, before he set course for home, that all were safely on the ground.

The hectic start to the month continued on the night of the 7/8th, with three Whitley sorties, two to France and the other to Holland. F/L Jackson took off at 20.08 to retrace the previous night's steps, and crossed the French coast near Berck-sur-Mer, noting intense flak from Boulogne some twenty miles to the north, where a Bomber Command attack was in progress. Visibility was excellent, and he experienced no difficulty in locating his target area, and completing the drop from 500 feet at 22.50, before turning east and commencing pigeon drops in the Valenciennes region of northern France. F/O Hockey and Whippy Nesbitt-Dufort, meanwhile, were engaged in a long range drop to the Pyrenees under Operation FENGLER, and had taken off first, in Z6473, at 20.00. They crossed the French coast at 21.53, and reached the River Loire at 23.00, with a further two hours flying time ahead of them before the drop zone was reached. Toulouse passed underneath at 00.53, and the drop zone, south of Carcassonne, was reached twenty-two minutes later. They turned for home at 01.20, and landed at St Eval in Cornwall five hours and forty minutes later with fuel tanks almost dry after eleven hours in the air. Finally, on this night, P/O Austin had taken off at 20.15 on Operation GLASSHOUSE, and crossed the Norfolk coast at Cromer, heading for the Dutch Frisian island of Terschelling. Within minutes he observed a light on the water, which turned out to be a dinghy, whereupon he transmitted an SOS message, which was received by the Hull radar station. He circled the dinghy until help arrived, and then continued on his journey at 22.55, reaching his pinpoint near Zwolle in fine weather conditions. The agents dropped away at 23.32, their parachutes observed to open, and the crew believed them to have arrived safely on the ground.

Two nights later, the Hockey/Nesbitt-Dufort combination was sent on another long range trip, this time to Denmark under Operation ESMOND/COLUMBUS. They took off at 20.00 in T4166, with Lt Sneum on board and a wireless operator by the name of Christoffersen. They flew through cloud and heavy rain all the way to the target area, which they reached at 10,000 feet, before admitting defeat. They turned for home, and eventually landed at Leuchars in Scotland after nine hours aloft, fog having denied them access to stations nearer home. Similar conditions hampered operations on the night of the 10/11th, and kept two of the three aircraft involved airborne for between ten and eleven hours. P/O Austin took off on Operation BARTER at 19.45, and headed for the French coast, where he failed to obtain a fix, but found one at Chinon in north-western France at 00.30. The reception committee consisted of two fires and flashes by torch, and the two agents dropped away safely at 00.40, and were seen to be standing on the ground. Initial task completed, he flew on southwards for a further 130 miles to deliver leaflets to the Perigueux area, east of Bordeaux, before turning for home, pinpointing on Brighton, and landing at Newmarket after eleven hours and five minutes aloft. F/L Jackson was airborne for ten and a half hours, when engaged on Operation SARDINE. He had taken off at 20.10, and, likewise, found visibility to be very poor over France, preventing him from pinpointing his position until reaching Agen, situated on the River Garonne in southern France at 00.17. From there he set course for the target area near Toulouse, shedding altitude as he headed south-south-east, and reached the drop zone at 00.46. The operation was completed from 500 feet between 00.50 and 00.57, after which, he circled Toulouse at 2,000 feet delivering leaflets. Having crossed the enemy coast homebound, he set course for Tangmere, which he reached at 04.40, but bad weather kept him airborne for a further two hours before he eventually landed back at Newmarket. Meanwhile, F/L Murphy, who had been last to take off at 20.17, crossed the English coast at 21.21, and made landfall at Cabourg on the Normandy coast. He pinpointed first on Saumur on the River Loire, and then Chateauroux further to the south-east, finally reaching St-Amand-Mont-Rond at 23.57. The two agents parachuted down five minutes later to complete Operations GYPSY/VERMILION, and they were observed to be safely on the ground, before F/L Murphy headed for home, crossing the English coast at Bognor at 02.20, and finding conditions to be very challenging. Rockets were fired from Stradishall to aid his navigation, and he eventually landed at Newmarket at 04.12, after a round trip of a mere seven hours and fifty-five minutes.

The final operation, before a lull of almost three weeks, was conducted by Sgt Reimer on the night of the 11/12th. He took off on Operation COLUMBUS at 19.45, and headed for Esbjerg on Denmark's west coast, where he encountered searchlights and flak. He reached his drop

P/O Wilkin was posted to 138 Squadron from Abingdon on 30 September 1941. (K. Szrajer)

zone at 23.33, and successfully delivered his agents by parachute, before landing at 03.40 after an uneventful return flight. P/O Wilkin was posted to the squadron from Abingdon on the 30th, the day on which operations resumed. P/O Smith was introduced to operations as second pilot to F/O Hockey on this night, taking off on Operation LUCKYSHOT at 18.55, and heading for Berck-sur-Mer on the French coast, which was reached at 20.40. Cumulus cloud was encountered, which persuaded F/O Hockey to reduce height from 7,500 to 3,500 feet, but heavy rain forced him down to 2,000 feet, and, with the ground obscured, the attempt was abandoned. Sticky Murphy took off at 19.22 on Operation TEAMAN, to deliver an agent into Holland. The Dutch coast was crossed just south of Amsterdam, and course set for Hoofddorp, then Meppel and Drenthe in northern Holland, where an agent was dropped at 21.12.

Meanwhile, P/O Austin had taken off at 19.25 on Operations MOSJID/OUTCASTE and BALACLAVA, and was heading for Belgium when the front and rear turrets were declared unserviceable. Undaunted, he continued on to encounter searchlights at Courtrai, which were lost after evasive action was taken. The drop zone for Operation MOSJID was located at 22.16, and the agent's parachute was seen to open, as was that of his package, but nothing was observed of them on the ground. The remaining two operations, supply drops, were carried out in the Champlon area, where leaflets were also dispensed, and a safe return was completed at 02.40. 138 Squadron's first full month ended with the impressive total of nineteen Whitley sorties and one by a Lysander.

October 1941

Some time earlier, a call had gone out for Polish airmen to volunteer for special duties operations over their homeland, and the response was, of course, magnificent. Crews were initially drawn from 301 Pomeranian Squadron, which had been formed as a Fairey Battle unit at Bramcote in north Warwickshire in July 1940. After contributing to the campaign against the invasion transports in the occupied ports, the squadron had converted to Wellingtons in October, and was now a standard front-line 1 Group unit commanded by W/C Rudkowski. He, however, was to lead the special duties contingent of his compatriots, whose training was completed during September.

A busy first night of October saw 138 Squadron launch three sorties, beginning with F/L Jackson departing Newmarket at 18.30 on Operation BEAU GESTE. He was flying over eight to nine-tenths cloud, which made pinpointing difficult, and he found himself west of track when approaching the French coast. He turned east-north-east, identified the coastline at 21.05, and was able to set course for the drop zone, which was positively identified at 21.33. Reducing altitude to 1,500 feet, he watched his agent's parachute open at 21.36, but was unable to confirm sight of him on the ground. He returned home, where he was assisted at the English coast by searchlights, and landed at Newmarket thirty minutes after midnight. Sgt Reimer had taken off shortly after F/L Jackson, heading for Belgium on Operation LUCKYSHOT, which P/O Hockey had failed to complete twenty-four hours earlier, and Operations HIRELING/RHOMBOID. He arrived at the French coast at le Crotoy in the Bay of the Somme north-west of Abbeville at 20.30, before setting course for the drop zone. He reached the target area an hour and twenty minutes later, but low cloud made the task impossible, and he abandoned all three drops. P/O Austin lifted his Whitley off the ground at 22.25 on Operation BINDER, and crossed the enemy coast at 00.10, reaching Cambrai in north-eastern France at 01.31, where leaflets were dropped. The visibility was poor, and the light of the moon failed to improve matters, but the target area was eventually identified after a further fifty minutes flying, and the agent's parachute was seen to open, but there was no confirmation of him on the ground. A safe return was made after a round trip of seven hours.

On the following night, S/L Nesbitt-Dufort took off in a Lysander at 21.15, to carry out Operation BRICK on behalf of the SIS. His destination was a disused airfield in occupied France, from where he was to pluck a Polish Air Force officer, and bring him safely back to Tangmere. The French coast was crossed at le Treport at 21.55, and course set to the south-east to cover the seventy miles to Estrees-Saint-Denis, forty miles north-east of Paris. A signal from the ground was seen and acknowledged at 22.30, and the Lysander was on the ground four minutes later, before becoming airborne again with its passenger at 22.37. There was a little flak over the exit point at Dieppe, but an otherwise uneventful return trip culminated with a safe landing.

Three operations were mounted on the night of the 3/4th, but only two are documented in the 138 Squadron ORB. W/C Knowles was the first to take off, at 18.19, bound for France on Operations SABOT/SPEED, and reached the English Channel at 19.25. He set course for Cabourg on the French coast, north-east of Caen, which he found to be hidden by fog and haze, but the poor visibility did not conceal the shooting down in flames of a Hudson by flak ships.

The enemy coast was crossed at 20.19, and the nose of the Whitley pointed towards Tours, which was reached at 21.21 in conditions of ten-tenths cloud and haze. There were many lights of an unspecified nature around the drop zone, and the agents agreed to being dropped some ten miles east of the intended pinpoint. Once they were safely away, W/C Knowles dropped leaflets over Chateauroux and sundry townships and villages as he made his way to the coast, and landed at Newmarket shortly after midnight.

There had been two unsuccessful attempts to complete Operation LUCKYSHOT, a container drop over Belgium, and P/O Austin took off six minutes after W/C Knowles for another try. He was also carrying two agents to deliver under Operations RHOMBOID/HIRELING, which had also not been completed at the first time of asking. The enemy coast was crossed in poor visibility at 20.39, and the first recognisable pinpoint was picked up at 21.57, from where a course was set via Namur, Liege and Verviers. The visibility had improved by the time that the drop zone drew near, and the LUCKYSHOT reception committee made contact at 23.23. Four containers and a package were delivered a minute later, and the parachutes were seen to deploy. P/O Austin then continued on eastwards to the Lac de la Gileppe, which he reached at

W/C Rudkowski, the first CO of 301 Polish Bomber Squadron. In July 1941 he was released from Polish Air Force and transferred to the HQ of Chief Commander of Polish Armed Forces, General Sikorski. There he was responsible for organisation of special operations to Poland. Portrait painted by Frank E. Beresford. Thanks to the Polish Institute and Sikorski Museum archive. (PISM via P. Hodyra)

23.44, and delivered his two agents three minutes later. There was still work to carry out, however, and course was set to Namur to dispense leaflets, and then to a further pinpoint for the release of pigeons. His night's work done, P/O Austin crossed the enemy coast homebound at 00.50, and landed safely at Tangmere an hour later.

F/O Hockey was also aloft on this night, undertaking what became and remained the squadron's longest duration flight in a Whitley. This operation is not recorded in the ORB, and the details come from Freddie Clark and his book, Agents by Moonlight. The destination was an area south of Pardubice in Czechoslovakia, into which a Czech Army NCO was to be parachuted. At 19.10, Z9158 took off from Tangmere after refuelling, and headed across occupied territory to meet up with the Rhine deep in southern Germany. From here a course was set for Prague, thence to the Elbe, and further still to the drop zone, which was reached shortly after 01.00 hours. Visibility was poor, but the drop went ahead, and, on the return flight, bombs were delivered onto a railway line in Germany. Most of the flight was undertaken in heavy cloud, and it was the low, rain-bearing variety, which greeted the crew's return to home airspace. Hockey brought the Whitley in beneath the cloud base, and landed back at Tangmere at 06.30, almost eleven and a half hours after take-off. For this magnificent effort, the crew members were awarded a Czech War Cross.

This was the first successful operation to Czechoslovakia, and it would open the way for more, to which end, Czechoslovakian pilot, P/O Bala, and two gunners were posted in from 19 O.T.U on the 7th, and P/O Anderle and crew on the 9th. The first Polish crew, that of F/O Jasinski, who had completed a tour with 300 Squadron, was also officially posted in on the 9th, but they would have to undergo conversion training on Halifaxes at Linton-on-Ouse for the remainder of the month, before becoming operational. Among their future tasks would be the dropping of Russian agents, members of the NKVD, into occupied Europe, in line with a top secret agreement between Britain and the Soviet Union. In view of the murder and exile of many Poles by Russians, something known to the Polish airmen, it is to their eternal credit, that they would subjugate their personal feelings for the greater good of the war effort.

The night of the 10/11th saw four sorties launched, F/L Jackson departing Newmarket first at 18.12 on Operations CORSICAN/TRIPOD/DIVINER. The ORB provides no details of pinpoints or the destination, recording only that the enemy coast was crossed at 20.14, after flying through rough weather. The target area was reached at 23.45, and four agents left the aircraft by parachute four minutes later. The second part of the night's work was completed at 00.03, and the enemy coast crossed homebound at 02.15, followed by a safe landing at 04.03. Six minutes after F/L Jackson's departure, P/O Austin took off on Operation MAINMAST, and headed for the French coast, which he crossed at 20.19. He set course for Tours with the ground obscured by cloud, but was able to locate it anyway, before turning onto the three hundred-mile leg south to Toulouse, during which the cloud dissipated. He reached Toulouse at 00.30, to undertake the final short leg to the drop zone, where he saw lights, but failed to identify a reception committee. He circled the area, and made every effort to complete the drop, but in the absence of a signal from the ground, he was forced to abandon the attempt, and he landed at Tangmere at 06.05, after a round trip of almost twelve hours without reward.

Operations INTERRALLE/SUZANNE were handed to Sgt Reimer, who took off in Whitley Z9159 at 20.55, and reached the French coast two hours later. He set course for Angers, on the River Loire, but had to fly at 700 feet to be able to spot his pinpoint. The reception committee flashed the letter K, and the packages were dropped on the first run, both parachutes being observed to deploy. Satisfied, he flew on to Berthegon, some fifty miles to the south-east of Angers, and set course from there to the next drop zone. The agent was delivered about three miles north-west of the intended pinpoint, and after seeing his parachute open, Sgt Reimer headed for home, and landed safely at 03.35. The last to depart Newmarket on this evening was F/O Hockey, who took off at 21.20 on Operation PEAR. He crossed the French coast at Cabourg at 23.27 at 3,000 feet, before heading south for the 150-mile leg to Tours, which he reached at 00.26. Cloud became a problem, but he made his final course changes, followed a road, and dropped his agent, while flying in a westerly direction at 01.55. Having seen the parachute open, F/O Hockey retraced his steps to Tours to drop leaflets (nickels), before crossing the French coast near le Havre and being engaged by heavy flak, which he evaded, and landed safely at Newmarket at 05.50.

Operation MAINMAST was rescheduled for the night of the 13/14th, and handed to Sticky Murphy, who took off at 19.10, and reached the French coast at Cabourg at 20.21. He set course for Tours, and, in the absence of a blackout in occupied France, the city was well-lit. He pinpointed on Limoges on his way to Toulouse, which was reached at 23.31, and, as he passed over the city at 4,000 feet, the lights went out street-by-street. At 23.44, he picked up a signal from a car light just north of the planned pinpoint, and the drop was carried out. Only one parachute was seen to deploy, and it was initially thought, that the lack of moon and darkly camouflaged canopy had hidden it from view, however an investigation revealed that the port container had hung up, and despite efforts to dislodge it, it refused to fall away. Murphy turned for home, noting that Toulouse was now blacked out as he passed by, and the remainder of the homeward journey was completed without incident and with a safe landing at 05.10. This brought the end of the moon period, and before the next one, three Halifaxes would be added to the squadron's strength.

F/L Jackson was promoted to squadron leader rank on the 20th, and having now recovered from the injuries sustained in the crash in April, F/L Oettle returned to the squadron on the 28th. On the following day, he took Whitley Z9223 for a local flight, presumably to re-acquaint himself with the type before resuming operations. The aircraft stalled during its final approach to Stradishall and crashed, killing Oettle and two other members of the crew. The new moon period began on the last night of October, when Sticky Murphy took off at 18.45 on Operations EMILE/LOUIS. The English coast was crossed at 20.50, and course set for Chalons in north-eastern France, by following the River Marne, but a heavy snowfall rendered the ground featureless, and made map-reading to a precise pinpoint all but impossible. The two agents were dropped about eight miles south-west of the intended target area at 22.14, before the Whitley was turned back towards Abbeville to release some pigeons, and what is referred to in the ORB as "the usual low flying diversion" was carried out. The English coast was crossed homebound at 00.03, and a safe landing made at 01.15.

November 1941

S/L Jackson and P/O Austin had each flown a Whitley, Z9159 and Z9158 respectively to Portreath in Cornwall on the 29th of October, as a staging post for the long flight to Malta, from where they were to participate in supply drops to partisans in Yugoslavia. They landed at Portreath at 13.30 in a gale, and foul weather over the continent delayed their intended departure that night. The following day was spent preparing the aircraft, and marking up maps and charts, while severe icing conditions kept them on the ground for another two nights, and it was not until 08.15 on the 1st of November, that they finally set off for the first leg to Gibraltar. The Isles of Scilly passed beneath at 08.39, Cape Finistere at 12.03, and the Spanish/Portuguese coast at 14.51, before Gibraltar was spotted a little over an hour later, and a safe landing completed at 17.10, after a number of failed attempts in a strong crosswind. The flight to Malta took place that same evening, with a take-off from Gibraltar at 21.15, and a course set from Europa Point at 21.33. Thunderstorms lay across the route, and course changes were made at 22.48, 23.08 and 23.17 to circumnavigate them. A star-fix on Polaris showed them to be north of track, and another course change at 02.28 had them heading for the North African coast, from where the final leg to Malta began at 04.03. They arrived there safely two hours later, in the middle of an air raid, but got down intact, and, as events turned out, they would have to kick their heels for almost a week before an operation could be scheduled. There was a tendency on Malta, for visiting combat aircraft and crews to be commandeered by the military authorities for unauthorized operations, and the 138 Squadron crews had been issued with strict instructions, that their aircraft and equipment was for the sole use of SOE.

While they were absent from Newmarket, F/O Hockey was promoted to flight lieutenant in charge of the long range work of the squadron, and three more Whitleys were taken on charge to supplement the Halifaxes. Sgt Reimer took off at 18.55 on the 1st to carry out Operation CHILBLAIN over Denmark, crossing the English coast outbound at 19.35, and homebound at 02.10, with nothing to show for his endurance after being defeated by cloud and icing conditions. P/O Weeks was posted in from 11 O.T.U on the 6th as the latest pilot to join the squadron. That night, Sgt Reimer took off at 18.20 on Operations OUTCLASS/FABULOUS. On reaching the French coast he climbed to 8,000 feet, picked up a pinpoint on the River Loire, and set course for Toulouse, which he reached at 23.15. The reception committee was found without difficulty, and the drop completed at 23.50, and he was safely back on the ground shortly after 05.00. Eleven minutes after Sgt Reimer's departure from Newmarket, F/L Murphy took off for south-western France on Operation FIREFLY. He crossed the French coast at Cabourg at 20.37, reached Limoges at 22.15 and Perigueux at 23.36, where he picked up the lights of the reception committee, and completed the drop two minutes later. The return flight was uneventful, and he landed back home at 04.21. *According to Freddie Clark's account, Whippy Nesbitt-Dufort also attempted a Lysander operation to France on this night, but was defeated by the weather. However, the squadron ORB makes no mention of this sortie, and F/L Murphy appears to have enjoyed favourable weather conditions.*

The night of the 7/8th was of great significance to Bomber Command, and its ramifications would bring into question the continued existence of a strategic bomber force. Frustrated by a prolonged period of poor weather, C-in-C Peirse decided to launch a record number of sorties in an attempt to score a major success. The main effort was to be directed at Berlin, and involve more than two hundred aircraft, but AVM Slessor of 5 Group expressed grave doubts about the conditions for such a long-range operation, and was allowed to withdraw his forces, and send them instead to Cologne. A third operation was to be directed at Mannheim, and together with a host of minor operations, there would be 392 aircraft airborne, not to mention those from 138 Squadron, the existence of which was not yet alluded to in Bomber Command reports. In the event, 169 aircraft set off for Berlin, seventy-five for Cologne and fifty-five for Mannheim, while ninety-three others took care of the minor operations. The night turned into a disaster, which cost the Command a record thirty-seven aircraft, more than twice the previous highest in a single night, and not one operation had produced any damage. Peirse would be summoned to a meeting with Churchill on the following evening to explain himself, and, on the 13th, was ordered to restrict further operations, while the future of the Command was debated at the highest level.

Meanwhile on this night, and according to Freddie Clark, but not confirmed in the ORB, S/L Nesbitt-Dufort re-flew the Lysander operation from the previous night, and, this time, succeeded in delivering one agent and picking up two others. F/L Murphy was also on duty, and took off for the Dutch coast at Egmond on Operation CATARRH with two SOE agents on board. He made landfall at 100 feet at 23.36, from where he set course for Ommen, and picked up a pinpoint at 00.05. The drop was completed two minutes later, after which he descended again to 100 feet, dispensing pigeons and leaflets over towns and villages as he retraced his steps to the coast. As he crossed the shoreline, he came upon a German convoy of twenty large ships, which immediately took evasive action, while firing upon him, but he landed safely at 02.45.

Earlier in the day, and many, many miles away, a conference had taken place on Malta in the office of the island's military commander, attended by Major Mackenzie, who was in charge of the Army's contribution to whatever was going on, along with other army personnel, two Serbian pilots, the senior officers of a flight of three Wellingtons from the Middle-East, and S/L Jackson. They had been informed that the equipment for the SOE drop would be brought in by flying boat and submarine, the latter having arrived that very morning. It was decided, that strong winds and icing conditions made it inadvisable to operate over mountainous terrain at night, and the Wellington captains considered it impossible to locate pinpoints over Yugoslavia. The Air Ministry was contacted about carrying out the operation by day, but, with only two containers ready, P/O Austin took off at 21.50, with an experienced Serbian pilot on board, who was familiar with the region, and set course from Dellimara Point on the island's south-eastern extremity. He reached his next pinpoint, an island, at 00.47, and, at the Balkan coast, he headed inland to another navigation point, which was reached at 02.14. He finally reached the drop zone at 02.50, observing the reception committee lights some five miles ahead. A number of fires were burning on the hilltops, and more were set alight when the letter R was flashed from the Whitley and answered. The containers fell away at 02.56, and the rear gunner observed the parachutes opening. Task completed, P/O Austin turned for Luqa, and landed safely at 07.35, after a round-trip of almost ten hours. A further drop was planned for the 9th and 10th, but one of the Whitleys became unserviceable, and a forecast of poor weather conditions persuaded the station commander to cancel them. Two agents had arrived on the 9th, without parachutes, but the 138 Squadron crews were ordered home as soon as conditions allowed, which would not be for a few days more.

This night of Friday/Saturday the 7/8th also brought the first of many operations by Polish crews, for which F/O Jasinski, late of 1 Group's 300 Masovian Squadron, was the pilot, with a former 301 Squadron crew, and that unit's first commanding officer, W/C Rudkowski, on board as an official observer, who would report back to HQ. Rudkowski had arrived in England late in 1939, and, following his operational tour, had been posted to Polish Air Force HQ, where his new role was to liaise between the Polish Air Force authorities and SOE. The operation was launched from Linton-on-Ouse, and involved three Polish agents, among which was Jan Piwnik, who would become famous among his people as a resistance commander. The round trip to the outskirts of Warsaw of around two thousand miles was only slighter shorter than the Halifax's range, but this was of little concern to the Polish crew, who were ecstatic at having the honour and opportunity to contribute to their nation's struggle against the Nazi oppressors. Even had they known there was no chance of surviving, they would have gone just the same, and felt themselves privileged to do so in such a just cause. This was the spirit typifying the Poles where-ever they fought, and none served in Bomber Command with greater fervour.

L9612 took off from Linton-on-Ouse on Operation RUCTION at 18.30, first, to cross Denmark to pinpoint on Bornholm Island, lying south-east of Sweden, and then to make landfall near Danzig, from where course was set for Charzykowskie Lake near Chojnice, some sixty miles inland. They were flying above cloud at 11,000 feet, and, at around 21.00, it was decided to drop down to below the cloud base at 6,000 feet to confirm their position. While descending they picked up some ice, but the ground soon came into view, and the River Vistula was identified and followed towards Bydgoszcz, 150 miles north-west of Poland's battered Capital City. A tail wind and a cruising speed of 250 mph drove them to the drop zone in a creditable four hours and ten minutes, and, having received the appropriate signal from the reception committee, the flaps and undercarriage were lowered to help the Halifax to slow down to something more comfortable for the departing agents. They parachuted into the darkness, along with radios, containers of arms and ammunition, and other essential items, and the wireless operator sent a message back to base to confirm that the drop had been successfully carried out. Attempts were then made to retract the undercarriage for the return journey, but, unfortunately, the hydraulics system had fallen victim to the numbing cold, and the undercarriage resisted all attempts to retract it. This massively increasing the drag effect on the aircraft, as the tail wind became a head wind, and wiped out the already fine margin of endurance. Sgt Sobkowiak took over the controls to allow F/O Jasinski some respite, and they climbed again to 10,000 feet to just above the clouds, and set course for the east coast of Denmark, where they were fired upon by flak. A calculation of their situation informed them that England lay three and a half hours away, but they had fuel only for seventy-five minutes, and this prompted a decision to make for Sweden, where a forced-landing was carried out successfully four miles west of Ystad, near Malmo, at around 06.00, without crew casualties. The Halifax sustained damage, and was set on fire by the crew and destroyed. The crew was taken to an internment camp at Falun, internment in Sweden usually representing a pleasurable experience, and the crew members were gradually returned to England, W/C Rudkowski arriving home first within two weeks. F/O Krol and Sgt Mol landed at Leuchars on the 7th of January, and F/O Jasinski two days later. When F/O Jasinski came home, he re-joined 300 Squadron, and would complete another tour of operations.

Having undertaken a long-range double operation to France on the night of the 6/7th, the newly-promoted F/Sgt Reimer brought the moon period to a close on the night of the 8/9th, with another double, although shorter range drop over the same country. Operations ARBORETUM/IRRADIATE began with a departure at 19.40, and the crossing of the French coast at 21.35. Givet, on the Franco/Belgian border, was reached at 22.33, and, seven minutes later, the first agent parachuted down. It took a further fifteen minutes to locate the next pinpoint, where a reception committee signalled its presence, and the second agent was delivered at 22.59, before a safe return concluded with a landing at 02.20. Meanwhile, S/L Jackson and P/O Austin and their crews were kicking their heels on Malta after the weather closed in, and they had to wait until the 15th, before being able to head home. They departed Luqa at 17.25, and P/O Austin landed at West Malling at 03.15, while S/L Jackson put down at Newmarket at 04.30.

Thus far, it had been a bad year for the Command, its deficiencies encapsulated in the damning Butt Report released on the 18th of August. This, in its broadest terms, had highlighted the inability of the crews to locate and hit targets at night, but the Command had suffered other setbacks, particularly with regard to the new aircraft types introduced into operational service early in the year. Each had promised much, but had failed to deliver, and had spent lengthy periods under grounding orders, while essential modifications were carried out. The weather had also been unfavourable during the final quarter of the year, at precisely the time that Peirse would have been hoping to gain some successes to cleanse the Command's besmirched reputation. It must have been a frustrating time, and his eagerness to operate, even in doubtful weather conditions, more than once resulted in recall signals being sent, while the bombers were outbound over the North Sea. Clearly, to navigate over a blacked-out hostile country at night, with cloud obscuring ground features, was a problem without solution until the advent of the electronic devices which would be the Command's salvation later in the war. However, one has to ask, how the magnificent men in their 138 Squadron flying machines, were able to locate tiny drop zones and landing grounds under similar conditions? Perhaps the difference was the moonlight, but at this stage of the war, before the Luftwaffe night fighter force became such a potent weapon, bombing operations were frequently conducted during the moon period anyway.

During the stand-down period before the next moon, 138 Squadron bade farewell to W/C Knowles and S/L Jackson. The former was appointed station commander at Jurby on the Isle of Man, where, sadly, his tenure and his life would be brought to an untimely end. Taking advantage of the presence on his station of a Whitley in transit to Belfast, he borrowed it to take some friends for a jaunt, and died when it crashed on take-off. He was replaced at 138 Squadron on the 17th by the familiar form of W/C Farley, the original commander of 419 Flight, now fully recovered from his broken leg. Two new Halifaxes, L9613 and L9618, were added to the strength, as was a Polish crew and two Polish pilots to replace those interned in Sweden. Operations resumed on the night of the 26/27th, when W/C Farley undertook his

(Above) The wreckage of Halifax L9612 which was destroyed by her crew after force-landing near Ystad in the morning of 8 November 1941. (Bo Widfelt. Thanks to Swedish Forced Landing Collection via W. Zmyslony). (Below) The Polish crew of Halifax L9612 celebrating New Year's Day, 1942 in Falun, Sweden. The captain of the crew, observer F/O Krol, is third from the left. (PH)

first sortie since returning to SOE operations. He took off on Operations DASTARD/DAICE at 19.20, and headed for the French coast at Cabourg, which he reached at 22.00, before turning towards Paris. He pinpointed over the French Capital at 23.15, but found the bad weather too challenging, and aborted the sortie. Low cloud prevented him from pinpointing on the French and English coasts on the way home, and it took a considerable search before he eventually located Newmarket to land at 03.20. F/Sgt Reimer, meanwhile, had taken off at 19.45 in Z9287, to deliver an agent to France under Operation PLAICE. He crossed the French coast at 21.40, and set course for the River Loire for his next pinpoint. This was reached at 23.10, and the drop zone at midnight, but it took a further forty-five minutes to raise the reception committee. The triangular light arrangement was not very bright, and those on the ground only signalled when the Whitley was directly above. The agent eventually fell away, his parachute seen to open, and F/Sgt Reimer turned for home at 01.00, dispensing leaflets over Tours and other areas as he went.

On the following night, P/O Gibson carried out his first sortie since joining the squadron, taking off at 18.30 to try to complete Operations DASTARD/DAICE. Once over France, he encountered mist, which prevented him from picking out anything on the ground, and he, like W/C Farley, was compelled to give up and return home after more than nine hours aloft. On the 28th, F/L Laurent, a French former naval and fighter pilot, took Lysander T1771 for a

The Westland Lysander is probably the aircraft type most often associated with the cloak-and-dagger work of SOE in Occupied Europe. 138 Sqn operated a number of Lysander III aircraft, which contributed 64 sorties, for the cost of three of their number. Photos of 138 Sqn Lysanders being very scarce, this aircraft was, in fact, operated by the other significant SD unit at Tempsford, 161 Sqn. V9673, MA-J, was shot down at Berry-au-Bac, Aisne, France, on 11th December 1943, with the loss of the three occupants. (Crown Copyright).

The first five experienced Polish crews who, before they were assigned as volunteers to 138 Squadron, had completed their first tours of duty in 301 Squadron. From right: pilot P/O Zygmuntowicz (KIA during special operation on 20/21 April 1942), third - future CO of Polish C Flight in 138 Squadron, observer F/O Krol. Photo was taken on 27 June 1941 at RAF Swinderby. (PH)

Two other Polish pilots who later served in 138 Squadron; from right: Sgt Klosowski and Sgt Jensen. The third airman, decorated by General Ujejski, Inspector General of the Polish Air Force in Great Britain, is Sgt Janik who was flying in 138 Squadron as wireless operator in F/O Kuzmicki`s crew. (PH)

From the right: wireless operator Sgt Wasilewski, who in 138 Squadron flew in the crew of F/O Krol, and pilot Sgt Pieniazek, a member of the second Polish crew assigned for flying special operations. (PH)

W/C Rudkowski, CO of 301 Bomber Squadron passes his congratulations after the presentation of a decoration to pilot Sgt Jensen. 4th from the right - Wireless Operator P/O Bator. After the tour in 301 Squadron he completed a couple of special operations in 138 Squadron and volunteered to became a special agent. He was dropped to Poland on 25/26 January 1943 by the crew of F/L Krol. He was killed during the Warsaw Uprising in September 1944. (PH)

practice flight, and collided with trees at Farnham in Surrey in bad visibility, killing himself and his two ground crew passengers. Also on this day, six Polish airmen were posted in from 301 Squadron, including pilots P/Os Zygmuntowicz and Dobromirski, who had been with their previous units since April and May respectively. Sticky Murphy and F/L Lockhart volunteered to join the Lysander flight, and both would prove to be well suited to the task. Guy Lockhart was another character, who had been with the squadron for some time, flying frequently as second pilot to W/C Knowles. He was considered by some to be an eccentric, but this seemed to be a pre-requisite for successful Lysander pilots anyway.

P/O Gibson took off at 19.10 on the 30th, for a second attempt to complete Operation IRRADIATE, which had defeated F/Sgt Reimer's best efforts at the end of the previous moon period. He crossed the French coast at 21.40, but encountered ten-tenths cloud, and it was 22.17 before he set course for Chimay on the Belgian side of the border in the Ardennes. The drop zone was at Sury, less than thirty miles to the south-east on the French side, which was reached at 23.10, but no reception committee lights were seen, and the operation was abandoned again. A safe landing was carried out at Abingdon at 02.30.

December 1941

There were no operations during the first week of the new month, but further postings from 301 Squadron on the 6th brought in six new recruits, including pilots, Sgts Klosowski and Pieniazek. P/O Gibson was assigned to Operation COOL, for which he took off at 20.15 on the 8th, and headed for English coast south of Tangmere. He pinpointed on the French coast at 22.06, before setting course for Tours via le Mans, reaching the latter at 22.24. He dropped down to 3,000 feet to get below the ten-tenths cloud, and found the visibility then to be good. He obtained a pinpoint on the River Loire south-west of Tours at 23.02, and, twenty minutes later, found Chateauroux, from where a course was set to the target area. This was reached at 23.30, but no reception committee was waiting, and after circling for fifteen minutes, the agents parachuted one mile west of Montriol (unable to locate), before P/O Gibson set a reciprocal course, delivering nickels over Chateauroux on the way. He crossed the French coast homebound at 01.38, and landed safely at Newmarket at 03.36.

F/Sgt Reimer departed Newmarket twenty minutes after P/O Gibson, to undertake Operations CLAUDIUS/BERYL. He crossed the English coast at 21.45 and the French coast at 22.27, but it was not possible to obtain a pinpoint because of cloud. Course was set for Blois, situated on the River Loire, south-west of Orleans and south-east of le Mans, and height reduced to 2,000 feet to allow for map-reading. He arrived at Blois at 23.14, before setting course for the drop zone, where the reception committee signalled its presence, and the agent's parachute was seen to open at 23.23. With the first task completed, F/Sgt Reimer flew back over Blois to deliver leaflets, and then dropped a second agent at a different location, before dispensing more leaflets over Chateauroux, and returning home to land at 03.44.

F/L Murphy took off at 22.10 on the same evening to undertake one of the few Lysander pick-up operations to be laid on outside of France. Operation STOAT required him to land at an airfield at Neufchâteau in Belgium, close to the frontiers with Holland and Germany. He set course initially for Abbeville, a dozen miles inland from the French coast at Cayeux-sur-Mer, but cloud prevented him from obtaining a pinpoint, and he set a new course on e.t.a at 23.00. He flew eastwards for a further fifty minutes, before setting course for the landing zone, assisted by snow on the ground, which allowed wooded areas to stand out clearly. He circled the airfield until a light was seen to the south at 00.40, and this was followed by another light in a steady beam five minutes later. The first light continued to flash an incorrect identification letter, and, under standing orders, Sticky Murphy should, perhaps, at this point, have abandoned the sortie. There could be any number of reasons for an incorrect signal, including a genuine mistake on the part of the sender, but its immediate effect was to put Murphy on his guard. He concluded that the agents were being chased, but decided to go in anyway, signalling his intent by blipping the engine twice. Twenty yards short of the flare path, his landing lights revealed the ground to fall away sharply in front of him, so he applied power and went round again. This time he opted to land away from the flare path on the eastern side of the aerodrome, in case it was a trap, and taxied round to face the reception committee, before readying his revolver. He flashed his landing light, and caught in its glare an approaching gaggle of enemy soldiers, firing as they came. Murphy gunned the throttle as rifle rounds peppered the Lysander, and as he left the ground at 01.00, he felt one strike him in the neck. No vital parts of the aircraft were hit, however, and he made good his escape, binding his wound with one of his wife's silk stockings, which he always carried with him on operations as a mascot. As a postscript, both agents eluded their pursuers, although one was captured a few days later, and was sent to Berlin for trial. Amazingly, he escaped, and ultimately returned to England.

Finally, on this night, Sgt Wilde took off from Stradishall at 22.30 on Operation OVERCLOUD, and, within ten minutes, was in ten-tenths cumulus cloud, which hid from his view both the English and French coasts, which were crossed at 8,700 feet. At 23.20, a gap in the clouds revealed a flashing beacon, which could not be identified. Sgt Wilde reduced altitude to 4,000 feet, but visibility remained poor, and he decided to abandon the sortie. He landed first at Tangmere, but took off again at 02.50, and reached base at 04.15. The final operation of the moon period brought the SOE debut of one of the Czech pilots, P/O Anderle. Flying in Whitley Z9125, he took off at 20.47 on the 12th, and crossed the French coast near Caen at 22.40. He was unable to see the ground, and altered course to the south-west on dead reckoning (DR) for the 150-mile leg to his final destination of Vannes on the west coast. He flew through clouds and snowstorms most of the way to Rennes, then, continuing on, he crossed the coast into the Bay of Morbihan, south of Vannes, before turning back to locate the drop zone. He eventually received a signal from the ground, and successfully delivered his containers at 00.40, returning safely home thereafter via the French coast at 02.24, and the English coast at 03.18, and landing at Newmarket at 04.57.

During the stand-down, 138 Squadron changed address by moving to Stradishall on the 16th, one of the former homes of both 419 and 1419 Flights. It would prove to be a temporary arrangement, however, and, when the next move came, it would be to an airfield dedicated to secret operations. Christmas Eve was characterized by inhospitable weather, into which a number of sorties to Belgium were launched. F/Sgt Reimer took off first, at 20.00, on Operation NUSSICK 1, which was combined with Operation PERIWIG, being flown by Sgt Jones, who departed Stradishall thirty-three minutes later. Sgt Jones had reached Southampton when a recall signal was received at 21.52, and he landed back at base two hours later. F/Sgt Reimer was already well into his sortie by this time, and had crossed the south coast of England at 21.07, and the French coast near le Crotoy at 21.44. Cloud prevented him from seeing the ground, but he circled, hoping to elicit some response from a reception committee. Nothing was observed, however, and, consequently, he set course for his second pinpoint, which he should have reached at 22.50. Ten-tenths cloud persisted, forcing him to abandon the attempt and turn for home, and he took the opportunity to drop leaflets near Cambrai and Henin-Beaumont on the route to the coast.

Christmas and Boxing Days passed in relative peace, but a number of sorties were mounted on the night of the 27/28th, amongst which was Operation CHILBLAIN, a dual purpose undertaking, to bomb a transformer station, (described in the ORB as electrical works) at Vordingborg, south-west of Copenhagen, and deliver two agents and a package. Sgt Jones and crew flew out over the east coast at 21.12, and made landfall over Denmark at 00.06, but without being able to obtain a pinpoint. At 00.27 they were able to establish their position on Denmark's eastern coast, and, at 00.52, set course for the target and reduced height to 3,000 feet, and then 2,000 feet, to allow map-reading across the islands. The electrical works was sighted at 01.20, and a bombing run into wind attempted at 1,000 feet, but the bombs were not dropped. They were released on a second run, however, and fell about 150 yards short, the crew surmising that the transformers probably sustained damage from the concussion, and also from the four bursts of fire from the rear turret. A course was then set for the second pinpoint, while much motorized activity took place on the roads below. The second pinpoint was located by means of a signal from the ground at 01.55, and both agents and the package dropped away from 500 feet. The rear gunner reported all three parachutes to have deployed, despite the fact that one of the static lines was found by the dispatcher to be missing, and news would be received, that one of the agents had, indeed, fallen to his death. A homeward course was set, and ground detail identified, and leaflets were dispensed over fairly well-populated area at 02.43. It became apparent later, that they had been provided with an incorrect beacon list, and low-lying fog prevented any chance of map reading. To add to their woes, the second pilot reported that the elevator trimming was fully forward, and the aircraft was difficult to control. Sgt Jones took over, and drained all of the fuel from the fuselage to the wing tanks, and moved all personnel forward to counter the tail-down-nose-up tendency. The emergency "Darkie" call was sent, and answered by Oakington, which lit up its flare path, and after considerable difficulty, and both pilots pulling on the control yoke, a dangerous but ultimately safe landing was carried out at 07.50, after more than eleven hours in the air. They remained at Oakington until 16.51, when, refuelled and mechanically checked-out, they took off for Stradishall.

Not mentioned in the ORB were sorties on this night by a Polish crew in Halifax L9618, and F/Sgt Reimer in Whitley Z9385. The Halifax took off from Lakenheath at 21.20 on Operation JACKET, and, according to Freddie Clark's account, was an attempt to deliver six agents and two containers to the crew's homeland, where a navigation error led to the drop taking place in the wrong area. Polish historian Piotr Hodyra writes, that the Halifax was fired upon over Denmark, but continued on towards the drop site in central Poland, where, confirming the navigation error in very difficult weather conditions, the agents and stores left the aircraft about twenty-five miles north-east of the intended pinpoint, near Sochaczew, some forty miles west of Warsaw. The weather may have persuaded the crew to adopt a more direct course home, which took them over Bremen. This was, in fact, familiar territory to the experienced bomber crew, who had flown to and from Bremen on numerous occasions in recent months, and they arrived safely on the ground at Stradishall at 09.10 after a long round trip of almost twelve hours. The success of the drop was confirmed later by the Polish Home Army HQ. Certainly the weather was bad as F/Sgt Reimer approached Stradishall on return from his sortie, and the Whitley crashed onto the airfield, killing three of the occupants outright, and severely injuring Reimer. There are conflicting reports concerning the cause of the crash, but it seems likely, that Reimer and his crew fell victim to an enemy intruder, and that the aircraft was already on fire before the impact. Sadly, F/Sgt Reimer, a Canadian, would succumb to his injuries two weeks later, and the loss of such an experienced SOE pilot would represent a major blow to the squadron.

W/C Farley and F/L Hockey brought down the curtain on the year's operations with sorties on the night of the 28/29th. In a case of extremes, W/C Farley's turned out to be, perhaps, the shortest on record, while Hockey's was among the longest. Farley became airborne in Whitley Z6728 at 20.10, but, within ten minutes, he had lost the use of his airspeed indicator, TR9 radio equipment and W/T, and the sortie was immediately abandoned. Attempts to contact Stradishall by R/T were unsuccessful, leaving Farley with no choice but to come in unannounced. The containers were jettisoned over the airfield, before a safe landing was carried out, and Farley's prudence was made manifest, when both engines failed on touchdown, and all brake pressure was lost.

Blood on his hands. SS Obergruppenführer Reinhard Heydrich.

F/L Hockey's task was to transport an assassination team to Czechoslovakia, at the request of the Czech government in exile. Their brief was to kill the SS chief Reinhardt Heydrich, a ruthless, ambitious, high-ranking officer and one of Hitler's inner-circle, who had been installed as the governor, and was the embodiment of Nazi evil. Two other teams were to be dropped at other locations to set up communications and a training function. It was, therefore, a fully laden Halifax L9613, NF-V, which lifted into the air from Tangmere at 22.00, and headed for the French coast, which was crossed at le Crotoy. From there, a course was set towards Darmstadt in southern Germany, shortly after which, an enemy night fighter appeared astern on the port quarter, and dropped two flares. No attack was carried out, and because of the heavy loading, F/L Hockey took no evasive action, and contact was lost after twenty minutes. Darmstadt was reached at 00.42, but, the deeper the penetration into enemy territory, the thicker the cloud became, and the heavier the snow lay on the ground, blotting out useful features needed for navigation. Altitude was reduced in an attempt to get beneath the cloud, and, at 02.12, flak was seen ahead, where Pilsen was believed to be, and this provided the pinpoint for the next stage of the flight to the first drop zone, to the south of the city. There were to be no reception committees, and it was entirely Hockey's responsibility to select the terrain within the briefed area. The two assassins parachuted at 02.24, after which, the visibility deteriorated in low cloud, making it almost impossible to recognize the landscape. Within twenty-two minutes of the first drop, however, the remaining two teams, one of three men and the other of two, got away from 800 feet, and it was estimated, that each landed within a dozen miles of the planned landing grounds. The return flight was equally difficult to navigate, but the French coast was eventually crossed at 07.20, shortly after which, the cockpit escape hatch blew open and jammed. The second pilot, hung on to it to prevent it from flying away and, perhaps, damaging the tail, and the speed was reduced to 140 mph. Selsey Bill passed beneath at 08.07, and the exhausted crew touched down at Tangmere at 08.19, after ten hours and nineteen minutes in the air.

Many accounts have been written about the assassination attempt, which was not carried out until the end of May. It was carefully planned to take place at a sharp bend in the road, where, each day, Heydrich's open-top limousine was forced to slow down en-route to his Prague office. On the appointed day, one assassin carried a submachine gun, and the other a hand grenade, but the gun jammed at the vital moment, and the grenade exploded in the gutter beside the car. Heydrich had risen to his feet to draw his pistol, and sustained shrapnel wounds, which, while quite serious, were not believed to be life-threatening. He had, in fact, even been able to give chase to the fleeing assassins before collapsing. Fortunately, a piece of horsehair from the car seat had penetrated his body, and this caused blood poisoning, which ultimately resulted in his death on the 5th of June. Sgts Jan Kubic and Josef Gabcik were eventually betrayed, and died during a gun battle with German soldiers, while they were trapped in the basement of a church.

The loss of F/Sgt Reimer and the unfortunate Danish agent made it a sad end to the year, which had seen a major escalation in SOE/SIS operations, and a creditable ratio of successes to failures for an organisation still in its relative infancy. For the Command in general, however, the year was turning with the black cloud of failure still suspended above it, and with few solutions for its troubles in prospect. There was, however, one ray of light, and this was currently occupying the airfield at Waddington in Lincolnshire. The first production examples of the new Lancaster had been handed to 44 (Rhodesia) Squadron for introduction into operational service in the near future. This would prove to be the "Shining Sword" as far as the bombing offensive was concerned, but it would be a considerable time yet, before the Command redeemed its reputation under a new leader.

January 1942

The New Year began for the Command as the old one had ended, with a series of ineffective operations against the German cruisers at Brest. More than a dozen raids of varying sizes were mounted in December, and only a few less in January, but, at least, this annoying itch would soon be scratched for the last time. The restriction order, imposed following the debacle on the 7/8th of November, would remain in place for a further six weeks, until the arrival of a new commander-in-chief. Sir Richard Peirse departed on the 8th of January to become Commander-in-Chief of Allied Air Forces in India and South-east Asia, and he was replaced temporarily by AVM Baldwin, the 3 Group A-O-C. The year began for 138 Squadron with a very long-range operation to southern France on the night of the 1/2nd of January, for which Sgt Jones was volunteered. He departed Stradishall on Operation MAINMAST at 16.20, and landed at St Eval as a staging post at 18.45. After refueling, he took off again at 20.48, and set course for the French coast, where, at 21.50, they ran into slight but accurate heavy flak, and a night fighter was spotted. At 22.05 a course was set for Limoges, and height reduced from 9,000 to 2,000 feet, but, even so, a thin layer of stratus cloud rendered the ground barely visible. Ultimately, it became impossible to obtain a pinpoint, and the course was calculated according to DR. At 01.36, it was estimated that the River Rhone pinpoint lay below, and a due south course was adopted to reach the coast at the Gulf of Lyon. At 02.10, a mountain range became visible ahead, and, by flying alongside the highest peak, it was possible to obtain a firm fix of position. A new course was set accordingly, and it became possible to map-read to the drop zone, where the three passengers and stores took to their parachutes, which were observed by the rear gunner to open. It had been intended to return directly to Stradishall, but cloud persuaded Sgt Jones to put in at St Eval, where a safe landing was carried out after a flight lasting three minutes under twelve hours.

On the following night, P/O Smith undertook his first Whitley sortie as captain with a particularly arduous trip to Norway under Operations CHEESE/FASTING. He took off at 20.25, and crossed the coast at Cromer at 20.59 at 2,000 feet. Despite concerns about the port propeller during the outward flight, landfall on the Norwegian coast was made ten miles south of Flekkefjord at midnight in conditions of two-tenths cloud and patches of mist. The target area was found to be clear, however, and the agents were dropped from 2,900 feet at 00.23, two camouflaged and one white parachute being observed to deploy. Leaflets were dispensed over Feda and Rorvig, and the enemy coast crossed homebound near Vanse at 00.40. Stradishall was reached at 04.42, and a safe landing carried out three minutes later.

Sometime in late December, two Whitleys, Z9140 and Z9295, had been detached to Malta, presumably for SOE operations over the Balkans. During a Luftwaffe attack on the airfield at Luqa on the 3rd, both were destroyed at their dispersals, but no casualties were reported among 138 Squadron personnel, and nothing relating to these aircraft is recorded in the ORB. On the morning of the 5th, W/C Farley and Sgt Jones were detailed to fly a Whitley each and passengers to Wick, as a staging post for Operations ANVIL/LARK, but weather conditions were very unfavourable, and the operation was abandoned.

The operation to Poland, SHIRTJACKET, previously flown on the night of the 27/28th of December, was rescheduled to take place on the 6th, when a Polish crew captained by F/O

Wodzicki, was briefed to deliver six men and stores to a location about fifteen miles east of Warsaw. The operation was launched from Lakenheath, where an overloaded Halifax L9618, with an all-up weight of 61,198lbs, struggled into the air at 19.55. They set course for Esbjerg on the west coast of Denmark, which was reached at 23.07, and then turned for the island of Bornholm in the Baltic, some forty miles off the south coast of Sweden. This passed beneath at 00.25, and a course was then set for Grudziadz, Modlin and, finally, the target area, around 275 miles inland to the south-east. It took and hour and forty-five minutes to reached the drop zone near Minsk Mazowiecki, to the east of Warsaw, a journey completed without incident at 02.10, but F/O Wodzicki was forced to orbit the area for forty minutes, searching in vain for signals from the anticipated reception committee. When these were not forthcoming, the drop was carried out blind at 02.50, and it seems, that a number of parachutists fell close to a German patrol and were injured in a firefight. The main problem for those on the ground thereafter, would be to locate the containers. The Halifax crew knew nothing of this, of course, and began the long flight home, passing by Warsaw at 03.15. The Polish coast was crossed at 04.46, a pinpoint was obtained on the Danish coast at 05.45, and Esbjerg passed by ten miles to the south at 06.40. At last, the English coast slipped reassuringly beneath the Halifax, and, after a trip lasting 12¾ hours, and with the last reserves of fuel, a safe landing was carried out at Attlebridge in Norfolk at 08.40.

It was late on the 7th, 23.37, when P/O Anderle took off on Operations MOUSE/VERMILION in a Whitley, and crossed the English coast at 00.38. He reached the French side of the Channel at 01.18, and set course for Heures. He flew into a heavy storm, and technical difficulties began to present themselves, beginning with an erratic air speed indicator (a.s.i.). While using the reserve fuel tanks, both engines cut out five times, and, finally, a valve burned out in the W/T transmitter, rendering it unserviceable. P/O Anderle gave in to the inevitable, and abandoned the sortie to return home, landing at Tangmere at 03.15. P/O Smith brought the current moon period to a close when taking off at 01.08 on the 10th in Whitley Z9287 on Operations TENTERHOOK/HORNBEAM/TRIPOD 2. He crossed the English coast at 4,000 feet at 02.11, and the enemy coast at Pointe de la Percee forty-nine minutes later, before setting course for the first target area. He reduced height to 2,000 feet in conditions of thick mist up to 3,000 feet and horizontal visibility of 850 yards, and reached the target area at 03.40. Unable to make a positive identification, he decided to press on to the second one, with an initial pinpoint on the River Loire, which was reached at 04.00, and from where the second pilot was able to map-read to HORNBEAM, arriving ten minutes later. P/O Smith circled for fifteen minutes, but in the absence of a reception committee, he headed for the second part of the operation, to deliver leaflets to Ligniers in central France, and Ranes, south of Caen. He crossed the French coast homebound at 10,000 feet at 05.26, and landed safely at base at 07.56.

January proved to be another disappointing month for the bomber squadrons, particularly where its efforts over Germany were concerned. Operations to Hamburg, Bremen, Hanover and Münster resulted in few crews reaching the general target areas, and little significant damage was inflicted. The new moon period brought a return to operations for 138 Squadron on the night of the 22/23rd, when P/O Smith was once more on duty, this time for Operations MARMOSET/PERIWIG 1. He took off in Whitley Z9286 at 20.05, and crossed the English coast ten miles east of Beachy Head. He was able to pinpoint on the enemy coast and set course for the target, which was reached at 00.35, but on receiving no signal from a reception committee, he abandoned the sortie and returned home. Later on the 23rd, six Czech airmen arrived from 311 Squadron, including pilots Sgts Janek and Politzer, and two days later, 51 Squadron contributed two more, including pilot, P/O Austin. That evening, P/O Anderle took off at 19.15 in Whitley Z9158 for another attempt at Operation HORNBEAM, and also to carry out Operations DACE/CYPRUS. He was over the target area from 21.40 to 22.35, and delivered DACE at a position two kilometres south of Mulsanne, just to the south of le Mans, and the others at Verneit, further to the west, and north of Rennes. Four parachutes were seen to open, but no reception committees, and after completing his drops, he returned home without incident, and landed at 01.30.

Sgt Wilde took off in Whitley T4166 at 19.20 on the evening of the 25th, to carry out Operation OVERCLOUD 2, but he was defeated by the weather conditions over France, and landed back at base at 22.15. On the following night, P/O Smith left Stradishall in Whitley Z9287 at 21.48 to carry out Operation TURNIP over Holland. The target area was reached at 00.43, and the exact pinpoint for the drop established, but the Dutch agent refused to parachute into the snow-covered landscape below, possibly, because no reception committee had been arranged to spirit him away, and he returned with the aircraft to land at base at 03.04. Inevitably, during a period of bad weather, a backlog of operations developed, and this unfinished business had to be slotted into the new schedule. This led to a busy night on the 28/29th, when six Whitleys and a Lysander were detailed for operations, three to France and the others to Belgium. Sadly, the night's efforts would do little to ease the pressure on the schedule, as the weather again took a hand. Operations began with the departure of Z9287 at 19.00 for Operations MOUSE/VERMILION/WHITSUN. The name of the pilot is not recorded, but severe icing and electrical disturbances caused the sortie to be abandoned at 20.40, and the Whitley landed back at base at 23.16. At 19.01, Z9158 lifted off, with P/O Anderle at the controls, and headed for France to carry out Operations LUCKYSHOT/WEASEL. Having crossed the French coast north of Dieppe at 20.52, he set course for St Quentin in the north-eastern region, but encountered such challenging weather conditions, that he was unable to pinpoint the drop zone. He retraced his steps to the coast, dropping leaflets over a small town two miles south of Amiens on the way, and arrived safely home at 23.26.

P/O Austin was the next to take-off on this night, at 19.10, in Whitley Z9232, having been briefed for Operations BALACLAVA 1/CANTICLE/DUNCAN. He had reached the Lens area of north-eastern France before the weather compelled him to turn back, and he delivered leaflets there, before returning to land at Newmarket at 01.07. Sgt Wilde left the ground at 19.15 in Z9286 to undertake Operations PERIWIG 1/MARMOSET/MAN FRIDAY/INTERSECTION, and crossed the French coast at 21.03, before setting course for Valenciennes. From there he followed the course of a canal east-north-east to Mons, across the border in Belgium, and soon located the drop zone, where three agents parachuted away. On the way to the French coast homebound, he delivered leaflets over Douai, twenty miles west of Valenciennes, and attracted the attention of a few flak guns as he departed enemy territory at 22.56. T4166 took off from Stradishall at 19.22, in the hands of Sgt Peterson and crew on Operations BRANDROLL/BALDRIC. The target area was located, but not the precise drop zone, which was blotted out by the snow, and this became yet another abortive sortie, which ended with a safe landing at 01.44. Sgt Jones, meanwhile, was struggling back on one engine from an abortive sortie over Belgium, and failed by twenty miles to reach the English coast.

Two bodies came ashore two weeks later, it is believed in a dinghy, and, it seems, therefore, that Whitley Z6728 was successfully ditched, and that most, if not all of the eight men on board survived the impact, and either drowned or succumbed to exposure. This operation is not detailed in the ORB for this night, but the entry for the 29th records the aircraft and crew as missing.

This was to be an eventful night for Whippy Nesbitt-Dufort, who had taken a Lysander to central France to pick up two agents from a field near Issoudun. This operation is also not recorded in the ORB, and the details come from Freddie Clark's account. With his passengers on board, he took off, and found his path blocked by weather conditions so severe, that they were quite impossible to circumnavigate. With his engine icing up, he opted to return to the field he had recently departed, but was forced to land in a different one, which had a ditch running across it. T1508 came to a stop with its nose in the ditch and its tail in the air, but virtually undamaged, and its occupants emerged entirely unscathed. Nesbitt-Dufort would be forced to spend a month as a guest of the French underground, until being picked up by Sticky Murphy on the 1st of March, in an Anson borrowed from 10 O.T.U., and, on his return, he would be awarded a well-earned DSO. The Lysander was less fortunate, however, and was totally destroyed by a train as it was being towed across a railway line. Whether this was an unfortunate accident, or an inventive way of preventing it from falling into enemy hands is uncertain. This proved to be the final Lysander pick-up sortie undertaken by 138 Squadron, as responsibility for this type of operation would be assumed by the soon-to-be-formed 161 Squadron.

The 29th brought an influx of new pilots to the squadron, and the promotion to squadron leader rank of F/L Hockey. P/O Russell and F/L Outram arrived from Abingdon, while F/Os Krol and Jasinski were posted in from the Polish Depot, and F/L Davies DFC from Kinloss. The month's operational activity ended on the night of the 31st with two container drops, carried out by P/O Simmonds and Sgt Peterson. The former took off first in Z9232 at 19.35, to carry out Operation OVERCLOUD 2, and reached the drop zone at 23.35 to successfully deliver four containers. On return, the poor weather conditions persuaded him to land at Steeple Morden in Cambridgeshire. The latter was airborne on Operation OVERCLOUD 3 at 21.04 in Z9282, and reached his target area at 00.55, before also dropping four containers and returning safely home to land at 03.54.

February 1942

The Armstrong Whitworth Whitley Mk. V was the mainstay of the squadron in the first two years of operations. The type flew 219 sorties for the loss of 12 aircraft (Crown Copyright).

There would be no SOE/SIS operations for almost the entire month, until a flurry of them was mounted during the final few days, and the Command's bomber squadrons were also sparsely employed. Attacks on the Scharnhorst, Gneisenau and Prinz Eugen at Brest were mounted on the evenings of the 6th, 10th and the 11th, and, shortly after the last mentioned, the cruisers slipped anchor, before heading under a strong escort into the Channel in an audacious bid for freedom. The poor weather conditions were helpful to Vice-Admiral Otto Ciliax, the fleet commander, whose flag was on Scharnhorst, and it was not until 10.30 hours on the morning of the 12th, that the enemy fleet was first spotted by a pair of Spitfires. In accordance with orders, the two high-ranking pilots from Kenley did not report their findings until landing, at which juncture only 5 Group was standing by at four hours readiness. A plan had been prepared to deal with this eventuality under the code name Operation Fuller, but it ground painfully slowly into action, and it was 13.30 before the first sorties were launched. Thereafter, while the light lasted, a record number of 242 daylight sorties were dispatched against the warships, but the low cloud base and squally conditions prevented most crews from locating their quarry. Some attacks were carried out, but no hits were scored, and fifteen Bomber Command aircraft and crews were lost, mostly without trace in the sea. The enemy fleet made good its escape into the North Sea, and by the following morning, all elements had reached home ports. The episode caused major embarrassment to the government and the nation, but brought a welcome end to a long-running saga, which had been a costly distraction for the Command.

A few days earlier, on the 10th, the armed merchant ship Alcantara had departed Boston, on America's eastern seaboard, and set course for England, carrying among its passengers ACM Sir Arthur Harris. He had spent the previous eight months as part of a diplomatic and military mission to the United States, and had played a major role in cementing relations between the two nations. He was coming home to assume the post of Commander-in-Chief Bomber Command, having spent the war up to November 1940 as A-O-C 5 Group. From then until the American interlude, he had been a Deputy Chief-of-the-Air-Staff to Sir Charles Portal, and was a bomber baron to the core. He had been a squadron commander in the twenties and thirties in the Middle East, and spent much of his time developing the theory and practice of bombing by both day and night. He would take up his appointment on the 22nd, but, in the meantime, a new Air Ministry directive was issued on the 14th, which stated quite unequivocally, that the primary objective of bomber operations from now on should be the morale of the enemy's civilian population, particularly the workers. Harris would pursue this policy with a will, and was one of its most vociferous advocates, but he was not, as many believe, the architect of area bombing. Area bombing had been a fact since late 1940, but the new directive swept away all pretence, and, for the time being at least, would allow the Command to be free of non-strategic distractions.

On the same day as the new directive was issued, 161 Squadron was formed at Newmarket around a nucleus of 138 Squadron personnel, but would move to Graveley after just two weeks. The commanding officer was W/C "Mouse" Fielden, who had formerly commanded the King's Flight, and he was able to call upon the services of Sticky Murphy and Guy Lockhart, as these were posted in along with 138 Squadron's Lysanders. The 138 Squadron ORB records Murphy's posting to 161 Squadron on the 14th, but states his destination to be Graveley rather than Newmarket. On the 16th of June, Murphy would relinquish his command of the Lysander Flight in favour of Guy Lockhart, on posting to the Air Ministry, and this was to keep him away from the operational scene for a year. In June 1943, he would begin a Mosquito conversion course, and, in September be posted to 23 Squadron in Malta, where he would soon become a flight commander, and ultimately the commanding officer. A man of enormous popularity for his charm, good nature, bad singing and love of life, he would lead by example from the front, where his courage and daring could act as an inspiration to the rest of the squadron. Shortly after returning to England in May 1944, 23 Squadron would be posted to 100 Group Bomber Command as one of seven similar units employing the "Serrate" electronic device to home-in on enemy night fighters. This highly effective bomber support work was to bring rich rewards in terms of shot-down enemy night fighters, but it would also cost "Sticky" Murphy his life in early December 1944.

Guy Lockhart would fly his last Lysander sortie with 161 Squadron on the 22nd of December 1942, before handing the flight over to S/L Hugh Verity. Later he would serve at the Air Ministry, before, in November 1943, being appointed as a flight commander with the newly formed 627 Squadron, a Pathfinder unit operating Mosquitos out of Oakington. Six weeks later, on New Year's Day 1944, he would, at last, be given his own command, with the formation of another new Mosquito squadron, 692, as a member of the Pathfinder's Light Night Striking Force. However, following the loss of 7 Squadron's commanding officer in mid March, Lockhart would return to Oakington as his replacement, and be killed, when his

Lancaster was lost during an operation to Friedrichshafen at the end of April. Whippy Nesbitt-Dufort would also be drafted into 161 Squadron on his return from France, while Gordon Scotter would arrive in May for a brief stay. The latter began a career as a test pilot shortly afterwards, and after the war joined Rolls Royce, where he remained until his untimely death in 1969.

Two more Halifaxes had been added to the strength of 138 Squadron, by the time that operations resumed from Stradishall and Lakenheath on the night of the 25/26th. F/Sgt Pieniazek lifted L9618 into the air from the latter at 18.50 to begin Operation COLLAR over Poland. Carrying six agents, two containers and two packages, he adopted the standard route out via Schleswig-Holstein and the Baltic, but found heavy cloud all the way to the target area near Wyszkow, thirty miles north-east of Warsaw. This prevented the crew from being able to identify pinpoints on the ground, but did not discourage heavy flak batteries from taking pot-shots at the Halifax when over Sylt, Kiel and Stettin. Despite the huge effort and commitment to reach the drop zone, and after circling for ten minutes, no reception committee presented itself, and the operation had to be abandoned, a safe return culminating with a landing at base after eleven hours and thirty-five minutes aloft. S/L Hockey had taken off in L9613 five minutes after Sgt Pieniazek, and set course for Norway to carry out Operation CLAIRVOYANT, hoping to pinpoint on the Norwegian coast. Sadly, the cloud that had defeated the Polish drop, thwarted also S/L Hockey, for whom icing conditions added to the difficulties, and he abandoned the sortie to land at base at 03.50. Whitley Z9230 was the third aircraft to depart Stradishall on this night, lifting off at 20.59 in the hands of F/L Davies for Operation CATARRH over Holland. He became another victim of the conditions, after finding it impossible to see either land or sea, and abandoned his sortie to return for a safe landing at 01.20. The final operation to be mounted on this night was CARROT, for which P/O Smith took off at 21.08 in Whitley Z9287. He crossed the English coast at Southwold, before swinging to port to pinpoint on Vlieland, from where he set course for Zwolle, some eighty miles to the south east. Once there, the conditions also prevented him from identifying ground detail, and he returned home to land after a relatively short flight of four and a half hours.

By the evening of the 27th, the weather conditions had improved somewhat, setting off another night of intense activity to try to clear the backlog of outstanding operations. First off the ground at 18.50 was Halifax L9618, with F/Sgt Pieniazek at the controls, and bound for Poland for a second attempt at Operation COLLAR, the drop site for which, on this occasion was eight kilometres north-east of the railway station at Konskie, south of Warsaw. All went well until the Danish coast was reached at 21.23, when engine problems forced an early return. S/L Hockey took off at 18.55 in Halifax L9613 to carry out Operation BOOT, also over Poland, and this was the first British crew to attempt a drop into that country. They took the experienced F/O Krol to help with navigation to the target area near Piotrkow Trybunalski, south of Lodz, but encountered ten-tenths cloud fifty miles out over the North Sea. This persisted over Denmark and the German Baltic coast, where the severe cold deposited ice on the control surfaces and propellers, forcing S/L Hockey to turn back. He landed back at Stradishall in the most appalling blizzard conditions, and, while taxying back to his dispersal on the frozen and rutted track, he had the misfortune to run over a member of the ground crew, Cpl White, fatally injuring him. P/O Simmonds was the last to set off, at 21.33, in Whitley Z9232, bound for Holland and Operations CARROT/CATARRH. The Dutch coast was crossed in ten-tenths cloud north of Alkmaar, but the skies cleared over the mainland, and the drop zone was reached at 23.36. The agent parachuted into a clearing in a wood, after which, course was set for Meppel, from where a railway line was followed to reach the next drop. Two containers were delivered to a reception committee at 00.07, before a safe return ended with a landing at base at 02.50.

During his first week as C-in-C, Harris contented himself with a continuation of the small-scale attacks on German ports, which had been the fare since the start of the year. At Kiel on the 26/27th, the Gneisenau was struck by a high explosive bomb intended for the floating dock, and her sea-going career was ended for good. This was somewhat ironic, as she was now supposedly in safe haven after enduring and surviving almost a year of constant bombardment at Brest. Her main armament was removed subsequently for use as a shore battery. Harris had arrived at the helm with firm ideas already in place, on how to win the war by bombing alone. He was under no illusions about the current state of the Command, however, and recognized, that the transformation to war-winning potential would be a long and painful process. Never-the-less, a start had to be made, and his first large-scale operations would employ new tactics to increase their effectiveness. Until now, multiple targets had been attacked by smallish numbers of aircraft, each operating at an individual height, heading and even time, thus diluting the effort and limiting the damage inflicted, while allowing the defences to concentrate on individual aircraft. Harris believed that the way forward lay in concentration, in pushing the maximum number of aircraft across the aiming point in the shortest possible time, thus overwhelming the defences and the emergency services. Thus was born the bomber stream, which would form the basis of all major Bomber Command night operations over Germany for the remainder of the war. Harris also knew, that urban areas are more efficiently destroyed by fire rather than blast, and it would not be long before the bomb loads carried by his aircraft reflected this thinking. One drawback of Harris's single-minded commitment to the all-out bombing of Germany, was his intense dislike of any distractions, and his resentment towards any who wanted to siphon off one of his aircraft for a purpose other than bombing. This was not good news for those with interests in SOE and SIS matters, although with Churchill's backing, they would always get the necessary equipment. To be fair to Harris, though, whenever he was overruled by higher authority in areas where he was left with no room to manoeuver, he generally played the game.

March 1942

S/L Romanoff arrived on posting from Ringway on the 1st, to assume the role of B Flight commander, and there was a promotion to squadron leader rank for F/L Davies. It was a busy day for the "moon" squadrons, firstly for 161 Squadron, as it moved from Newmarket to Graveley, and, secondly, for both units in preparing for a night of operations. In the event, 138 Squadron put just two Whitleys into the air over France, in an attempt to clear up some of the outstanding operations abandoned over the past month through weather or technical problems. W/C Farley took off at 18.32 in Whitley Z9287 to carry out Operations MOUSE/VERMILION, and crossed the French coast near Caen at 8,500 feet, before pinpointing on the River Loire, four miles east of Blois. He ultimately delivered one agent from around 600 feet about ten miles south-south-east of the intended drop site, and also released a package and a pigeon. The remainder of the trip was uneventful, and he landed initially at Tangmere at 03.27.

The ORB provides a confusing picture of Sgt Wilde's activities on this night, with two separate entries on different pages describing Operations CANTICLE/DUNCAN & MASTIFF/INCOMPARABLE on one, and Operation PERIWIG on the other, both undertaken in Z9286, with a take-off time of 18.48, and a landing time of 01.50. Details for PERIWIG, which appears to be his first drop, are more comprehensive, and describe him crossing the French coast at 8,000 feet north of the River Somme, before pinpointing on Douai at 2,000 feet, and descending to 400 feet over the drop site. He circled from 21.50 to 22.40, but received no signal from the ground, and eventually gave up, presumably, then setting course for his next briefed location. The entry for this other operation suggests that he found the target area without undue difficulty, and delivered his agents successfully, but pigeons under Operations CANTICLE and DUNCAN became detached, and one remained in the aircraft. On the way home on a reciprocal course, leaflets were dropped over Douai. The likelihood is, that PERIWIG was accidentally omitted from the original entry, and added out of sequence on the following page between operations for the nights of the 2/3rd and 3/4th.

Three Whitley operations were launched on the night of the 2/3rd, beginning, it is believed, with BALACLAVA, for which, no take-off time is recorded. Sgt Peterson was the pilot of Z9282, which crossed the French coast south of Abbeville at 5,000 feet, before descending to 2,500 for the 150-mile leg to Sedan in eastern France. The drop site was close to a wood, where a single white light was being waved by a man on the ground. The containers were released in a single salvo, and the Whitley was back on the ground at Stradishall by 23.30. Operations BRANDROLL/BALDRIC were undertaken by S/L Davies in Z9230, which took off at 18.56 with two SIS agents on board. The English coast was crossed near Tangmere, and landfall made over France north of the Somme, probably at Berck-sur-Mer. From there, an easterly course was set to Douai, and altitude reduced to 800 feet, from where the drop site was clearly visible. The passengers were delivered, and a safe return completed at 00.22. Finally, T4166 took off at 22.50 on Operations COLLIE/TIGER/TERRIER, with Sgt Thompson at the controls on his first sortie since joining the squadron. The details as recorded in the ORB are sparse, mentioning only that he crossed the French coast near Abbeville, and successfully delivered his three passengers and pigeons, before returning safely home.

The night of the 3/4th brought five operations, with departures from Stradishall spread throughout the evening, beginning, it is believed, with Halifax L9618, which took off at 18.38 for Operation COLLAR, with F/Sgt Pieniazek at the controls, and F/Sgt Klosowski as second pilot. This was the third attempt to complete the drop near Wyszkow, and retraced the steps of F/Sgt Pieniazek's previous effort a week earlier which had been thwarted by engine problems. This time, the Halifax behaved impeccably, crossing Denmark and the frozen Baltic to reach the planned drop zone in good weather conditions and moonlight. It was only during the fourth circuit that lights appeared on the ground, upon which, the agents parachuted down from 900 feet, and a reciprocal course was set for home. A safe return was made to conclude another twelve-hour round trip. The persistence and determination of special operations crews was remarkable. After sometimes long and arduous outward flights, they would be prepared to stooge around in the target area, awaiting the appearance of a reception committee, and widen their search if no signal was forthcoming, all the time exposing themselves to the risk of being picked up by a night fighter. This was the case for P/O Smith and crew, who took-off at an unspecified time in Whitley Z9275, to carry out Operation ADJUDICATE. The French coast was crossed at Caen at 6,000 feet, before height was reduced to 1,500 feet for the pinpoint on a wood north of Levron (*difficult to decipher hand-written entry*). The crew searched for an hour for a reception committee, before observing signal lights fourteen miles south of the briefed drop site. A package was delivered from 600 feet, and a safe return made on a reciprocal track to land at 02.49.

Operation RUM began with the take-off of Whitley Z9158 at 20.27, piloted by P/O Anderle. He crossed the French coast at 2,000 feet, before climbing to 6,500 feet to clear the mountains in the central region. The three passengers were Russian NKVD agents, one of whom was a woman, a fact to which the crew members were oblivious, and they were disgorged over the

Pages from Sgt Pieniazek's Log Book with entries referring to special operations flown by his crew in March 1942. (J. Pieniazek via PH)

drop site from a height of 600 feet. Task completed, a course was set for home, and a safe landing carried out at 05.36. Also operating on this night for the first time was F/L Outram, who took off at 21.00 in Whitley Z9286 on Operations BREVET/BRAVERY/PERIWIG 1. The French coast was crossed at 4,000 feet at Point Haut-Banc, and a course set for north-eastern France, following the line of the Oise canal to the pinpoint for the first two components of the night's work. The drop site was picked up, and the three agents sent on their way from a height of 600 feet, before a new course took them over the frontier into Belgium. A triangular display of lights on the ground identified the waiting reception committee, and the containers fell away accurately to complete PERIWIG 1. F/L Outram brought the aircraft home via the north bank of the Somme and Tangmere, and landed safely at 02.35.

Another of the newer recruits to special operations was P/O Frank "Bunny" Rymills, a tall, fair-haired pilot in his very early twenties, who already had a bomber tour behind him as a sergeant pilot, and a DFM to show for his efforts. He was, reputedly, a first class poacher, a hobby pursued purely as a distraction from the war, and had the war not interfered with his plans, he would have graduated as an architect. He and his crew were last away on this busy night, taking off in Whitley Z9230 at 23.19, bound for Operation TURNIP over Holland, hoping to deliver the agents, who had declined to parachute onto the snow-covered terrain at the end of January. They crossed the Dutch coast at 6,000 feet over the dunes north of Ijmuiden, before dropping down to 2,000 feet to search for the drop site. The ground was still concealed under a covering of snow, and, in the face of continued reluctance to jump on the part of the agents, P/O Rymills was forced to bring them back home. On the way, eight pigeons were released over Hoorn, on the eastern side of the Den Helder peninsular, and a safe landing was completed at 04.10.

This night's intensive activity by 138 Squadron had been masked to an extent by Harris's first major operation as C-in-C. He had sent a force of 235 aircraft, a record to a single target, against the Renault lorry factory at Billancourt in Paris, in a carefully orchestrated three-wave attack, which would form the basis of most future operations. Led by experienced crews, and with extensive use of flares to provide illumination, the raid inflicted damage on every building within the complex, and halted production for a month. Over 220 crews reported bombing as briefed, many of them from low level in the face of a weak flak defence, and the operation was an outstanding success for the period, gained for the loss of a single Wellington. The satisfaction was marred only by the heavy casualties visited upon the civilian population in adjacent residential districts, and this was a problem that could never be satisfactorily addressed. It was something of a paradox, that Harris, as a champion of area bombing, should gain his first victory by way of a precision raid.

Back at Stradishall on the night of the 8/9th, Sgt Wilde took off at 23.20 in Whitley Z9286 to carry out Operation FRENSHAM, a container drop over Belgium. Everything was proceeding according to plan as he crossed the English coast at 4,000 feet, but he was forced to turn back shortly afterwards, when his altimeter failed. The moon period was about to end, when the new B Flight commander, S/L Romanoff, attempted to repeat the operation two nights later. Almost immediately after take-off, Whitley Z9125 returned to earth in a nearby field, and exploded after catching fire. Romanoff and all but the rear gunner in his Czechoslovakian crew were killed, and this bitter blow to the squadron was most keenly felt by his close friend, S/L Hockey. The front-line squadrons of the Command had also been active over the three nights from the 8/9th to the 10/11th, as Harris attempted to deliver a decisive blow against the mighty industrial city of Essen, home of the giant Krupp armaments manufacturing concern. Essen was to feature prominently in his future plans, but, despite dispatching a total of 524 aircraft over the three nights, those in the vanguard equipped with the new Gee navigation device, the raids were a major disappointment, inflicting only slight superficial damage. Better results were obtained at Cologne on the night of the 13/14th, but, it would be a long time yet, before technology provided the answers to the problems of navigation and target identification through cloud and industrial haze.

Whitley Z9125 which was lost on 10/11th March when the aircraft crashed shortly after take-off, with the loss of S/L Romanoff and three of his crew.

During the monthly stand-down on the 14th, 138 Squadron moved to a new and permanent home, where it would remain until a matter of weeks before the end of hostilities. Tempsford lay nine miles to the east of Bedford, and was built on what might be termed a reclaimed bog. As time was to prove, this was a fact that would be difficult to ignore for pilots who put a wheel off the concrete taxy ways. Built by John Laing and Sons between late 1940 and the last days of the summer of 1941, it spread across Gibraltar Farm, a name that would persist throughout its occupation by the RAF. A few of its buildings were retained and used as offices and stores, and they acted as a natural camouflage to casual onlookers from the air. To these were added the necessary hangers, a control tower and nissen hut accommodation, and a standard triangulation of runways, two of which terminated just short of the main LNER railway line from London to Edinburgh.

Tempsford was not the first choice of those seeking a permanent home for the two moon squadrons. Graveley, the current home of 161 Squadron, had been preferred. but someone suggested that it was not ideally suited to the launching of heavily laden Halifaxes, and the rest is history. It should be mentioned, however, that 35 Squadron experienced no difficulty in launching its heavily laden Halifaxes and later Lancasters from Graveley from August 1942 right through to the end of the war. One senses, perhaps, the hand of Harris manipulating matters, for he was, after all, the C-in-C Bomber Command, and, in the overall scheme of the strategic bombing offensive, the moon squadrons were, in his eyes at least, entirely alien entities, with no useful part to play. The temptation in such a situation was probably to find a backwater for them to play in, and this was Tempsford. Ironically, as the war progressed, and the Allies began preparing to invade Fortress Europe, Harris would actually find himself lending aircraft and crews to Tempsford, particularly from the Stirling squadrons of 3 Group, although this was only after they had been withdrawn from operations over Germany.

Two pilots, P/Os Turnham and Newport-Tinley, were posted in from 10 O.T.U on the 20th, and they would experience the customary bedding-in period of mushroom treatment and heel-kicking, until the "powers-that-be" decided to bestow enlightenment upon them. The honour of being the first to operate from Tempsford fell to P/O Smith, who took off at 19.00 on the 23rd in Whitley Z9286, to undertake Operations LUCKYSHOT/WEASEL. He crossed the French coast at le Crotoy, and found increasing haze to be blotting out ground detail for twenty miles on approach to the drop site near Givet, on the Belgian border. He reached the target area at 22.21, and searched in vain for an hour and forty minutes for a signal from a reception committee, before giving up and returning home to land at Tangmere at 02.03. P/O Miller took off at 19.05 in Z9230 to carry out Operation FUERTY, but a problem with his port engine curtailed the sortie, and he landed at Tangmere at 20.30, after jettisoning the containers over the airfield.

The first success of the moon period came at the hands of P/O Russell on the following night, the 24/25th, when he took off at 19.01 in Z9232 on Operation MINK. He crossed the French coast at 7,000 feet near le Touquet, and pinpointed on a large wooded area north of Abbeville, from which a course was set for Douai. The final leg from Douai to the drop site was covered without incident, but it was only after circling for forty minutes, that the passenger parachuted away from a height of 600 feet. The same route was adopted for the return flight, and a safe landing was carried out at Abingdon at 00.49. S/L Davies took off in Z9282 at 19.15 for a second attempt to complete Operations LUCKYSHOT/WEASEL, and he crossed the French coast at 4,000 feet over Berck-sur-Mer at 21.00, before setting course for the target area. He reached the drop site on the Franco/Belgian border at 22.15, and observed a triangle of lights. However, these were extinguished almost immediately, and he circled for an hour in the hope of completing the job. Unfortunately, the lights did not reappear, and the attempt was ultimately abandoned, and a safe return made to a landing at Tangmere at 01.20.

Coincidentally, Tangmere was the station from which P/O Kingsford-Smith had set off in Whitley Z9275 at 20.30 that evening, for another crack at Operation FUERTY. P/O Kingsford-Smith was a relative of the famous pioneering Australian aviator, Sir Charles Kingsford-Smith, who had set many records in the twenties and thirties, including trans-Pacific Australia to America flights in both directions, and had also pioneered airline routes across the globe. He had disappeared without trace between India and Singapore in 1935, while attempting another record. A number of family members would fly with Bomber Command during the war, one of them being appointed as the first commanding officer of 5 Group's 463 Squadron RAAF in November 1943. This was 138 Squadron's Kingsford-Smith's first SOE sortie as crew captain, and, he was, no doubt, optimistic about his chances as he crossed the French coast and made for Tours. From there he set course for Vannes to the west, and thence to the drop site, but, despite circling the target area for half an hour, then returning to tours and retracing his steps to Vannes, and stooging around between Vannes and the drop site for a considerable time, no signals were received from the ground, and he brought the Whitley back to a landing at Tangmere at 01.30. Finally, Sgt Owen, who was also flying as captain for the first time, departed Tempsford at 19.38 in Whitley Z9159, to carry out Operation PERIWIG over

Belgium. He crossed the French coast at le Crotoy at 21.28, and set course for Douai, and beyond to the drop site. He arrived in the target area at 22.29, and circled for an hour at 700 feet, from where the ground was visible, despite a covering of haze. Sgt Owen did see a light, but it was extinguished almost instantly, and he eventually gave up and headed for the coast at Berck-sur-Mer, before landing at Tangmere at 01.07, to bring the curtain down on a disappointing night.

The frustrating start to the new moon period continued on the 25/26th, with a night of heavy activity for both front line bomber units and 138 Squadron. The former went back to Essen with a record force of 254 aircraft, and destroyed one house, while the latter dispatched six aircraft, three Whitleys and three Halifaxes, and also ended up with nothing to show for their endeavours. The first to venture out from Tempsford at 19.55 was Whitley Z9287, captained by P/O Smith, on Operation ADJUDICATE 3. The French coast was crossed at 21.57, and a course set for Limoges, before a pinpoint was obtained on the River Loire at 23.00. Thereafter, the track was lost, and P/O Smith found himself at 8,000 feet over mountainous country to the east of the intended course. He eventually got back on track and reached the drop zone at 01.06, but, in the absence of a reception committee, abandoned the sortie at 01.52, and set a course for home, where a safe landing was carried out at 05.35 with the containers still on board.

Meanwhile, a Polish crew, captained by F/O Zygmuntowicz, had taken off at 20.00 in V9976, bound for Austria on Operation WHISKEY, and carrying the last two of the five NKVD agents, who had recently been landed in Scotland. The Halifax slid over the French coast at Le Touquet at 21.27, and set course in good weather conditions until south of Mannheim, where ground mist developed, and blotted out the terrain. The general target area, some twenty miles south-west of Vienna, was eventually identified at 01.30, but not the precise location for the drop, and the operation was abandoned after an hour-long search. The French coast was crossed homebound at 04.45, and a landing made at Tangmere after ten hours aloft. There were two departures logged at 20.15, Whitley Z6959 and Halifax L9613, the former heading for Denmark on Operation TABLETOP captained by F/L Outram. The Danish coast was crossed north of Esbjerg at 23.49, and a course set for the drop zone, which was identified and circled for thirty minutes before the task was abandoned in the absence of a reception committee. The long, cold sortie was completed with a safe landing at home at 05.20.

S/L Hockey was bound for Czechoslovakia on Operations BIVOUAC/ZINC, and crossed the French coast at 9,000 feet over Le Crotoy at 21.45. Increasing haze and fog gradually reduced visibility to the point where it became impossible to continue, and the decision was taken to turn back for Tangmere, where a safe landing was made at 06.40, after a trip lasting almost eleven hours. Whitley T4166 had taken off at 20.19 in the hands of Sgt Thompson and his crew to carry out Operations BURR/BOUQUET, an SIS drop over France. Half way across the Channel the port engine developed a problem, which was not terminal, but would persist for the remainder of the flight. The French coast was crossed at Le Crotoy at 7,000 feet at 22.08, and a new course set for Cambrai, but ground haze made it impossible to identify it, or, for that matter, any other urban area. The sortie was abandoned, and the French coast re-crossed homebound north of Dieppe at 00.27, before a safe landing was carried out three hours later. Finally on this night, F/Sgt Pieniazek, who, like S/L Hockey, had been briefed for a trip to Czechoslovakia on Operations STEEL/IRON, took off at 20.25 with five agents on board, and crossed the French coast at le Crotoy at 22.10. A course was set for Metz in north-eastern France, and then Langenburg in southern Germany, and the target area near Pilsen was reached at 01.30. Haze and poor visibility caused the crew to run out of identifiable features on the ground, and, after circling the general area of the first drop zone for twenty-five minutes, they were forced to throw in the towel and head for the second one, at Kolin, south-east of Prague. Here, the conditions were even worse, with mist filling the valley and obscuring the river pinpoints. The attempt was abandoned, and a safe return made at 05.45.

While Harris tried and failed again at Essen on the night of the 26/27th, 138 Squadron plugged away at what was becoming a serious backlog of operations. P/O Kingsford-Smith was first to take off at 19.45 in Whitley Z9159, to undertake Operations BOUQUET/ BURR/BREACH/BLOCK. The French coast was reached at Berck-sur-Mer at 7,000 feet at 21.20, before a gliding descent was carried out to 2,000 feet, and a course set for Cambrai. Four agents successfully dropped away and pigeons were released, before leaflets were delivered over Arras to the north-west on the way home. Z9158 and Z9286 were both recorded as taking off from Tempsford at 20.00, the former on Operation SHAKESPEARE captained by P/O Russell. The French coast was reached at 21.38 at Fecamp, and a south-easterly course set to overfly Paris, although the capital was shrouded by haze. The route to the drop zone passed over Macon, where there was no blackout until the Whitley circled to pick up the next pinpoint, when the lights were extinguished. The River Saône was picked up and followed south to Lyon, where the lights remained on, and a triangulation of lights was identified from 3,000 feet, accompanied by the flashing of the letter K to confirm the presence of a reception committee. Packages were dropped accurately, before a course was set for home, which was reached at 04.11, pigeons having been released fifteen miles inland from the French coast on the way.

Sgt Wilde, meanwhile, piloting the latter Whitley on Operation PERIWIG 2, passed over the French coast at 7,000 feet at an indeterminate point in conditions of ground haze. A course was set for Douai en-route to Belgium, but, at 22.08, when about sixty miles inland and at 3,000 feet, persistently poor visibility persuaded him to abandon the sortie and turn for home. He re-crossed the French coast, again without obtaining a pinpoint, and reached the south coast of England some fifteen miles east of Tangmere, before landing at Tempsford at 00.10. Finally, Whitley Z9282 took off at 20.20 to carry out the combined SOE/SIS Operations ADJUDICATE 2/MERRY, with F/L Davies at the controls. The French coast was crossed east of Caen at 21.19 at 4,000 feet, and a new course set for Limoges, which was reached and circled until a pinpoint was identified and packages dropped. The second drop was in the Perigueux region, and lights were spotted when eight miles away, but no recognizable signal could be confirmed from the ground on arrival. A search was carried out from 500 feet for thirty-five minutes, before the attempt was abandoned and a course set for home, which was reached at 04.24.

The 27/28th was the night of the famous St Nazaire raid by commando and naval units, supported by elements from Bomber Command. The icing conditions and 10/10ths cloud that hampered the bombers' efforts, also defeated P/O Miller's attempt to clear up one of the outstanding operations to Belgium. He took off at 20.50 in Whitley Z9159 on Operations

LUCKY SHOT/WEASEL, but shortly after crossing the French coast, decided the prudent decision was to turn for home, and he was back on the ground at Tempsford at 00.33.

The above was actually the last of five operations for the night, the first of which, an attempted re-run of PERIWIG 2, having been launched at 19.45 in Whitley Z9286, with Sgt Wilde again in the pilot's seat. He crossed the south coast of England at 21.00, and set course for le Crotoy, encountering ten-tenths cloud and icing at 4,000 feet on the way. He climbed to 8,000 feet in an attempt to lose the cloud, but was unsuccessful, and, on reaching the French coast at 21.42, descended to 700 feet, where cloud was assessed at three-tenths. Lights from two aerodromes were spotted, possibly at Arras and Douai, and enemy aircraft could be seen circling at around 300 feet. With little prospect of completing the sortie in the prevailing conditions, Sgt Wilde reluctantly admitted defeat for the second time, and turned for home with his "cargo". Ten minutes after Sgt Wilde's departure from Tempsford, F/Sgt Pieniazek and his all-Polish crew lifted Halifax L9618 off the ground, with six agents on board bound for Czechoslovakia on Operation ZINC/STEEL. They crossed the French coast at 11,000 feet in ten-tenths cloud with icing conditions, before heading for Metz in eastern France, Passau in south-eastern Germany, and then Vienna, where they turned to the north to cross into Czechoslovakia. Navigation proved to be a nightmare during the entire outward flight, but the general area for the drop was eventually reached, although mist in the valleys continued to provide a challenge. The three ZINC agents were dropped with radios about twenty-four miles south-west of Jihlava, and, although the STEEL drop is not detailed in the ORB, three more agents and radio equipment were parachuted down into open country close to woods seven miles north-east of Kyov. On the way home, flak was encountered south of Mannheim, and intense and accurate light flak at Calais at 06.00, when the Halifax was at 5,000 feet. Only one of the agents was destined to survive, and it was he, who would help the Gestapo to hunt down the assassins of Heydrich.

F/O Zygmuntowicz and his crew took off at 20.00 in Halifax V9976 bound for Poland for another attempt to carry out Operation BOOT. They crossed over the island of Sylt at 22.25, and headed for Denmark, and then, from the Baltic towards the next navigation point, before deciding whether or not to continue. The weather proved to be good, and the decision was taken at 02.00 to press on to the drop zone. A course was set to Sieradz, south-west of Lodz, and then the drop site itself east of Czestochowa, some fifty miles further south. They were able to map-read to the target area, where a reception committee was identified, and the delivery of six agents completed successfully. They returned via a reciprocal route, experiencing hydraulics problems on the way, and running into searchlights over Copenhagen, and almost into seven enemy fighters over Sylt, but cloud and good fortune kept them safe until landing at Leconfield in Yorkshire at 08.00, after exactly twelve hours in the air.

There is some confusion concerning a sortie undertaken by F/Sgt Thompson and P/O Widdup, the latter flying as second pilot. The squadron ORB mentions only the loss of Whitley T4166 and its crew on the 28th, but provides no time of take-off, which presumably took place on the evening of the 27th. The operation was part of CATARRH/WATERCRESS, which involved a supply drop and the delivery of an agent to Holland. The agent, A. A. Baatsen, was parachuted over Steenwijk, east of the Ijsselmeer, and into a German trap, which ensnared him almost immediately on landing. The network had been under German control for some time, and it was they, who were making the arrangements with unsuspecting London contacts. The agent would be held and interrogated for more than two years, before eventually being executed at

Pilot F/O Zygmuntowicz (second from the right) with aircrew from 301 Bomber Squadron. First from the right pilot F/Sgt Waszak who served in 138 Squadron as well. The third in the back row is wireless operator Sgt Wilmanski, who was KIA with the entire crew of F/O Zygmuntowicz during the special operation on 20/21 April 1942. (W. Wawrzecki via PH)

Mauthausen concentration camp in September 1944. The drop had been observed by the enemy, who were able to monitor the supply drop at the second location also, and, presumably, prime the flak batteries on the island of Texel to prepare a reception for the homebound Whitley. The aircraft failed to return home, after crashing into the sea off Den Helder, and its fate only became clear after the body of the rear gunner, Sgt Wood, was washed ashore for burial.

On the night of the 28/29th, Harris dispatched a force of 234 aircraft to the Baltic port city of Lübeck, a target selected for its ease of location on an identifiable coastline, the paucity of its defences, and the half-timbered construction of the houses in the narrow streets of the old centre. The predominantly incendiary bomb loads reflected the fire-raising intent of the raid, which was conducted along the lines of the successful assault on the Renault works in Paris earlier in the month. The operation was an outstanding success, the first for the area bombing policy, and after the flames had done their work, 3,400 buildings were left either totally destroyed or seriously damaged. 138 Squadron took advantage of this activity to fly three sorties to Holland and two to Norway, beginning with TURNIP/LEEK, which were assigned to P/O Russell and crew in Whitley Z9286. They were airborne at 19.30, and were soon crossing the English coast at Cromer heading for Texel, at which point they flew down the Zuider Zee, pinpointing on Oosterdijk, Elburg and Deventer, before map-reading to the TURNIP drop zone. The passengers were delivered safely, and a course set for LEEK, where there turned out to be many houses, which unsettled the agents. They decided, that the area was too heavily populated to guarantee a secret drop, and opted to remain on board and return home.

Before the Russell crew had even reached the Norfolk coast outbound for Holland, Whitley Z9230 was racing down the runway at Kinloss, on the Moray Firth of north-east Scotland, and lifting into the air at 19.53 to head for Norway. Sitting in the pilot's seat in charge of Operation CHAIN was F/L Davies, and, two hours after take-off, he was able to watch Raege Fjord slide beneath as landfall was made. The coastline was followed to the next pinpoint, an undecipherable island, from where a course was set to the drop zone. The only illumination to be observed came from the headlights of a car parked off the road, and a dim orange glow in the bushes, about five miles south-south-east of the pinpoint. While F/L Davies circled the area, the car driver flashed a torch repeatedly, before driving onto a track and turning several times. Once satisfied that this was, indeed, the reception committee, the containers were dropped, and the car driver was observed to run towards them. Job done, F/L Davies turned for home, and landed safely at 05.55. Also launching from Kinloss on this night was P/O Smith, who took off in Whitley Z9287 at 20.18 on Operation GROUSE. Landfall over Norway was made without opposition between Sola and Stavanger, and the flight proceeded from there without incident to the drop zone. A container was dropped, but the passenger was reluctant to leave, and there was a delay before he could be persuaded to jump some two to four miles south-west of the intended pinpoint. Lights were seen on the ground, apparently from cottages a mile or so away to the north and south, but the crew did not hang around, and set course for home, landing at Acklington in Northumberland at 04.22.

P/O Kingsford-Smith and crew were assigned to Operation LETTUCE, and took off from Tempsford in Whitley Z9159 at 20.28, before crossing the English coast near Cromer and then the centre of Vlieland at 2,000 feet. They pinpointed on Staveren, Elburg and Deventer, from where it was possible to map-read directly to the target area. The passengers were dropped successfully, and a reciprocal route was adopted for the return flight, during which, a good many lights were noted in Zwolle railway yards. The last departure from Tempsford on this busy night was by S/L Outram and crew in Whitley Z9232, who took off at 23.40 on Operation NASH. They crossed the English coast at 00.25, and made landfall over Terschelling at 01.47, although they were not entirely sure of their exact location. They continued on eastwards, until a landmark was recognized, and then turned south, leaving Leeuwarden to port, and followed the railway line to the drop zone, where the passenger parachuted out. A safe return was completed with a landing at base at 04.40. All of the agents and containers were delivered as planned, but a number of the former would not survive the night.

Further attempts were made to clear up two quite long-standing operations to Belgium on the night of the 29/30th. P/O Miller was first away at 19.55 in an unspecified Whitley bound for Operation PERIWIG 2 over France. He crossed the French coast north of the mouth of the River Somme at 21.35, before setting course for Douai, from where he was able to map-read to the drop zone. Ground details were clearly visible, but no reception committee was evident, and lights from traffic on surrounding roads and nearby houses had an unsettling effect on the crew. While circling, the front hatch was inadvertently opened, and as efforts were being made to close it, the Whitley wandered off track towards the north-east, and found itself in a flak and searchlight zone over the Scheldt Estuary. Course was set for home, and a safe landing made at Tangmere at 01.10. P/O Bunny Rymills took off in Whitley Z9232 at 20.00 on Operations LUCKY SHOT/WEASEL, and crossed the French coast at le Crotoy at 21.30, before setting course for Aublain and then Givet on the Franco/Belgian border. From Givet, he was able to map-read to the target area, which was reached at 22.30, and, after circling for a time, located the drop point, where no reception committee presented itself. Some red and while lights were observed, but they were believed to be from a railway. Rymills was certain about his location near St-Hubert, but map-read to Beausaint and back, before abandoning the sortie, and returning by the same route to land at Boscombe Down at 05.00, after jettisoning the containers.

Some compensation was gained on the following night, however, when F/O Zygmuntowicz and F/Sgt Pieniazek each flew successful Halifax sorties to Poland to deliver a total of twelve agents and stores. The former lifted L9613 into the air at 19.05 to carry out Operation LEGGING, and crossed the enemy coast over the Danish island of Mandø, before entering Poland and pinpointing on Sieradz, south-east of Lodz, and map-reading to the target area. The drop zone was reached at 01.00, and the precise pinpoint easily located, upon which the agents were dropped from 1,200 feet ten minutes later. Thereafter, a homeward course was set, which took them over the Baltic to Denmark and out over Esbjerg, and the operation was successfully concluded with a landing at Langham in Rutland at 06.50. L9618 took off at 19.45 on Operation BELT, and crossed the Danish coast north of Esbjerg at 22.15, and the German coast near Kolberg at 23.24. F/Sgt Pieniazek pinpointed on the River Vistula and reached the target area near Tluszcz, north-east of Warsaw, at 01.15, before dropping the agents from 1,200 feet at 01.55. The homeward course took the Halifax out over Stettin, which was reached at 03.47, and the tired crew finally landed at Bodney in Norfolk at 07.35.

April 1942

The first operation of the new month took place on the night of the 1/2nd, when S/L Davies and crew took off in Whitley Z9230 at 21.23 on Operations ADJUDICATE 2/SYCAMORE. The French coast was crossed near le Havre at 23.10, from which point it was possible to map-read towards Limoges, where lights could be seen through a break in the cloud. The passenger was dropped right on schedule, before a new course was set for Perigueux, some fifty miles to the south-west, which was reached at 1,200 feet, but obscured by cloud extending down almost to ground level. At 01.54 the attempt was abandoned, and a return course was adopted, which took the Whitley via Caen and Worthing to a safe landing at Tempsford at 06.36. P/O Miller and crew took off at 22.35 in Whitley Z9158 on Operation FUERTY. They crossed the French coast at 00.28 and set course for Tours, which they pinpointed, before heading towards Chateau la Vellins and ultimately Vannes. All of the landmarks were clearly visible, and P/O Miller flew up and down the neighbourhood for an hour in search of a reception committee. Sadly, no signal was received from the ground, and P/O Miller eventually gave up and headed home, where he landed at 05.35.

On the following night, two Whitley flights were scheduled, the first by P/O Kingsford-Smith and crew, who took off in Z9295 at 22.27 to undertake Operation BALACLAVA. They crossed the French coast at Abbeville at 23.58, and set course at between 2,000 and 3,000 feet for Soissons, forty miles north-east of Paris. Ground features stood out clearly, particularly so the double bend in the River Meuse, and the line of a forest edge with gaps near Saint-Leger, which meant that the crew was able to map-read to the drop zone. A train was seen travelling north as they located the pinpoint and delivered the container in response to a flashing light, which was immediately extinguished once the container was on the ground. A homeward course was set via le Touquet and Beachy Head, and a safe landing carried out at Tempsford at 04.32. Three minutes after Kingsford-Smith's departure, P/O Russell and crew took off in Whitley Z9275. They had been given Operation MANDAMUS to complete, and reached the French coast at Pointe Haut-Blanc at 23.57. They set course for Roye, Soissons and the River Aisne in north-eastern France, and then to the drop zone on the Belgian side of the frontier, but the inability to identify landmarks, despite searching at 1,500 feet until 02.18, forced the abandonment of the sortie. They returned home via an unidentified point on the French coast, and made landfall on the friendly side of the Channel over the Needles, at the western end of the Isle of Wight. The containers were jettisoned over Tempsford after permission to do so was obtained, and a safe landing was carried out at 05.47.

Five Whitleys were detailed for operations over Belgium on the night of the 5/6th, three of them trying to complete operations, which, by now, had failed repeatedly. There were to be late departures for all, beginning with P/O Russell, who took off in Z9146 at 23.50 on Operation MANFRIDAY. He reached the French coast without incident at Berck-sur-Mer at 01.39, and proceeded on an east-south-easterly course towards Cambrai. However, when eight miles short, the port engine began to fail, and this demanded an immediate abandonment of the sortie and an attempt to return home on a single engine. A message was sent to base as the ailing Whitley passed five miles to the south-west of Arras, at which point a single-engine enemy aircraft was reported by the rear gunner. P/O Russell had limited options in terms of evasive action, but ran through the tops of clouds, and the enemy aircraft was lost. The Whitley lost height steadily, and the containers were jettisoned to save weight as the nearest point on the English coast was sought. In the event, the starboard engine and altitude lasted until Abingdon was reached, and a safe landing was carried out at 06.10. P/O Smith was handed Operation MANDAMUS, for which he and his crew took off at 23.57 in Z9275, and crossed the French coast at le Crotoy at 01.49. Intense darkness enveloped the Whitley, rendering map-reading impossible, and the first one hundred miles over France was flown without any navigational aid. On reaching the general target area, a search was carried out for an hour and a quarter without success, and the attempt was abandoned, before a safe return culminated with a landing at Tempsford at 07.23.

P/O Miller and crew departed Tempsford at 00.05 in Whitley Z9158, to carry out Operation PERIWIG. They, too, crossed the French coast near le Crotoy, at 01.48 at an altitude of 5,000 feet, and proceeded to the target area in zero visibility. Despite descending to 1,200 feet, no ground detail could be seen, and the first pinpoint they positively identified was the beacon at Abingdon at 04.55, after returning from yet another failure with the pigeons and stores still on board. P/O Kingsford-Smith and crew were in Whitley Z9159, and took off at 00.26 on Operation LUCKYSHOT/WEASEL. They crossed the French coast at 01.49 while flying at 3,000 feet, before shedding a thousand feet in the hope of picking up some ground detail. Visibility remained at zero, however, and the flight continued on dead reckoning, with a turn onto a planned heading on e.t.a at 02.45. To continue was futile, and they turned back to land at Tempsford at 05.38 with the cargo still on board. F/L Outram and crew were the last to take to the air, lifting off from Tempsford in Z9232 at 01.05 to undertake Operation LEEK over Holland. It took just under ninety minutes to reach the Dutch coast north of Alkmaar, from where pinpoints were picked up at Oosterdijk and Enkhuizen. From Enkhuizen they flew back to the west a few miles directly to Harderwijk, which was clearly recognized and circled for forty minutes just to make sure. Finally, two agents parachuted to earth, and the Whitley turned for home, passing over Hoorn and Callantsoog in an indirect route to the safety of the North Sea, before landing safely at Tempsford at 06.00. Sadly, it would be only a matter of weeks before both agents were betrayed and arrested.

On the 8th, 161 Squadron began to remove itself from Graveley, for its transfer to Tempsford, which would be completed by the 11th. The two moon squadrons would remain together from this point, until an impending war's end ultimately reduced the need to support resistance organisations. The night of the 8/9th brought two long-range Halifax operations, one to Poland and the other to Austria, and the first to take off, at 19.35 for the former, Operation CRAVAT, was L9618, bearing the crew of F/Sgt Pieniazek and six agents, four containers and a package. They crossed the English coast at 19.35, and the enemy coast over Denmark at 21.44, meeting no opposition on the way. The first pinpoint was identified at Malmo, in south-western Sweden, where six or seven searchlights sprang into action and searched in vain for the intruder. A new course was set for Kelberg, and the German coast was crossed in ten-tenths cloud at 10,000 feet, without gaining a pinpoint. The poor visibility persisted all the way to the River Vistula, where matters improved as they turned towards the target area and descended to 3,000 feet. Midway between the Vistula and the drop zone a pinpoint was picked up at Plock, which enabled them to navigate to their ultimate destination, seven miles south-west of Lowicz. A PoW camp was clearly identified, and the lights of a reception committee appeared where expected. The agents and packages were parachuted into their arms from 1,000 feet at

01.20, but the lights were extinguished before the four containers could be delivered, and they had to be brought home. Heavy flak was encountered as they flew over Stettin at 12,000 feet on the way home at 02.55, and eight minutes of violent evasive action was required before they emerged safely on the other side. The Danish coast was crossed at Esbjerg at 05.15, and the Halifax touched down at Tempsford at 07.47. P/O Anderle and crew took off at 20.25 in L9613 to undertake Operation WHISKEY, and crossed the French coast at 21.42, before setting course for the target area in Austria, encountering heavy cloud and icing conditions on the way. They continued on south of Mannheim at 23.15, but could pick up no pinpoints, and the decision was taken to turn back on a reciprocal course. Paris passed beneath unseen, but la Roche-Guyon was recognized to the north-west of the French capital, before the coast was crossed at 03.30. Conditions over the Channel were very bad, but Tangmere eventually hove into sight, and a safe landing was carried out at 04.40 with the two NKVD agents still on board.

On the night of the 12/13th, S/L Davies and crew took off in Whitley Z9230 at 23.00 to carry out Operation TABLETOP over Denmark, which had first been attempted at the end of March. They crossed the English coast near Cromer thirty-eight minutes later, but twenty miles inland over enemy territory encountered thick fog, which persisted as they continued on eastwards until the e.t.a. for the drop was reached at 05.30. In the face of insurmountable odds, they turned back five minutes later, and landed back at Tempsford at 07.28. This seemingly ill-fated operation was rescheduled for the night of the 15/16th, when responsibility was handed to Sgt Wilde and his crew. Whitley Z9282 took off at 22.37, but immediately experienced an engine problem, which, although not instantly terminal, was a concern. Sgt Wilde persevered with it for an hour in the hope that it would clear, but, when thirty miles north-east of Cromer, and with no sign of an improvement, he decided to turn back. Possibly conscious of Harris's irritation at the hiving off of perfectly good bombers for non-bombing duties, the SOE authorities apparently assigned a single aircraft and crew to a bombing sortie also on this night. F/Sgt Pieniazek and his crew boarded Halifax L9613, before taking off at 19.35 and heading for the port of Königsberg in east Prussia. They carried six 500lb bombs, which they delivered as briefed from 1,000 feet, and returned safely after more than eleven hours in the air. It was one of the longest flights yet recorded for a bombing sortie. There is no mention of this operation in the squadron ORB, and the details come from Piotr Hodyra and Freddie Clark.

On the following night, F/O Smith and crew clambered into Whitley Z9287 along with three agents and two packages, and took off at 21.56 for yet another attempt at TABLETOP. They crossed the Danish coast north of Nissum at 02.11, and map-read across country to the target area, which was reached at 03.10. After circling for a short time, the lights of a reception committee were noticed, but not at the expected location. The agents parachuted from 800 feet, the opening of their canopies confirmed by the rear gunner, but he would not have known that two of them would sustain injuries by falling into trees. The Danish coast was crossed homebound at 04.10, and the English coast at 06.11. On the night of the 18/19th, F/O Zygmuntowicz and his crew took off at 20.30 in Halifax V9976, with four agents and stores on board, bound for Norway on Operations RAVEN A and RAVEN B. They crossed the enemy coast near Stavangar at 00.45, and map-read to the target area, which was something of a feat over a land dotted with lakes. Once in the general area of Voss at 01.30, it was impossible to establish the precise pinpoint, and they back-tracked to Sognefjord to try to re-orient themselves. Map-reading back towards the south, the drop zone was eventually identified, and once it was certain, that they were within an accepted radius of the pinpoint, the agents, containers and packages were delivered at 02.30. The return journey to a landing at Lossiemouth at 05.10 was accomplished without incident.

Observer F/L Voellnagel was the senior officer of Polish crews in 138 Squadron, assigned to the unit as the third crew from 301 Bomber Squadron. He was KIA on 20/21st April 1942 during Operation WHISKEY. (PISM via PH)

Two nights later F/O Zygmuntowicz and his crew were on duty again, this time to try once more to get the two NKVD agents into Austria after two previous failures of Operation WHISKEY. W/C Farley decided to name himself among the crew, to fulfil the role of dispatcher, and it proved to be a fateful decision. Flying in dense fog, Halifax V9976 smacked into the side of a Bavarian hill, south of the Teegensee, and within sight of the Austrian border, killing all eight crewmen and their Russian passengers. This was the first Polish crew to fail to return from SOE operations. Meanwhile, three of the squadron's Whitleys were engaged in leafleting sorties (nickels) over France, and this too was to lead to tragedy. The first of the trio to take off, at 20.45, was Sgt Wilde in Z9287, bound for Lyons. The French coast was crossed near Bayeux at 22.45, but severe icing was encountered, which caused an engine problem that threatened to compromise the operation. Flying on in a southerly direction, the Whitley reached the vicinity of Bourges in central France, but with more than a hundred miles still to go to Lyon, Sgt Wilde decided to deliver the leaflets, and seventeen packets were duly released from 6,500 to 7,000 feet. An arduous return flight through ten-tenths cloud was completed with a landing at Boscombe Down at 03.15.

P/O Russell and crew took off at 20.55 in Z9275, and reached the French coast near Caen at 22.53, and set course for Toulouse, pinpointing on Poitiers and Perigueux on the way. They picked up the lights of Toulouse at 00.47, and spent twenty-five minutes dispensing, what Harris had once referred to as toilet paper, to its inhabitants. The return trip was undertaken without incident, until two trawlers fired light flak at them off Whitby, and a safe landing was carried out at Tempsford at 08.08. P/O Miller and crew were last away at 21.00 bound for St-Etienne in Z9158, passing out over the English coast at Selsey Bill, and entering enemy airspace at the mouth of the Somme. Conditions in the target area were clear, and the blackout in this part of unoccupied France particularly ineffective. Cloud increased to ten-tenths for the return journey, and heavy mist at Tangmere resulted in a diversion to Boscombe Down. On approach over Wiltshire from the south-east, Z9158 struck high ground at the Porton experimental site, and crashed, bursting into flames. P/O Miller and all but one of the occupants lost their lives, and only rear gunner, Sgt Hubbard, survived to be taken to hospital with injuries.

The loss of W/C Farley was clearly a blow to 138 Squadron, but, at least, in S/L Hockey, it would find the perfect replacement, and he was promoted to wing commander rank on the 21st to fill the breach. At the same time, F/L Outram was promoted to squadron leader rank to take over the Halifax flight. Operations continued on the night of the 23/24th with two Whitley sorties to France undertaken by S/L Davies and P/O Smith. The former took off first at 20.49 in Z9230 on Operation ADJUDICATE 2, and crossed the French coast at Cabourg at 22.28. A course was set for Limoges, and then Perigueux. On arrival, the town and its surrounds were found to be well-lit, with lighted traffic on the roads, and the drop zone was circled for about thirty minutes before a triangle of lights appeared. The containers were dropped from about 800 feet, before course

The grave of W/C Farley and F/L Voellnagel's crew in the War Cemetery at Durnbach shortly after the war. (W. Wawrzecki via PH)

was set for Tangmere, which was overflown at 03.15 en-route to Tempsford, where a safe landing was carried out at 04.47. P/O Smith and crew took off at 21.05 in Z9287 on Operation ADJUDICATE 3, and crossed the French coast at 23.15. They set course for Limoges, pinpointing on the River Loire and River Lot near Villeneuve, and map-read at 1,800 feet to Cahors, observing the ruins of Chateau Rousillon clearly below. Despite circling for thirty minutes, no reception lights were evident, and the drop was abandoned, upon which, a course was set back to Limoges, where nickels were dispensed. Homebound, a fix was obtained on the French coast near Cherbourg, and a safe return to Tempsford was completed at 06.42.

Four Whitley sorties were scheduled for the night of the 24/25th, three of them recorded as departing Tempsford at 21.30. Still unaware that drops over Holland were at the behest of the enemy, P/O Russell and crew took off in Z9275 on Operation CATARRH 3, and crossed the coast over Southwold at 22.26. The enemy coast was reached north of Harlingen, and the coastline followed south to Hindeloopen and on to the target area. A triangle of lights was seen at 00.38, but, because of their location in a wood, it was impossible to keep them in sight while running in for the drop. After circling for forty-five minutes, the lights were picked up again, and the containers and packages were delivered into the hands of the enemy. Throughout the operation, the Whitley was under observation from the ground, and had flak guns trained upon it, but it was allowed to return home via Enkhuizen and a point on the coast north of Alkmaar, and landed at 03.05. Sgt Owen and his crew were on board Z9282, briefed to undertake Operations LAMB/MULE/SABLE/RETRIEVER, and they crossed the French coast at le Crotoy at 22.25. The next pinpoint was a wood north of Valencienne, which was located at 00.14, with thirteen minutes to fly to the drop zone, which is believed to be across the border in Belgium. However, no further fix could be obtained, and despite circling the general target area until 01.45, the poor visibility rendered the sortie unsuccessful, and a course was set for home. The containers were jettisoned over Tempsford, and a safe landing made at 04.15 with the passengers still on board.

Sgt Wilde and crew were in Z9286 as they took off on Operation PERIWIG 2, and headed for le Crotoy, which was reached at 23.16. A course was set for Douai and beyond, but searchlights and flak were encountered, which persuaded Sgt Wilde to abandon the sortie at 00.12, and turn for home on a reciprocal course, and land at Tempsford at 02.55. S/L Outram and crew were the last to take off on this night, lifting into the air in Z9232 at 21.42 on Operation DASTARD. It took an hour and two minutes to cross the Channel and reach le Crotoy at 23.37, but the W/T receiver became unserviceable, and poor visibility prevented any certainty in navigation. Heavy flak from an unexpected direction added to the doubts about the Whitley's precise whereabouts, and, after considering his options for ten minutes, S/L Outram took the decision to turn back, landing safely at 01.20.

On the following night, the 25/26th, P/O Anderle and crew undertook a trip to Czechoslovakia in Halifax L9618, taking off at 20.55 on Operations BIOSCOPE and BIVOUAC, and crossing the French coast at Abbeville at 22.21. They set course for the target area, pinpointing on the River Rhine, but flew over cloud most of the way, which caused them to overshoot Pilsen by ten minutes. Turning eastwards, they observed flak a few miles to the north at 01.40, but, because of the cloud, it proved impossible to deliver the agents and stores, and they returned to land at 06.04, having seen nothing of the ground on the way. S/L Davies and crew took off at 21.23 in Whitley Z9275 for Operation PERIWIG 2, and reached the French coast at Berck-sur-Mer at 23.16, before setting course for Douai and the drop zone at Ath in Belgium. The search for the pinpoint lasted ninety minutes, before it was abandoned, and a course set for home, where they landed at 04.43 without further incident. Finally on this night, P/O Smith and crew departed Tempsford in Whitley Z9282 at 21.43 to undertake Operations SPANIEL/WEASEL, and crossed the French coast at St Valery at 23.36. A course was set for Rivier on the River Meuse, south of Namur, and then, it seems, a westerly course was set, which provided further pinpoints on a wood south of Amiens and a railway south of St Quentin. In the event, the exact drop zone was not identified after an eighty-minute search, and the French coast was re-crossed homebound at le Crotoy at 03.44, followed by a landing at Tempsford at 04.50.

One of the relatively few successes of this period came at the hands of P/O Russell and crew on the following night, when they took off in Z9275 at 20.59 on Operation CHEESE I, bound for Norway. The English coast was crossed at Cromer at 21.49, and the passage across Norway conducted by map-reading at between 5,000 and 6,000 feet under bright moonlight, pinpointing on lakes, rivers and Ardal Fjord, until the e.t.a expired. They continued on, picking up a lake just west of the pinpoint, and Berdal was identified in the Telemark region in the south of the country. Six containers were dropped, and an uneventful return made, which culminated with a landing at Tempsford at 06.28.

Undaunted by the previous failure of Operations BIOSCOPE/BIVOUAC, P/O Anderle and crew took off in Halifax L9613 at 20.57 on the 27th, bound for Czechoslovakia to try again, and they were the first of six departures from Tempsford over the ensuing fifty-three minutes. The French coast was crossed at le Crotoy at 22.20, and a course set for Givet on the Belgian border, which was pinpointed forty minutes later. Karlsruhe was reached at 00.03, and then Nuremberg at 00.45, before Pilsen passed by to the south and the crew map-read the final leg to the target area. Seven agents and stores were successfully parachuted over the briefed drop zone, before a safe return was carried out, culminating with a landing at Tempsford at 05.57. The second sortie to depart on this evening was undertaken by Sgt Owen and crew in Whitley Z9282 (or Z9232), which lifted off at 21.30 on Operation MANFRIDAY. They crossed the French coast also at le Crotoy, at 23.45, before setting a course for Arras and the Arleux Lakes further to the east. A pinpoint was gained on a wood at 00.41, from where a search for the precise drop zone commenced at 1,000 feet and lasted for forty-eight minutes without success. The attempt was abandoned, and a safe return made to land at Tempsford at 03.50.

Two Whitleys were recorded as taking off at 21.33, one was Z9287, and the other is believed to have been Z9275, although the serial number is omitted from the ORB. The former contained the crew of F/O Smith, who were engaged on Operations SPANIEL/WEASEL. After crossing the French coast, a course was set for Revin, close to the Belgian frontier, but it proved impossible to find pinpoints on the ground, and they overshot the River Meuse. They ran into a cone of searchlights north of Mezieres, which took fifteen minutes to escape through violent evasive action taking the Whitley almost to ground level. It was decided to back-track to St Quentin, where a pinpoint was identified, which enabled them to reach Givet and then Dinant, where the lights of a reception committee were observed after a fifteen-minute search. The cargo was delivered, and a reciprocal course set for base, where a landing was carried out at 05.35. The other Whitley, captained by S/L Outram, was bound for France on Operation DASTARD, and crossed into France at le Crotoy at 23.20. A course was set for la Ferte, near Paris, and a pinpoint gained on the River Oise, where a course change took them to further pinpoints on the Rivers Yonne and Seine. The drop zone was identified and circled at 1,500 feet for thirty minutes, but the only lights observed emanated from railway signals rather than a reception committee, and the sortie was subsequently abandoned.

P/O Rymills and crew took of at 21.35 in Whitley Z9159 on Operation LUCKYSHOT 2, and crossed the French coast at St Valery at 23.28 at 3,000 feet. They set course for the target area, pinpointing on Amiens and a bend in the River Meuse at Givet, and then flew up and down the River Ourthe, south-east of la Roche in Belgium, before identifying the clearing in which the triangle of lights should have been visible. After searching for thirty minutes, they back-tracked to Givet, before returning to the drop zone for another look. They remained for a further twenty minutes before giving up, and returning safely home to land at 05.40. The final departure from Tempsford on this night was by Whitley Z9282 (or Z9232) on Operation CARP at 21.50. P/O Gibson and crew were charged with the responsibility of carrying it out, and they crossed the French coast south of Bayeux at 23.45. They pinpointed on the River Loire and located Angers, before following the river back to Saumur, which was recognized by the passengers. Over the target, a yellow flashing light was observed one or two miles from the pinpoint, but this was extinguished as the Whitley approached to investigate it. The operation was subsequently abandoned, and a safe return made to land at base at 04.35.

Operations for the night of the 28/29th involved three Whitley sorties, the first by Z9275, which lifted off the ground at 20.50 bearing the crew of S/L Outram on Operation CHEESE 2. They crossed the Norwegian coast at 01.30, and map-read to the target area. The specific village for the drop was identified and circled once, before the containers were dropped and seen to land. The return flight was incident-free, and a safe landing was carried out at 06.20. S/L Davies and crew followed S/L Outram into the air at 20.55 in Z9230 on Operation COCKEREL, and crossed the English coast at Wells at 21.36 heading for the Norwegian coast. Once there, they navigated their way to the target by pinpointing on fjords, lakes, roads and railway lines, and, after locating the specific lakeside for the drop, they circled to see if a reception committee could be raised. There was no response from the ground, but the two passengers and stores were delivered, anyway, from 800 feet on the east side of the lake, before a new course was set to Lindesnes, near the southern tip of the mainland, a few miles to the north-west of which, nickels were delivered over Lyngdal. An uneventful return trip ended with a landing at 05.20, by which time, P/O Russell and crew had already landed from their shorter-range sortie. They had taken off at 21.59 in Z9282 to undertake Operation MANFRIDAY over Belgium, and crossed the French coast at 23.45, before proceeding without incident to the target area. A flashing light signalled the presence of a reception committee, into the arms of which the passengers were delivered, their parachutes confirmed to have opened, and the Whitley returned safely to land at 03.02.

With the short nights of summer fast approaching, Poland, Czechoslovakia and Norway would soon be out of range, and the first of three operations to take place on the night of the 29/30th, involved P/O Anderle and crew setting off for their homeland of Czechoslovakia for the third time in the space of five nights. They took off at 20.58 in Halifax L9618 on Operations IRON/INTRANSITIVE/STEEL, and crossed the French coast at 22.21, before setting course for the Rhine between Mannheim and Karlsruhe. Nuremberg passed beneath en-route to the drop site, which was located in bright moonlight and circled once, before the five passengers and stores parachuted away from 400 feet while on an easterly track. An uneventful return trip ended with a landing at Tempsford at 05.35. An hour after Anderle's departure, Whitley Z9159 was climbing into the night sky bound for Belgium on Operation PERIWIG 2. While outbound over the Channel, an engine began to develop problems, and P/O Bunny Rymills decided to turn back. Whitley Z9287 took off at 22.04 bound for Belgium on Operation LUCKYSHOT 2, with Sgt Owen at the controls. The French coast was crossed at 00.18 in conditions that aided map-reading, and the River Meuse was located easily, as was the drop zone at a wood to the west of Champlon. Containers were dropped and pigeons released, and two men were observed to run towards the former to retrieve them. According to Freddie Clark's account of this night's operations, S/L Outram was also out and about, delivering six containers to Norway in clear visibility, but there is no mention of this sortie in the squadron ORB.

April ended with a further four operations on the last night of the month, beginning with the departure of Halifax L9618 at 21.00 on Operation VEGA. F/Sgt Pieniazek and crew were bound for Norway, and, at 22.14, passed over the lighthouse at Flamborough Head on the

Yorkshire coast near Bridlington. On reaching the Norwegian coast, they followed it to Narestø, before crossing inland at Boraa at 01.10. From there they continued on to Vegår Lake and beyond to the drop site, where a forty-minute search revealed the lights of a reception committee. (None of the above Norwegian locations has been located on a map). A flashing letter K identified the precise location, over which two runs were made, releasing two containers on each occasion. A return course took the Halifax over Langesund, south-west of Tonsberg, and then back over Flamborough Head to a landing at Tempsford at 03.50. P/O Russell and crew took off at 21.49 in Whitley Z9232 to undertake Operation BASS. They crossed the French coast east of Caen at 23.22, and set course for le Mans, which was reached at 01.10. The next pinpoint was at Langon, which was located easily, leaving just the final leg to the drop site, but, because of the vast number of clearings, which were not on a map, it proved difficult to find the correct one in the absence of a reception committee. An hour's search raised no response from the ground, and it was decided to abandon the attempt and return home, where a landing was carried out at Boscombe Down at 08.05.

S/L Davies and his crew were in Whitley Z9230 on this night, and they took off at 21.55 to carry out Operation LAMB/MULE/SABLE/RETRIEVER. After crossing the French coast at 23.45, they set course for Douai and Valenciennes, and, as they approached the drop site, could already pick out the triangle of lights from a reception committee. The passengers were disgorged, and an uneventful operation was completed with a safe landing at Tempsford at 03.26. The final departure on this night was that of Whitley Z9287, which was airborne at 22.05 bound for Belgium, bearing the crew of F/O Gibson on Operation PERIWIG 2. They crossed the French coast at the same time at S/L Davies, at 23.45, passing over a lighthouse flashing a white light, before setting course for Aubigny and the Arleux Lakes. Approaching the drop zone on e.t.a., they picked up the lights of a reception committee, and delivered containers from 700 feet. They returned home without incident on a reciprocal route, and landed at Tempsford at 03.50.

April had been another sobering month for the Command generally, in which Harris had continued his assault on Essen. In eight raids during March and April, over fifteen hundred sorties had produced no significant damage within the city, and a total of sixty-four aircraft had been lost in the process. Other attacks on Cologne, Hamburg and Dortmund during the course of April had been almost equally unimpressive, and Harris's hostile attitude towards the sidelining of two complete squadrons for SOE/SIS work hardened. However, a four raid series against the Baltic port of Rostock on consecutive nights from the 23/24th had been an outstanding success, which left over seventeen hundred buildings in ruins, and restored some self-belief. Whilst this was, of course, very positive, the success was largely attributable to the coastal location of the target. The bulk of Germany's industrial might lay further inland, in towns and cities concealed beneath an almost ever-present blanket of industrial haze, and they were proving to be elusive in the extreme.

May 1942

May began with two Whitley sorties on the night of the 1/2nd, Z9232 taking off first at 21.40, with Bunny Rymills at the controls on Operation BASS. He crossed the French coast at 23.15, and set a course for Langon in the unoccupied zone, flying over the River Loire at midnight, and pinpointing on Beaufort-en-Vallee, Cognac and Libourne, where many lights were found to be on. Langon was identified, and all villages to Roquefort pinpointed, before he came upon the main Bordeaux to Bayonne road, where the passengers and packages were parachuted away. He crossed out over the western coast of France homebound at Biscarrosse-Plage near Bordeaux, and landed safely at St Eval in Cornwall at 06.05. Sgt Owen and crew departed Tempsford at 22.01 in Z9159 to undertake Operation DASTARD I. They crossed the English coast at 23.00, and set course for la Fuerte, map-reading there at 2,000 feet. They circled the area to identify the drop site, and saw lights immediately. The containers were dropped, and, after they arrived on the ground, a man was seen standing beside them flashing O.K. They returned by the same route, releasing pigeons over Beauvais on the way, and landed safely at base at 04.15.

On the following night, S/L Davies and crew climbed into Whitley Z9230, and took off at 21.55 to carry out Operations CAMELIA/ASPEN. They entered enemy airspace north of Caen at 23.24, and set course for Tours, from where they followed rivers, roads and railways until the lights of a reception committee were picked up. The passengers were dropped from 400 feet at 01.01, before steps were retraced to Tours and the coast, and a landing completed at Tempsford at 04.05. Not mentioned in the ORB for this night is a sortie by Halifax W1012 with a Polish crew, who were to service a reception point near Lyon in south-eastern France. They took off at 22.30, but unfavourable weather conditions in the target area prevented the drop from taking place, and a safe return was completed at 08.45. The final trips to Norway for the time being were flown by Bunny Rymills and F/O Gibson on the night of the 3/4th, but bad weather would render their efforts void. F/O Gibson took off first, at 21.32, in Whitley Z9287, to undertake Operation WOODCOCK. He crossed the English coast at 22.21, and started to climb to put himself above the cloud. He continued on at 8,000 feet until just before the first e.t.a. over Norway, at which point, he dropped down to 1,000 feet, before climbing back to 4,000 feet over the target area. Cloud continued to be a problem, and he descended again to 3,000 feet in an attempt to break through it, but was unsuccessful. Over a mountainous terrain, he was left with no alternative other than to abandon the sortie, and returned home to land at 06.30 with passengers and stores on board. P/O Rymills was on duty again on this night, and took off with his crew at 22.35 in Halifax W1012, to carry out Operation CRANE. They flew out over the English coast at Cromer at 23.12, and continued on over cloud to Norway, where they descended to 6,000 feet without breaking free of the white stuff. Without sight of the ground, the operation could not be completed, and the Halifax returned home to land at 07.10.

F/O Krol was the captain and navigator, and F/Sgt Klosowski the pilot of Halifax L9613, which took off for France at 23.20 on the night of the 6/7th, with an all-Polish crew on board charged with carrying out Operation ADJUDICATE 3. Unlike in the RAF, where the pilot was always crew captain, in Polish crews, the senior officer was designated as crew captain, irrespective of his role. They crossed the French coast near Caen at 00.26, and set a southerly course to the target area near Cahors, where the Chateau-de-Roussillion was identified. The hoped-for triangle of red lights was not observed, however, although many scattered lights were, including one flashing the letter V. They circled the target area for thirty-eight minutes at 3,000 feet, but attracted no signal from a reception committee, and decided to press on to Limoges, where fourteen packets of leaflets were dispensed at 03.37. As they flew back from Limoges to Caen, they observed many lights from the notoriously ineffective blackout, and completed the uneventful return trip at 06.35. This was the final operation of the moon period, and the stand-down period would last until the night of the 24/25th. During this period, fresh blood arrived from 10 and 18 O.T.Us and 301 Squadron.

When operations resumed on the evening of the 24th, 138 Squadron put up five aircraft for sorties over France and Belgium. Two Whitleys were recorded as taking off at 22.00, Z9282 on Operation LUCKYSHOT 3, and Z9288 on Operation CHROME, with the crews of Sgt Owen and F/O Gibson respectively. The former reached the French coast at le Crotoy at 23.51, and set course for a loop in the River Meuse south of Givet, which was easily located. They continued on to the drop site, where lights were seen and the containers dropped from 600 feet. Leaflets were delivered on the return route to Givet, and six pigeons released near Cambrai, before the aircraft returned to land safely at 04.52. The latter crossed the French coast at Cabourg at 23.56, and set course to the south-east and Orleans, which was pinpointed at 00.49. According to the ORB, they then flew north-eastwards to Corbeil and, afterwards, the drop site, where the containers were delivered from 600 feet, before a reciprocal course returned them to Tempsford at 04.57.

S/L Outram and crew took off in Z9232 at 22.03 to carry out Operations MANFRIDAY 2/COYOTE. They crossed the English coast at 23.22, and the French coast at le Crotoy at five minutes after midnight, and set course for a wood south-east of Valenciennes. From there they headed for the drop site, picking up lights when three miles short, and the passengers and containers were delivered without incident, after which, leaflets were delivered onto the outskirts of Mons. F/O Russell and crew were the next to depart Tempsford, at 22.10 in Whitley Z9159, bound for Operation PERIWIG 3 over Belgium. However, engine trouble soon struck the aircraft, which had a history of exactor problems, and they were soon back home after abandoning the sortie. Now that the longer-range operations had been shelved, Halifaxes became available for trips to France, and P/O Bunny Rymills and crew took W1012 there on this night to drop an agent and stores into the south-central region of the country. They departed Tempsford at 22.20 on Operation GORSE, and passed over Cabourg on the French coast at 00.08, before setting course for Tours, which was pinpointed at 00.56. Once there, they flew straight on to Montlucon in central France, passing Chateauroux on the way. At Montlucon they followed a road to a river pinpoint, where a triangle of lights was picked up after twenty minutes. The passenger and stores were dropped from 600 feet, and a safe return made to Tempsford, where they landed at 05.30.

The frustrating spate of Whitley engine problems persisted on the night of the 28/29th, when Sgt Owen and crew took off for Belgium on Operation PERIWIG 3 in an unspecified aircraft at 22.08, for a flight that lasted just fifty-nine minutes. First off on this night was Halifax W1012, which became airborne at 21.50 with P/O Bunny Rymills and crew on board, bound for Operations EEL/ARBUTUS. They crossed the French coast at Cabourg at 23.35, and set course for Lyons, map-reading to the Loire, before encountering cloud and rain, which they broke through in time to pinpoint on St Etienne. Lyons was identified, and, subsequently, the drop site, where the containers were delivered, although on return to Tempsford at 06.12, one was found to have hung-up. The Whitley of F/L Smith and crew followed Sgt Owen down the runway at 22.09 to carry out Operation SPANIEL 2. They crossed the French coast at le Crotoy at 00.16, and set course straight to the target area, pinpointing on Doullens, Cambrai and a lake near Bois de Chimay on the way. They flew over a loop in the River Meuse south of Givet, and, finally, pinpointed on a tunnel near Beauraing, where the lights of a reception committee were picked up. They made one circuit before dropping the containers accurately, and delivered leaflets over the Givet area on the way home to a landing at 04.27.

P/O Anderle and crew departed Tempsford at 22.15 in Halifax W1002 on Operation ELDER. They reached the French coast at Isigny-sur-Mer, west of Caen, at 23.45, setting course then for the target area near Perigueux, and crossing the River Loire near Saumur. They had to descend almost to ground level to get beneath the cloud base in the drop zone, and recognized the location at Chateau le Rocque on arrival. However, despite searching for thirty minutes, no reception committee lights greeted them, and they were forced to bring their passenger home. They dispensed leaflets between the drop site and the Loire, and landed back at Tempsford at 04.50. The final departure on this night was that of Whitley Z9286, which took off at 22.45 with the crew of F/O Russell on board, bound for Holland on Operation LETTUCE. The English coast passed beneath at 23.16, after which, a course was set for Harderwijk, where all landmarks were clearly visible, but no reception committee revealed itself. In fact, the crew received confusing signals from the Dutch countryside, including the headlights of a stationary car on a road north of Putten, which began to travel slowly towards the north. After circling for thirty minutes, F/O Russell opted to abandon the sortie and come home, and landed at Tempsford at 03.45.

Another busy night followed on the 29/30th, when six sorties were mounted, beginning with F/O Gibson and crew taking off at 21.55 in Whitley Z9688 to carry out Operations YEW/CHESTNUT. They crossed the French coast at Cabourg at 23.45, and set course for le Mans, pinpointing on the Loire on the way, and reaching la Fleche to the south-west, before following a road north-west a few miles to Sable, and then back-tracking and dropping the passengers and cargo. Nickels were delivered over le Mans on the way home, and a safe landing was carried out at 04.42. Sgt Freeland and crew undertook their first sortie with the squadron, when taking off in an unspecified Whitley at 22.00 on Operation BALACLAVA 3. They made landfall over le Crotoy at 23.36 flying at 2,000 feet, and set course for a bend in the River Meuse, before heading for the tunnel at Beauraing in Belgium, and picking up the railway that would lead them to the drop site. The reception committee lights were visible from five miles away, and the cargo dropped, after which, nickels were delivered over the Wellin/Rochefort area on the way home to a landing at 03.55. F/Sgt Owen and crew were in Whitley Z9287, which took off at 22.13 bound for Belgium on Operation MANDAMUS, but returned at 23.44 after a dead engine ended the sortie early.

F/O Krol and crew took off from Tangmere at 23.12 in Halifax W1002, bound for Operation ELDER, and, after crossing the French coast near Caen, set course for Perigueux in the south-west. They pinpointed on the River Loire and map-read to the target area, where they searched in vain for thirty minutes for the lights of a reception committee. Despite the absence of a signal from the ground, the passengers were dropped from 800 feet at 00.57 near a chateau, woods and a river. It was only as they turned away at 02.16 that the first light was observed, which triggered the dropping of the containers and packages from 700 feet on a north-east to south-west heading. They returned by the same route, and landed back at base at 05.15. P/O Sutton and crew took off at 22.20 in Whitley Z9159, to try to complete Operation PERIWIG 3 over Belgium, which had been abandoned by F/Sgt Owen twenty-four hours earlier, and had now failed three times. They crossed the French coast over the mouth of the Somme at 00.07, and set course for Ath, map-reading their way south and then west to the drop site, where they circled once before delivering the cargo. Leaflets were dispensed in the Mons area on the way to the coast homebound, although cloud prevented them from identifying their precise exit point, and they landed at Tempsford at 04.00. S/L Davies and crew were the last to depart Tempsford on this night, lifting off the runway at 22.39 in Whitley Z9230, bound for Holland and Operations CATARRH/BEETROOT. They crossed the enemy coast at Callantsoog, south of Den Helder, at three minutes after midnight, and set course for the target area via Enkhuizen. They slightly overshot the drop site to the north, and turned back to pick up and follow a railway line until lights were spotted. They circled twice, before parachuting two agents into the Dutch network now being controlled by the Gestapo. By the time that S/L Davies and crew were retracing their tracks to Enkhuizen, the agents had been arrested, and their radios and new electronic beacon device had fallen also into enemy hands.

Four sorties were planned for the night of the 30/31st, beginning with the departure of S/L Outram and crew at 22.12 in Whitley Z9232 for Operation MANDAMUS. They crossed the French coast at le Crotoy at 23.55, and pinpointed on the loop in the River Meuse south of Givet, before following a road and railway past Rochefort and Marche to the drop site. The reception committee lights were identified, and, whilst circling in preparation for the run-up, the containers were released prematurely, and fell about three miles south-west of the pinpoint. Leaflets were delivered east of Givet on the way home, and a safe landing was carried out at 05.10. F/O Bunny Rymills and crew left Tempsford three minutes after S/L Outram, in Halifax W1012, and set course for the French coast at le Crotoy on Operation EEL. They crossed into hostile territory at 23.43, and headed directly for the target area, pinpointing on Orleans and Lyon on the way, and dropping leaflets at the latter. They followed the Saone Valley to the reception site, and dropped the passengers from 600 feet, before adopting a reciprocal course home, and landing at Tempsford at 05.40. P/O Pieniazek and crew had been handed Operations PRIVET/BLACKTHORN to complete, and they took off at 22.30 in Halifax W1007, before crossing the French coast at 23.54. They set course for the target area near Le Mans, gaining a pinpoint on the River Loire from 1,000 feet in rain, but the precipitation had ceased by the time the drop site was reached in ten-tenths cloud. The passengers and package were delivered from 800 feet, and a reciprocal course adopted, which took the Halifax through continuing poor weather conditions to a landing at Tempsford at 05.30. F/O Russell and crew completed the night's SOE activities, when taking off in an unspecified Whitley at 22.55 to undertake Operation LETTUCE over Holland. They crossed the enemy coast over Vlieland at 00.36, and flew at 400 feet down the Zuider Zee to the target area. Lights were picked up, and the cargo dropped, before a return course was adopted via Oosterbeek and Callantsoog at an altitude of 250 feet. Whether or not it was noticed by the operating crews on this night, it would be fair to say, that they were not entirely alone over occupied Europe.

After a busy first eight nights of May for the Command generally, the pace had slackened markedly as Harris prepared for his masterstroke, and a disappointing raid on Mannheim on the night of the 19/20th was the only major outing before the final days of the month. On taking up his appointment as C-in-C, Harris had stated that he needed four thousand bombers with which to win the war, and, whilst there was not the slightest chance of getting them, he needed to ensure at least, that those earmarked for him, were not spirited away to what he considered to be less deserving causes. In view of the Command's continuing generally uninspiring performances, Billancourt, Lübeck and Rostock apart, there was still a question mark hanging over the future of an independent bomber force. Harris needed a major victory, with, perhaps, a dose of symbolism, to demonstrate the war-winning potential of a large, genuinely heavy bomber force, ideally consisting mainly of Lancasters.

Out of this was born the Thousand Plan, Operation Millennium, the commitment of a thousand aircraft in one night against one of Germany's premier cities, for which Hamburg was pencilled in. Harris did not have a thousand front-line aircraft, however, and, therefore, needed to rely on the goodwill of other Commands, principally Coastal and Flying Training, which, in letters to Harris on the 22nd and 23rd respectively pledged generous support. Sadly, the Admiralty, one of Bomber Command's most ardent critics, intervened, and Coastal Command was forced to withdraw its contribution. Undaunted, Harris, or more likely his able and affable deputy, AM Sir Robert Saundby, scraped together every airframe capable of controlled flight, or something akin to it, and pulled in the screened crews from their instructional duties. In this way, come the night, not only would the magic figure of one thousand be reached, it would be comfortably surpassed.

Only the weather now remained in question, and as the last days of May ticked inexorably by, this seemed in no mood to play ball. A motley collection of aircraft from the training units had joined the bomber squadrons on operational stations from County Durham to the south Midlands, and Harris was acutely aware, that this giant fleet might draw attention to itself and compromise security. The time was fast approaching, when the operation would either have to be launched or be abandoned for the time being, and it was in this tense atmosphere of frustration and hope, that "morning prayers" began at Harris's High Wycombe HQ on the 30th. All eyes eventually turned upon Harris's chief meteorologist, Magnus Spence, who ultimately was able to give a guarded forecast of clear weather over the Rhineland after midnight, with a chance of moonlight, but dashed any likelihood of favourable conditions over north-western Germany and Hamburg. Thus did the fates decree, that Cologne would bear the dubious honour of hosting the first one thousand bomber raid in history.

Late that evening, 1046 aircraft took off, some of the older training hacks lifting somewhat reluctantly into the air, powered more by the enthusiasm of their crews than by the power of their tired engines. A few of them would be unable to climb to a respectable height, and would fall easy prey to the defences, or simply be brought down by mechanical failure. Those aircraft reaching the target city, however, almost 870 in total, contributed to an outstanding success, which left over 3,300 buildings completely destroyed, and many thousands more damaged to some extent. The loss of forty-one bombers was a new record high, but in conditions favourable to attackers and defenders alike, it represented an acceptable 3.9%.

While his massive force remained assembled, Harris was eager to employ it again against Essen, and allowed just one night's rest in between. It was in less crowded skies, therefore, that F/Sgt Owen and crew took off at 22.45 in Whitley Z9288 on the night of the 31st, to embark on Operation CATARRH 5 over Holland. They headed for the Afsluitdijk across the Zuider Zee, but thick haze prevented them from map-reading, and it was not until they eventually identified a pier north-west of Kampen, south of the Ketelmeer, that they were able to re-set their course. Even so, they missed the next pinpoint, and backtracked to the Elburg promontory, and this time flew straight on to the reception lights. They completed two circuits before dropping the six containers, and returned home, for a change on two engines, to land at 03.55.

June 1942

From left: Czechoslovak observer P/O Krcha of F/O Anderle's crew along with Poles; observer F/O Walczak and pilots; P/O Pieniazek and F/O Dobromirski (killed on 17 December 1942). (K. Szrajer via A. Jackowski)

Only 956 aircraft were available for Essen on the night of the 1/2nd of June, when, in contrast to two nights earlier, the operation was a major disappointment, which sprayed bombs all over the Ruhr, and left the target city relatively untouched. 138 Squadron launched two Halifax sorties on this night, both recorded as taking off at 22.15. Bunny Rymills was at the controls of W1012 as it headed for France on Operations CRAB/MINNOW/PERCH, and reached the French coast at Cabourg at 23.53. A course was set for Tours, from where they flew direct to Montlucon in central France, which was reached at 01.30. They flew up and down the nearby rail and road links five times, seeking the lights of a reception committee, but, in the absence of a signal from the ground, it was decided at 02.00 to turn for home, where they landed at 05.25 with the passengers and stores still on board. W1007 contained the crew of F/O Walczak, who had been briefed to attempt Operations PALM/SPRUCE over France. F/Sgt Klosowski was occupying the pilot's seat as they lifted off at 22.15, and headed towards the French coast near Caen, before setting course for Lyon in the south-east, which, once reached, provided the final pinpoint before the drop site near Villefranche. They circled the area for an hour and nine minutes before finally sighting a signal from a reception committee, whereupon, the passengers and stores were dropped from 600 feet, and the lights were extinguished. An uneventful return flight ended with a safe landing at Tempsford at 05.45.

Four follow-up operations by forces of conventional size were sent against Essen over the succeeding two weeks, beginning on the night of the 2/3rd, but produced no improvement in accuracy, and the five-raid series cost eighty-four aircraft. There was just a solitary 138 Squadron sortie on the night of the 2/3rd, flown by F/O Gibson and crew in Whitley Z9288. They took off at 22.50 on Operation LETTUCE, and reached Vlieland at 00.34, before setting course for the target area via Stavoren, but overshot Harderwijk to the south. They searched northwards along the coast, until picking up a flashing beacon, and set course from there to the drop site, where a triangle of lights signaled the presence of a reception committee. The cargo was dropped from 500 feet, and an uneventful return trip carried out, with a landing at Tempsford at 04.15.

F/O Walczak, observer who flew in the Polish crews of F/S Jensen and P/O Szrajer. (K. Szrajer via A. Jackowski)

On the following night, P/O Anderle and crew took Halifax W1002 on Operation SNAKE, and crossed the French coast at 23.44, before setting course for Nevers, pinpointing at les Vallees on the way. Nevers was identified, after which they map-read to the drop site, five miles short of which, a flashing letter P could be seen. The passengers and stores were delivered to the reception committee, and the return trip completed without incident at 05.15. W/C Hockey and crew took off at 22.20 in Halifax L9613, in an attempt to complete Operations CRAB/MINNOW/PERCH, which had defeated Bunny Rymills two nights earlier. They crossed the French coast at four minutes after midnight, and set course for Tours, where they arrived at 01.02, before heading towards Montlucon and finding the marshalling yards there well-illuminated. They followed the railway lines to the drop site, where a half-hour search culminated in the delivery of three agents and stores. They returned by a reciprocal route, and landed at Tempsford at 05.20. F/Sgt Owen and crew took off at 22.27 in Whitley Z9275, and headed for Belgium on Operation MANDAMUS 2. They crossed the French coast near the mouth of the River Somme at 00.20, flying at 2,000 feet, and flew on to the loop in the River Meuse south of Givet, where they were unable to establish their precise position in the extreme darkness. With no prospect of completing the sortie, they turned back at 01.27, and landed at base at 04.07.

According to Freddie Clark's account, Harris pressed the moon squadrons into service in early June, first as postmen, and then as bombers. 161 Squadron was, apparently, the more put-upon unit, and its Whitleys were sent nickeling on the last night of May and first night of June, and bombing railway yards in France on the night of the 2/3rd. 138 Squadron's Halifax W1007 was included in such an attack at Tours with F/Sgt Pieniazek at the controls and W/C Rudkowski on board. Taking off at 23.30, they delivered fifteen 500 pounders onto the railway station, and returned safely after a trip of a little over six hours. Freddie Clark states, that, before the month was over, even the Lysanders would be carrying bombs to targets in France. He further states, that 138 Squadron delivered leaflets to France on three consecutive nights from the 7/8th, completing eight sorties in all, but was then left in relative peace, carrying out just one more nickelling sortie before the new moon period began around the 20th. There is no mention of any of these sorties in the Squadron ORB, and it is, therefore not possible to confirm them. A new Czech adjutant had been posted in from 311 Squadron on the 5th, who was probably responsible for maintaining the diary of events. As the sorties mentioned by Clark occurred around this "bedding-in" period, perhaps he was not yet up to speed, and unintentionally failed to record them.

The entry in F/S Pieniazek's Pilot Log Book referring to the bombing operation against Tours on 2/3rd June 1942, which due to unknown reason, was not mentioned in 138 Squadron's Operations Record Book. (J. Pieniazek via PH)

According to the ORB, operations resumed on the night of the 21/22nd, when F/L Smith took off at 23.18 in Whitley Z9287 to undertake Operation PERIWIG 2. Le Crotoy passed beneath at 01.15, and a course was set for Conde in north-eastern France as a pinpoint before the drop site in Belgium. A large wood to the west of Conde provided the necessary navigation reference for the final leg, but intense darkness thwarted all efforts to locate the drop site, and the attempt was ultimately abandoned. A dozen pigeons were released and leaflets delivered, but the containers were brought back to a landing at 04.45. S/L Davies and crew took off at 23.32 in Whitley Z9230 on Operation BARSAC, a "Pickaxe" operation, which was the code for the delivery of an NKVD agent, not necessarily of Russian nationality, into Europe. They crossed the Dutch coast at Callantsoog on the Den Helder peninsular at 01.04, and pinpointed on Hoorn and Harderwijk, before carrying out a sixteen-minute search for the drop site, close to one of the "Englandspiel" (England Game) areas now being controlled by the enemy. Major Hermann Giskes of the Abwehr would be responsible for the capture of more than fifty agents dropped into Holland, beginning with Hubertus Lauwers in early 1942, upon whose person were found ciphers, which Giskes would use under Unternehmung Nordpol (Operation Northpole) until 1944, to lure unsuspecting agents into his net, and ultimately, mostly, to their deaths. On this night no reception committee had been planned, and the agent, Nicolai Kravets, was dropped blind from 500 feet, seven kilometres east of Harderwijk in a clearing in a wood. However, despite the close proximity of an enemy-controlled drop zone, there is no report of an agent being captured on this night.

On the following night, F/O Gibson and crew rolled down the runway at Tempsford in Whitley Z9288 bound for Operation PERIWIG 4, and took to the air at 23.01 to head for the French coast. They reached the south side of the Somme Estuary at 00.33, before proceeding to Frevent, Arras and the Arleux Lakes, from where the final run to the drop site commenced at 01.04. The target area was reached at 01.26, and a search carried out until 02.07, when the sortie was abandoned in the face of intense darkness, and a homeward course adopted. F/O Russell and crew, meanwhile, were over Holland, having taken off from Tempsford at 23.30 in Whitley Z9287 to carry out Operations LETTUCE 3/SPINACH/PARSNIP. They crossed the Dutch coast near Callantsoog at 01.07, and set course for Harderwijk, before heading for the drop site close to Rijssen. Reception lights were seen, and the two agents, Lt Jan Jakob van Rietschoten, and his radio operator, Johannes Buizer, parachuted down from 650 feet, leaving the containers, initially, on board. The lights were doused, but then re-appeared, and the six containers were then delivered, like the agents, into the hands of the Gestapo. F/O Russell set course for home, and landed at 04.10, an hour before F/O Gibson, and, of course, was oblivious to the events on the ground in Holland.

The night of the 23/24th brought a single sortie, carried out by F/O Krol and crew in Halifax W1007, which took off at 22.50 on Operations DORY/PERCH 2. They crossed the French coast at Pointe de la Percee at 00.06, and set course straight to the target near Clermont-Ferrand. They were able to map-read from 3,000 feet, and identify pinpoints on the River Loire at Blois, before running in directly on the drop site, where reception lights were observed. The passengers and cargo were delivered from 1,200 feet on a north-south heading, and the successful operation culminated with a safe landing at 05.20. S/L Davies and crew were handed the task of trying again to complete Operation PERIWIG 4 on the night of the 24/25th, and took off at 22.50 in Whitley Z9230. The crossed the French coast at Berck-sur-Mer at 00.35, before heading first for Valencienne, and then the drop zone in Belgium. They ran into patchy cloud near Messines, which persisted right across the target area, but the drop zone was identified, and the cargo delivered from 600 feet. F/Sgt Owen and crew carried out the night's other successful sortie to Belgium in Whitley Z9232, having taken off at 22.27 on Operation SPANIEL 3. They crossed the French coast at 00.30, and headed for the loop in the River Meuse south of Givet, pinpointing on the lakes at Trelon and then Chimay across the frontier. They ran straight in on the reception lights, and dropped the containers, although one failed to release, and had to be brought back to a landing at 04.50.

This busy night of SOE activity continued with the departure of Halifax W1012 at 23.00 in the hands of P/O Bunny Rymills and crew. Their brief was to carry out Operation AD-GLOVE, (this may be an abbreviation for ADJUDICATE/GLOVE), and they reached the French coast at Cabourg at 00.23 while flying at 2,000 feet. They set course for Limoges, pinpointing on Le Mans and Tours on the way, but aborted the sortie for an unspecified reason at 01.40, and returned home. Whitley Z9275 departed Tempsford at 23.05 with the crew of F/L Sutton on board, bound for Belgium on Operations MANFRIDAY 3/KOALA. They crossed the French coast over the mouth of the River Somme at 00.50, and flew on for a further ninety minutes, before running into low cloud, which obscured ground detail, and forced the abandonment of the sortie. The final departure from Tempsford on this night was that of Whitley Z9287 at 23.07. It contained the crew of F/O Smith, who reached the French coast at Le Crotoy at 00.53 bound for Belgium on Operation BURGUNDY, another "Pickaxe" operation. They set course for Givet, and then the drop site, but low cloud obscured the ground and made map-reading impossible. Despite this, the passenger decided to take to his parachute at 400 feet, about six miles west of the briefed location, and a package was also dropped, after which, the Whitley returned safely to land at 05.20.

The final use of the Thousand force came on the night of the 25/26th, when 960 Bomber Command aircraft took off for Bremen, accompanied by 102 others from Coastal Command, in what was recorded as a separate operation. Churchill personally ordered the Coastal Command participation, and the actual numbers converging on the target exceeded those going to Cologne at the end of May. While not achieving anything like the success of that operation, results at Bremen far surpassed the debacle of Essen, and 570 houses/apartment blocks were destroyed, and some important war industry concerns were damaged. Under cover of this massive distraction, 138 Squadron dispatched two aircraft to France, beginning with Halifax L9618 at 22.58. P/O Pieniazek and crew were assigned to Operations MACKERAL/ROACH, and crossed the Normandy coast at Grandcamp-les-Bains at 00.15, before setting course for the unspecified target area. The sortie was ultimately abandoned, after the reception lights were extinguished during the approach. The responsibility for maintaining the squadron ORB now passed to a new scribe, whose entries provide scant detail of each sortie. Whitley Z9232 took off at 23.00 with S/L Outram at the controls bound for Belgium to try to complete Operations MANFRIDAY 3/KOALA, previously attempted by F/L Sutton. The French coast was crossed at 00.45, and a course set for the drop zone, a mile and a half east of Baugnies, and just over the border with France, where the passengers and containers were delivered from 500 feet, before an uneventful return ended with a landing at Tempsford at 04.35.

The night of the 26/27th saw four Whitley sorties, and one by a Halifax, with destinations in Belgium, Holland and France. First away from Tempsford at 22.40 was Whitley Z9282, carrying the crew of F/Sgt Owen on Operation LUCKYSHOT 4, a supply drop. They crossed the French coast at le Crotoy at 00.23, and set course for the loop in the River Meuse south of Givet, before pinpointing on the tunnel at Beauraing and running across the lights of a reception committee. The stores were dropped, but one container was found to have hung up, and the reception committee had departed the area before it could be released. At 22.42, Halifax W1007 took off in the hands of P/O Anderle and crew on Operation SYRINGA, and crossed the French coast at Pointe de la Percee at 23.52. They proceeded to the target area, which was recognized by the abundance of lakes, and searched in vain for a reception committee for more than thirty minutes. Finally, at 02.15, the sortie was abandoned, and the four-hour return trip undertaken. F/Sgt Freeland and crew took off at 22.45 in Whitley Z9286, bound for the French coast on Operations LYNX/MONGOOSE/CHAMOIX. Le Crotoy passed beneath at 00.15, as a new course was set for the Belgian frontier and Libramont beyond, where trains could be seen running towards Rolley. The drop site was identified, and passengers, pigeons and leaflets were delivered before a safe return culminated with a landing at 05.15. Whitley Z9288 took off at 23.25 in the hands of F/O Gibson and crew, and headed for the Dutch coast on Operations CATARRH 6/MARROW. They pinpointed on a lock in the Zuider Zee dam, and proceeded via Stavoren to Elburg, before finding the lights of a reception committee at the first attempt.

The passengers and stores were dropped from 600 feet, and a return course set for home, passing over Oosterbeek and Callantsoog. Both agents, George Jambroes, and his radio operator, Joseph Bukkens, fell right into the laps of Dutch collaborators, who handed them over to the Gestapo. The final departure from Tempsford on this night was also to Holland, and involved Whitley Z9287 and the crew of F/O Russell on Operation TURNIP 1. They lifted off the runway at 23.30, and entered enemy territory ninety minutes later, before setting course for Oosterbeek and Harderwijk. Having established their track, they continued on to the drop site, where the lights of a reception committee beckoned, and six containers and nickels were dropped, probably into the hands of the enemy. The Dutch coast was crossed homebound at 02.29, and, when sixty miles out from the English coast, fires could be seen in Norwich, resulting from a German fire-raising attack, as part of the series on cities appearing in the famous Baedeker guide books.

On the following night, S/L Davies and crew took off at 22.42 in Whitley Z9230 bound for France on Operation MONKEYPUZZLE. They crossed the enemy coast near Caen at 00.19, before setting course for Alencon and the drop site beyond. The passenger, Raymond Flower, was to open a new circuit in the Loire Valley in the Tours area, and was dropped close to the village of St Paterne from 500 feet, before the Whitley made a safe, uneventful return, culminating with a landing at 04.15. On the night of the 28/29th, W1007 and L9613 took off at 22.40, the former on Operation TULIP carrying the crew of F/O Krol, with F/Sgt Klosowski at the controls, and the other on Operation AD-GLOVE with the crew of F/O Walczak, for which, F/Sgt Jensen was the pilot. Navigator Krol gave a course for Limoges and the drop site beyond, which was reached at 02.09, and a search of the area conducted for sixteen minutes, before the absence of a response from the ground led to the drop being abandoned. The Walczak crew crossed the French coast at 23.52, and also headed for Limoges,

Pilot F/O Szrajer was one of the most experienced Polish pilots who flew in 301 Squadron and later in special operations. By the end of the war, he had completed the impressive number of 100 bombing and special operations. (K. Szrajer via A. Jackowski)

which was reached at 01.13, before they embarked on the final leg to the drop site. A reception committee signalled its presence with lights, and the passengers parachuted into the darkness.

A reciprocal return course took the Halifax back to Limoges, where leaflets were delivered, and the sortie ended with a safe landing at Tempsford at 05.00.

On the following night, Halifax W1007 was the first of two 138 Squadron aircraft to depart Tempsford, lifting off at 22.35 in the hands of F/O Krol and crew to undertake Operation BUFFALO. They crossed the French coast at 23.56, and set course for the target area, taking advantage of the good visibility to pinpoint on Orleans and other towns on the way. They ran straight in on the drop site, where lights from a reception committee were clearly visible, and the passengers and cargo were parachuted away, before a new course was set for Macon, where leaflets were delivered. F/L Sutton and crew took off in Whitley Z9275 at 22.44 on Operation SHALE, and the ORB provides no details as to destination, stating only that the sortie was concluded successfully. Unfortunately for history, the ORB entries from this point on provide minimal information, specifying in most cases only the destination country and the outcome. On the last night of the month, P/O Anderle and crew took off at 22.45 in Halifax W1007 on Operation SYRINGA, and landed at Tangmere at 04.50 after a successful sortie. On the same night, Bunny Rymills and crew took off at 23.04 in Halifax W1012 bound for France on Operations ILEX/ALMOND/GREENHEART, and also landed at Tangmere, at 04.10, after successfully delivering three agents and a package.

July 1942

138 Squadron's schedule for the first night of the new month involved Halifaxes L9613 and L9618, which took off at 22.45 bound for France with the crews of F/O Walczak and F/O Krol on Operations PIMENTO and SYRINGA 2 respectively. The brief for the former was to deliver a twenty year old English agent, Anthony Brooks, into the Limousin region of west-central France, and he would be the youngest yet to be dropped by the SOE squadrons. He slept in a sleeping bag during the outward flight, and was woken with coffee and sandwiches, before preparing for his departure. On a clear, moonlit night, he parachuted from 800 feet, and suffered a heavy landing, which left him with a sore knee and back. Some local people had watched his descent, and they carried him into a farm house, where his injuries were tended to, while others buried his parachute. This was the start of what would become a highly successful career in the field, which would ultimately earn him a DSO and a Military Cross. Both 138 Squadron aircraft returned safely to Tempsford after 05.00 to report successful outcomes. Last off on this night, at 23.25, was Whitley Z9232 with the crew of S/L Outram, who headed for Holland on Operations LETTUCE 4 and LEEK A. The sortie was unsuccessful for an unspecified reason, and the Whitley returned to Abingdon at 05.10. According to Freddie Clark, the enemy had the aircraft under surveillance throughout its time over occupied territory, but the German policy of firing at some incursions, while allowing others to escape, kept the SOE authorities oblivious to the fact that the network was under Gestapo control.

Two sorties were dispatched to Holland on the following night, F/O Gibson and crew taking off at 23.40 on Operation TURNIP 2 in Whitley Z9288, to be followed ten minutes later by F/Sgt Freeland and crew in Z9286 on Operation CATARRH 7. According to Freddie Clark, F/O Gibson was unable to complete his cargo drop because of the weather, despite which, the unreliable ORB records his sortie as successful. F/Sgt Freeland found himself in the middle of an accurate flak barrage after dropping his containers, probably having been under enemy surveillance from the moment he crossed the coast. The Whitley sustained some damage, but returned home safely, and was soon back in harness. The final operation of the moon period involved Halifax L9618, which took off at 22.35 on the night of the 5/6th with P/O Pieniazek at the controls, bound for France on Operations ROACH/MACKEREL. The ORB states simply that the Halifax landed at 03.35 after an unsuccessful sortie.

The 10th brought an influx of ten new aircrew from 19 O.T.U at Kinloss, including two NCO pilots. During the stand-down period, Harris turned his attention upon Essen's Ruhr neighbour, Duisburg, beginning a five raid series on the night of the 13/14th. Bad weather contributed to another frustrating night, which left the city with only minor damage, and the remaining four operations between the nights of the 21/22nd and the 6/7th of August would be equally disappointing. During the same period, however, Emden, Hamburg and Saarbrücken were subjected to highly effective attacks, in which much damage was inflicted, and the signs were there to show, that the Command was, perhaps, at last emerging from the dark cloud of failure. On the night of the second Duisburg raid, the 23/24th, the moon squadrons resumed operations after their stand-down. 138 Squadron dispatched the crew of F/O Krol in Halifax W1007 at 22.50, to bomb an electric power station at Folligny, near Granville, on the south-western coast of the Cherbourg peninsular. The short-range operation took just three hours and fifty minutes to complete, on a night when five 161 Squadron Whitleys were bombing marshalling yards at another location in France. Also on this night, 138 Squadron dispatched three SOE Whitley sorties to Holland, each of which was described in the ORB as successful. It began with S/L Davies and crew taking off at 22.54 in Z9230 on Operations LETTUCE 4/LEEK A, which S/L Outram had failed to complete earlier in the month. They delivered Lt Gerard Hemert into the hands of Giskes and his gang, along with six containers, inside one of which, was a wireless transmitter, the sixth to become available as a link between the gestapo and Baker Street. P/O Newport-Tinley and crew departed Tempsford at 23.00 in Z9146 on Operation LEEK I, and successfully delivered six containers, and they were followed away at 23.30 by P/O Wilkin and crew in Z9248 on Operation TURNIP 3, which was also successful in delivering four containers.

The ORB records two Halifax sorties being launched on the night of the 24/25th, both to France, piloted by P/O Pieniazek (P/O Wodzicki's crew) and P/O Rymills in L9618 and W1012 respectively. P/O Rymills successfully delivered three agents under Operations CRAYFISH/BRILL, but the Wodzicki crew failed to complete Operations ROACH/MACKEREL. They were given another opportunity to complete it twenty-four hours later, however, on what would be the third attempt. P/O Szrajer and crew took off at 22.20 in Halifax W1012, with F/Sgt Jensen at the controls, and delivered three agents and two containers, under Operations JUPITER/SYRINGA 6. The ORB goes on to record another Halifax sortie to France on this night, involving W1007 and the crew of F/O Krol, who were handed Operation SYRINGA 4, which, apparently, was successfully concluded.

It was also on this night, although not recorded in the ORB, that 138 Squadron put up four of the nine Tempsford Whitleys sent against a power station south-east of Nantes. Z9282 failed to return from the operation, and F/Sgt Owen and his crew were duly posted missing. It was learned later that the Whitley had crashed near Vire in the Calvados region of north-western France, and that only the rear gunner had survived to fall into enemy hands. There had always been a danger of losing experienced SOE crews if they were called upon to fly bombing operations, and now it had happened. Never-the-less, seven 138 Squadron Halifaxes took part in a bombing raid on a target, believed to be a base for enemy tanks, at Gien on the Loire on the night of the 26/27th. According to Freddie Clark, five of them were crewed by Poles, who were eager for any opportunity to hit at the enemy, and P/O Anderle and Bunny Rymills were invited to join the party. (A Polish source can find no reference to these sorties in logbooks of some of those serving with the squadron at the time) It was the Polish element that developed the plan of attack, which involved a left hand circuit and line astern bombing from 2,000 feet. They also planned to shoot up the airfield at Chateauroux on the way home, although Bunny Rymills considered this to be a risk too far, and would not get involved. All returned safely from what was believed to be an accurate attack, which was confirmed by photo-reconnaissance. Unfortunately, the photos also revealed an absence of tanks, and it was discovered that the attack had been based on outdated intelligence. This caused anger at Bomber Command HQ, and brought an end to bombing operations by the moon squadrons. S/L Davies also made it safely home from Denmark on this night, for which destination he and his crew had taken off at 22.09 in Whitley Z9230 on Operations TABLETALK/TABLELEG. Their efforts were in vain, however, after failing to locate a reception committee for their passenger.

Evidence of the multinational character of 138 Squadron aircrew. From left to right: F/O Wilkin (Canada), S/L Boxer (New Zealand), P/O Anderle (Czechoslovakia). Photo from archive of another pilot who served in 138 Squadron, P/O Szrajer (Poland). (K. Szrajer via A. Jackowski)

The first of three sorties to take off for Belgium on the evening of the 28th was Whitley Z9232, carrying the crew of S/L Outram on Operation LUCKYSHOT 5. They got away from Tempsford at 22.00, and landed at 04.35 after an apparently successful operation. F/Sgt Freeland and crew were airborne at 22.05 in Whitley Z9288 on Operation BALACLAVA, five minutes before F/L Sutton and crew lifted off in Whitley Z9275 on Operation SPANIEL. Both landed safely after 04.00, to report successful sorties. The night of the 29/30th was one of major activity involving seven sorties, three by Halifaxes to France, and four by Whitleys to Holland. The Halifaxes departed at ten-minute intervals, beginning with L9613 at 21.50 with the crew of W/C Hockey on Operations CLAM/PERCH. W1012 followed at 22.00 captained by F/O Wodzicki on Operation SYRINGA 5, and W1007 brought up the rear at 22.10 with the crew of F/O Walczak on Operation SYRINGA 3. The Whitleys, crews and operations were Z9230, S/L Davies, Operation Lettuce, Z9428, F/O Russell, Operation TURNIP 4, Z9146, P/O

Turnham, Operation CATARRH 8 and Z9287, P/O Newport-Tinley, Operation LEEK 2. Three sorties were successful in terms of delivering their stores and returning safely, but the arrival back at Tempsford of S/L Davies DFC and his crew was awaited in vain. Z9230 had been shot down by a night fighter flown by Lt Geiger of III.NJG/1, while on final approach to the drop zone, and had crashed at 00.58 on the edge of the Haarlerberg wood, four miles west-north-west of the town of Rijssel. There were no survivors from among the seven occupants, and, it seems likely, that as the drop had been arranged by the Gestapo, the night fighter was waiting to spring the trap. Thus was lost another highly experienced SOE crew and a flight commander. As a result, F/L Boxer would be posted in from 161 Squadron on the 3rd of August, and promoted to the rank of squadron leader to fill the breach.

There was just a single sortie on the night of the 30/31st, carried out by P/O Anderle and crew, whose brief was to undertake the long trip to the Nîmes region of southern France to deliver two agents, Claud de Baissac, and his wireless operator, H Peuleve, under Operations SCIENTIST/AUTHOR. They took off at 21.55 in Halifax W1012, and dropped their passengers blind, possibly from too low an altitude. Baissac broke his ankle, although soon recovered, while Peuleve sustained a multiple leg fracture. The Halifax returned a little over eleven hours later, and the crew, unaware of the events on the ground, reported a successful sortie. The night of the 31st brought two Whitley sorties, beginning with the departure for Denmark of Z9288 at 22.30 with the crew of F/Sgt Freeland on board. They were to carry out Operation TABLETALK/TABLELEG, which had previously been attempted by the now missing S/L Davies five nights earlier. They dropped three agents, Hans Hansen, Peter Nielson and Knud Petersen, into a field near Farsø in northern Jutland, along with two containers, which fell some distance away, and were recovered by the enemy. The Whitley landed safely at Tempsford after a round trip of eight hours and fifteen minutes, and the crew was able to report a successful operation. W/O Walker and crew took off at 22.48 in Whitley P5029, bound for France on Operation MANFRIDAY. The sortie, to deliver an agent and stores to the Valenciennes area, failed, but the ORB does not offer any insight into the reasons. This was Walker's first sortie as crew captain.

August 1942

During the August stand-down period, a new era was dawning at Bomber Command. Before the Pathfinder Force came into existence, however, a useful attack was carried out on the town of Osnabrück on the night of the 9/10th, which was followed by two highly destructive raids on Mainz on the nights of the 11/12th and 12/13th. On the 15th, the four founder Pathfinder heavy squadrons, 7, 35, 83 and 156, began the move into their respective stations at Oakington, Graveley, Wyton and Warboys, and prepared for war under the leadership of the brilliant, but humourless, Group Captain Don Bennett. Bennett, an Australian, was a master aviator, with specialist skills in navigation, and recent experience of operations as the commanding officer of 4 Group's 10 Squadron. Earlier in the year he had been shot down over Norway, while attacking the Tirpitz, and had evaded capture to return home, within weeks, to resume his command. The selection by Harris of such a junior officer to lead the new force was both controversial and inspired, and more than a few feathers were ruffled by his appointment. Until being granted group status in its own right, the fledgling outfit would occupy 3 Group stations, and fall nominally under 3 Group control. From January 1943 the Pathfinder Force would become 8 Group, taking over its stations from 3 Group, and gradually expanding to occupy other airfields in the region.

The moon squadrons thus found themselves on the south-western fringe of what, in 1943/44, would become a kind of Spaghetti Junction of the air, with almost constant activity and overlapping circuits. There are no entries in the squadron ORB between the promotion of S/L Boxer on the 4th, and the 17th, when the death of F/O Gibson is recorded. It states simply, that he was killed, but offers no circumstances, and Bomber Command losses for 1942 makes no mention of a 138 Squadron aircraft being involved in an incident. In an inauspicious beginning to what would become an illustrious career, the Pathfinders led their first raid on the night of the 18/19th, against the port of Flensburg. Situated on the eastern coast of the Schleswig-Holstein peninsular, where Germany and Denmark meet, it should have been easy to locate, but the complete failure to identify it led to bombs falling instead onto Danish towns.

Operations from Tempsford resumed on the night of the 23/24th, when F/O Wilkin and P/O Newport-Tinley undertook Whitley sorties to France and Belgium respectively. The former took off first at 20.25 in Z9428 on Operation LUCKYSHOT 6, and returned to Tangmere a little over six hours later, having been unable to complete the drop, after failing to raise the expected reception committee. The latter took off at 20.41 in Z9287 to carry out Operations BALACLAVA 5, WALLABY and SPRINGBOK, with two agents, six containers, ten pigeons and a supply of nickels on board. They crossed the English coast at Littlehampton at 2,000 feet, and maintained that altitude over the Channel, passing by Berck-sur-Mer at 22.19. They set course for the target area in good conditions with some ground haze, and were at the southern edge of Cambrai, when they stumbled into a dozen searchlights and accurate light flak from a number of positions. The Whitley sustained hits, which caused the fraying of a rudder cable, a punctured hydraulics pipe and damage to the agents' parachutes. The drop was abandoned, and the pigeons released sixteen kilometres inland from the coast on the way home to a landing at Tangmere at 01.05.

Officers of 138 Squadron. Photo taken at Tempsford between June and September 1942. (W. Zmyslony)

On the following night, eight sorties were dispatched to France with mixed fortunes, the five SYRINGA trips all to deliver supplies. The first to depart Tempsford, at 19.55, was Whitley Z9288 with the crew of P/O Turnham, who were engaged on Operation SYRINGA 11. They flew deep into southern France, and returned at 05.05 to report an unsuccessful sortie. W/O Walker and crew were the next to take off, at 20.09, in Whitley Z9275 to attempt Operation SYRINGA 13. They landed twenty minutes after P/O Turnham, and also reported being unsuccessful. Z9286 took off at 20.10 with the crew of F/Sgt Freeland on board bound for Operation SYRINGA 12. They landed back at Tempsford at 05.00 to report a successful drop. By this time, the four Halifaxes, with their greater speed, had returned from their sorties, three having successfully delivered their agents and stores. P/O Anderle and crew had taken off at 20.17 in W1002 for Operation SPRUCE 1, P/O Rymills at 20.27 in W1012 on Operation DIRECTOR 1, and P/O Szrajer in L9613 at 20.35 on Operation CRAB 2. F/L Sutton was carrying out his first sortie in a Halifax, having converted during the "dark period", but, on arrival at the drop site, west of Nevers in central France, the signals from the ground were indistinct and only visible from directly above. This difficulty was compounded by the failure of the intercom system, and the attempt had to be abandoned. S/L Outram was briefed to carry out Operation SYRINGA 7, a stores drop, in Whitley Z9232, but, at 00.30, he force-landed on the south bank of the River Cher, a dozen or so miles from Vierzon, happily without injury to the five occupants. Fortunately, they were in unoccupied France, and, having ensured that the aircraft had been completely consumed by fire, they put their escape and evasion training into practice, and all eventually made it back home through Spain and Gibraltar, S/L Outram returning first at the end of September.

The night of the 25/26th brought four more sorties to France, three of them supply drops, while S/L Boxer had an agent to deliver as well. P/O Newport-Tinley and S/L Boxer were both recorded as taking off at 20.00 in Whitleys Z9286 and Z9288 on Operations MARS and DETECTIVE/BLACKTHORN respectively, the latter crossing the French coast at Cabourg at

7,000 feet, above ten-tenths cloud, which began to dissipate as he headed inland towards Vouvray on the River Loire. From there he found the first pinpoint, and three parachutes were seen to drop away from 600 feet, which may have been the agent, Henri Sevenet, and two packages. The second drop site was nearby, but no parachutes were observed there, and, finally, leaflets were released over Loches on the way home, which was reached at 03.00. P/O Newport-Tinley and crew also returned safely to land at 01.50, and likewise reported a successful outcome. The Halifaxes, L9618 and W1012, departed at 20.20 and 20.31 on Operations PLANE 1 and SYRINGA 10 with the crews of P/O Pieniazek and F/Sgt Klosowski respectively, and they returned at 03.25 and 04.28 to complete a rare night of 100% completed sorties.

The night of the 27/28th proved to be the busiest yet for 138 Squadron in SOE terms, with eight sorties departing Tempsford between 19.55 and 20.25, all bound for France. P/O Turnham and crew started the ball rolling in veteran Whitley P5029, when setting off on Operation SYRINGA 11, which they completed successfully, and from which they returned at 05.05. F/Sgt Freeland and crew took off at 20.05 in Whitley Z9286 to try to complete the Operation SYRINGA 7 supply drop, from which S/L Outram had gone missing three nights earlier, and they returned at 04.35 also to report a successful outcome. Following them into the air had been Halifax W7775, with the Polish crew of F/O Walczak, piloted by F/Sgt Jensen, who were on their maiden sortie to carry out Operations SUPPLY/SPINDLE. They flew out over Selsey Bill, and crossed the French coast thirty-five minutes later at 3,000 feet over Isigny-sur-Mer. A new course was set, which took them south to the village of Montsoreau on the southern bank of the Loire, and, at 00.40, a triangle of red lights was picked up, and a white light flashing the letter Z. A total of five packages dropped away during two circuits, before they headed for the second pinpoint, which was reached at 00.55, when the agent, Peter Churchill, parachuted into the French countryside. This was a new experience for him, after previously being inserted into France by submarine. The Halifax and crew made it safely home to land at 04.45.

P/O Pieniazek and crew were in Halifax W7773, and took off at 20.10 to undertake Operation GEOLOGIST 2. They were chased down the runway two minutes later by Halifax L9618 with the crew of F/Sgt Sobkowiak, who were undertaking their maiden sortie, Operation SYRINGA 8. A further three minutes thereafter, and Halifax L9613 took to the air, captained by P/O Anderle, and bound for Operation DIRECTOR 5. The departures were completed at 20.22 and 20 25 by Bunny Rymills in Halifax W1012 and F/O Wilkin in Whitley Z9428 on Operations DIRECTOR 2 and LUCKYSHOT 6 respectively. Another night of 100% success was thwarted by the failure of P/O Rymills to raise a reception committee, but that apart, it had been a good night for the SOE.

There were mixed fortunes on the following night, when four sorties were dispatched, beginning with the departure at 19.52 of Whitley P5029 in the hands of P/O Newport-Tinley and crew, who were bound for southern France to undertake Operation GEOLOGIST 1. They returned two minutes short of ten hours later to report an unsuccessful attempt. P/O Anderle and crew enjoyed better luck, having taken off for France at 20.05 in Halifax L9613 on Operations WALNUT/DIRECTOR 4. They landed back after a round trip of eight hours and fifteen minutes, and reported completing the first part of their assignment, but failing the second. P/O Pieniazek and crew departed Tempsford at 20.07 in Halifax W7773, and headed also for France to carry out Operation CATALPHA. They crossed the French coast near Isigny-sur-Mer, pinpointing afterwards on the Loire and Meximieux, before reaching the drop site at St Etienne-de-Saints-Geoirs, where the agent was delivered. They returned at 03.43, to confirm that the drop had proceeded according to plan. Finally on this night, W/O Walker and his crew took off at 20.21 in Whitley Z9428 on Operation SPANIEL 6 over Belgium. This was the shortest range sortie, and they landed back at base at 02.28 to give the thumbs-up on their efforts.

Two Whitley sorties were launched to Belgium on the night of the 29/30th, one of them taking F/O Wilkin and crew on Operations MINK/OCELOT in Z9426, from which an agent and six containers were dropped, and forty-three pigeons released. The other involved W/O Walker and crew in Z9275 on Operation SYRINGA 9, and they, too, returned to report a successful endeavor. The squadron ORB is both undecipherable and unreliable as a source of information for the last night of August, but the sorties launched were all devoted to France. Bunny Rymills and crew took off at 19.55 in Halifax W1012 on Operations AMETHYST/DIRECTOR 2, and, the first part, to deliver an agent, was concluded successfully, but they were unable to complete the second element, after failing to raise a reception committee. This was a common theme, which had led to all but one of the previous DIRECTOR operations failing. P/O Newport-Tinley and crew were in Whitley Z9426, and briefed to carry out Operations CLAM/OUTCAST. This required them to deliver five containers, one package, three bundles of leaflets and a dozen pigeons, which, it seems, they accomplished, before returning safely home.

Armstrong Whitworth Whitley V, Z9428 of No. 138 Squadron, in 1942. The aircraft eventually wound up at 24 OTU and met her end on 26th September 1943 when she exploded over Stoke Orchard whilst on a Bullseye exercise. F/Sgt GM L'Hommedieu RCAF and his four crew died (Crown Copyright).

September 1942

For the front-line squadrons of Bomber Command, September began with an intended attack on Saarbrücken on the night of the 1/2nd. The Pathfinders posted a "black" by illuminating the nearby small and non-industrial town of Saarlouis, which, to the chagrin of its inhabitants, was pounded by the main force crews. This could have been an ill-omen for the remainder of the month, but, in fact, the following night saw the Command embark on an unprecedented series of effective raids, which would extend into the second half of the month. During the period, Karlsruhe, Bremen twice, Düsseldorf and Wilhelmshaven were all subjected to heavy and accurate attacks, and only Frankfurt escaped with minor damage. Even the notoriously elusive cities of Duisburg and Essen were hit harder than before, although neither was severely damaged. The raids on Düsseldorf and Bremen, on the 10/11th and 13/14th respectively, produced a level of destruction only exceeded by the thousand bomber raid on Cologne at the end of May. It can be no coincidence, that these successes came at a time when the Pathfinder crews were beginning to come to terms with the demands of their exacting role after an unconvincing start. From the Düsseldorf operation, they also had at their disposal "Pink Pansies", the first rudimentary form of target indicators.

The moon squadrons were also busy during the early part of the month, 138 Squadron launching "INTONACJA" (intonation) a new season of flights to Poland with three Halifax sorties on the night of the 1/2nd, all undertaken by Polish crews. Each of the drop sites in Poland was within eighty kilometres of Warsaw, which, itself, was more than three hundred miles east of Berlin. *(There is always confusion when writing about Polish crews, which were captained by the senior officer on board, and not, as in the RAF, by the pilot. There are also discrepencies between the ORB accounts and those of Freddie Clark, who had access to the debriefing reports, with regard to the pilots. In addition, the ORB tends to name the pilot, rather than the official crew captain, and for the purposes of this account, therefore, crews will be referred to, where it is known, by the pilot's name.)* P/O Pieniazek and crew were first away, at 18.44 in W7773, to carry out Operations SMALLPOX/MEASLES, which involved delivering six passengers and four containers into an area roughly a dozen miles north-east of Grojec, and twenty-five miles south of Warsaw. They flew out at 10,000 feet in cloud, passing through storms as they pressed on eastwards, but matters improved somewhat as northern Germany slid by to starboard. The Halifax was hit by flak over Denmark, which damaged the oxygen system and a radio antenna, but they arrived in the target area to find a typically well-organized reception committee, and the drop was completed successfully. The crew enjoyed a safe and uneventful return flight, to land after a round trip of twelve hours and six minutes. W7775 had followed them into the air at 18.55 with F/Sgt Jensen at the controls, carrying five agents and stores, bound for their homeland on Operation CHICKENPOX. Outbound for the drop site near the village of Mariew, situated about fifteen miles north-west of Warsaw, the Halifax had an encounter with a ME110 night fighter, which left it with damage to its wings, fuselage and tail-plane. Despite that, the drop was carried out over reception committee lights at 00.33, with just one container hanging up as a result of damage to the electrical release gear. A safe return was eventually made to Tempsford, after a round trip of almost twelve hours. The last to depart of the Poland-bound Halifaxes was W7774, at 18.57, with F/Sgt Klosowski in the pilot's seat. They were to carry out Operation RHEUMATISM, the drop site for which lay to the west of SMALLPOX, where they were to deliver six agents and four containers. Sadly, having reached the target area, they were unable to raise a reception committee, and were forced to return home with their passengers and stores. It speaks volumes for the fortitude of these Polish crews, who might fly a twelve-hour round trip to achieve nothing, and then go again with renewed enthusiasm within days.

While these operations were in progress, S/L Boxer and crew took off at 22.30 in Whitley Z9146 on Operation MONGOOSE 1 over Belgium. The brief was to deliver eight containers, leaflets and pigeons, en-route to which, they crossed the English coast at Orfordness at 3,000 feet, and headed for the Scheldt Estuary. Here, having reduced altitude to 1,500 feet, they were met by inaccurate light flak from Haamstede aerodrome, and again from Woensdrecht, and were forced off course as they followed the Dutch/Belgian frontier. They attracted more flak and searchlights from Hellevoetsluis on the north bank of the Haringvliet, and, now down to between 1,000 and 300 feet, it was decided to abort the sortie and turn for home. The stores were jettisoned over the airfield, and a landing made without hydraulics and flaps, suggesting that at least one flak shell had found the mark. Finally on this night, P/O Turnham and crew took off for Holland at 23.15 in Whitley Z9275, to undertake Operations MANGOLD/PARSLEY. They were carrying two agents, four containers and a package as they headed out over the Norfolk coast bound for Vlieland. It was two hours later when they crossed the island at 1,500 feet and set course for Stavoren in ideal weather conditions, before making for the drop site near Assen. As they approached, the lights of about half a dozen vehicles were visible at points around the site, but they were extinguished before the Whitley passed over. While making a wide circuit, the crew watched the lights come on again, only to be doused yet again as the Whitley flew towards them. Not wishing to give up too early, P/O Turnham flew along the railway to Assen and back a number of times, but, ultimately, he was uncomfortable with the activity on the ground, and set course for Enkhuizen, at 1,500 feet, dispensing leaflets on the way. They ran into searchlights and light flak from Alkmaar aerodrome, but crossed the enemy coast to the south at 500 feet, before safely crossing the North Sea and returning home. P/O Turnham offered the opinion that the drop site appeared to be compromised, but his warning would go unheeded.

F/Sgt Klosowski and crew returned to Poland in Halifax W7774 on the night of the 3/4th, and, this time, were able to complete Operation RHEUMATISM, which involved the dropping of six agents. Meanwhile, P/O Pieniazek and crew, who were in W7773, completed Operation MEASLES, and both aircraft returned safely home after more than twelve hours aloft. The single sortie on the night of the 6/7th was carried out by F/L Sutton and crew in Halifax L9618. They took off at 20.08 on Operation CHAFFINCH, which was a drop over Norway, but the absence of a reception committee forced them to return home nine hours later with their load intact. Fresh blood arrived from 12 O.T.U on the 8th, and among the ten new recruits were two pilots, Sgts Harrop and Reardon.

There were no further operations until the night of the 12/13th, when F/Sgt Jensen was at the controls of L9613 bound for Norway on Operation GROUSE 2, the purpose of which, was to insert the first components of the force that would eventually carry out the audacious attack on the German heavy water plant at Vemork in the Telemark region, west of Oslo. Unfortunately, engine problems prevented the drop from taking place, and the Halifax returned early to land at Peterhead in north-eastern Scotland. The ORB entries for this period are illegible, but it appears that four sorties were mounted on the night of the 18/19th, three of them over Belgium, beginning with the departure of Whitley Z9286 at 19.45 with the crew of F/Sgt Freeland on board. They were to undertake Operations PERIWIG 5/MARMOT, but it is not possible to decipher the report to confirm their success or otherwise. Whitley Z9275 took off at 20.00 on Operation MANFRIDAY with the crew of W/O Walker, and they were followed into the air at 20.22 by Z9159 with the crew of P/O Turnham. The operations to Holland, MANGOLD/PARSLEY, which had previously been attempted by P/O Turnham on the night of the 1/2nd, were given to F/O Wilkin and crew on this night, and they departed Tempsford at 21.00 in Whitley Z9288. P/O Turnham's uncertainties concerning the security of the drop site, had clearly gone unheeded, but, in the event, a reception committee failed to appear, and the attempt was abandoned.

According to the ORB, there were three Whitley sorties on the following night, two to Belgium, sandwiching one to France. However, Freddie Clark's account has the French drop, Operation HAGFISH, taking place on the night of the 22/23rd, and he is a more reliable source. The proceedings for the night of the 19/20th began with the departure from Tempsford at 18.52 of Z9275 and the crew of P/O Newport-Tinley on Operation SPANIEL 5, from which they returned safely at 01.55 to report a successful drop. P/O Kingsford-Smith and his crew took off at 19.04 on Operation BALACLAVA 6, and, it is believed, that this sortie was concluded successfully. As far as it is possible to decipher from the ORB entries for the night of the 21/22nd, two Whitley sorties were carried out, involving the crews of F/O Wilkin and F/Sgt Freeland in Z9428 and Z9286 respectively. Their brief was to undertake Operations TERRIER 7 and INCOMPARABLE, for which they took off for Belgium shortly before 20.00, returning either side of 01.00 with nothing to show for their efforts. Not mentioned in the ORB for the reason stated above, was the sortie to France by F/L Russell on the night of the 22/23rd. They had taken off for France on Operation HAGFISH at 18.55 in Z9428, but, if the ORB entry for the wrong night is to be believed, they failed to complete the drop.

Pilot F/O Anderle, one of a number of Czechoslovak airmen who served in 138 Squadron. (J. Rajlich)

There was much activity at Tempsford on the 23rd, as four Halifaxes and two Whitleys were prepared for operations over France that night. P/O Rymills started the ball rolling, when taking off in W1012 at 19.37 on Operation DIRECTOR 13, which he failed to complete. Whitley Z9275 was the next to take off, at 20.01, carrying the crew of F/O Walker on Operation CRAB 5, which they completed successfully. F/L Sutton and crew departed Tempsford at 20.05 in Halifax L9618 on Operation SYRINGA 14, and they returned from the seven hour-long trip to report a successful drop. They had been followed into the air at 20.10 by F/L Russell and crew in Halifax W7774 on Operation SYRINGA 15, which, it is believed, they failed to complete. F/O Anderle and crew were on board Halifax W7776, as it took off at 20.15 bound for Operation CRAB 3, but they, too, failed to complete their sortie as briefed. At 20.20, P/O

Turnham and crew rolled down the runway in Whitley Z9159 to carry out Operations WHITEBEAM/MONKEYPUZZLE 1 and ARTIST, which involved the transportation of two female agents, Lisé de Baissac and Andrée Borell, to the Loire-et-Cher region of north-western France. On arrival over the drop site, the signal lights were observed to be laid out correctly in a triangle, but they were white, rather than the red expected by the crew, and it was decided to bring the agents home.

The female agents, the first members of the First Aid Nursing Yeomanry (FANY) to be parachuted into France, had only to wait twenty-four hours for their second chance, and their departure would be one of nine scheduled for the night of the 24/25th, the first six of which were to destinations in France. Proceedings got under way at 20.35 with the departure of Halifax W1229 in the hands of P/O Szrajer and crew, who had been briefed to carry out Operation PLANE 2, but they returned at 03.55 to report being unable to complete the drop. Halifax W7773 was airborne at 20.40, bearing F/O Dobromirski and crew on Operation OUTCLASS 2, which they were able to complete, before returning safely to land at 04.05. Bunny Rymills and crew were on board Halifax W1012, and took off at 20.45 on Operation SYRINGA 17, which they failed to complete. Halifax W7774 took off at 20.49, to undertake Operations GEOLOGIST 6/REDWOOD/LIME/AUBRETIA with F/Sgt Sobkowiak at the controls, but, it appears from the minimal information available, that they were unsuccessful. The last of the France-bound departures took place at 20.52, as Whitley Z9428 departed Tempsford in the hands of F/O Wilkin and crew to try again to deliver the two female agents brought home the night before under Operations WHITEBEAM/MONKEYPUZZLE 1 and ARTIST. They crossed out over Bognor Regis, and reached the French coast at Pointe de la Percee at 22.34, while flying at 2,500 feet. They set course for Orleans and the River Loire, and continued south until arriving at the drop site at 00.35, in conditions of low broken cloud. As on the previous night, the triangle of lights was seen clearly on the ground, but they were still white, rather than red. However, the flashing light gave the correct signal, and the agents were dropped from 500 feet on the second pass across the target, their safe arrival on the ground confirmed by the dispatcher. Twenty-two-year-old Andrée Borell would make her way to Paris to work as a courier, but would fall into enemy hands in January 1944, and be executed in July. Lisé de Baissac, who was thirty-seven years old, went south to Poitiers to set up a reception organization for incoming agents, and she would be successfully brought home by S/L Verity in a 161 Squadron Lysander on the night before the Peenemünde operation in mid-August 1943.

The remaining three operations on this night involved drops over Holland in Whitleys, and were, therefore, on behalf of Hermann Giskes and the Gestapo rather than SOE. Z9286, on Operations KALE/CAULIFLOWER/LETTUCE 6, took off first, at 21.25, captained by F/Sgt Freeland. Their brief was to drop two agents and six containers each at two locations, one near Wijk bij Duurstede, and the other near Amerongen, both south-east of Utrecht. All four agents and their supplies fell into enemy hands, including an eighth transmitter. P/O Newport-Tinley, meanwhile, had lifted Z9287 off the ground at 21.32 to deliver two agents and containers under Operations MANGOLD/PARSLEY, and had headed for Vlieland, where they came under fire

F/Sgt David Freeland, pilot (Peter Green)   F/Sgt Eddie Hayhoe, second pilot (Stuart Smith)   WOP/AG F/Sgt Fred Green (Peter Green)

W/O Peter Moore, air gunner (Sally Strachan via Peter Green)   F/Sgt George Wall (right) with another member of 138 Sqn, Johnny Martin. The photo was taken at Newmarket in late 1941. (John Coleman via Peter Green)   F/Sgt John Charrott, the crew's regular navigator, (John Charrott via Peter Green)

Pilots F/Sgt David Freeland and F/Sgt Edmund Hayhoe (centre), along with WOP/AG F/Sgt Fred Green lost their lives when Z9275 was shot down near Merville, France. W/O Peter Moore, air gunner, and W/O John Cox, navigator, survived as POWs. F/Sgt Green had previously completed two tours of ops with 38 Sqn before a spell at 11 OTU, Bassingbourne. F/Sgts Hayhoe and Freeland had been with 78 Sqn from Autumn 1941 before their posting to 138 Sqn in January 1942. Two members of Freeland's regular crew were not present on his final operation. F/Sgt George Wall (below, centre photo standing to the right of 138 Sqn crew man Johnny Martin) was the usual air gunner whilst F/Sgt John Charrott (below, right) was the crew's navigator. Photos: Peter Green and Stuart Smith via Aircrew Remembered.

while flying at between 1,500 and 800 feet. A course was set for Stavoren and the drop site beyond, and, after cruising around for a few minutes, lights were observed on the ground. All of the containers hung up on the first pass, but four fell away on the second, along with both agents and a package from 450 feet. The Whitley was fired on again as it passed south of Alkmaar, and the return flight was made in conditions of thunder, lightning and rain. Finally on this night, P/O Kingsford-Smith and crew took off at 22.25 in Z9275 on Operation MARROW 1, and presented Giskes with a further six containers to add to the ever-expanding stockpile of SOE equipment in Nazi hands.

The night of the 25/26th brought just a single sortie to Norway under Operation BITTERN, which was handed to F/Sgt Sobkowiak and crew in Halifax W7774. They took off from Tempsford at 19.25, but, despite committing almost nine and a half hours to the endeavor, the drop could not be completed. The final sorties of the month took place on the night of the 26/27th, beginning with W/O Walker and crew taking off at 19.25 for Holland in Whitley Z9286 on Operation MARROW 2. The drop was completed as planned, and a further six containers found their way into the possession of Hermann Giskes. Shortly after 22.00, P/O Turnham and crew took off for France in Whitley Z9428 to attempt Operation HAGFISH, and they returned some five hours later to confirm a successful sortie. As midnight approached, P/O Newport-Tinley and crew set off for Belgium in Whitley Z9287 to carry out Operation MINK 2. They landed at Stradishall at 05.25, after what the illegible scrawl in the ORB suggests was an unsuccessful attempt. The fourth sortie of the night, which is not mentioned in the ORB, cost the squadron another experienced crew, who were trying to complete a recently failed attempt to deliver stores to Belgium under Operation INCOMPARABLE 1. Whitley Z9275 crashed near Merville in France, close to the border with Belgium, and F/Sgt Freeland and two of his crew, 19-year-old second pilot F/Sgt Edmund Hayhoe and WOP/AG F/Sgt Fred Green, lost their lives, while the two survivors, W/O JH Cox, navigator, and W/O Peter Moore, Air Gunner were taken prisoner. Eyewitness accounts state that the aircraft was hit by flak at about 0600hrs, making a controlled crash-landing avoiding nearby houses and powerlines, However the aircraft then hit the bank of a small stream, ripping off the undercarriage[1]. There was an enemy airfield nearby, and, it is possible, that the Whitley stumbled across it, and was brought down by its defences.

---

[1] Account by Peter Green, http://www.aircrewremembered.com/freeland-david.html

October 1942

The 1st of October brought a number of personnel changes to Tempsford. Firstly, 161 Squadron's commanding officer, W/C "Mouse" Fielden, was promoted to Group Captain rank and appointed station commander, and secondly, W/C Percy "Pick" Pickard arrived as his replacement. It will be recalled, that during a lull in his operational career, he had accompanied his good friend, Ron Hockey, on 138 Squadron's first operational sortie from Tempsford a little over a year earlier. This night of the 1/2nd brought what amounted to a maximum effort for 138 Squadron involving nine sorties, with targets in France, Poland and Holland. The Polish contingent was the first to depart Tempsford, with the prospect of twelve hours or more flying ahead of them. Each Halifax also carried as many bombs and incendiaries as its all-up-weight allowed, and these were to be employed against railway targets. At 17.58, F/Sgt Sobkowiak lifted Halifax W7774 into the air on Operations GIMLET/SPANNER, and headed for the Danish coast en-route to the drop site near Deblin, on the eastern bank of a loop in the River Vistula, some fifty miles south-east of Warsaw. The operation was completed successfully, and a safe landing made at Hemswell, home of their compatriots of 300 and 301 Squadrons. Halifax W7776 was next to take off, at 18.00, bearing the crew of F/Sgt Klosowski and passengers to the drop site near Siedlce, east of Warsaw, on Operation CHISEL. They experienced difficulty in finding the exact pinpoint, but successfully delivered six agents and four containers, before heading for home. They had also been briefed to bomb the railway station at Warka, south of Warsaw, which would have added considerably to the duration of the flight, and whether or not they complied, is unknown. What is certain, however, is that they reached the Yorkshire coast at Flamborough Head with empty tanks, and the Halifax was force-landed by F/Sgt Klosowski near Whitby without injury to the occupants after spending thirteen and a half hours in the air. The last of the Polish element to take off was F/Sgt Jensen with the crew of F/O Walczak in W1229, which was bound for a drop site at Gloskow village near Garwolin, again south-east of Warsaw, on Operation HAMMER. They delivered four agents and four containers onto the briefed location, and returned safely, again after more than thirteen hours aloft.

Bunny Rymills and crew were handed a trip to Norway, for which they departed Tempsford at 20.30 in Halifax L9618. There are no details available, other than a barely legible scrawl that suggests the sortie failed. The first of two sorties to France was dispatched at 21.19 in the form of Halifax L9613 with the crew of P/O Anderle on board. They were to undertake Operations CRAB 3/PHYSICIAN/CHEMIST, the first part of which required the delivery of three containers to the Vire region of Normandy. That accomplished, they set course for Chateauroux and then Bourges, which they pinpointed before fog spread across the ground. Once in the general area of the drop site, the two passengers, F A Suttill and J F Amps, became reticent to jump without knowing their precise location, but, after four circuits, they were persuaded that they were close enough to the target, and dropped away. Their task was to set up a new circuit in the Paris area under the codename PROSPER, but, after their arrest in June 1943, the organization collapsed. P/O Anderle and crew made it safely back to England, and landed at St Eval in Cornwall. The final Halifax departure on this night was that of W1007, which took off at 23.20 in the hands of F/L Russell and crew to carry out Operations TIGER/REDCROSS/BLACKTHORN over south-eastern France. The TIGER element involved a drop on behalf of the SIS, but this failed through the absence of a reception

W/C Hockey's Halifax, L9613 NF-V, photographed in October 1942. The aircraft joined the unit in November 1941. The aircraft earned a place in history the following month when used to drop an assassination team into Czechoslovakia. They successfully killed leading Nazi official, Reinhard Heydrich. L9613 went on to join 1660 CU after her stint on special duties. (J. Rajlich)

committee. The remaining two element, the delivery of five containers and two packages, was completed successfully, however, and this aircraft also landed at St Eval. The night's remaining three sorties were all by Whitleys to Holland, and began at 22.30 with the take-off of Z9286 and the crew of P/O Turnham on Operation MARROW 3. Their brief was to deliver six containers, which, it appears, was accomplished, before a safe return brought them to a landing at Wyton. W/O Walker, meanwhile, was engaged in Operation MARROW 5, having taken off last at 22.42 in an unspecified Whitley, but he was defeated by ground fog in the drop zone, and had to abandon the attempt. P/O Newport-Tinley and crew had lifted off at 22.37 in Z9428 on Operation CABBAGE/CATARRH, and contributed another brave young Dutch agent to the rapidly growing roll-call of the damned in Gestapo hands.

On the following night, the 2/3rd, while almost two hundred aircraft from the Pathfinder and main force squadrons went to Krefeld, 138 Squadron was also active over various regions of the continent. The night's activities began with the departure of Halifax W7773 at around 18.30, with F/O Pieniazek at the controls, operating for the final time with 138 Squadron. The crew captain, undertaking his first sortie since joining, was F/O Kuzmicki, and they were heading for their homeland on Operation LATHE, to drop three agents and four containers to a site near Mokobody village, a dozen or so miles north-west of Siedlce. The weather conditions outbound were good, but extreme darkness hampered the search for pinpoints. Never the less, the operation was successful, and the Halifax returned to a landing at Dyce in north-eastern Scotland after a flight duration of five minutes short of twelve hours. Two Whitley sorties to Holland, by Z9287 and Z9428, took off at 21.38 and 21.43 on Operations MARROW 6 and MARROW 5 with the crews of P/O Kingsford-Smith and, it is believed, P/O Rymills respectively. The latter, a supply drop, was successful, while the former failed for an unspecified reason. Finally, P/O Anderle and crew took off at 22.00 in Halifax L9613 to return to France to complete the SIS drop, Operation TIGER, from the previous night. Conditions were good, and they identified the drop site after circling Givors, south of Lyon. An agent and two packages were delivered into the hands of a reception committee, before a safe return culminated with a landing at Tangmere.

The moon period was brought to a close on the night of the 3/4th, with an eight hour trip in a Halifax by F/L Sutton and crew to Norway, to deliver an assassination team to deal with known collaborators. Operation BITTERN was to be a blind drop into an area between Honefoss and Hole, near Lake Tyrifjorden, and could only take place if the crew captain was certain, that they were within five kilometres of the specified pinpoint, and that the agents knew the lie of the land. Another proviso, was that the operation should not take place on a Saturday, because of the likelihood of locals being out walking in the area. They took off at 23.05, on a murky night with a forward visibility of a thousand yards, and a cloud base at 1,000 feet. They crossed the Norfolk coast at 23.33, and headed towards the Danish coast in hazy, cloudy conditions and occasional showers. Visibility had become good by the time they made landfall, and they experienced no difficulty in identifying ground detail as they made their way to the drop site. The agents jumped out at 700 feet, to be followed by six containers, and the Halifax returned on a reciprocal route to land at Acklington in Northumberland.

The rest of Bomber Command was involved in heavy raids on Aachen, Osnabrück and Kiel on the nights of the 5/6th, 6/7th and 13/14th respectively, and produced a moderate degree of damage, but a force of over 250 aircraft managed to leave Cologne almost untouched on the night of the 15/16th. 5 Group carried out a massed daylight raid on the Schneider armaments works at Le Creusot and the nearby transformer station at Montchanin on the 17th, and, although the sight of over ninety Lancasters in a gaggle over France must have made an impressive sight, and returning crews were convinced of the accuracy of the attack, the target had actually escaped serious damage. The 138 Squadron ORB records three operations by Whitley Z9428 to Holland, taking place on the nights of the 11/12th, 14/15th and 15/16th, with the crews respectively of P/O Kingsford-Smith, P/O Turnham, and F/O Wilkin. The operations were TURNIP 5, which was apparently successful, and TURNIP 6 on the two latter occasions, which failed. The ORB also records that W/O Walker and crew took off in Whitley Z9286 at 23.15 on the evening of the 17th, to carry out Operation MONGOOSE 3 over Belgium, but were unable to complete. There was a flight by F/O Walczak and crew in a Halifax to Gibraltar to deliver passengers on this night, but this is not mentioned in the ORB, and Freddie Clark makes no mention of any of the above sorties. The outward leg was completed safely in eight hours, and they returned to England on the 24th.

Freddie Clark records 138 Squadron returning to action on the night of the 18/19th with four sorties to Scandinavia. Three of these were by Halifaxes to Norway, beginning with the departure of P/O Rymills and crew in W1012 at 18.45 on Operations CASTER/CORONA. They successfully delivered two agents and two packages, before returning safely to base to land at 03.55. Before the other Norway-bound departures took place, Whitley Z9288 left Tempsford for Denmark with the crew of P/O Kingsford-Smith on board. They were to carry out Operation TABLETOP A, the first water jump to be attempted. Having lost contact with the Danish SOE, it was decided by London to employ this unusual method of insertion, which required the agent, Morgans Hammer, to wear a newly-developed waterproof suit over his civilian clothing. Once on land, he was to take over the running of the TABLE group. He was dropped into the waters of the Kattegat off the coast of Tisvilde, twenty-five miles north-west of Copenhagen, and all seems to have proceeded according to plan. W/C Hockey and crew took off at 19.06 on Operation GROUSE 2, the purpose of which was to insert four agents into Norway as part of the build-up of the sabotage force preparing to attack the German heavy water plant at Vemork. They crossed the English coast outbound at 19.38 flying at 5,000 feet, and reached the Norwegian coast a thousand feet higher at 22.16. They pinpointed on Ardals Fjord and Totak Lake, and found the drop site on a small mountain plateau at Flarfeit in the isolated region of Hardangervidda, some sixty miles inland from Bergen. The agents, Claus

Helberg, Jens Poulson, Arne Kjelstrup and Knut Haugland, were safely delivered from 1,000 feet, along with six containers and two packages, after which, leaflets were delivered over Ardal from 6,000 feet at 23.45. They passed over the Norwegian coast homebound at 00.02, and reached the English coast at Burnham two and a half hours later.

The squadron ORB records three sorties taking place on the night of the 20/21st, and a further seven twenty-four hours later. Freddie Clark, however, writes that nine sorties were dispatched on the night of the 21/22nd, but details only two. Those cited in the ORB as taking place on the night of the 20/21st were all bound for France, and involved Whitley Z9159 departing Tempsford at 20.10 with the crew of P/O Turnham on Operation SPRUCE 4, Halifax W1012 taking off fifteen minutes later with Bunny Rymills and crew on Operation PLANE 2, and P/O Anderle and crew in Halifax W1002 at 20.28 on Operation SPRUCE 5. All returned safely after successfully carrying out their assigned tasks. Of the seven remaining sorties dispatched over the two nights in question, six had business over France, and one over Holland, and, in chronological order according to take-off times, they began with Whitley P5029 becoming airborne at 20.13 in the hands of P/O Newport-Tinley and crew on Operation SPRUCE 2, a stores drop. By the time they approached the south coast of England, after successfully fulfilling their brief, they were very low on fuel, and were forced to ditch off Eastbourne. This was accomplished without injury to the crew, who were soon picked up and taken ashore. Two Halifaxes were recorded as taking off at 20.20, W1007 and L9613, with the crews of F/L Russell and W/C Hockey respectively. The former was to carry out Operation SYRINGA 19, and the latter ACTOR/SCIENTIST 1, but neither was successful, in the case of W/C Hockey, through the failure to raise a reception committee. There were two departures also at 20.25, those of Halifaxes W1229 and W7773, with the Polish crews of F/L Krol, pilot, the newly-promoted W/O Klosowski, and P/O Wodzicki, pilot, F/Sgt Sobkowiak, on Operations SYRINGA 18 and CRAB 4 respectively. The former was successfully completed, the latter not, but no details are available. The final departure on this night was that of Whitley Z9428, which contained the crew of F/O Wilkin, and took off at 22.07 bound for Holland on Operations CELERY A/PUMPKIN/MARROW 9/TOMATO A. Two agents, Peter Kamphorst and Meinart Koolstra, and their wireless operator, Michael Pals, like so many before, parachuted down into the arms of the waiting Gestapo, who were presented also with six containers.

On the night of the 22/23rd, Bomber Command began a series of operations against Italian cities in support of Operation Torch, the Allied landings in North Africa, which would ultimately lead to the complete defeat of the Afrika Korps. Genoa and Milan were each attacked twice before the end of the month, the latter somewhat audaciously by 5 Group in daylight on the 24th. That night 138 Squadron launched four Halifaxes and four Whitleys on widely dispersed operations across Europe, and with the greatest distance to travel, W7773 was the first to depart, taking off from Linton-on-Ouse at 17.55 bound for Estonia on Operation BLUNDERHEAD. F/Sgt Sobkowiak was the pilot, with W/O Zaremba as a much-needed second pilot to take some of the strain of what would be a mammoth feat of endurance. They crossed out over the Yorkshire coast at 2,000 feet, and, because of the cloud conditions, would not climb higher during the entire course of the operation. They pinpointed on the northern tip of Denmark, before setting course across Sweden to Gotska Sandön, a small island in the Baltic, north of Gotland. At 23.05 they passed over Naissaar Island, a dozen or so miles north-west of Tallinn, and reached the target area to the east of the capital ten minutes later. The site for the blind drop was situated between Kiiu and Leesi, but the English agent, Roland Seth, chose not to leave the aircraft there, as the ground was clearly marshy. Another site was chosen in a clearing between woods, onto which he parachuted from 800 feet, before signalling his safe arrival on the ground. In fact, his parachute had caught on telephone wires and a tree, and he had landed close to a German field post, which dispatched soldiers to arrest him. He would later escape, be betrayed and recaptured, but, would, ultimately, and, perhaps, miraculously, survive his captivity. The Halifax returned via a reciprocal course, crossing the Danish coast near Ringkobing and the English coast near Sheringham, before landing safely at Tempsford after a round trip of thirteen hours and thirteen minutes duration.

Another ultra long-range operation on this night involved Halifax W1002 and the all-Czechoslovakian crew of F/O Anderle, who took off at 18.42 on Operation ANTIMONY. They were carrying three agents, who were to re-establish contact with the Home Army, and a bomb load consisting of four 250 and two 500 pounders, each with an eleven second delayed fuse. They had attained 6,000 feet by the time they crossed the Suffolk coast at 19.30, and they continued to climb as they headed for the Franco/German frontier at Strasbourg. By this time they were cruising at a little under 10,000 feet, but unable to map-read because of ten-tenths cloud. At 21.24 they made a course change on e.t.a, when at 11,000 feet, and it was only when they were about forty miles north of Prague, that they obtained their first actual pinpoint, at Terezin on the River Elbe. From there they proceeded via Roudnice nad Labem and Melnik to the first drop site, where haze prevented them from identifying it. Flying on to the second drop site, all three agents, Frantisek Zavorka, Stanislav Srasil and Lubomir Jasinek, parachuted away from just 400 feet at 23.08. It took ten minutes to reach Pardubice aerodrome, the target for the bomb load, some sixty miles east of Prague, and half were delivered onto the hangars on the first circuit, the remainder onto the barracks on the second. Not content, they made two further low-level runs across the target to allow the front and rear gunners to strafe parked aircraft, and the Halifax was hit by accurate return fire from the ground. They followed a reciprocal return course, crossing Germany at 9,000 feet, and landed safely at 05.21. Sadly, the agents would retain their freedom only until January 1943, when two would commit suicide, while Szrasil became a collaborator.

The next two departures from Tempsford were by Halifaxes bound for Norway. W1007 and W1229 took off at 20.03 and 20.20 with the crews of S/L Boxer and F/L Sutton respectively. They were to undertake Operations THRUSH and GANNETT, but neither was completed, and it is believed, that adverse weather conditions were responsible for the failures. Whitley Z9286 was the next away with the crew of W/O Walker at 20.24, with a destination somewhere in Belgium to carry out Operation MONGOOSE 3. This is recorded to be a successful sortie, but, again, no details are forthcoming. The remaining three sorties on this night were flown in Whitleys with Holland as their destination, and involved the crews of P/O Turnham on Operations MARROW 6/TOMATO A & B in Z9159, F/O Wilkin on Operation MARROW 6/CELERY B & C in Z9428, and P/O Kingsford-Smith on Operation MARROW 4 in Z9288. They took of at 21.30, 21.35 and 21.47 respectively, and their efforts resulted in a further four agents, Jan Hofstede and Horst Steeksma, and their wireless operators, Max Macare and Charles Pouwels, falling into enemy hands as soon as they touched down, along with eighteen containers.

The night of the 27/28th was devoted to France and Holland, and would be only partially successful as far as those at Tempsford were aware, although, in fact, it was a night when nothing of benefit to SOE was achieved. The four France-bound Halifaxes were first away, with two departures logged at 20.05, those of F/O Walczak and crew, pilot, F/Sgt Jensen in W7774 on Operation ALMOND 1, and F/L Russell and crew in W1007 on Operations ACTOR/SCIENTIST. W1012 took off at 20.12 with the crew of P/O Rymills on board to carry out Operations MONKEYPUZZLE 3/GARTERFISH, and they were followed into the air at 20.20 by L9613 and the crew of F/O Idzikowski, pilot, F/O Dobromirski, on Operation PRUNUS 2. Not one of these sorties was completed, for which there is no explanation, but it seems likely that the weather conditions proved unfavourable. They were certainly unhelpful to returning crews, three of which put down at Tangmere, and the other at Boscombe Down. P/O Turnham and crew began the departures for Holland at 21.27 in Whitley Z9159, intending to undertake Operation MARROW 8. W/O Walker and crew were next away at 21.38 in Whitley Z9286 on Operations MARROW 10/CUCUMBER A & B, and they were followed at 21.43 by F/O Wilkin and crew in Z9428 on Operation MARROW 11. All three were able to deliver their agents and stores, but those of CUCUMBER, Capt Jan Dane and Jacob Bakker, fell into the hands of the enemy, along with eighteen containers. All three Whitleys returned safely to land at Downham Market.

The night of the 29/30th was attended by a major effort on the part of the Polish contingent, but sadly, it would be a night of failure and loss. There would also be two sorties to Holland and one to Denmark, but it was the Polish contingent that started the ball rolling to take advantage of as many hours of darkness as possible. Halifax W1229 took off at 17.45 on Operation BRACE with the crew of F/O Walczak on board, and F/Sgt Jensen at the controls. They were also carrying six agents, four containers and two packages. Among the agents was W/C Roman Rudkowski, the first commanding officer of 301 Squadron, who had been on the first Polish SOE sortie to his homeland almost a year earlier. Once back in Poland, he was to assume a command role in the Air Force arm of the Home Army. The drop site was about five miles to the east of Radzyn, some eighty miles south-east of Warsaw, but, on arrival, the signals from the ground were indistinct, and it was decided to press on to a reserve site, which also proved to be incorrectly lit. With great disappointment, the attempt was abandoned, and W/C Rudkowski opted to return to England, rather than risk the possibility of jumping into enemy hands. A head wind on the way home suggested they may not complete the North Sea crossing, but radio communication was established with Bircham Newton in Norfolk, and seconds after the Halifax landed, with a record duration of fourteen and a quarter hours aloft to its credit, the engines cut.

F/L Krol was the captain of Halifax W7774, which set off on Operation WRENCH at 17.54 to bomb the Gestapo HQ in the centre of Warsaw. The operation was in response to requests from the commander of the Polish Underground Movement, General Rowecki, for attacks on Warsaw. The idea was backed by the commander of all Polish forces, General Sikorski, in London, and SOE chiefs approved the request on the 22nd of October. Some sources put W/O Klosowski at the controls, which may have been the case, but a Polish source names P/O Szrajer as first pilot, and, as a native of Warsaw, his knowledge of the topography would be invaluable to the success of the operation. They reached the target apparently without incident, but, after making a number of runs across the city, hampered by poor visibility, F/L Krol decided that an attack would endanger his countrymen in the vicinity of the HQ building, and decided instead to bomb the nearby airfield at Okecie with the four 250 and two 500 pounders. As they approached, the pilot switched on his landing lights, and the Germans responded by lighting up the runway, which greatly aided the attack. This done, the Halifax turned for home, and was attacked by two ME110s over the sea some fifty miles out from the Danish coast. Damage was sustained to the engines, intercom, fuel tanks and dinghy, but the wireless operator maintained an SOS signal throughout the remainder of the flight, and second pilot, W/O Klosowski, eventually put the aircraft down on the sea between Sheringham and Cromer, very close in to the beach. The coastguard had observed the ditching, and the crew was brought ashore by the Sheringham lifeboat after ninety minutes, and the Halifax was towed to the shore.

The other Halifax to head for Poland on this night was W7773, which took off at 17.55 on Operation PLIERS, but this is not recorded in the ORB. The drop site was located about ten miles north of Opole, near Rogow village, and it seems certain that the target area was reached, although the evidence suggests that the drop did not take place. The Halifax crashed between Hellern and Refsland in southern Norway, and all on board, including the three Polish agents, were killed. The pilot of the all-Polish crew of F/O Wodzicki was F/Sgt Sobkowiak, with W/O Zaremba as second pilot, and crew captain, F/O Wodzicki, the navigator. These would be the final sorties conducted to Poland in 1942. The Poles weren't the only crews flying on this night, as three Whitley sorties also took place, although they too failed. W/O Walker and crew took off at 21.38 in Z9286 and headed for Denmark on Operations TABLEMAT/TABLETOP I, where, despite circling both drop sites for ten minutes, no reception committee was encountered. They were fired upon through the cloud by enemy ships on the way home in poor weather conditions, and they returned to a landing at Bodney ten hours after take-off. F/Sgt Weatherstone undertook his first sortie as crew captain on this night, taking off at 23.45 in Z9288 on Operation MARROW 13, which he and his crew failed to complete. Finally, Z9428 lifted off two minutes before midnight to carry out Operation MARROW 12 with another pilot acting as crew captain for the first time. P/O Bunting would be disappointed on this occasion, and like F/Sgt Weatherstone, landed at Mildenhall.

The experienced P/O Bunny Rymills completed his service with 138 Squadron on the last night of the month, when he and his crew took off at 23.10 in Halifax W1012 to carry out Operation GARTERFISH, which was to be combined with Operation MONKEYPUZZLE 3/ACTOR/BUTCHER. They successfully delivered three agents, four containers and four packages, before returning safely to land at 04.15, the short duration of the flight suggesting that the target area was in northern France. After a short rest, Rymills would return to special duties at Tempsford in January to complete a second tour, only this time as a Lysander pilot with 161 Squadron. By the time of his posting, he would have amassed a total of fifty bombing and special duties operations. Also operating over France on this night were P/O Turnham and his crew in Whitley Z9159 on Operation PRODUCER 2. They were undertaking their sixth operation of the month, but failed to return, and, it was later established, that all had been killed, when their aircraft crashed in the Abbeville coastal region.

70 years after the crash, the remains of Halifax W7773 are still at the crash site on private land near Egersund, Norway. W7773 was lost with the entire crew of F/O Wodzicki on 29/30 October 1942 during the Special Duties operation to Poland. (M. Przybylowicz via PH)

Above left: Pre-war photo of observer F/O Wodzicki, the captain of Polish crew which was lost during operation PLIERS on 29/30 October 1942. Above right: Another member of F/O Wodzicki's crew, pilot F/Sgt Sobkowiak. Below: The DFC awards to Polish airmen which took place on 5 October 1942 at RAF Hemswell. 4th from the right - Wireless Operator P/O Pantkowski from F/O Wodzicki's

November 1942

November's SOE operations began on the night of the 9/10th, when F/O Walczak and crew took off at 17.40 in Halifax W1229 with F/Sgt Jensen at the controls to carry out Operation NEPTUNE I, which involved the dropping of an agent into a lake in France. No details of the sortie are provided in the ORB, but the duration of the flight, in excess of eight hours, suggests that the drop site was to the south of the demarcation line. On the 16th, S/L Boxer, with P/O Kingsford-Smith as second pilot, set off for Gibraltar in DG252, as the spearhead of a contingent of seven 138 Squadron Halifaxes tasked with delivering much needed equipment to Maison Blanche in Algeria in support of Operation Torch. The other pilots were W/C Hockey, F/L Russell, F/Os Anderle and Dobromirski, P/O Pieniazek and W/O Klosowski, each of whose crews included a second pilot, and the aircraft, L9613, L9618, W1002, W1007, W1012 and W1229, also carried ground crew. It seems, that they departed on the 17th, having flown first to Hurn as a staging post, and, after refuelling at Gibraltar, took off again for the three-and-a-half-hour flight to North Africa. W/C Hockey twice experienced engine problems, but he made it safely home with the others around the 19th and 20th.

In the meantime, the single sortie from Tempsford on the night of the 16/17th was carried out by F/Sgt Weatherstone and crew in Whitley Z9288. They took off at 18.35 to undertake Operation JOURNALIST, combined with Operation PHYSICIAN, the destination for which was in France, a country now under complete occupation after Hitler ordered his "boys" into the Vichy region on the 11th. No details are available, but the operation, which took six and a quarter hours to complete, was logged in the ORB as successful. Sgt Smith and crew led the way on the night of the 17/18th, when taking off at 18.57 in Whitley Z9288 on Operation SCIENTIST 2. For an unspecified reason, the operation over France, which occupied in excess of eight hours flying, and ended at Tangmere, was not completed, but P/O Bunting and his crew enjoyed better fortunes on Operation PHYSICIAN I. They had taken off at 19.35 in Whitley BD260, and arrived back to land at Stanton Harcourt at 01.15 to report a successful sortie. Also on this night, W/O Walker and crew took off at 19.53 in the newest Whitley, LA764, to carry out Operations BABOON/DINGO/LUCKYSHOT 8 over Belgium. They delivered two agents and ten cases of coffee, before returning safely home to land at an unspecified time. W/O Walker completed his tour with 138 Squadron with another Whitley sortie to France in LA764 on the night of the 19/20th. He took off at 22.06 bound for Holland on Operation LETTUCE 8, which he duly completed, before returning to Tempsford to land at 03.15. In the course of time, W/O Walker would return to the squadron for a second tour, but this time as a commissioned officer.

There was a busy night of operations for both Tempsford squadrons on the night of the 22/23rd, four of them involving 138 Squadron Whitleys. F/Sgt Weatherstone and crew were first off the ground at 19.31 in Z9288, bound for Operations CRAB 6/GUNARD/CHUB MINOR over France. They returned to Tangmere at 03.19 to report being unable to complete their brief. P/O Bunting and crew took off at 19.50 in BD260, also bound for France on Operation PIMENTO I, and they had better news on their arrival at Tangmere at 03.36, reporting a successful sortie. Sgt Smith and crew were next away, at 20.50 in LA763, to carry out Operations PERCH 3/WHALE and GUDGEON over France, and they also were successful. Finally, Sgt Reardon and crew departed Tempsford at 22.02 in LA764 bound for Holland on Operation TURNIP 5, which they were able to complete before returning to land at Wyton. The squadron dispatched two Halifaxes to France on the night of the 23/24th, one containing the Czechoslovakian crew of P/O Anderle, and the other the Polish crew of W/O Klosowski. The former set off first at 20.09 in W1002 on Operations CRAB 7/LLAMA, and was followed into the air ten minutes later by the latter in DT543 on Operation SYRINGA 19, but neither was able to complete their drops.

Norway provided the focus for the squadron on the night of the 25/26th, when three Halifaxes sorties were planned and briefed. S/L Boxer and crew took off at 18.54 in DG254 on Operation GANNET, carrying an agent. They arrived over the drop site, where the agent declined to jump because of the strength of the wind, and the operation had to be aborted. They landed at Marham after more than nine hours in the air, and one can only the imagine the frustration of the crew to return empty-handed after such a mammoth effort. P/O Szrajer was at the controls of W1229 as it departed Tempsford at 19.45 with F/O Walczak's crew on board, along with two agents and one package to be dropped blind on Operation ORION I. On reaching the Norwegian coast at 4,000 feet in the Farsund area, they were approached by a twin-engine aircraft, which was lost after taking evasive action, and, shortly afterwards, about ten flak guns opened up on them without effect. They dropped down to 2,500 feet in good weather conditions, and picked up a solid pinpoint at Flekkefjord, which led them directly to the drop site. The terrain looked rather uneven, and the decision was taken to parachute the two agents onto flatter ground two miles to the east. They left the aircraft at 800 feet, the rear gunner confirming their safe arrival on the frozen earth, and the Halifax returned to a landing at Waterbeach at 02.30. They were joined there at 03.19 by F/O Anderle and crew, who had taken off last, at 19.49 in W1002, to undertake Operation THRUSH. They had also successfully delivered two agents, along with six containers, during an apparently incident-free sortie lasting six and a half hours.

Just two Halifax sorties to France were carried out on the night of the 26/27th, beginning with the take-off of W1012 at 21.25 with the crew of W/O Klosowski on board. They were to carry out Operation GEOLOGIST 12, but returned to Tangmere at 05.10 with the load intact. F/L Sutton and crew took off at 21.37 in L9618 on Operations STATIONER/CRAB 7/DESIGNER, and also returned to Tangmere at 05.25 to report success only at the CRAB drop site. The weather was unfavourable during the period, and was probably responsible for the failure of many of the drops during the final week of the month. Among four Polish airmen posted to the squadron on the 27th, were two pilots, F/Sgts Mierniczek and Peczek. Three sorties on the night of the 27/28th involved two by Halifax to France, and one by a Whitley to Holland. S/L Boxer and crew took off at 21.05 in DG253 on Operations DESIGNER, STATIONER and SYRINGA 19, but failed to complete, and F/O Dobromirski and crew were also unsuccessful, after taking off at 21.33 in DT542 to carry out Operations CRAB 6/GURNARD/CHUB MINOR. Whitley LA763 was the last to take off in the hands of Sgt Smith and crew, who had been briefed for Operation LEEK, and they returned at 02.25 to report a successful drop.

Two Whitley sorties were carried out over Holland on the night of the 28/29th, but the first departure from Tempsford was that of Halifax L9618 at 22.30, bound for France and Operation SCIENTIST I with the crew of F/L Sutton on board. Sadly, the effort put into the five-hour-fifty-minute flight was in vain, as was that in putting together Operations TURNIP

8/BROCCOLI/MUSTARD, flown by F/Sgt Weatherstone and crew in Whitley LA763. They had taken off at 22.34 for the drop site in Holland, and, on arrival, delivered Lt Johann de Kruyff and his radio operator, George Russell, into the hands of Hermann Giskes. The other operation on this night was PARSNIP I, undertaken by P/O Ruttledge and crew in Z9286, which took off for Holland at 22.55, and returned six hours later to report a successful drop. The four sorties launched on the night of the 29/30th were divided equally between Whitleys and Halifaxes, and those conducted by the venerable Whitley would be the last by the type in 138 Squadron hands, as crews were now converting to the Halifax. The Holland-bound Whitleys would have to wait until the early hours before their departure, and were preceded by hours by the Halifaxes taking off for Norway. F/L Russell and crew departed Tempsford at 20.50 in W1007 on Operation GANNET, and, despite low cloud for most of the outward flight, they were able to identify the blind drop site, with the help of the agents, who were familiar with the region, and the two men parachuted down. P/O Szrajer, again piloting for F/O Walczak's crew, lifted W1229 off the ground at 21.40 to attempt to deliver three containers on behalf of the SIS under Operation ORION 2. They encountered heavy rain storms during much of the outward flight, and the cloud base was down to 2,000 feet, but matters had improved markedly by the time the search for the drop zone began, and they map-read their way easily in what became excellent visibility. Sadly, there was no reception committee to greet them, and it was assumed that the deep snow had prevented access to the area.

It was 01.32 before LA764 lifted off with the crew of Sgt Reardon to carry out Operations LETTUCE 4/CHIVE/CRESS over Holland. On board were Hermann Overes and Johann Ubbink, who parachuted themselves into the arms of Giskes and his gang. Ubbink would escape at the end of August 1943, and, after reaching Berne in Switzerland, would inform London that the Dutch organization had been compromised. This was something that London, having received many warnings, should already have known, and its failure to act on the warnings resulted in forty-three British agents falling into enemy hands, and, in most cases, execution. P/O Bunting and crew brought the night's departures to an end, when taking off at 02.40 in BD260 on Operation Sauterns. The brief was to deliver stores, possibly on behalf of SIS, and this was apparently accomplished without incident.

December 1942

At the beginning of December seven crews were sent on attachment to 511 Squadron, a transport unit at Lyneham in Wiltshire. They, and two others from 161 Squadron, were to assist in the transportation to Egypt of around 70,000lbs of supplies, including medicines for the Eighth Army in Libya. W/C Hockey was again to command the flight, although he departed for the Middle-East a few days after the first crews. W/O Klosowski and P/O Szrajer left for Malta and or Cairo in DT543 and W1229 respectively on the 3rd, and they were followed on the 6th by F/L Sutton in L9618. The remaining four crews, those of W/C Hockey, F/O Dobromirski, F/O Anderle and F/L Russell, departed Tempsford on the 7th in L9613, DT542, W1002 and W1007 respectively, although the last-mentioned was recalled. It was not destined to be a happy detachment, and not all of those setting out would return.

The crew of Czechoslovak pilot F/O Anderle (standing third from right) who were lost after taking off from Malta on 15 December 1942. (P. Vancata)

There wasn't a great deal of activity by those remaining at home during this moonless period, but S/L Boxer and crew took off for Holland at 23.14 on the 9th in W1012 on Operation PARSLEY A, and returned four hours later having failed to complete the drop. The flight seemed to attract more than the usual amount of attention from searchlights and enemy aircraft, as if it were being tracked, although without any actual hostile incidents taking place. The drop site was on the coast on the eastern side of the Den Helder peninsular, east-south-east of Hoorn, but, in the event, stronger-than-forecast winds and intense darkness produced unfavourable conditions, and the operation was ultimately abandoned. W/C Hockey had arrived at Cairo on the 8th after staging at Hurn and Malta, but encountered a servicing problem associated with a

Above: Five of the crew of DT542, NF-Q which crashed in Malta on 17th December 1942 shortly after taking off on a ferry flight to England. All seven crew and ten passengers lost their lives: F/O Krysztof Dobromirski (pilot), F/O Stanislaw Pankiewicz, 2nd pilot; F/Sgt Alfred Kleniewski, wireless operator; second row: F/O Zbigniew Idzikowski, navigator; Sgt Roman Wysocki, WOP/AG. Below: Major (Lord Apsley) Bathurst, DSO, MC, TD in the light coat was amongst the passengers, which comprosed military personnel returning to England (all photos Aircrew Remembered except F/O Idzikowski – PISM via PH)

tyre. This was to delay his departure home, and require him to off-load two of his intended passengers to other aircraft. AVM d'Albiac was returning to the UK to become A-O-C 2 Group, while Major the Lord Apsley DSO was a member of the Royal Armoured Corps. F/O Anderle set off for Malta on the 15th in L9618, with his all-Czech crew and two RAF ground crew, but failed to arrive. The Halifax is presumed to have crashed into the sea with the loss of all on board, and the names of the seven aircrew and two ground crew are commemorated on the Alamein Memorial.

F/O Dobromirski arrived at Luqa airfield on Malta without incident, and, in the very early hours of the 17th, took off for Gibraltar. Having barely become airborne, DT542 crashed just beyond the runway, killing all seventeen occupants, among them Lord Apsley. F/L Sutton elected to remain over land on his way to Gibraltar in W1002, and his decision was soon vindicated. As they flew across the Algerian desert, an engine began to lose oil pressure and eventually had to be shut down. Soon the other engines were displaying the same symptoms, and one burst into flames. A successful belly-landing was carried out, after which the Halifax was consumed by fire. It was later established, that the wrong type of oil had been used. The crew was not marooned for long, and returned home on the 21st, the day before W/C Hockey. In the meantime, on the night of the 16/17th, P/O Kingsford-Smith and crew took off at 23.23 in DG271 to undertake Operations CRAB 4/CRAB 8 over France. They returned to Tempsford at 05.35 to report being unable to complete the drops. On the following night, P/O Newport-Tinley and crew took off at 21.12 in DG272 to carry out Operation COCKLE, a jump into a lake in France, but the weather proved to be unhelpful, and the attempt was abandoned. The purpose of the jump into water, (according to Freddie Clark), was to reduce the impact on landing for agents of more advanced years.

It was rescheduled for the night of the 20/21st, and handed to F/O Kuzmicki and crew, for whom the pilot was W/O Jensen. They took off in W7775 at 21.36, and crossed the French coast at Pointe de la Percee, before heading towards Avranches, and then the drop site at Lake Duc, some sixty miles further to the south-west. They overshot the mark initially, but pinpointed on a river, and soon found themselves over the northern tip of the lake, into which G Chartier and A Rapin parachuted safely, the dispatcher reporting one man to be wading ashore, and the other to be swimming towards him. The Halifax arrived home after a round trip of four hours and twenty-five minutes, that would have taken a Whitley six hours to complete. F/L Russell and crew took of at 21.40 in DG253 to carry out Operations GIBBON, BORZOI and LUCKYSHOT 8 over Belgium. They landed at Manston at 02.35 to claim success on the first two elements, but failure on the third. P/O Newport-Tinley enjoyed better fortunes on this night, when undertaking Operations CARACAL/SHREW/PERIWIG 7 over Belgium. They took off at 21.48, and reached the drop site without incident, whereupon the two agents, about to be given a ten-minute warning, jumped out without instructions. They were travelling at 200 miles per hour at the time and at 900 feet, considerably faster and a little higher than would have been the case had they waited. The Halifax landed at Manston at 03.00, where, according to the ORB, the crew reported failing to complete the PERIWIG element. The busy night continued with the departure from Tempsford at 22.54 of P/O Kingsford-Smith and crew in DG271 on Operations TURNIP 2/TURNIP 9 over Holland. This they failed to complete, and the final sortie of the night, by S/L Boxer and crew, who took off at 22.58 in

DT627 bound for Denmark on Operations TABLEMAT/TABLETOP I, also failed, and no details are available to shed light on the reasons.

An event of great significance on this night for the Command, and the bombing war in general, took place unnoticed by all except those involved. As more than two hundred aircraft of the Pathfinder and main force squadrons attacked the city of Duisburg, towards the western edge of the Ruhr, six Mosquitos of 109 Squadron departed Wyton in Cambridgeshire bound for a power station at Lutterade in Holland. Their task was to deliver the first Oboe-aimed bombs on enemy territory as a calibration test, in order to establish the blind-bombing device's margin of error. Three crews carried out successful attacks, but the unexpected presence of craters from stray bombs intended for Aachen back in early October prevented the plotting of the Oboe bombs, and further calibration tests would be required. These were to provide the necessary information, and the device would be ready for use in the coming year's first major campaign. W/C Hockey arrived back from Malta on the 22nd, pleased to have put Malta behind him, after days of being bombed.

On the night of the 22/23rd, four Halifax sorties were mounted to Holland. P/O Newport-Tinley and crew were first off at 21.45 in W7775, to undertake Operation MARROW 12, which was a drop site under the control of the Gestapo. They failed to return, and, it was later established, that the Halifax had crashed near De Wijk about four miles east-south-east of Meppel in northern Holland. Six of the eight occupants, including the pilot, lost their lives, and just two survived as PoWs. One of these, Sgt Bloxham, sustained serious leg injuries, and this probably led to his repatriation in September 1944. On their return, F/L Russell's crew would report seeing an unidentified aircraft being engaged by flak in the vicinity of Texel shortly after midnight, and, perhaps, this was W7775. They had experienced a torrid time of their own, after taking off at 22.55 in DT620 on Operation MARROW 13, with a dozen containers to deliver. While flying over the centre of Texel at 75 feet in bright moonlight, they were engaged by light flak and machine guns, which inflicted damage upon the port-inner engine, starboard flaps, bomb doors and the bomb-bay fuel tank. The port-inner failed soon afterwards, and the containers were jettisoned into the Zuider Zee as they turned for home. Having climbed to over 1,000 feet, they were fired on again from a flak ship, and the port-outer engine began to show signs of failing also. An SOS was sent out, but the Halifax struggled across the coast near Southwold, and landed safely at 02.35. Meanwhile, P/O Kingsford-Smith and crew had taken off at 23.09 in DG252 to carry out Operations TURNIP 9/PARSNIP 2. They returned to Tempsford shortly after 03.00 to report a successful sortie. Finally on this night, F/O Wilkin and crew set off at 23.25 in DG271 on Operations MARROW 14/ MARROW 15. They had twelve containers to deliver, and they also landed back minutes after 03.00 to report a successful sortie.

The weather closed in for the festive period, and all six sorties attempted on the night of the 23/24th would fall victim to the conditions. Take-offs began at 21.00, with the departure of P/O Kingsford-Smith and crew in DG252, to undertake Operations CRAB 4/CRAB 8/BUTLER/BARBER/FARRIER over France. They were followed away at 21.07 by the recently-returned S/L Gibson and crew in DG271 on Operations GLAZIER/SCULPTURE/PHYSICIAN 2. Next off the ground at 21.15 were F/Sgt Twardawa and crew in W1229 on Operations PERCH 6/PRAWN, to be followed at 21.27 by F/O Wilkin and crew, who were bound for Belgium in DG253 to carry out Operation LUCKYSHOT 8. The last of the four sorties to France on this night involved the crew of W/O Jensen, who took off at 21.40 in DT543 on Operations BOOKMAKER/SCIENTIST I, the first element of which is believed to have been in the la Rochelle region of western France. Finally, S/L Boxer and crew took off at 22.28 in W1007 bound for Denmark on Operations TABLEMAT/TABLETOP I, and, just like the others, returned to admit defeat.

138 Squadron's final sorties of the year were undertaken by F/O Kuzmicki, with F/Sgt Mierniczek at the controls, and S/L Gibson over France on the night of the 29/30th. The former took off with his crew at a minute before midnight in DG252 bound for Operations BUTLER, BARBER, FARRIER, CRAB 4 and CRAB 8. They returned in under three hours as the weather conditions defeated them. The latter took off at 01.00 in DG271 on Operations GLAZIER/TOBACCONIST, and successfully delivered two agents and two packages, before returning safely after a round trip of five hours. It had been a tough final quarter of the year for the SOE squadrons, during which, some highly experienced 138 Squadron crews had gone missing. The New Year was to bring a whole new dimension to the bomber war through greater numbers of aircraft, new electronic devices, improved tactics and well defined campaigns. However, the enemy would counter in time with a more efficient defensive system, and this would make life even harder for those involved in clandestine operations.

January 1943

The New Year began slowly for many of the front line squadrons, as the Oboe trials programme was given priority. This involved the Mosquitos of 109 Squadron marking for Lancasters of 1 and 5 Groups in small-scale attacks on Essen seven times and Duisburg once during the first two weeks of January. The Canadian 6 Group came into existence on New Year's Day, and a week later, the Pathfinders at last achieved Group status as 8 Group. On the 14th, a new Air Ministry directive called for another all-out assault on U-Boots in response to mounting losses in the Atlantic. To this end, the major French ports providing bases and support facilities for the craft were to be area bombed, beginning with Lorient that very night. This operation by over a hundred aircraft was somewhat disappointing, but was only the first in what would be an eight-raid series over the succeeding four weeks, which would leave the town a deserted ruin.

138 Squadron also opened its 1943 account on this night with eight sorties, according to Freddie Clark, although the ORB records only six, all of which went uncompleted because of the weather conditions. They were Operation GEOLOGIST 12 flown over France by S/L Gibson and crew in DG271, between 20.45 and 04.58, Operations WATERTIGHT/LIME I flown by F/O Wilkin and crew over France in DT543? between 21.05 and 03.15, Operations KER/GUDGEON 6 flown by the recently-returned F/L Austin and crew also over France in W1012 between 21.12 and 04.43, Operation LUCKYSHOT 8 flown by P/O Kingsford-Smith and crew over Belgium in W1007 between 21.40 and 02.45, Operations LABRADOR, CALF, BORZOI, and CARACAL flown by F/L Russell and crew over Belgium in DT725 between 21.40 and 02.00, and Operations PARSNIP 3/PARSLEY A/RADISH flown by S/L Boxer and crew over Holland in DT627 between 00.18 and 03.31. A Polish source has Operation MARROW 17/MARROW 20 being flown on this night over Holland, DG253 taking off at 23.25, with the crew of F/O Kuzmicki on board DG253, and W/O Mierniczek at the controls. They returned early, after just two hours and twenty-five minutes, for which engine trouble was responsible. F/L Austin reported, that the area in France designated for his drop site was flooded.

Each of the four sorties to France on the following night produced a similar result, only this time through the absence of reception committees. F/O Kuzmicki and crew were first away, at 20.50 in DT543, to attempt Operation PRUNUS 5. Seven minutes later, DT725 took off with the crew of P/O Kingsford-Smith on board, they having been briefed for Operation PRUNUS 4. DT725 was next away at 21.00 with the crew of S/L Boxer on Operation GUDGEON 6, and, finally, DG253 departed Tempsford at 21.30 with the crew of F/O Walczak to carry out Operations CRAB 13/11. Both Polish crews spent over seven hours in the air, and cited poor weather conditions for their failure to make contact with a reception committee. The main force undertook its first major operation of the year over Germany on the night of the 16/17th, with a less than convincing assault on Berlin. The destruction of the Deutschlandhalle, the largest covered arena in Europe, and the loss of just one aircraft, were the only highpoints, and when the operation was repeated on the following night, damage was only minor, while the losses shot up to twenty-two.

There was an improvement in SOE fortunes on the night of the 18/19th, when 138 Squadron dispatched eight sorties to four countries. The process of getting them off the ground began at 18.50, with the departure for Denmark of F/O Wilkin and crew and four agents in W1007 on Operations TABLEMAT/TABLEMANNERS. They crossed the Danish coast at about 22.10, and, shortly afterwards, ran into four searchlights and flak while at 600 feet. They dropped down to 500 feet, and soon came under fire again, before, forty-five minutes later, when at 450 feet, being latched on to by a JU88. Evasive action and a response from the rear gunner lost the enemy fighter, but despite the effort to reach the area of the drop site, and good visibility, snow blotted out all ground detail, and the attempt had to be abandoned. The longest-range sortie of the night involved S/L Boxer and crew, who had been briefed to undertake Operation MERCURY, a joint venture with Operation IRIDIUM, being flown simultaneously by S/L Hodges of 161 Squadron. Their destination was Czechoslovakia, and each Halifax carried four agents and ten bundles of leaflets. Their drop sites were within 30 kilometres of each other, and they departed Tempsford with ten minutes between them. DT725 was airborne at 19.00, passed over the English coast at Beachy Head at 4,000 feet, climbing over the cloud-covered Channel to 7,000 feet by the time the French coast was crossed at Cayeaux. Once over France the cloud thickened, and they were fired upon by heavy flak as they traversed Paris at 6,000 feet at 00.47. Icing conditions saw them climb to 8,000 feet, with an expectation of diminishing cloud as they flew towards the east, but the cloud thickened further, preventing them from pinpointing on the ground. The approach of high ground kept them at altitude, and they ended up stooging around the Alps region, where mist and fog filled the valleys up to 5,000 feet. All attempts to identify Lake Constance failed, and the fuel situation ultimately forced the abandonment of the sortie. S/L Hodges, meanwhile, had remained low, and made it as far as the Pilsen area, before also being forced by the conditions to give up. Further efforts to complete this operation would take place in the ensuing weeks.

The four sorties to France on this night began with the departure at 20.00 of S/L Gibson and crew in L9613 on Operation PIMENTO 6. They returned at 03.00 to report a successful outcome. F/O Ruttledge and crew were next away at 20.27 in DT726, with a brief to carry out Operation PERCH 8, and they also came back with good news at 03.45. Taking off at 20.40 was DT627 with the crew of F/L Austin on board, who were briefed to undertake Operation PERCH 9. They returned at 03.35, and reported being unable to complete the attempt, the only one to fail over France on this night. Before the last of the France-bound Halifaxes took off, two sorties were dispatched to Belgium, the first at 21.35 in the form of W1229 with the crew of P/O Kingsford-Smith on board. They were to carry out Operations BORZOI I/LEMUR I/COAL/TURTLE, and were successful in completing three elements, failing only on BORZOI I. DT543 took off at 21.40 carrying F/O Kuzmicki and crew on Operation CARACAL I/LABRADOR/CALF/GIBBON, and returned at 02.40 to report a 50% success, with the completion of the second and third elements. The night's final sortie, the fourth one to France, departed Tempsford at 22.04. On board DG253 was the crew of F/O Walczak, who had been briefed for Operations CRAB 17/WATERTIGHT, and they returned safely after more than eight hours in the air, having completed the drops.

Among new recruits to 138 Squadron on the 21st and 22nd were pilots, F/Sgt Zabicki and F/O Machej. F/L Boxer's recent frustrations were eased to some extent on the night of the 22/23rd, when he and his crew took off at 21.10 in DT627 to undertake Operations CRAB

11/JUGGLER/FARRIER over France. They crossed the enemy coast at Pointe de la Percee at 5,000 feet, found the Loire, and, in good conditions, continued on to Montargis, forty miles east of Orleans, where the two agents and two packages were dropped blind from 500 feet at a speed of 125 mph. With the JUGGLER/FARRIER elements now complete, S/L Boxer headed south to his next pinpoint at Chateauneuf-sur-Cher in central France, where he found reception lights, which he circled twice before dropping six containers from 450 feet. Having completed all three elements of his night's work, he returned to a safe landing at Exeter after a flight of almost ten hours. *(One of the men parachuted in by S/L Boxer was Henri Dericourt, whose job was to set up aircraft landing sites in the Loire region, and arrange the transport of SOE agents to and from England. He would develop close ties with the German Sicherheitsdienst (secret service), and a number of SOE agents would be arrested as a result. After the war, he would be put on trial as a double agent and traitor, but ambiguous evidence concerning his management by MI6, which encouraged him to gain close contact with the Germans, would cause the trial to collapse. To this day, no one can say for certain, whether he was a British or German agent. He would survive the war, but his reputation had, by then, been destroyed.)* The only other operation on this night was carried out by F/O Ruttledge and crew in DT726. They took off at 21.28 bound for Belgium on Operations GIBBON I/LUCKYSHOT 8/CARASAL I, and also landed at Exeter, at 03.46, having completed the second and third elements only.

Norway was the destination for four of six 138 Squadron Halifaxes on the night of the 23/24th, two of them containing Polish crews captained by the observers, F/O Kuzmicki and F/O Walczak. DT543 took off at 19.50, with the former on board, bound for Operation GANNET I, which required them to drop seven containers. They completed the sortie as briefed over Gudbrandsdalen Valley, and returned to land safely at Kinloss at 04.50, after a round trip of nine hours. Next away, at 19.55, to carry out an operation of utmost importance, were S/L Gibson and crew in BB281. The purpose of Operation GUNNERSIDE was to insert a team of six saboteurs into the Telemark region of Norway, with a brief to destroy the German heavy water plant at Vemork, and so end the enemy's quest to build an atomic bomb. If no reception committee made contact, the men, Joachim Ronneberg, Knut Haukelid, Kasper Idland, Fredrik Kayser, Birger Strømsheim and Hans Storhaug, were to parachute blind within a twenty kilometer radius of the planned drop site. The southern tip of Norway was found to be covered in low cloud and fog, and, when landfall was made at Kragerø, the crew could find no recognizable pinpoints. They seem to have backtracked to Lindesnes, and from there found the Tinnsjø area of Telemark, but, with the lakes covered by snow, even the saboteurs were unsure of their whereabouts, and after more than ninety minutes over hostile territory, they abandoned the sortie. They were fired upon at Farsund on the way home, but made it safely back to Kinloss to register a flight of eight hours and fifty minutes.

The second Polish crew took off at 20.00 in W1229 on Operation CHAFFINCH, and passed out over the Norfolk coast near Blakeney, before undertaking the North Sea crossing and reaching the Norwegian coast at Soknald at 22.50. Unlike S/L Gibson, they were able to pinpoint their progress to the drop site by identifying lakes, and, on arrival, circled for twenty-five minutes awaiting a signal from the ground. When this did not materialize, and sure of their location, the three agents agreed to drop blind from 600 feet, and were followed out by three packages and six containers. At this point, the rear gunner reported seeing lights on the slope of a hill a thousand yards away, and, also, a signal from the agents confirming their safe arrival on the ground. They, too, were diverted to Kinloss, where they arrived at 04.15 after an uneventful return trip. P/O Kingsford-Smith and crew were the last of the Norway-bound departures, taking off at 20.10 in DT725 for Operation CHEESE 3. The purpose of this was to help establish W/T contacts and secret army links in southern Norway, but a cloud base at 1,000 feet made it impossible to establish accurate pinpoints, and the containers were brought home to a landing at Harwell. The two remaining sorties to France, by F/L Austin and crew in DT727, and F/O Wilkin and crew in DG253, were unsuccessful. The former took off at 20.04 on Operations PRUNUS 3 and STONEMASON, and the latter at 20.43 on Operation GEOLOGIST 12, and both landed at Tangmere. The ORB offers no insight into the reason behind their failure to complete.

There was an early start for three of the four crews in action on the night of the 25/26th, all of whom were bound for Poland on operations with a woodworking theme. The first to leave the ground at 18.40 was DT725, in the hands of F/O Kuzmicki and crew, who had been briefed for Operation SPOKESHAVE. They were carrying four parachutists, who were to be delivered to a drop site about ten miles south-east of the railway station at Piotrkow Trybunalski. When the Halifax arrived, there was no reception committee waiting to receive the men, who refused to jump blind, and came back to Tempsford after a round-trip of twelve and a half hours. DT726 was the second to take off on this night, at 18.48, with P/O Kingsford-Smith and crew on board for Operation SCREWDRIVER. Their drop site was a dozen miles or so south-east of Lowicz, fifty miles west-south-west of Warsaw, which they reached after the long flight out by the usual route over Denmark and Sweden. They circled the target area for ten minutes, without raising a reception committee, and the four agents were eventually dropped over a "safe" area, one of them carrying $243,000 in a money belt. A light was flashed from the ground, and a car was seen speeding past the pinpoint towards it. The six containers were brought home, where a safe landing was made after another mammoth flight of more than twelve hours. F/L Krol and crew took off at 18.52 in DT727 to carry out Operation BRACE. They were carrying four agents, including the previously-mentioned Roman Rudkowski, former 301 Squadron commanding officer, and liaison officer between 138 Squadron and Polish HQ. The drop site was located about ten miles east of Bialobrzegi, sixty or so miles south-east of Warsaw, and, despite receiving no signal from the ground, the agents jumped blind, leaving the containers on the aircraft to be brought home. Finally, S/L Boxer and crew set off at 20.22 in DT627 to undertake Operation VICE, carrying a group of parachutists. Their drop site was at a location twenty miles west of a railway station at Wloszczowa, roughly between Lodz and Cracow, which they reached, but were unable to establish their precise position. The failure of an engine persuaded them to turn back, and they limped home on three engines, jettisoning the containers into the sea, before landing at 08.55.

Departures from Tempsford on the night of the 26/27th were spread over six hours and involved three Halifaxes, each heading for a different country. *(The squadron ORB has these sorties taking place on the night of the 26/27th, while Freddie Clark cites the 28/29th. Bomber Command War Diaries has no entry for the 28/29th.)* The early start was handed to F/O Walczak and crew, whose pilot was F/Sgt Twardawa. They took off at 18.45 in DT727 bound for Poland on Operation GAUGE, to deliver four agents to a drop site about ten miles north-west of Kielce, situated a little to the east of Wloszczowa. The agents' task was to explain to the Polish Home Army why the help they urgently needed could not yet be provided. After a long outward leg across Denmark and Sweden flown on dead-reckoning, they picked up their first visual pinpoint on the River Vistula at Grudziadz, some fifty miles south of Gdansk, and followed its course south-west to Fordon. They found the reception lights, and the four agents left the aircraft, their opened parachutes being confirmed by the rear gunner. He failed to notice six other chutes belonging to the containers, however, and it was only after arriving back at Tempsford, that they were found to have hung-up, and were still on board. The next departure from Tempsford was not until 23.51, when L9613 took off for France with the crew of F/L Austin on Operations ROACH I/MUSSEL/TENCH I. They returned at 05.33 to report being unable to complete the drop through the absence of a reception committee. DT627 took off for Denmark at 00.45 on Operations TABLEMAT/TABLEMANNERS, for which the crew of S/L Gibson had been briefed, and they also were thwarted by the failure to locate a reception committee, and landed back home at 07.28.

As far as the Command's bomber squadrons were concerned, the night of the 27/28th brought another advance in target marking, with the first ground marking by Mosquitos, flying in at high level ahead of the Pathfinders. The target was Düsseldorf in the Ruhr, and the degree of damage was an indication of things to come for the region in a campaign to begin a few weeks hence. F/O Walczak and crew were, hopefully, sufficiently rested after their recent long-range sortie, when being called to the briefing room on the 29th, to receive instructions for an operation that night over Norway. They took off at 03.55 in DG252 on Operation CARHAMPTON I, but adverse weather conditions prevented them from carrying out the drop, and they returned home after a six-hour round trip to complete a generally frustrating month. The Command ended the month with a raid on Hamburg on the night of the 30/31st, in which Stirlings and Halifaxes of 7 and 35 Squadrons respectively introduced the new H2S rudimentary ground-mapping radar system to main force operations. It was by no means a convincing debut, but in time, the device would make a valuable contribution to the Command's effectiveness.

February 1943

The new month began for 138 Squadron with and influx of new aircrew members between the 1st and the 6th. The squadron also had to contend with the departure on the 2nd of W/C Hockey, who, having concluded his highly successful tour as commanding officer, was posted to the Air Ministry. It would be the end of the month before his replacement arrived, and in the meantime, the burden of responsibility doubtless fell upon the shoulders of S/Ls Boxer and Gibson. As far as operations were concerned, the early part of the month was dogged by failure through difficult weather conditions, and it would be mid-month before any serious business could be concluded. P/O Kingsford-Smith and crew carried out the first sortie of the month, when taking off at 21.43 in W1012 to head for France on Operation PERCH 6. They returned at 04.20 to report failing to complete their assigned task. Also on this night, a pair of Oboe Mosquitos prepared the way for the H2S-equipped Pathfinder element at Cologne, as the search continued for effective target-marking techniques. It was another unconvincing attack, which was repeated at Hamburg on the following night. At 15.00 on the afternoon of the 4th, F/O Hogg was in the process of taking off from Tangmere in DG271 for a transit flight to Tempsford. As he accelerated along the runway, a swing developed, and the undercarriage subsequently collapsed, writing-off the Halifax, but without damage to the occupants.

It was not until the night of the 9/10th that operations resumed, when two Halifaxes were dispatched to France. S/L Gibson and crew set off at 20.18 in DG252 to carry out Operations PHYSICIAN 2 and 7, and they were followed into the air at 20.44 by P/O Clow and crew in DG253, the pilot undertaking his first sortie as crew captain since joining the squadron. They had been briefed for Operations PHYSICIAN 4/6, but neither crew was able to complete their drops, for which the weather conditions were probably responsible. One of two sorties launched on the night of the 12/13th produced the first modest success of the month, and was probably a confidence booster for P/O Clow and crew. They had taken off at 00.19 in HR665 and set course for Holland on Operation MARROW 21/16, and had managed to complete the first element. F/L Austin and crew had preceded them into the air at 23.59 in DG253 to carry out Operation MARROW 22/PARSNIP 3, but they returned after five and a half hours to report an unsuccessful trip.

The night of the 13/14th proved to be extremely busy for 138 Squadron, with nine sorties scheduled to be carried out over five countries, including, surprisingly, Germany. The first two departures were those of DT543 and DT727 at 19.10, with the crews of F/O Kuzmicki and F/O Walczak on Operations IRIDIUM and MERCURY respectively. These were to be carried out over Czechoslovakia, and had previously been attempted by S/L Boxer and 161 Squadron's S/L Hodges in January. They returned home after nine and ten hours in the air, with their agents and stores still on board. They were long-gone on their outward flight when Sgt Smith and crew took off for France in HR665 at 19.48 on Operation TENCH I/2, but they, too, would return with a report of defeat. DT726 was the next to depart Tempsford, at 20.05, bearing the crew of F/O Ruttledge to Germany on Operation TONIC, the purpose of which was to deliver two NKVD agents and a package blind into a location close to the frontier with France. They passed over Beachy Head, and made landfall over France at Pointe du Haut-Banc, before heading for a large wooded area south-west of Valenciennes, thence to Lachaussee, south-west of Metz and on to the drop site near Endingen. They spent forty-five minutes searching for their precise position with poor vertical visibility, and an estimated wind speed at ground level of 30 mph prompted the decision to abandon the attempt.

Almost ninety minutes elapsed before the next take-off, which was that of P/O Kingsford-Smith and crew in DG252 at 21.30. Their destination was Belgium, where they hoped to complete a whole host of drops under Operations LEMUR 2 and 3/BORZOI I/GRIFFIN/BADGER/CARASAL 2/GIBBON I. They returned six hours later to confirm partial success, the delivery of two agents, four containers and two packages on the last four-mentioned elements. F/O Wilkin and crew were also heading for Belgium, having taken off in W1012 at 21.40 to undertake Operations LUCKYSHOT 9/ELKHOUND/GOFER, and when they returned at 04.50, it was to claim completion only of the first element. F/L Dodkin and crew had arrived on posting at the start of the month, and undertook their first sortie on this night. They took off at 21.57 in DG253 bound for France on Operations PHYSICIAN 4/6, but experienced a disappointing debut and failed to complete their drops. S/L Gibson and crew took off at 22.50 in BB281 to deliver an agent and stores to locations in Holland under Operations PARSLEY I/RADISH/MARROW 16/CATARRH 10/CHICORY. The first two elements were uncompleted, but a female agent, Beatrix Terwindt, a former KLM stewardess, who was acting on behalf of MI9 to attempt to set up an escape route between Holland and Belgium, was dropped as planned, along with six containers, four packages and four boxes of chocolate. Sadly, this was an enemy-controlled site, despite which, Miss Terwindt survived the war, and gave evidence to the Dutch Commission of Enquiry set up at the end of hostilities. The final departure on this night was that of F/O Gebik and crew, who took off in DT725 bound for France on Operation SEXTO. It took just four hours to deliver two agents and return safely to complete a night of mixed fortunes for the squadron, which saw the backlog of operations expand.

Two nights later, on the 15/16th, France provided the focus for four of the five sorties scheduled, with Belgium the destination for the fifth. P/O Clow and crew took off first, at 19.24, in HR665 to carry out Operations PHYSICIAN 2, 8 and BREWER. The first two elements were stores drops, which were not completed because of the weather conditions, but the third element, the delivery of two agents into France, was successful. F/L Dodkin and crew were the next into the air, at 21.45, in DT620, briefed for Operations ARTIST 2/BUTLER/BARBER over France, which they failed to complete. F/L Austin and crew had a four-element sortie to occupy their attention, and took off at 21.50 in DG253 heading for Belgium on Operations LEMUR 2/3/BORZOI/FARMER 1. They arrived back at 03.35 to report another failure. Sgt Smith and crew were airborne at 21.54 in DG252, which was to carry them to southern France on Operations ARTIST 1/CRAB 10/PHYSICIAN 7. They arrived back a little over seven hours later with the good news that all three elements had been completed. Finally on this night, F/O Gebik and crew set out at 22.22 in DT725 on Operations FANFARE/COCKLE 1, and returned at 04.00 to report a successful sortie.

On the night of 16/17th, as the eighth and last of the heavy raids on the port of Lorient was in progress, 138 Squadron was in the process of dispatching ten aircraft to widely dispersed destinations in Poland, Norway, Denmark, Holland and Germany. Half of them took off in a flurry of activity either side of 18.30, the first four bound for Poland, and carrying identical loads of a group of paratroopers, six containers and two packages. Departures from Tempsford began with DT726 at 18.19 in the hands of F/O Ruttledge and crew, who were briefed for Operation RASP. They were to deliver their passengers and stores to a drop site near a railway station at Wloszczowa, however, after being unable to find the precise pinpoint, the passengers jumped, leaving the stores in the Halifax, which returned home safely after a round trip of thirteen hours and sixteen minutes. DT727 took off at 18.25 with the crew of F/O Walczak, who were to undertake Operation VICE, the drop site for which was north-west of a railway station at Minsk Mazowiecki, thirty miles east of Warsaw. Reception lights were picked up, and the delivery of the men and stores proceeded according to plan, before a safe return brought the Halifax to a landing after another mammoth flight lasting more than thirteen and a half hours. F/O Gebik and crew were the next to take off, at 18.29 in DT725 on Operation SAW. Their drop site was north-east of a railway station at Piotrkow, where they found a reception committee waiting. Sadly, one of the jumpers died after his parachute failed to deploy properly. DT543 took off at 18.30 with the crew of F/O Kuzmicki on board, whose pilot was W/O Mierniczek. They were bound for a drop site south-east of Minsk Mazowiecki to carry out Operation SPOKESHAVE, but a starboard engine problem over Denmark forced them to turn back, after which, the other starboard engine also cut. Despite the difficulties, they made it back home on two engines, and landed at 22.15.

The last of the early take-offs was that of S/L Boxer and crew in DT627 at 18.38, whose destination was Denmark to fulfil Operations TABLEMAT and TABLEMANNERS. On board the Halifax were four agents, Ole Geisler, Hendrik Larsen, Adolf Larsen and the radio operator, Gunnar Christiansen, who were to be dropped blind between 21.00 and 21.30 GMT under camouflaged parachutes into an area east-north-east of Mariager. They crossed the English coast at Cromer, and set course for Ringkøbing, on Denmark's western coast, which they reached while flying at 500 feet in excellent visibility under bright moonlight. This enabled them to map-read their way to the target area, which they found at 22.41, and the drop was carried out from 700 feet. The return journey across Denmark was undertaken at low level, and they were at 100 feet as the passed over the Jutland coast, but climbed for the North Sea crossing, and were at 2,000 feet as they reached the Norfolk coast at Holkham

Pilot F/Sgt Peczek flew as navigator in F/O Kuzmicki's crew. (PISM via PH)

Bay. The next two departures from Tempsford were those of S/L Gibson at 19.10 in BB281, and F/L Austin at 19.50 in DG253, who were both bound for Norway to carry out Operation GUNNERSIDE and Operation CARHAMPTON I respectively. As previously mentioned, the purpose of GUNNERSIDE was to deliver saboteurs into the Telemark region to attack the heavy water plant at Vemork, and it was an operation previously attempted by S/L Gibson back in January. He reached the target area, guided by the Rebecca direction-finding system, and delivered six parachutists, six containers and five packages onto the frozen surface of Bjornos Fjord from 700 feet. The saboteurs would meet up with the now exhausted GROUSE team towards the end of the month, and carry out a successful demolition job, which would effectively eliminate any threat of Germany developing an atomic bomb. Operation CARHAMPTON, the original purpose of which had been to seize a convoy of merchant ships near Abelsnes in Flekkefjord, had also been carried out at the end of January, but the ground element of the plan had failed. The commandos had remained in place, however, with the intention of attempting further operations. On this night, F/L Austin dropped a dozen containers and four packages, before returning safely after a round trip of seven and a half hours.

F/O Wilkin and crew took off at 20.00 in DT620 to deliver an NKVD agent to Germany, but heavy cloud in the target area prevented identification of the drop zone, and the agent found himself back on English soil a little over six hours later. There was a lull in departures for the next two hours, until P/O Clow took off at 22.09 in HR665 bound for Holland on Operation MARROW 23/CALVADOS/PARSNIP 3. The first and third elements were supply drops, involving seven containers at the first, and then seven containers and four boxes of chocolate at the second, all of which fell into enemy hands. The second element was the delivery of an agent, possibly of the NKVD, across the border between Lingen and Dalum in Germany, but a communications problem between the flight engineer and the dispatcher resulted in the agent leaving the aircraft earlier than intended, some eight miles south-west of the drop site, and from a little higher and at a greater speed than was customary. Nothing could be done, of course, and the Halifax turned for home, crossing the Dutch coast at 200 feet south of Egmond. It was not until 00.28 that F/L Hooper and crew took off in W1012 to complete the night's work by fulfilling Operations TURNIP 10, ENDIVE, PARSLEY A and RADISH. He dropped three more agents, Klaas Bor, Cornelius van Hulsteyn and Cornelius Braggaar into the Gestapo death-trap in Holland.

Poland was on the agenda again on the night of the 17/18th, occupying the efforts of two Halifaxes, while a third had Belgium as its destination. S/L Boxer and crew took off first at 18.40 in DT627 on Operation FLOOR, carrying four agents and six containers, which were successfully delivered to a drop site attended by a reception committee. F/O Kuzmicki and crew took off ten minutes later in DT725 on Operation WALL, and, aided by good weather conditions and visibility, likewise, found a reception committee waiting for their four agents and containers. F/L Dodkin and crew took off in DT620 at 20.10 to carry out Operations ELKHOUND, GOFER and TONIC over Belgium and Germany. The last element was the "Pickaxe" operation involving an NKVD agent, attempted a few nights earlier, but the drop site could not be located, and the agent and stores were returned to Tempsford. According to Polish sources, F/Sgt Smith and crew took off to carry out Operation RIVET over Poland on this night in DT727, but a.s.i failure forced them to return soon afterwards to try to effect a repair. By the time they were ready to go again, ninety minutes had elapsed, and it was too late to complete the operation under cover of darkness.

Five sorties were scheduled initially for the night of the 18/19th, but a re-run of Operation TONIC was cancelled at the last minute. Of the four remaining, three were to take place over Holland and one over Belgium, and it was the last-mentioned that started the ball rolling at 21.34. P/O Clow and crew were in HR665, assigned to Operations LEMUR 4/BORZOI I/FARMER I, but they encountered poor visibility, and were unable to locate the drop site. Sgt Smith and crew were next away at 22.37 in DG252 to carry out Operations MARROW 20 and 19, HOCKEY and TENNIS over Holland, and, together with F/L Austin and crew, who took off in DG253 at 23.53 on Operations MARROW 18/PARSNIP 4/BROADBEAN/GOLF, delivered four agents, Gerard van Os, William and Pater van der Wilden and Capt John Kist into the hands of Giskes, along with twenty containers, four packages, eight boxes of chocolate and two more transmitters, to bring the total up to sixteen sets. The other sortie over Holland on this night was attempted by F/O Gebik and crew in DT725, who took off at 23.19 to deliver three agents to a drop site near Ermelo under Operations MARROW 17/SPROUT/KOHLRABI/SEAKALE. They returned at 04.10 to report failing to complete the drop, it is believed because of poor visibility, and this probably deprived the Germans of further bounty. Pathfinder and main force elements, meanwhile, began a three raid series in six nights against Wilhelmshaven, which would all result in failure.

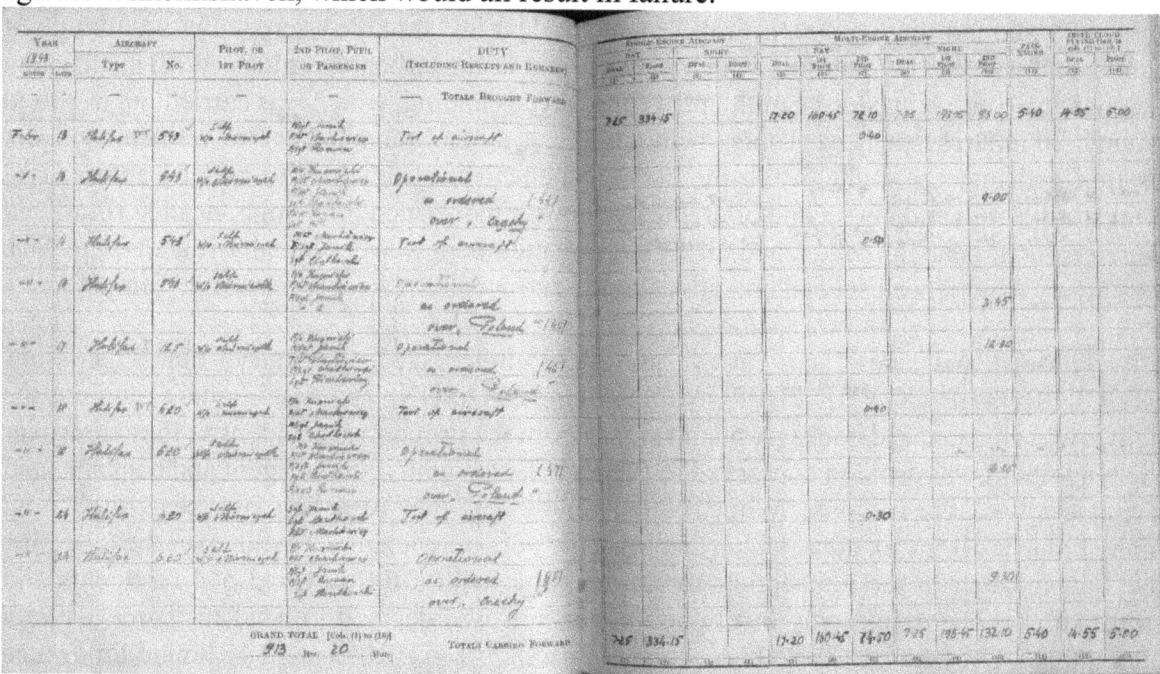

Page from the logbook of F/Sgt Peczek with entries referring to special operations flown by his crew in February 1943. (J. Penczek via G. Korcz)

The night of the 19/20 was another busy one for 138 Squadron, which would dispatch eight sorties, half of them to France, and the others on long-range forays into Czechoslovakia, Austria and Poland. Those with the furthest to fly took off first, beginning with F/O Ruttledge and crew, who left the ground in DT726 at 18.27 bound for Czechoslovakia on Operation MERCURY, but failed to complete in the face of adverse weather conditions. S/L Boxer and crew were next away at 18.30 in DT627 on Operation SODAWATER over Austria. This was a re-run of the Pickaxe operation to deliver two NKVD agents and two packages blind onto a drop site near Endingen, but, while still outbound, and probably on the leg between the

Lachausee and Lake Constance, the port-outer engine began to overheat, prompting the decision to feather it and turn for home. Finding it difficult to maintain height, they jettisoned the stores over a wood north-east of Freiburg, and eventually made a safe return to Tempsford. F/O Kuzmicki and crew took off in DT620 at 18.45 on Operation SPOKESHAVE, to deliver four passengers, six containers and two packages to an unnamed drop site in Poland, which was probably the one south-east of Minsk Mazowiecki. The weather proved to be good, the drop site was located, and the operation completed according to plan. The newly-promoted F/L Wilkin and crew were the last to take off for eastern Europe, climbing away at 19.10 in DT727 on Operation IRIDIUM over Czechoslovakia, where the adverse weather conditions, which defeated F/O Ruttledge, thwarted also this sortie.

The remaining four sorties had France as their destination, and one of them involved P/O Kingsford-Smith and crew. The ORB does not provide any details of the sortie, Operation BURGANDY/BUTTERCUP 2/DIRECTOR 4, which was carried out in W1012, and would have begun with a departure sometime after 20.00. The first two elements were on behalf of the SIS, with drop sites believed to be in the Lyon area, and they are thought to have been completed. It was while on the way to the final drop, and searching for a pinpoint at low-level over a fog-bound north-western France, that the Halifax stumbled across the aerodrome at Tours, and was hit by light flak, which knocked out both starboard engines. With insufficient height to bale out, Kingsford-Smith opted for a forced-landing, which was carried out in a field twenty kilometres south of Tours, without injury to the occupants. The remaining agent disappeared into the night, while the crew dispersed in an attempt to evade capture. P/O Kingsford-Smith and his second pilot, the previously mentioned P/O Hogg, headed south, but were captured near Bordeaux, and all eight crew members were eventually rounded up. This was a very experienced special operations crew, and would be keenly missed at Tempsford.

S/L Gibson and crew got away at 20.35 in BB281 to carry out Operations STOCKBROKER/GOAT/RAT/PRUNUS 3/STONEMASON. The first element required the delivery of an agent and package, but no signal from the ground was evident as they flew over the pinpoint. It was decided to proceed to PRUNUS, also with a single agent and package, and a course was set via Toulouse. While flying at 1,000 feet, they were held by a searchlight, and hit by light flak from six guns, which damaged the port-outer engine. Flying over the drop site, they again failed to see a reception committee, and, with a full payload of four agents and stores still on board, and only three good engines, it was decided to head for home without attempting GOAT and RAT. P/O Clow and crew took off in HR665 at 20.45 bound for France and Operations LIME 1/2/3, which were stores drops. On flying over a railway junction south of Isigny at 1,500 feet, they were picked up by two searchlights, and came under accurate fire from about eight guns, but managed to avoid damage. Undaunted, they set course for the Loire, then Limoges and the first drop site. The skies were clear and the visibility good, and the first drop of four containers and two packages was completed from 600 feet. Conditions remained good for the second drop of five containers, which took place from 1,500 and fell into the arms of the reception committee. The third site was more difficult to find because of its location in relation to the surrounding countryside, but four containers and a package found their way to earth, and the Halifax returned safely home. F/L Dodkin and crew were the last to depart Tempsford on this night, doing so at 21.24 in DG252. They had also been briefed for a multiple drop over France under Operations BEAUNE/CRAB 4/PERCH 6, and completed the first element, the delivery of an agent. There was no sign of a reception committee at the two remaining locations, where stores were to be dropped, and these elements were abandoned.

An influx of new airmen, mostly Poles, began on the 20th, and continued until the 25th. There were just two sorties on the night of the 20/21st, both to Poland by all-Polish crews. That of F/O Walczak took off first in DT620 at 18.35 on Operation RIVET, carrying four passengers, six containers and two packages to a drop site located about nine miles south-east of a railway station at Koniecpol, some fifty miles south of Lodz. The drop was carried out according to plan, and the Halifax returned to a safe landing at Middleton-St-George after a round trip of thirteen and a half hours. F/O Gebik and crew took off at 18.52 in DT726 to carry out Operation FILE, which required the delivery of four passengers, six containers and two packages to a drop site ten miles north-west of Pinczow, some thirty miles south-east of the RIVET pinpoint. Again, all proceeded according to plan, and, despite taking off seventeen minutes behind the Walczak Halifax, and penetrating a fraction deeper into Poland, they arrived back at Middleton-St George thirty-six minutes ahead of their squadron colleagues.

The 24th was a day of high intensity for the 138 Squadron ground crews, who had ten aircraft to prepare for dispatch that night to Austria, Germany, Czechoslovakia and France. Sadly, much of their effort would be rendered ineffective by the weather over France. The night became something of a benefit for the NKVD, however, and thus was cleared a number of operations that had defied previous attempts to complete them. F/O Gebik and crew got matters under way, when taking off at 18.50 in DT725 to fly Operation SODAWATER over Austria, the drop recently attempted by S/L Boxer. They crossed the French coast at Berck-sur-Mer, and followed the same route as S/L Boxer to Lake Constance, before setting course for Lake Chiem and then pinpointing on the Neusiedlersee, to the west of which was the drop site near Eisenstadt. The two agents parachuted from 650 feet at 00.26, and, apart from being fired upon by accurate heavy flak when south of Linz, the return journey was accomplished without incident, and the Halifax landed back home after a trip of ten hours and forty minutes. F/O Kuzmicki and crew were next away from Tempsford, at 19.00, in DT620, for a further, and, ultimately, vain attempt to complete Operation IRIDIUM over Czechoslovakia. On a positive note, F/Sgt Twardawa and crew finally managed to deposit the NKVD agent into Germany at the third time of asking. They took off at 21.05 in DT727 on Operation TONIC, and crossed the French coast at 500 feet en-route to the Valencienne area, before setting course for Lake Lindre, situated close to the German frontier in north-eastern France. From there they flew to the drop site near Endingen, where two agents and a package were successfully dropped at 00.40.

The remaining seven sorties on this night had destinations in France, and can be dealt with quickly, as not one was completed. F/Sgt Smith took off at 21.03 in W1007 on Operation PERCH 12, and was followed into the air at 21.32 by S/L Gibson in BB281 on Operations STOCKBROKER/LUCERNE/GOAT/RAT/PERCH 15, at 21.56 by F/L Hooper in BB313 on Operations GUDGEON 3/PERCH 6, at 22.03 by F/O Ruttledge in DT726 on Operations SCIENTIST 4/OAKTREE/HAYSEED, at 22.06 by F/O Clow in HR665 on Operations LIME 4/VERTU/SHRIMP I, at 22.32 by F/L Dodkin in DG252 on Operations PITINETTE/PHYSICIAN 6/4, and, finally, at 22.51 by F/L Austin in DT627 on Operation GUDGEON 9. The PITINETTE element of F/L Dodkin's brief involved the dropping of F/L

Yeo-Thomas of the SOE, who, with another agent, was to assess the resistance forces in France, obtain their allegiance to De Gaulle, co-ordinate their military and intelligence activities, and examine the possibility of setting up a central management committee. Although returning to England on this night, he would land in France twenty-four hours later courtesy of 161 Squadron. This brought to an end another intensive period of operations.

The Command sent over three hundred aircraft to Nuremberg on the night of the 25/26th, and they deposited most of their bombs into the city's northern fringes and outlying communities. 138 Squadron, meanwhile, prepared four Halifaxes for a late take-off, possibly to take advantage of any distraction caused to the enemy defences by the returning bomber fleet over France. Sgt Cook and crew were the first to depart Tempsford, doing so at 01.05, on their maiden operation since joining the squadron. They were to head for Holland in DG252 to undertake Operation MARROW 22/18, but, in the event, they failed to complete it, and, in so doing, probably deprived the enemy! A minute after their departure, HR665 took off for Belgium with the crew of F/O Clow on board, bound for Operations PERIWIG 7/LEMUR 2/3/BORZOI I/FARMER I, which became another wasted effort. S/L Gibson and crew were assigned to Operations PHYSICIAN 2/PHYSICIAN 8, and took off at 01.15 in BB281 bound for France. They returned at 07.10 to report being unable to complete the drop. A second sortie to Holland involved F/L Hooper and crew, who took off at 01.38 in BB313 with the intention of carrying out Operations MARROW 17/24/SPROUT/KOHLRABI/SEAKALE, but this, also, was unsuccessful.

The following night brought a moderately successful attack by four hundred aircraft on Cologne, but results were still disappointing as the start of the Ruhr offensive loomed a week hence. 138 Squadron launched three sorties on this night, beginning with the departure for Holland at 01.00 of F/O Ruttledge and crew in DG252, who were hoping to complete Operations MARROW 22/18, which had thwarted Sgt Cook twenty-four hours earlier. They were partially successful, returning at 07.50 to report the completion of the first element. F/L Austin and crew took off at 01.10 in HR665 bound for France and Belgium to carry out Operations FARMER I/PERIWIG 7/LEMUR 2/3/BORZOI I, but they were unsuccessful, as were Sgt Smith and crew, who were last away at 01.32 in BB313 for another attempt at Operations MARROW 17/24/SPROUT/KOHLRABI I/SEAKALE. This concluded a frustrating month, which had seen a number of long-running outstanding operations cleared up, but the majority of the effort expended had been rendered ineffective, largely by the weather.

The new commanding officer, W/C Batchelor, took up his appointment on the 28th, having thus far enjoyed a wartime career remarkably similar to that of W/C Pickard, the current 161 Squadron commander. Firstly, both had served as flight commanders with 9 Squadron, and Batchelor had succeeded Pickard as British adviser and commanding officer of 311 Czech Squadron in May 1941. Now, both were at Tempsford running a squadron engaged in special duties.

March 1943

Bomber Command opened its March account at Berlin on the night of the 1/2nd. Three hundred aircraft set off, and those reaching the Capital delivered a scattered but effective attack, which left almost nine hundred buildings in ruins, and severely damaged twenty factories. 138 Squadron's operational programme for the month began on the night of the 3/4th, when two sorties were dispatched to Poland to deliver stores. DT725 took off at 18.30 with the crew of F/O Miszewski, who had been briefed for Operation ROSE. They were transporting six containers and four packages to a drop site about five miles east of Gora Kalwaria, situated on the west bank of the Vistula, south of Warsaw. Two minutes later, F/Sgt Smith and crew took off in DT727 to carry out Operation TULIP on behalf of the SIS, the drop site for which was located five miles east of Wyszkow, some forty miles north-east of the capital. The early part of their approach was masked by a four hundred-strong bomber force heading for Hamburg, where over a hundred fires were started, although the main weight of bombs fell a dozen miles downstream of the Elbe onto the small town of Wedel. Both 138 Squadron crews were able to raise a reception committee and deliver their stores, and a safe return was made to Tempsford and Leconfield respectively, after more that twelve hours aloft.

Two nights later, Harris sent over four hundred aircraft to Essen, to open the Ruhr campaign. This was the first offensive for which the Command was adequately prepared and equipped, with a predominantly four-engine force of heavy bombers, and the electronic device, Oboe, to provide the accuracy to bomb through the previously impenetrable blanket of industrial haze. 362 crews claimed to have reached and bombed the city, and the result was by far the most devastating assault on any Ruhr target to date. More than three thousand houses were destroyed, with two thousand others seriously damaged, and fifty-three buildings within the giant Krupp complex were hit. It was a major success for Oboe, and was a portent of things to come for Germany's industrial heartland. Before the next Ruhr raid, however, Harris switched his attention to southern Germany, raiding Nuremberg, Munich and Stuttgart on the 8/9th, 9/10th and 11/12th respectively. The first two enjoyed a degree of success, despite lying well beyond the range for which Oboe could be employed, and 138 Squadron took advantage of the large-scale activity on both nights to launch further sorties to Poland.

The attention of the enemy defences on the night of the 8/9th, therefore, was upon southern Germany, as F/O Machej and crew took off from Tempsford at 18.30 in DT725, and headed westwards towards Denmark and then Poland, to undertake their maiden SOE sortie. Operation DAISY was a supply drop consisting of six containers and four packages to be delivered to a reception site about seven miles north-west of Pulawy, and about seventy miles south-east of Warsaw. The operation was largely successful, but, on return to base at 07.10, one container was found to have hung-up. According to the 138 Squadron ORB, DT727 took off at 18.35 piloted by F/Sgt Twardawa, whose brief was to fly to his homeland to deliver stores under Operation LILY. Despite a huge effort, and after more than thirteen hours in the air, he returned to report failing to find a reception committee. Freddie Clark cites F/L Gryglewicz as the crew captain, and states, that the Halifax landed at Docking after fourteen hours aloft, having failed to deliver its cargo through a shortage of fuel. The truth is probably a combination of both scenarios, and the Halifax was probably running on fumes by the time it touched down. HR666 was the last to depart Tempsford on this night, taking off at 18.40, with the crew of W/O

Mierniczek on board, who were also bound for Poland on Operation ASTER. The drop site was again close to Wyszkow, and the operation proceeded according to plan, occupying twelve and a half hours of flight time. Operation LILY was rescheduled for the following night, and handed to F/O Ruttledge and crew. They took off at 18.41 in DT727, but failed also to complete the drop in the face of poor visibility caused by ground mist, and returned after a minute short of fourteen hours in the air. The other sortie on this night of the 9/10th was flown by F/L Austin and crew to Holland. They took off at 22.58 in HR665 to undertake Operations MARROW 17, SPROUT, KOHLRABI and SEAKALE, and presented the Gestapo with two more agents, Pieter Dourlein and Peter Bogaart, along with their radio operator, Pieter Arendse. This meant that Giskes now had seventeen radio links to London, and could add the contents of a further seven containers and four boxes of chocolate to his stock of SOE contraband. Dourlein would escape after six months in captivity, and would be the first SOE agent from Holland to get back to England.

The Stuttgart raid on the night of the 11/12th was a disappointing failure, and while it was in progress, S/L Boxer took W/C Batchelor as his second pilot, and Captain Charles Tyce, the instructor and "manager" of the agents, on a trip to Denmark. They took off at 19.13 in DT627 to carry out Operation TABLEGOSSIP/TABLETOP 1, which involved dropping four agents at the first pinpoint, and stores at the second. They crossed the western coast of Denmark near Svinklov at 500 feet, before proceeding to pinpoints south of Aalborg to deliver the passengers. S/L Boxer had been given a choice of two drop sites, the first of which appeared to be too wooded, prompting the second site to be chosen. Flemming Muus, Einar Balling, Verner Johansen and Poul Jensen left the Halifax at 550 feet at a speed of 120 mph, three landing safely, while Jensen sustained injury. Four packages were also dropped, each containing a bicycle, before the Halifax proceeded to the second location, where a reception committee was waiting to receive the stores as they parachuted down from 700 feet. They adopted a more or less reciprocal route home, crossing the west coast of Denmark at 200 feet, and enjoying clear skies as they traversed the North Sea to the Norfolk coast. There were also two supply drops to Holland on this night, beginning with Operation MARROW 18/LETTUCE 10, flown by F/L Hooper and crew. They took off at 22.36 in BB313, and had completed the first element of their sortie, before an enemy night fighter appeared on the scene to chase them off, perhaps at the behest of Giskes. F/O Clow and crew took off at 22.50 in HR665 on Operation MARROW 24/25, contributing to the night's tally of twenty-one containers, six packages and eight boxes of chocolate.

Round two of the Ruhr campaign was mounted on the night of the 12/13th, when Essen was again the target. The bombing was concentrated around the Krupp works, and 30% more damage was inflicted here than in the earlier raid, and almost five hundred houses were destroyed. 138 Squadron took advantage of the distraction to dispatch three Halifaxes to Norway, another two to France and one to Belgium. The first of the Scandinavian-bound Halifaxes, DT726, took off at 18.56 with the crew of F/O Gebik on board, piloted by F/O Machej. They were to undertake Operation PHEASANT, which involved the delivery of three agents, five containers and three packages, a task successfully accomplished during a round trip of eight hours and thirty-five minutes. S/L Gibson and crew took off in BB281 at 19.15 on Operation MARDONIUS, the purpose of which, was to put in place two agents to recruit and train local volunteers to become shipping saboteurs. They flew out over Cromer, and headed for the Skagerrak between northern Denmark and south-eastern Norway, making initial landfall over the island of Jomfruland, before setting course for Tyrifjorden, twenty miles north-west of Oslo. The final pinpoint before the drop site was at Enebakk, south-east of the capital city, and it was here that two agents, four containers and two packages were parachuted down from 600 feet. One of the agents was Max Manus, who would become celebrated in Norway as an SOE operative renowned for marine sabotage. Shortly before crossing the coast homebound at 800 feet, the Halifax was fired upon by medium to heavy flak, but no damage was done, and the sortie was also successfully concluded after five minutes short of nine hours aloft. HR666 took off for Norway on Operation CHAFFINCH at 19.20, piloted by W/O Mierniczek, who was a member of F/O Kuzmicki's crew. They failed to raise a reception committee, and thus, the effort of a nine-hour sortie yielded nothing. DT543 took off at 21.05 bound for France to attempt Operations SCIENTIST 5/GOAT/RAT. On board was the crew of F/L Gryglewicz, who were able only to complete the first element only, and returned after a flight of a little under eight hours. The Belgian operation, SAMOYED/PERIWIG 7/LEMUR 5/6, was given to Sgt Cook and crew, who took off at 21.15 in BB313. They managed to complete the first two elements, but neither of the LEMUR drops, and returned safely at 02.50. It was 22.35 when F/Sgt Smith and crew took off in BB316 bound for France on Operation COCKLE 2, and they returned at 03.02 with nothing to show for their endeavours.

As a lull in main force operations began, the following night brought eight sorties to Poland, six by 138 Squadron crews, and two by 161 Squadron. The 138 Squadron aircraft all departed in a thirty-minute slot from 18.30, each carrying four passengers, six containers and packages. They were led away by DT725 with the crew of F/O Gebik on board, who had been assigned to Operation TILE, the drop site for which was in familiar territory, near Kielce, sixty miles north-east of Cracow. F/O Kuzmicki and crew were in HR666, which took off at 18.35 on Operation WINDOW, to carry out its brief at a site near a railway station at Koniecpol, a similar distance north-west of Cracow. Next away, at 18.45, were F/L Gryglewicz and crew in DT727 bound for Mogielnica, some fifty miles south of Warsaw, on Operation AREA. At 18.50, DT726 took to the air on Operation STOCK with the crew of F/O Lawrenczuk on board, whose drop site was in the region of Minsk Mazowiecki, to the east of Warsaw. F/L Austin and crew were in BB281, which took off at 18.58 on Operation DOOR, and they were bound for a drop site north-west of Zwolen, some fifteen miles east of the city of Radom. Finally, S/L Boxer lifted DT627 into the air at 19.00 to carry out Operation BRICK, the reception point for which was located about ten miles north-east of Konskie railway station. All six sorties were successful, a rare event indeed, but, within twenty-four hours, the scales would tip the other way, as the fickle fortunes of war took a hand.

Tempsford was a hive of activity on the 14th, as eleven 138 Squadron aircraft were made ready for operations that night, along with others of 161 Squadron. Two sorties are not recorded in the ORB, and these would appear to be the first to take off, beginning, perhaps, with the one flown by S/L Gibson and crew, who got away at around 17.50 in BB281, bound for Czechoslovakia on Operation BRONZE, an SIS drop. They failed to return, and it was established later, that the Halifax had crashed near Munich, killing S/L Gibson DFC and all but one of the other seven occupants. The exception was the flight engineer, Sgt Hudson, who fought for his life before succumbing to his injuries on the 11th of April. There are no details available to explain the reason for the crash, or at what stage of the flight it occurred, and there is also no mention of agents among the dead, which lends weight to Ken Merrick's contention, that the purpose of the sortie was to deliver containers to a drop site north of Brno. The likelihood is, that the crash occurred outbound, perhaps while the crew was searching for a pinpoint in mountainous terrain. F/Sgt Smith and his crew took off at 18.50 in DT620, bound for Poland on Operation SLATE, to deliver six containers and six packages to a drop site near Wrona, situated between the previously-mentioned locations of Kielce and Koniecpol. They were outbound over Denmark, when they were shot down to crash without survivors at Store Heddinge on the Baltic coast, some twenty-five miles south of Copenhagen.

The next three departures, all to Poland, were all recorded at 18.15, and involved the crews of F/L Krol in DT543 on Operation STEP, F/O Kuzmicki in HR666 on Operation YARD, and F/O Lawrenczuk in DT726 on Operation PIPE. F/L Krol was to deliver three passengers, six containers and two packages to a location a few miles south of Grodzisk Mazowiecki, southwest of Warsaw. They adopted the usual route out over Denmark, and crossed the German coast near Swinemünde, before heading for the drop site and delivering their passengers and stores. They were fired upon by a flak ship on the way home and sustained a damaged rudder, but made it safely down to a landing at Cottam in Lincolnshire. The Kuzmicki crew was carrying six containers and six packages, which they dropped as briefed in what appears to have been clear conditions over north-eastern Europe, and they returned safely to Acklington. The Lawrenczuk crew was the only one of the trio to return with the load intact, after failing to locate the drop site.

A second sortie by 138 Squadron to Czechoslovakia on this night was undertaken by F/O Clow and crew, who took off at 19.08 in DT725 for another attempt to complete the thus-far troublesome Operation MERCURY. The sister operation, IRIDIUM, was handed to a 161 Squadron crew, who would fail to return. The route out was over Beachy Head, Pointe Haut-Banc, Laval, Lake Constance, Regensburg and thence to the drop site, and heavy flak was encountered as they passed at 5,000 feet through a dense belt of searchlights north of Augsburg. Fortunately they coned at 10,000 feet, and the Halifax was able to pick its way through the intense and heavy flak unscathed. The target area was reached, and the Moldeau River identified, but, although recognizing the general area, the passengers were not sufficiently sure of their precise location to risk a blind drop. This was the closest to success that Operation MERCURY would achieve. On the way home they were approached by a JU88 north-east of Lake Constance, and a brief engagement ensued, during which the enemy appeared to be hit, and was not seen again. On landing at Tangmere, the starboard wing was found to have sustained damage from a cannon shell.

The remaining five crews operating on this night would be plying their trade over France, where the weather turned out to be less favourable than that experienced by the long-haul brigade. W/C Batchelor took off at 20.30 in the newly-acquired LL119, as one of four 138 Squadron crews and two from 161 Squadron assigned to Operation DIRECTOR 34. This was his first operation as captain, and it would end in disappointment for him and for three others from the squadron. The route out took him to the French coast at Cabourg, thence in a south-easterly direction to Blois, Nevers, Tournos and the foothills of the Alps, before turning south to the drop site near Chalons. The entire outward flight was conducted in thick haze and cloud, and it proved impossible to identify pinpoints on the ground. The reception was to be four bonfires and a light flashing "P", but with no chance of picking it up, the sortie was abandoned. The other crews on this operation were those of S/L Robinson in HR665, F/L Hooper in BB313, and F/Sgt Cook in DG253, who had taken off at 20.38, 20.50 and 23.10 respectively, and had all been thwarted by the conditions. S/L Robinson was operating for the first time since joining the squadron. He had just relinquished command of 4 Group's 158 Squadron after a five-month tour of duty, and had elected to drop a rank in order to join 138 Squadron and remain on operations. The other operation on this night was IRIS/GUDGEON 1, which was flown by F/O Ruttledge and crew in JB802. They took off at 20.30 carrying one agent, six containers and three packages, which were delivered as briefed to unspecified drop sites in France. It was a bad night for Tempsford, which had lost three Halifaxes and crews, and two men from another 161 Squadron aircraft, which had crashed in Buckinghamshire shortly after take-off.

Poland dominated proceedings over the next few nights, with three sorties being scheduled for the 16/17th. S/L Boxer and crew were first away at 18.00 in DT627 bound for Operation PIPE. They were carrying six containers and six packages, which were successfully delivered to an unspecified drop site during a round-trip of twelve hours and thirty minutes. They were followed down the runway at 18.01 by F/L Gryglewicz and crew in DT727 on Operation ATTIC, which they, too, completed by dropping three passengers, six containers and two packages. Finally, F/O Polkowski and crew took off at 18.02 in an unspecified Halifax on Operation LOCK, and fulfilled their brief by delivering six containers and six packages. Of five sorties scheduled for the night of the 19/20th, four were to head for Poland and one to Norway. The Poland contingent began to depart Tempsford at 17.35, when JB802 lifted into the air carrying the crew of F/L Gryglewicz, along with three passengers, six containers and two packages under Operation CELLAR. They completed the outward flight, only to fail in their purpose after being unable to raise a reception committee. S/L Boxer and crew, which included the Polish navigator, F/O Izycki, were next away at 17.40 in DT627 on Operation KEY, to deliver six containers and six packages to two drop sites, one fifteen miles north-west of a railway station at Pionki, seventy-five miles south of Warsaw, and the other, east of Garwolin, some twenty-five miles further north. There was no signal from the ground at the first location, but the cargo was delivered at the second, and a safe return to Acklington was completed at 06.55. There were two departures logged at 17.45, those of F/O Lawrenczuk and crew DT726 on Operation KNOB, and F/O Polkowski and crew in BB340 on Operation BEAM. The former were tasked with delivering six containers and six packages to a reception point near Pulawy, fifty miles south of the above-mentioned Garwolin, and they returned to land at an airfield at Bulmer in Yorkshire, after a flight of thirteen hours, to report a successful outcome. The latter were carrying three passengers, six containers and two packages for delivery to a reception point south-west of Opoczno, located in another familiar resistance area between Lodz and Cracow. This was another successful sortie, which ended after thirteen hours with a landing at Driffield. Finally on this night, F/O Wrzesien and crew took off at 18.55 in

F/O Wrzesien who was navigator in the crew of pilot F/Sgt Waszak. (PISM via PH)

DT543 on Operation CHAFFINCH 1 over Norway. They returned safely to Kinloss after eight hours and thirty minutes aloft, to report failing to locate a reception committee.

As the break from main force operations continued, Sgt Brown and crew were posted in, and the four unsuccessful sorties to France from the night of the 14/15th were re-scheduled for the night of the 20/21st. The early departures, however, were by two Halifaxes bound for Poland, F/O Gebik and crew taking off first at 17.45 in BB340 on Operation GLASS. The reception point was again in the Garwolin region, where six containers and six packages were successfully delivered. F/O Kuzmicki and crew followed on five minutes later in DT726 on Operation BASIN, but an engine malfunction forced them to turn back when about four hours into the outward leg. The first of the four DIRECTOR 35 sorties to France took to the air at 19.40 in the hands of F/L Hooper and crew. They were in BB313, which landed at Predannack in Cornwall at 03.40, after an unsuccessful trip, for which no details are provided. However, as it was the first of the four DIRECTOR 35 aircraft to land at this airfield in the space of thirty-two minutes, all following flights of similar duration, it must be assumed that the target area was reached, but no contact was established with a reception committee. DG253 took off at 20.02 with the crew of F/L Austin on board, and landed eight minutes behind F/L Hooper to report a successful drop. F/L Rutledge and crew were next away at 20.18 in DK119?, followed at 20.28 by F/O Clow and crew in HR665, and both returned safely to Cornwall to report fulfilling their briefs. Sgt Cook and crew were the final departures from Tempsford on this night, taking off at 21.56 in BB329 bound for France to carry out Operations DAFFODIL/GUDGEON 5/6/LUCERNE. An electrical failure curtailed the sortie after the first and last elements had been completed, but a safe return was made to Tangmere at 05.10.

The front-line squadrons contributed over three hundred aircraft to a raid on St Nazaire on the night of the 22/23rd, an operation mounted in line with the January directive, and this was the first major outing for the main force since Essen. This attack took place three weeks after the first highly destructive assault on the port, and was deemed to be successful. During the course of the 23rd, 138 Squadron ground crews prepared six aircraft for operations that night, and the first to take off, at 19.12, was JB802, captained by Sgt Cook. He and his crew were to carry out Operation SEA URCHIN, and flew out via Tangmere, before crossing the French coast at 300 feet over Cabourg. They flew on in ten-tenths medium cloud to Orleans, Nevers and Lyon, where, having climbed to 2,000 feet, they were engaged by four searchlights and light flak. They were now in a thick band of cloud stretching from the ground up to 12,000 feet, and climbed gradually until reaching 8,000 feet over Cap Lardier. Once over the sea heading for

Corsica, the skies cleared, and they were able to pinpoint on the Gulf of Ajaccio, Propriano and Sartene, before reaching the drop site and circling for twenty-seven minutes. No reception committee made contact, and the six containers had to be brought home. Leaflets were dispensed on the way home near Dreux, west of Paris, and a safe return ended with a landing at Tempsford more than eleven hours after take-off.

F/O Clow and crew took off at 19.19 in DT726 to carry out Operations DIRECTOR 22/REPORTER/SURGEON, but returned thirty-four minutes later, presumably with serious technical difficulties. F/L Gryglewicz and crew were next away at 20.25 in DT727, bound for the Saumur region of western France to carry out Operations BUTLER/BARBER /PUBLICAN/STATIONER. The first three elements referred to the agents Francoise Garel, the organizer of the Butler reseau, Marcel Rousset and Marcel Fox, who were dropped blind from 900 feet along with their baggage and a wireless set. The baggage and wireless were not recovered, and the agents were arrested in Paris in April, shortly after which, the Germans began operating the BUTLER reseau. Garel and Fox did not survive their capture, but Rousset is believed to have escaped. The final element of this crew's work failed in the absence of a reception committee, and they returned safely to land at 04.00. W/C Batchelor's brief was a two-phase SIS drop over France, Operations LUPIN/JALOUSIE, for which he and his crew took off in DG252 at 20.45. The first element remained uncompleted, after the wrong colour of reception lights was displayed, and the white light flashed an incorrect letter. However, the second element, the dropping of six containers, was carried out successfully, and a safe return was made after a flight of seven and a half hours duration. F/L Austin and crew were on board DG253, which took off for France at 21.35 to carry out two drops under Operations ROACH 4/MUSSEL MINOR/WINKLE/GUDGEON 7/HADDOCK/SWORDFISH. They found the first drop site by map-reading their way in clear conditions along a railway line from Chartres, and finding a reception committee waiting for their two agents, four containers and three packages. The second reception point was in a bend in the River Loire more than two hundred miles to the south-east near Roanne, where the correct signal was flashed, and two agents, six containers and three packages dropped away. Leaflets were delivered over Roanne and Nevers on the way home, along with a total of fifteen pigeons. They were engaged by two searchlights and accurate light flak over Caen, which holed the fuselage in a number of places, but they returned safely after six hours in the air. F/O Ruttledge and crew completed the night's operations, when taking off for France at 22.06 in BB329 on Operations OAKTREE/CRAB 8/GUDGEON 2. They delivered two agents, fourteen containers and two packages onto two drop sites, before returning safely to land at 05.32.

The night of the 24/25th brought eight sorties, five of which had destinations in Poland. These took off in a flurry of activity between 17.48 and 18.00, led by F/O Polkowski and crew in BB340 on Operation BASIN. They had six containers and six packages to deliver to a reception point about twelve miles north-east of Pionki railway station, which they accomplished, before returning to land at Hemswell thirteen and a half hours later. F/O Gebik and crew were on board DT725, and took off at 17.50 to carry out Operation BATH. This was a supply drop consisting of six containers and six packages, but the Halifax was back in the circuit three and a half hours later with a dead engine. Also recorded as taking off at 17.50 was DT727 with the crew of F/L Gryglewicz, who had been assigned to Operation CELLAR. They were carrying three passengers, six containers and two packages to deliver to a reception point near Siedlce, a town situated to the south-east of Warsaw. The operation was entirely successful, and the Halifax returned safely to Tempsford after a round trip of exactly fourteen hours. S/L Boxer and crew were the next to take off, at 17.55, in DT627, and had with them a Polish second pilot, F/O Korpowski. They were to attempt Operation STONE, a supply drop of six containers and six packages onto a reception point five miles north of Rawa Mazowiecka, and, on return almost thirteen hours later, they were able to report job done. This was to be the final sortie of S/L Boxer's tour, although, his days of special duties work were not yet over, and when he returned to Tempsford a year hence, it would be as the commanding officer of 161 Squadron. The last of the Poland-bound departures was that of F/O Wrzesien and crew in DT543 on Operation DORIC. They had six containers and six packages to deliver, a task which they were able to accomplish, and also claimed a JU88 and BF109 as damaged by the rear gunner, following an encounter at some stage during the sortie.

The remaining sorties were to destinations closer to home, two to Holland and one to France. F/O Ruttledge and crew took off for the former at 22.23 in BB329, to carry out Operations LETTUCE 10/PARSNIP 5, the delivery of thirteen containers, a barrel of coffee and ten boxes of chocolate. The sortie proceeded according to plan, and the entire load dropped into the hands of the enemy, who were operating the site. F/L Hooper and crew took off for France at 22.38 in DG252 on Operations COCKLE 3/BARRACUDA/COCKLE 4, but adverse weather conditions persuaded them to turn back shortly after crossing the enemy coast. There is no mention in the ORB of F/O Clow's sortie, but we can assume, that he and his crew took off in HR665 some time around 22.30 to undertake Operations ST JOHN/ST ANDREW/LEEK 5 CATARRH 11, which involved the dropping of two agents, named Bergman and Gerbrands. They were outbound somewhere over the Dutch coast, when, according to Freddie Clark, the Halifax was shot down. Fortunately, F/O Clow, was able to maintain sufficient control to carry out a ditching in the Ijsselmeer, near Enkhuizen, without injury to the occupants. Sadly, Bergman drowned, while a Dutch fishing boat picked up Gerbrands, and he escaped. Not so the crew, however, who fell into enemy hands. F/O Clow, a Kiwi, had been with the squadron only since February, and this was his twelfth sortie.

The night of the 25/26th brought a unique operation for S/L Robinson and crew, who had flown out to Algeria in preparation for Operation KIPLING. They took off in an unspecified Halifax at 23.00 from Canrobert airfield, and headed for the drop site in Tunisia with two named passengers on board, Major Wooler and Staff Sgt Clark of the US Army, but others also. According to Freddie Clark, they flew to Pichon, then to the target, located fifty-five kilometres south of Sousse, on the eastern coast, and close to the railway line to the coastal city of Sfax. They were able pick up sufficient ground detail under a weak moon to identify ground detail, but lost the starboard-outer engine at this critical moment. Never the less, eight passengers and a container were parachuted down blind from 500 feet at a speed of 138 mph, to land just west of a road and rail junction situated eight kilometres north of La Hencha. The crew spent three hours fifty minutes in the air, almost an hour of which was in the target area, and landed safely back at Canrobert at 02.50.

Personnel of the Polish 'C' Flight of 138 Squadron photographed in early April 1943. The three senior officers in the comfortable chairs are, from left; S/L Krol, 'C' Flight's CO; W/C Batchelor, CO of 138 Squadron and navigator F/Lt Gryglewicz (J. Penczek via G. Korcz)

On the night of the 26/27th, Harris resumed his offensive against the Ruhr with a raid on Duisburg, the highly industrialized city nestling astride the Rhine towards the western fringe of the region. Like Essen, it had, hitherto, escaped serious damage at the hands of the Command, and the failure of the Oboe equipment in the bulk of the Mosquito marker force on this night led to another disappointing raid. The final two sorties of the month were carried out on the night of the 29/30th, with Poland as their destinations. F/O Lawrenczuk and crew took off at 18.29 in DT726 on Operation FURZE, and suffered the disappointment of reaching the target area, but not finding the reception point in the face of very unfavourable weather conditions. F/O Kuzmicki and crew had followed them into the air at 18.35 on Operation BALSAM, and also fell foul of the conditions to end the month on a downbeat note. During the course of March sixty-one sorties had been attempted, half of them over Poland, but the shorter nights would soon preclude any further long-range flights until September. For the Command in general the month ended with two disappointing attacks on Berlin on the nights of the 27/28th and 29/30th, which sandwiched another heavy assault on St Nazaire on the 28/29th. Also on the 29/30th, well over a hundred Wellingtons provided the main force for an attempt on the Ruhr town of Bochum, which, despite Oboe marking, escaped with minor damage on a moonless and cloudy night.

The 31st of March signalled the end of the line for the Wellington-equipped Polish 301 (Pomeranian) Squadron. On that day, it was withdrawn from Bomber Command operations, ostensibly because of a lack of available Polish airmen, but also as the result of a general reorganisation, and a week later it was disbanded. All of the redundant crews joined 1 Group's 300 or 305 Squadrons, while some of the ground crew were posted to the newly formed C Flight at 138 Squadron under the command of S/L Krol. This was a Polish undertaking, and most of the ground crew personnel were also Polish.

On 22 April 1943 RAF Station Tempsford was visited by Archibald Sinclair, the Secretary of State for Air (talking to W/C Batchelor on the photo). The Polish crew of navigator F/O Kuzmicki is standing on the right. From right to left: wireless operator F/Sgt Janik, 2nd pilot F/Sgt Peczek, 1st pilot W/O Mierniczek, air gunner F/O Markiewicz and navigator F/O Kuzmicki. (J. Penczek via G. Korcz)

April 1943

Halifax W1007, NF-U, stands on her nose after bursting a tyre on landing at Tempsford on 13th April 1943. Despite the apparent damage, the aircraft was repaired and returned to operational service. She was eventually transferred to 1666 CU and survived the war, being struck off charge on 1st November 1945 (Crown copyright).

As the coming spring brought fewer hours of darkness, the last sorties to Poland until the autumn were carried out on the night of the 2/3rd. F/O Polkowski and crew took off in DT725 at 18.03 on Operation FLAX, carrying three passengers, six containers and two packages, but a fault developed in the fuel pump during the crossing of the Baltic, and the sortie had to be abandoned. F/O Izycki and crew got away at 18.05 in BB340, with W/O Jensen at the controls, and with an identical manifest on board for Operation NETTLE. For whatever reason, they arrived thirty-five minutes late at the Danish coast, which meant, that the sortie could not be completed within the planned time window, and it, too, was abandoned. For the next week and a half, the moon squadrons stayed on the ground, while all around them the heavy squadrons of Bomber Command set about the destruction of industrial Germany. A return to Essen on the night of the 3/4th allowed the month to begin in promising fashion, as over three hundred aircraft destroyed more than six hundred buildings and seriously damaged almost as many again. In fact, this was a bright spot in an otherwise disappointing month, which would prove to be the least rewarding of the entire Ruhr campaign period. This was largely the result of the high number of operations being carried out against targets outside of the region, and, therefore, beyond the range of Oboe. The first of these was Kiel on the night of the 4/5th, for which a new record non-1,000 force of 577 aircraft was dispatched. In the event, the massive effort was in vain, as most of the bombs failed to find the mark, and damage within the town was fairly minor. Almost four hundred aircraft were employed against Duisburg on the night of the 8/9th, but even with the assistance of Oboe, they were unable to inflict more than modest damage. An all-Lancaster force tried again twenty-four hours later and fared only marginally better. The two last-mentioned operations cost twenty-seven aircraft between them, and a further twenty-one were lost from a force of five hundred raiding Frankfurt on the night of the 10/11th.

The ORB entries at this point become almost illegible, but other sources provide some insight into the "goings-on" on the 138 Squadron side of Tempsford. There were six sorties to France scheduled for the night of the 11/12th, beginning with the departure of F/O Lawrenczuk and crew in DT627 at 21.20 on Operations PRUNUS 5/SCIENTIST 24. They arrived back over seven hours later to report the failure of their brief, it is believed, through the lack of a reception committee. F/O Ruttledge and crew took off at 21.22 on Operation TRIREM/????EEPER/PHYSICIAN ??/PHYSICIAN 19/PRIVET, and completed all but PHYSICIAN 19. It is not known precisely what the Halifax was carrying in terms of passengers and supplies, but, along with the efforts of F/O Kuzmicki and crew, who departed Tempsford at 21.30 in DT725 to carry out Operations PERCH 4, SCALLOP, NAUTILUS, ROBALO and WHEELWRIGHT, of which all but the final element were completed, a total of five agents and fourteen containers reached their planned reception points. F/L Hooper and crew were assigned to Operation SCIENTIST 20/ARTIST ?/CRAB??, and took off in JB802 at 21.57, only to fail, again, it is believed, through the lack of a reception committee. DG252 lifted off the runway at 22.10 with the crew of F/O Wrzesien on board to carry out Operation LIME 6/CRAB 4, but they were also unsuccessful, as were F/O Izycki and crew, who were last away, at 23.05, in BB363 on Operations LIME 10/SHRIMP I.

France would continue to be the main focus for operations during this moon period, and the night of the 12/13th brought seven sorties by the squadron. BB340 took off at 20.30 with W/O Jensen as first pilot, F/O Korpowski as second pilot, and F/O Izycki as captain of the crew, which, on this night, included a number of RAF members. They were to deliver two agents to a reception point near Lyon under Operations DIRECTOR 22/REPORTER/SURGEON, and were crossing the French coast at 500 feet near Caen, with F/O Korpowski in the pilot's seat, when they were hit by a short burst of fire, which caused an engine to burst into flames. The damage was terminal, but the low altitude precluded any chance of baling out, and W/O Jensen took the controls for a forced landing at Douvres-la-Delivrande, five kilometres from the coast and twelve kilometres north-north-west of Caen. The wireless operator, F/Sgt Lesniewicz, had been killed by the flak, but all other occupants were able to scramble clear of the wreckage, before it was consumed by fire. F/O Korpowski was badly burned, but he and two British members of the crew, the flight engineer and a dispatcher, evaded capture, and the first two-mentioned arrived home via Gibraltar in early June. The two agents, Claude Jumeau and Lee Graham, would be arrested before long, and join the remainder of the crew in captivity. Jumeau would die in enemy hands, but Graham was to survive the war despite harsh treatment. F/O Korpowski's operational career was not done, and he would return to the fight with 1586 (SD) Flight at Brindisi, and complete his third tour on the 25th of July 1944.

The wreckage of Halifax BB340 flown by Polish crew of F/S Jensen (navigator F/O Izycki) which crashed near Caen, France on 12/13 April 1943. (T. Raykowski via PH)

Above left: Navigator F/O Izycki was severaly injured during the crash of Halifax BB340. Captured by German patrol together with pilot F/S Jensen was interrogated by Gestapo. Both later became prisoners in German concentration camp which was an evident violation of international agreements regarding prisoners of war. Above right: F/O Korpowski, the second pilot of F/S Jensen's crew, evaded capture and returned to England in June 1943. Below: The page from navigator F/O Izycki's logbook referring to the special operation to France on 12/13 April 1943. (Photos PISM via PH)

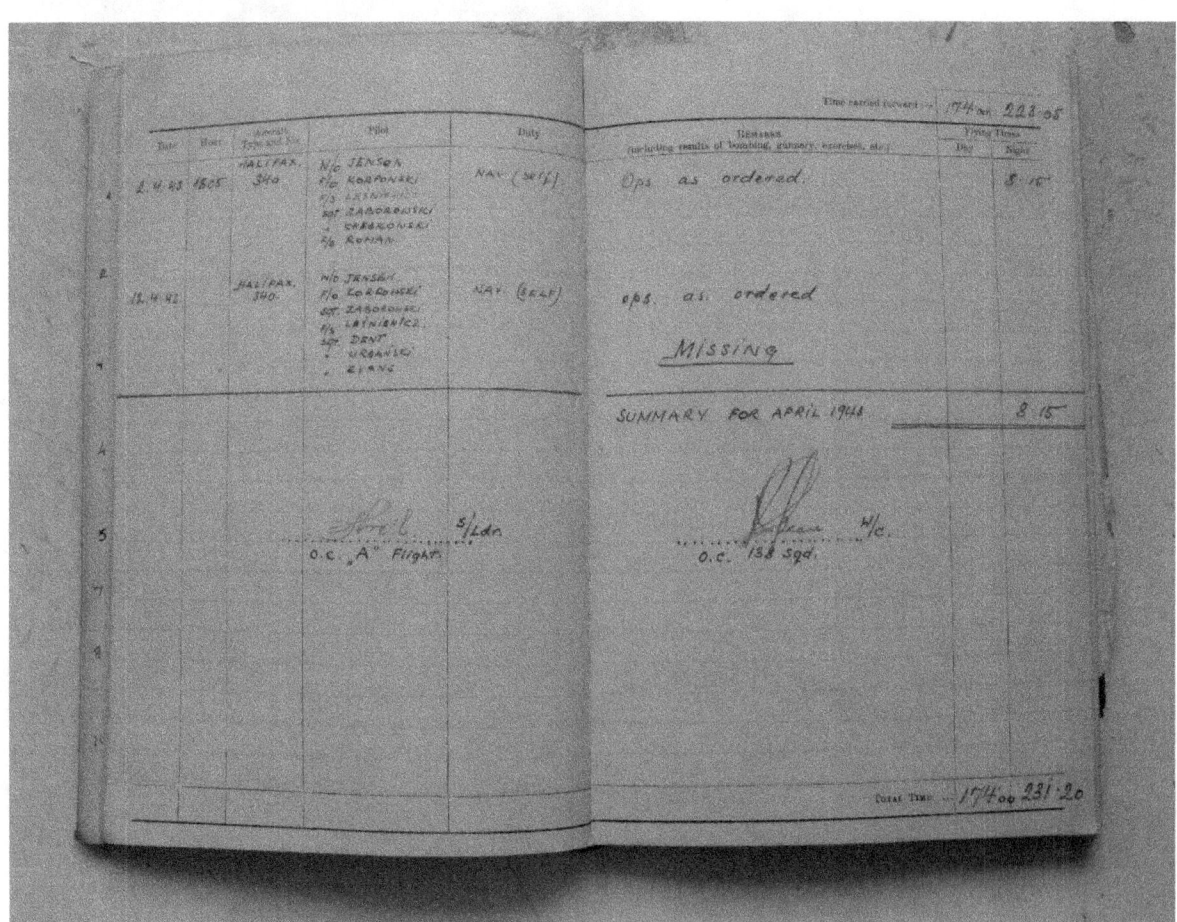

DT726 took off at 20.50 with the crew of F/O Lawrenczuk on board, bound for Operations STOCKBROKER/SHIPWRIGHT/STATIONER 2/PIMENTO 16, but not a single element was completed, and the round trip of more than nine hours was in vain. Next away, at 20.56, were F/O Gebik and crew in DT725 on Operation PRUNUS 3/STONEMASON/GUDGEON 9, They crossed the French coast at 100 feet east of Pointe de la Percee, and set course for Saumur, from where they headed for the reception point fifteen kilometres from Saint-Gaudens in the Gascony region of southern France. The drop site was difficult to locate in the mountainous terrain that reached up to 2,500 feet, but a reception committee was waiting, and an agent, Canadian C J Duchalard, parachuted into their arms, along with four containers and a package. Thereafter, a new course was set for GUDGEON, located near Foix, where, thirty minutes later, another reception committee flashed the correct signal, and five containers and two packages fell away. Task completed as briefed, the Halifax returned home on a reciprocal route to land safely after a round trip of eight hours. Within a week, the Germans had arrested the principal members of the PRUNUS circuit, but failed to catch Duchalard, who made his way back to England through Spain.

As far as it is possible to determine from the ORB entries, F/O Ruttledge and crew were the next to depart Tempsford, lifting off at 21.08 in BB364 to carry out Operations WHEELWRIGHT/SCIENTIST ?/6. It is believed that the first and last elements failed to be completed, but the second one was successful. F/L Hooper and crew took off at 21.17 in JB802 bound for Operations PIMENTO 14/18/PERCH 12, and only the last two elements were completed. F/L Gryglewicz and crew were on board BB330, which took off at 21.20 on Operations PHYSICIAN 19/STATIONER I/ SCIENTIST 14. The reception point was in the Chateauroux area, and the drop took place according to instructions. Finally, Sgt Cook and crew got away at 21.35 in BB363 to carry out Operations SCIENTIST 20/ARTIST 3/CRAB 13, but failed for an undisclosed reason to do so.

On the night of the 13/14th, a force of two hundred Lancasters set out for Italy to bomb the docks at La Spezia, and this activity helped to mask the approach of the clandestine operations to a number of occupied countries. 138 Squadron launched six sorties, beginning at 21.00 with the departure of F/O Kuzmicki and crew in Halifax DT726, bound for Italy to carry out Operation LOGANBERRY. They crossed the French coast at 400 feet at Pointe de la Percee, and noted heavy flak from the Caen area being directed at the Lancasters. A course was set for Nevers, and then Lac du Bourget, east of Lyon, before approaching the Alps, where the clear skies changed to ten-tenths cloud with a base at 8,000 feet. They circled for half an hour, climbing into clear air, before heading for the drop site, and descending on e.t.a to search in extreme darkness for a pinpoint on a lake. Once identified, they dropped six containers blind from 250 feet, and watched heavy flak being thrown up around Turin, as they made their way home to land after a round trip lasting ten hours.

Meanwhile, S/L Robinson and crew had departed for France in BB316 at 21.12 on Operations ROACH 3/FLOUNDER/PHYSICIAN 23/9, but returned to report being unable to complete their sortie for unspecified reasons. F/O Wrzesien and crew were in DT543, and took off at 21.15 bound for Belgium on Operations MOUFLON/JERBOA/CAPULET/BORZOI 1/LEMUR 2/3. They managed to complete the first three elements, delivering two agents and stores in a flight lasting five hours. At 21.21, DT725 left Tempsford carrying F/O Gebik and crew to France to undertake Operations GUDGEON 6/GOAT/RAT. The sortie was successful, although no details are available. At 21.23, it was the turn of F/L Dodkin and crew to set off for France in BB328 on Operations FARMER 1/PHYSICIAN ?/18, and they managed to complete the first and third elements. There is no mention in the ORB of the sortie to Belgium by Kiwi, Sgt Cook, and his crew, but we can assume that they took off in BB363 some time after 21.00 to carry out Operations GIBBON 2/CARACAL 3/PORCUPINE/MANDRILL. Their brief was to deliver two packages to a reception point south-east of Nivelles, and a container south of Brussels, before dropping two agents blind north-east of Namur. The fact that four bodies were recovered for burial, suggests that the Halifax came down in the Channel, somewhere off Bournemouth, with the loss of all nine airmen, two of whom were under training. It is not known whether the agents were still on board. Among those lost was F/Sgt Davidson DFM, who had been a member of P/O Leonard Cheshire's 102 Squadron crew, before Cheshire became a legend. It was during their epic Whitley sortie to Cologne, that Davidson was badly burned and temporarily blinded during the incident on the 12th of November 1940, and the harrowing account can be read in Cheshire's own words in his book, Bomber Pilot.

The southern city of Stuttgart played host to more than four hundred aircraft on the night of the 14/15th, but the centre of this somewhat elusive target escaped serious damage. The main weight of bombs fell across the north-eastern fringes, where almost four hundred buildings were destroyed, and many industrial premises were hit. 5% of the bomber force was lost, amounting to twenty-three aircraft, and from this point until the end of the summer of 1944, losses would remain grievously high, peaking in the first quarter of the coming year. With such a large bomber force approaching Stuttgart and withdrawing via southern France, 138 Squadron was able to feed six Halifaxes into French airspace, beginning with DT725, which took off at 20.30 with F/O Polnik at the controls for F/O Polkowski's crew. They were to undertake Operations STOCKBROKER/SHIPWRIGHT/STATIONER 2/PRUNUS 6 in the Pyrenees region. The route out took them from Start Point, on the south coast of Devon, to the Ile d'Oussant off Brest, across the Bay of Biscay, where the cloud base was down to 500 feet, and then to make landfall at Leon. From there a course was set to the first reception site, where two agents, Amedee Maingard and Mancunian, Harry Ree, were dropped, along with two containers and two packages, before they headed west to a second site, to deliver five containers. They returned via a reciprocal route, and landed safely after a round trip of ten hours.

S/L Robinson and crew were in DG252, which took off some time after 21.10 to carry out Operations JUGGLER I/CHESTNUT ?, and, as far as it is possible to discern from the ORB's illegible entry, they completed it. The next departure, that of F/O Ruttledge and crew in BB364, was at 21.39, after which they headed for Operation TRAINER I/LIME 10. They arrived back at 05.02 to report failing to carry out their brief, most likely through the lack of a reception committee. F/L Hooper and crew took off in an indecipherable Halifax at 21.42, bound for Operation STATIONER ?/LIME 1, which, it is believed, was not completed, also because of the absence of a reception committee. F/L Gryglewicz and crew took off at 21.50 in BB330, tasked with carrying out Operations SCIENTIST 7/17/22/A/WEAVER in the Angouleme region of south-western France. The first four elements were completed, but half an hour before reaching the final drop site, one of the agents was found to have left vital papers behind, and he had to be brought home, leaving his colleague to jump alone. BB329 lifted into the air at 22.00 with the crew of F/L Dodkin, who were bound for Operations PHYSICIAN 15/10/14, and succeeded in completing the first two elements only.

A busy night for Tempsford on the 15/16th saw thirteen sorties dispatched, all but one to France, and the bulk being entrusted to 161 Squadron. 138 Squadron's contribution to the night's work was four sorties, all supply drops, beginning with the departure of F/O Kuzmicki and crew in DT726 at 21.10. Their destination was southern France on Operation GUDGEON 8, which they completed during a round trip of just over nine hours. They were followed into the air at 21.15 by F/L Gryglewicz and crew in DG252 on Operations ROACH 3/FLOUNDER/PHYSICIAN 9/23. They were partially successful, completing the first two elements, before returning safely home after seven hours aloft. F/L Hooper and crew took off in JB802 at 21.22 to undertake Operations PHYSICAN 21/GUDGEON, and completed the first element only. Finally, F/O Ruttledge and crew got away at 21.40 in an unidentifiable Halifax to carry out Operations COCKLE ?/?/?, and, it is believed that all three were completed.

On the night of the 16/17th, Harris divided his strength in an attempt to confuse the defenders. The main operation, by over three hundred Lancasters and Halifaxes, was directed at the Skoda armaments works at distant Pilsen in Czechoslovakia, while a predominantly Wellington and Stirling diversionary raid took place at Mannheim. The former involved a complicated plan, in which the Pathfinders' target indicators were intended to act as route markers, to guide the main force crews to a visual identification of the target in conditions of moonlight. Unfortunately, the markers, which were correctly dropped seven miles from the aiming point, were bombed by the majority of the crews, and the target escaped damage. Not so the bomber force, which lost thirty-six of its number, split equally between the two types. The diversionary raid achieved significantly more damage, but a further eighteen aircraft were shot down, and this brought the night's casualty figure to a new record high of fifty-four. Two Tempsford Halifaxes, one from each unit, were able to slip into Norway under cover of the main event, F/O Gebik and crew having taken off at 20.57 in DT725 to carry out Operation PUFFIN. They were carrying two agents, eight containers and three packages, which they dropped blind from 900 feet at a location near Lake Tyrifjord, north-west of Oslo. F/O Polkowski and crew followed Gebik into the air at 21.00 in DT627, bound for Denmark on Operations TABLELAMP/TABLEGOSSIP. They crossed the Danish coast at 200 feet north of Sondervig, before setting course for the reception point north of Viborg. A reception committee flashed the correct signal, and Kai Lund parachuted down, along with four containers and a package. F/L Dodkin and crew took off at 21.30 in BB313 bound for Belgium to carry out Operations DORMOUSE/LEMUR 2/3/BORZOI 1. Despite clear skies, thick ground haze prevented the crew from identifying the pinpoint of a large wood south-east of Valenciennes, from where they were to hop over the frontier to the drop site. Ultimately, they lost their way, and abandoned the attempt. No departure time is recorded for S/L Robinson and crew, who, it is believed, were in DT727. The illegible entry is misleading, and the code letter is quoted as D, while DT727 should be K. Their destination was France, to undertake Operations SPRUCE 6/7/8, but, in the event, completed only the second element.

The main force stayed at home on the night of the 17/18th, while 138 Squadron sent six crews to France. Five of these sorties were successfully concluded, and will be dealt with first. F/L Gryglewicz and crew took off first in BB330 at 21.35, to conduct Operations PIMENTO 17/DIRECTOR 29. F/O Kuzmicki and crew were next away, at 21.42, in DT726 on Operations PIMENTO 2/SPRUCE 10, and completed the first element. BB328 took to the air at 21.44 carrying the crew of S/L Robinson on Operations ROACH 5/6/7, and they came home at 03.27 to give the "thumbs-up". F/O Ruttledge and crew were given the task of re-flying the DORMOUSE/LEMUR 2/3/BORZOI 1 operation, that had thwarted F/L Dodkin twenty-four hours earlier, and took off at 21.49 in DG252. They returned safely at 04.15, having completed all but the final element. F/L Dodkin and crew were handed three COCKLE operations, for which they took off in DG253 at 22.07, and returned to report complete success. We do not know what time F/L Lawrenczuk and his crew took off on Operation LIME 9, a container drop believed to be at Moulins in the Lons-le-Saunier region of eastern France, close to the Swiss frontier. We do know that F/O Ginter was at the controls, as DT725 was hit by flak at, or shortly after crossing the French coast, and crashed at Ussy, south of Caen, and a few miles north-west of Falaise. All on board are thought to have lost their lives, but, as only six names are listed in what should have been at least a standard crew complement of seven, some weight becomes attached to the unconfirmed report, that one crew member survived and evaded capture.

On the night of the 18/19th, force of 173 Lancasters and five Halifaxes returned to La Spezia on the Italian coast to bomb the docks area. Among the simultaneous four 138 Squadron sorties was one by F/O Gebik and crew, who took off at 21.47 in DT726, bound for east-central France on Operations SCULLION/PIMENTO 14. The drop site for the first element was about eight miles north of Autun, where a six-man team of saboteurs, led by Hugh Dormer, parachuted blind from 800 feet at a speed of 120 mph. A container and package accompanied them to the ground, containing the equipment necessary for an attack on a nearby synthetic oil plant. In the event, it would be found to be too heavily guarded for the sabotage to be attempted. The second drop site was forty minutes away, and benefitted from a reception committee, although their lights were poor and barely of assistance. More problematic, was the location in an area of high ground, which rendered it approachable only on a north-south or south-north heading. However, in the absence of opposition, the drop was carried out successfully, and they returned safely after a round trip of seven and a quarter hours. F/O Ruttledge and crew took off in BB328 at 21.49, and headed to France to conduct Operations WEAVER/ARTIST 7/SCIENTIST 10, returning at 03.45 as one of three crews on this night to be unsuccessful. The others were those of F/L Cooper, who departed Tempsford at 21.53 in JB802 to undertake Operations STATIONER 3/TRAINER 1 over France, and F/O Polkowski, who became airborne at 21.55 in DT627 on Operations LIME 4/ACROBAT 1/ACROBAT/JUDGE. No explanation is given for the lack of success of these sorties, so it can be assumed to be weather or reception-related.

On the following night, while the main force remained on the ground, F/O Kuzmicki and crew undertook the only 138 Squadron sortie. They took off at 21.00 in DT627 on Operations CENTAUR/CHAFFINCH 2, a long round-trip to Norway to deliver Captain Olaf Reed-Olsen. They crossed the Norwegian coast at Jomfeuland at 200 feet, before setting course for Hollen and the drop site. It was a blind drop from 800 feet, on an estimated position, slightly north of the intended pinpoint, and it nearly ended in disaster, as Reed-Olsen's parachute failed to release. He struck the tail-wheel, and was left trailing unconscious on his static line, which was not appreciated by the dispatcher, who assumed that all was well. Reed-Olsen regained his senses as he fell to earth beneath a partially opened canopy, which snagged on a tree and arrested his fall, but left him with a dislocated knee. Unaware of these events, F/O Kuzmicki carried on to the next pinpoint, a reception site eighteen minutes away, where he delivered nine containers. The other sortie from Tempsford on this night was also over Norway, and involved a 161 Squadron aircraft carrying out an SIS agent drop. This also suffered from a parachute malfunction, which, it is believed, had fatal consequences.

Over three hundred aircraft from the Pathfinder and main force squadrons went to Stettin on the night of the 20/21st, and severely damaged a large industrial area in the centre of the city. Stettin, on Germany's east Baltic coast, would be a fairly regular destination for the Command from this point on, and was, perhaps, the only urban target never to escape lightly. This was the last night of the moon period, and 138 Squadron concluded its month of operations with sorties to France, Denmark and Holland. It has proved impossible to decipher the ORB entries for this night, and Freddie Clark has these sorties taking place on the night of the 21/22nd. The ORB has ten entries, but a number of aircraft and crew captains are mentioned twice to create extra confusion. Take-off times are also illegible, and the following is the best that I can make of it.

At 20.32, F/O Polkowski and crew took off in DT627 bound for France on Operations SCIENTIST 21/PIMENTO 15, which they failed to complete during a round-trip of ten hours and thirty minutes. F/L Hooper and crew undertook Operations TABLETOP 2/TABLEHABIT to Denmark, taking off at 21,20 in an unidentified Halifax, and reaching the Danish coast at 800 feet over Lodbjaarg after a two-hour North Sea crossing. The drop site is believed to have been in the Viborg area, where four containers were delivered during the first pass at 00.33, and the agent, Proben Lok-Lindblad, during the second, three minutes later. They ran into deteriorating weather on approach to the Norfolk coast, and were diverted first to Elsham Wolds, and then to Leeming. BB330 took off at 21.30 with the crew of F/L Gryglewicz on board, who had been assigned to Operations PERCH 18/GUDGEON 4 over France, but this was another failure for which there are no explanations. Operations SPRUCE 8/6/SHRIMP 1 is also credited in the ORB to F/L Hooper, but, as good a pilot as he may have been, even he could not captain two aircraft at the same time! We do not know, therefore, which crew took JB802 to France, only that SPRUCE 8 was successful. S/L Robinson and crew had business to attend to over Holland, and took off sometime after 21.00 in an unidentified Halifax to deliver two agents, fourteen containers and five cases of chocolate under Operations NETBALL, GHERKIN and MARROW 27/28. While approaching the enemy coast, some fifteen miles north-west of Vlieland, and flying at 1,000 feet, they attracted the interest of a flak ship, and, five minutes later, having descended to 50 feet, a flak battery at the northern end of Texel joined in. They continued on the first drop zone, MARROW 28 at between 200 and 300 feet, and parachuted two agents into German hands, along with seven containers and two packages. At MARROW 27, the Germans welcomed a further seven containers and three packages into their stockpile.

F/O Gebik and crew were assigned to Operations PERCH 16/14/11, and took off in DG253 at 21.25 bound for France, where they completed the first two elements. BB313 was next to take to the air, at 21.47, on Operations PHYSICIAN 8/ALSATIAN/LEMUR 2/3, but it is uncertain which crew was on board, and only two elements were completed. At 22.00, BB364 departed Tempsford for France on Operations WEAVER/PERCH 18/11, possibly with the crew of F/O Ruttledge on board, although this is a hunch, rather than a firm belief. In the grand scheme of things, it is not important, and the operation was not completed anyway. The ORB logs the take-off at 22.05 of a Halifax and crew already assigned to another operation, and, therefore, the aircraft and its occupants sent to France on Operations COCKLE 12/13/ROACH ?, and completing the first two elements, will remain a mystery. F/L Dodkin and crew were in BB329, and were the last to take off at 22.50 for a supply drop to Holland under Operations MARROW 29/?? They were carrying fourteen containers, which they delivered as briefed, adding further to the enemy's bounty.

The month ended for the heavy brigade with another disappointing failure at Duisburg on the night of the 26/27th, before a moderately effective raid was unleashed upon Essen on the night of the 30th. On the two nights in between, extensive mining operations had taken place involving a record total for this kind of operation of 367 aircraft, which deposited 1,051 mines in the Biscay area and in northern waters.

A Bedford QLC fuel bowser replenishes a Halifax. Some 52,250 of these 3-ton 4x4 vehicles were produced, adapted to a variety of tasks including fire tenders, troop carriers, communications lorries and Bofors gun tractors, as well as conveying high octane petrol to the ever-thirsty bombers.

May 1943

After a less than satisfactory performance during April, May would bring a return to winning ways for the bomber brigade with a number of spectacular successes. It was not to be a particularly hectic period, however, and it was not until the night of the 4/5th that the first heavy raid took place. A new record non-1,000 force of 596 aircraft took off for Dortmund, and those reaching the city area destroyed over twelve hundred buildings, and seriously damaged over two thousand more. Thirty-one aircraft failed to return, and this was the highest loss at a Ruhr target since the campaign began. The deaths of almost seven hundred people on the ground was also a new record, but this figure included two hundred PoWs. It would be a full week before the next major foray took place, and in the meantime, preparations were in hand at Tempsford for the new phase of operations. 138 Squadron remained on the ground until the night of the 11/12th, when three sorties to Holland were briefed, along with one to Denmark. Although now written in a different hand, the ORB entries are still largely illegible, but, for the first time, include full crew lists. If only one could make them out!! F/L Austin and crew were in BB334, which took off at 22.07 for Operations TABLEJELLY/TABLEGOSSIP 2, the purpose of which was to deliver two agents and supplies to a reception point in Denmark. Clear skies afforded good visibility as they crossed the Danish coast at Vigso, and proceeded to the drop site, at a previously used location, where a reception committee was waiting to receive Paul Hansen and his colleague, along with two containers and two packages. On the way home, twenty-five pigeons were released, before the flaps began to deploy of their own accord, causing the Halifax to fly in circles. F/L Austin was able to stabilize the controls by adopting a full-flap configuration, which created enormous drag, and the North Sea crossing was carried out at 98 mph. It took almost four hours to reach the English coast, and a safe landing was eventually carried out at base at 06.11.

The supply drops to Holland departed Tempsford later, beginning at 22.40 with the take-off of BB313 and the crew of S/L Robinson on Operations MARROW/?? There are no details, and we are told only, that the sortie was successful. F/O Polkowski and his crew took off at 22.50, with F/O Polnik at the controls of DT627. They had been briefed for Operations LEEK 7/CATARRH 12, and were to carry out drops at 00.46 and 01.12. We cannot say for certain whether they were out or inbound when the Halifax crashed into the sea off the Dutch coast, killing all on board, but it was probably outbound, and possibly as the result of a trap set by Giskes, that had the defences lying in wait, but that is speculation. Apart from his 138 Squadron service, F/O Jan Polnik had completed twenty-eight operations with 300 Squadron, and served as a flight commander/instructor at 18 O.T.U. His body was one of four washed ashore, and he lies buried on West Terschelling with another member of the crew. The final departure on this night was at 22.56, and involved BB379 and the crew of F/O Gebik, who were to undertake Operations MARROW 32/31. Again, there are no details, other than, that the drops were successfully carried out during a round-trip of under four hours duration.

On the following night, the Command tried for the fourth time thus far in the campaign to nail Duisburg. 572 aircraft were involved, and for once, the Pathfinder marking and main force bombing were accurate, and concentrated around the centre of the city. Almost sixteen hundred buildings were completely destroyed, and sixty thousand tons of shipping was either

RAF Tempsford 1st May 1943. Top: The DFC is awarded to pilot W/O Klosowski who completed his second operational tour in 138 Squadron and stayed in this unit as a pilot instructor. Middle: The parade after the DFC decoration. P/O Szrajer, decorated in the same day, is marching on the right of W/O Klosowski. Bottom: Commander of Polish Flight C, F/L Krol, in the front of Polish aircrew who were flying in 138 Squadron in the first half of 1943. (Photos: PH)

sunk or severely damaged in Germany's largest inland port. Losses were again high, however, and amounted to thirty-four aircraft, a new record for the campaign. 138 Squadron mounted eight sorties to France on this night, four of them cargo drops, and proceedings began with the take-off of DT726 on Operations STATIONER 3/PERCH 11 at 22.03. It has not been possible to decipher the identity of the crew, however, the ORB does tell us, that only the first element was completed. BB329 was the next off the ground, at 22.05, with, it is believed, F/L Dodkin at the controls, bound for Operations LIME ?/ROACH 14/15, of which, elements two and three were completed. At 22.12, it was the turn of F/O Gebik and crew to take-off in BB379 on Operations PERCH 18/GUDGEON 19, and they completed the first element only. F/O Wilkinson and crew were next away at 22.17 in BB309, to undertake Operations SCIENTIST 20/ARTIST 2/3, in which endeavor, it seems, they were successful. It is not possible to determine the take-off time for DT727, or to identify the crew, but the brief was to carry out Operations GUDGEON 11/13, which were not completed.

Navigator F/O Polkowski was the captain of the crew lost on 11/12nd May 1943 over Holland (1st pilot F/O Polnik). (PISM via PH)

F/O Ruttledge and crew took off at 22.35, possibly in HR666, having been briefed for Operations ARARAT/CHESTNUT 3/ROACH 16/17. They found France to be under clear skies with good visibility, which enabled them to identify the first pinpoint, and deliver an agent and package blind from 600 feet. The next drop site was eight minutes away in the Rambouillet area, some twenty miles south-west of Paris, where a reception committee awaited the dropping of five containers from 500 feet. From there, they flew 130 miles to the southeast to Cosne, in the Burgundy region, where a further ten containers were delivered. A safe return was made, and the entire round-trip lasted just five and a quarter hours. According to Bill Chorley in Bomber Command Losses, S/L Robinson and crew also departed Tempsford at 22.35, in BB313, to carry out Operations DONKEYMAN 1/ROACH 10/LIME 16. It seems, that having completed the first two elements only, and while at low level on their way home, they were hit by light flak from an airfield, and caught fire. S/L Robinson gave the order to bale out, and the flight engineer and one gunner managed to do so before the Halifax was force-landed in a field near Troyes, some eighty miles south-east of Paris. S/L Robinson and other members of the crew sustained injuries in the process, but all of the crew survived, and having assisted his colleagues as best he could, the second pilot, Sgt Tweed, made good his escape, and ultimately evaded capture. He returned to the UK in September, the month following the arrival home of the gunner and flight engineer. S/L Robinson and the other members of the crew fell into enemy hands, the navigator and bomb-aimer having suffered quite serious injury, which led to their repatriation in February 1945. At 22.42, an unidentifiable Halifax took off on Operation PHYSICIAN 3?/CRAB 1?, with a sergeant pilot at the controls, and it returned later without completing its brief.

On the night of the 13/14th Harris divided his strength between Bochum in the Ruhr and the Skoda works at Pilsen, the latter an attempt by 5 Group to rectify the previous month's failure. The armaments factory again escaped damage, however, as most of the bombs found open country, while the Bochum raid was moderately successful, destroying almost four hundred buildings and seriously afflicting a further seven hundred. 138 Squadron ORB entries for this night are a nightmare to decipher, and Freddie Clark wisely decided to leave well alone apart from detailing the loss, for the third night running, of an aircraft and crew. F/O Noble and crew were in BB328, and attempting a two-element cargo drop over France. Their brief was to deliver ten containers at the first drop site, PHYSICIAN 10, and five at the second, ROACH 6, but they crashed at Pont-Audemer, around twenty miles south-east of le Havre, killing all six men on board. The other sorties on this night, as far as can be determined from the illegible scrawl, were as follows, and please excuse the number of ?s. At 21.51, Halifax ? with F/O Ruttledge on Operation SCIENTIST ??/SCIENTIST ??/???????, outcome unknown. At 22.09, DG253 with the crew of F/L Austin on Operation LUMBERJACK/LIME 1?/PHYSICIAN 33, of which the first two elements were completed. At 22.45, Halifax ? with the crew of Sgt Brown? on Operation CRAB 16/PHYSICIAN 32, not successful. At 22.50, BB330 on Operation COCKLE 11/12/??, S/L Griffiths and crew, two elements completed. At 23.08, DT726 on Operation PHYSICIAN 23/ROACH ?, crew unknown, both elements completed. At 23.14, F/O Wilkinson and crew in BB309 on Operation PHYSICIAN 27/ROACH ??/PHYSICIAN ??, which they completed. At 23.15, F/L Dodkin and crew in BB364 on Operation FARMER 2/ROACH 12/13, both of which were completed.

The squadron's run of misfortune extended into the very next night, when F/L Austin and his crew were almost lost during a two-element sortie to deliver three agents and stores to locations in France. They had taken off in BB329 at 22.03 to carry out Operations LIME 8/ACROBAT/JUDGE/COTTONWOOD/ROACH 31, which required them to deliver an agent and five containers to a drop site in the Lons-le-Saunier area of eastern France, close to the Swiss frontier. Afterwards, they were to take a north-westerly course to a reception point twenty miles north-west of Nevers in central France to drop a further ten containers. Also on board, were an extra navigator and dispatcher gaining operational experience. Five minutes after crossing the French coast at 600 feet, they were fired upon by a single gun in a field, and, two minutes later, they were coned by searchlights and fired upon again at Lisieux. This time the flak found its mark, knocking out the starboard-outer engine, and, after a further fifteen minutes, it became necessary to jettison the containers from around 250 feet, south-east of Caen (Mezidon), in order to maintain height and get home. The other sortie on this night involved F/O Gebik and crew, who took off at 23.00 in BB379 to carry out Operations SHAWL/PHYSICIAN 28. They were transporting two agents to an undisclosed reception point in France, where, despite the absence of the expected signal from the ground, the two men parachuted blind.

Over the course of the 15/16th and 16/17th, sixteen cargo drops over France were carried out by 138 Squadron, while 161 Squadron attended to SIS operations. Seven 138 Squadron crews were briefed on the 15th, and, once more, the ORB strives to conceal information behind an illegible scrawl. Happily, matters are about to improve in that department. What can be gleaned from the official record is as follows. Departures began at 22.10, with the take-off of HR666 on Operation CRAB 32/???? 4 with an unknown crew, the captain of which looks like F/O Puttridge, but this name, or one like it, does not appear again, and is not included in Freddie Clark's index of aircrew. The operations does appear to have been completed. At 22.27, DT726 took to the air, again with an unknown crew, on what appears to be Operations ROACH 31/11, one element of which was successful. At 22.14, BB309 took off with the crew of F/O Wilkinson on board, bound for Operations ARTIST 7/PERCH 11, which failed through the lack of a reception committee. The next to depart was BB317 at 23.05 with the crew of Sgt Brown, who were to undertake Operation PHYSICIAN 25, and, in this, they were successful. F/Sgt Norris and crew took off at 23.09 in BB330 on Operation PHYSICIAN 22, and they, too, achieved their objective. S/L Griffiths and crew were handed Operations COCKLE 15/18/PERCH 26, and took off at 23.10 in JD362 to complete the first two elements. Finally, at 23.17, F/L Dodkin and crew took off in BB364 to undertake Operations LIME15/PERCH 17, but were defeated by the weather, and brought their cargo home.

The night of the 16/17th is one which will live forever in the annals of Bomber Command. Operation Chastise was launched by nineteen specially modified Lancasters of the newly-formed 617 Squadron under the command of W/C Guy Gibson, against the Möhne, Eder and Sorpe Dams, situated east of the Ruhr Valley. The crews who took part in the epic attack, eight of which failed to return, wrote their own page in bomber folklore, and established the operation as the greatest feat of arms in aviation history. It has become an integral and inaccurate part of the story, that they were the only Bomber Command aircraft operating that night. In fact, almost seventy other aircraft were involved in a variety of operations, not counting nine belonging to 138 Squadron. Bomber Command records would make no diary mention of SOE and SIS operations until the night of the 4/5th of January 1944, almost three and a half years after the very first sortie took place. F/O Gebik and crew started the Tempsford ball rolling at 22.03, when taking off in BB334 to successfully carry out Operations GUDGEON 11/CRAB 24. At 22.08?, F/O Ruttledge and crew took off in HR666 on Operations ROACH 27/JUGGLER 3, but failed to make contact with a reception committee, and had to admit defeat. Sgt Brown and crew were next away, at 22.10, in BB378, having been briefed to attempt Operations LIME 7/CRAB 21, which were successfully completed. Logged as taking off at the same time, S/L Griffiths and crew were on board BB316, charged with attempting Operations PERCH 19/???? 13, the outcome of which is unclearly recorded, but, it is believed, that the second element was completed. F/L Dodkin and crew were the next to take-off, doing so at 22.14 in BB364 to attempt Operations SCIENTIST 15/27, the result of which is unclear. At 22.24, F/L Austin and crew got away in DG253 on Operations SCIENTIST 25/26, in which endeavor they were unsuccessful. F/O Wilkinson and crew were in BB330 as it became airborne at 22.43 on Operations ROACH 9/32/TINKER 1. They arrived back at 05.20 to give the "thumbs-up" on a successful venture. Sgt Bown and crew were in BB317, which took off at 23.00? on Operations ROACH 20/PHYSICIAN 26, which suffered from the lack of a reception committee, and failed. The last sortie on this busy night was that of F/Sgt Norris and crew, who took off at 23.10 in BB329 to carry out Operations COCKLE 17/18/19, returning in the small hours to report a successful outcome.

The 17/18th brought just three sorties by 138 Squadron, beginning with the departure from Tempsford at 21.54 of BB334, containing the crew of F/O Gebik. They were bound for Denmark on Operations TABLEMUSTARD/TABLEGOSSIP 3, and crossed the coast at

Ringkobing, before heading eastwards to Silkeborg, and a familiar reception site, used previously by other 138 Squadron crews in March and May. Three agents and four containers were parachuted in from 700 feet to a reception committee waiting on the ground. W/C Batchelor and crew took on Operation SCIENTIST 12/21 over France, and lifted off at 22.15 in HR666, before returning at 07.20 to report a successful outcome. F/L Austin and crew also had France as their destination, and took off at 23.17 in DG253 to attempt Operations ROACH 26/PHYSICIAN 24. They returned from the relatively short-duration round-trip at 03.48 to report completing the second element only. In the early hours of the 18th, F/L Hooper overshot his landing at Maison Blanche in Algeria, and wrote-off JB802. A number of crew casualties were reported, and, it is likely, that Arab workers occupying tents demolished by the aircraft, also became casualties. F/L Hooper's purpose for being in Algeria is not known, but two 161 Squadron aircraft had also shown up there on preceding days with stores and passengers.

Meanwhile, back at Tempsford, six sorties were mounted to France by 138 Squadron on the night of the 18/19th, beginning at 22.03 with the departure of F/O Ruttledge and crew in BB330. They were bound for Operation SCIENTIST 9, but failed to complete it for an undisclosed reason. F/O Wilkinson and crew were next off the ground at 22.14 in DT726. They were to undertake Operations GUDGEON 4/SCALERE, but also failed for an undisclosed reason, and landed at St Eval at 08.05, after almost ten hours aloft. F/L Dodkin and crew took off at 22.15 in BB334, now recorded in the ORB with the code-letter K rather than X. They were to attempt Operation SCIENTIST 13, and landed at Boscombe Down nine hours later to report a successful outcome. S/L Griffiths and crew were in BB316, which took off at 22.20, carrying agents and stores for delivery to two drop sites under Operations ROACH 33/LING/INKFISH/CARMEN. The first three elements, involving two agents, ten containers and three packages, were bound for the Chateau-Thierry area, forty miles east of Paris, while the remaining five packages were destined for another, undisclosed location. There was bright moonlight and excellent visibility as they crossed the French coast at Cayeux, and shortly afterwards, the Halifax came under accurate fire from about five rail-mounted guns in the marshalling yards at Serqueux. Shells found their way into the fuselage before exploding, causing injury to two of the crew and an agent, and S/L Griffiths was forced to abandon the sortie and turn for home, where he landed one hour and twenty-three minutes later. BB309 took off at 22.39 with the crew of P/O Bown on board, who had been briefed for Operations PHYSICIAN 37/JUGGLER 3/ROACH 22, and they succeeded in completing the first element only. The final departure on this night was that of F/Sgt Norris and crew at 23.00 in BB346 on Operations COCKLE 14/23/PRIVET 4, of which, only the first element was completed.

Despite this excitement, S/L Griffiths would be airborne again on the following night, flying one of six sorties to France assigned to the squadron. First off the ground at 22.10 were P/O Bown and crew in BB378, who were to attempt Operations LIME 19/TRAINER 3. Typically, no details are available, but only the second element was completed. F/O Gebik and crew took off at 22.12 in BB379, to re-fly a slightly modified version of a sortie originally attempted by F/L Austin on the night of the 14/15th. Operations LIME 21/8/ACROBAT/JUDGE/ACROBAT I had two reception points in the Lons-le-Saunier region of eastern France, en-route to which, and while flying at 200 feet some fifteen minutes after crossing the coast, they were fired upon from behind by a machine gun on the ground. They were not hit, and continued on to the first drop site, where John Starr and his Geordie wireless operator, John Young, parachuted down from 700 feet along with five containers. Starr would be betrayed by a double agent in July, but survive, while Young was to die in Mauthausen after his arrest in November. The second reception point was eight minutes flying time due south, where five containers were delivered in two sticks. F/O Ruttledge and crew took off in HR666 at 22.15 on Operation LIME 5, and returned at 04.57 to report a successful outcome. Also recorded as taking off at 22.15 was BB317 with Sgt Brown at the controls. He and his crew had been assigned to Operations ROACH 34/36, which they completed during a round-trip of a little over six hours duration. S/L Griffiths and crew were in BB305, and departed Tempsford at 22.20 in what would be a vain attempt to complete Operations PERCH 17/LIME 23. The final departure of the night was that of F/L Austin and crew in DG253, who took off at 22.33 to carry out Operations FIRTREE/CARMEN/ROACH 25, but succeeded only in completing the first element.

Five sorties were dispatched by 138 Squadron on the night of the 20/21st, four to France and one to Belgium. F/Sgt Norris and crew were the first to take-off, at 22.23 in BB334, to carry out Operations ROACH 39/DONKEYMAN I over France, an endeavor in which they were unsuccessful. F/O Gebik and crew were in BB317, and took off for France at 22.32 to attempt Operations CHESTNUT 4/BRICKLAYER A/PHYSICIAN A. They landed safely at 03.36 to report a successful outcome. F/L Austin and crew were in DG253 again, and departed Tempsford at 22.47 bound for France on Operations ROACH 28/MACDUFF/TEAL/IBEX/GIBBON 3. They landed safely at 03.16, and were able to report, that all but the first element had been completed. F/L Dodkin and crew had a drop site in Belgium as their destination, and took off at 22.50 in BB329 to undertake Operations LEMUR 6/5/BORZOI 1/ROACH 40, completing the first two elements only. Last away on this night were F/O Wilkinson and crew in BB309 at 23.00, to attempt Operations ROACH 37/24/TENCH 1. They were partially successful, but the ORB is not specific. Freddie Clark writes, that the night's operations delivered three more SOE and two SIS agents, along with twenty-two containers, to where they were needed in occupied territory.

Seven sorties were mounted on the night of the 21/22nd, three of them to France, according to Freddie Clark, and two each to Holland and Belgium. However, the ORB records three Belgian drops, and perhaps the confusion arises from the standard practice of delivering agents onto the French side of the frontier in the south, and for them to cross, and then make their way north. We are not provided with a take-off time for F/Sgt Norris and crew in BB329, but are told, that they were assigned to Operation MARROW 35/36, the delivery of seven containers and two packages each at two German-controlled "Nordpol" drop sites in Holland. At 02.00, the Halifax was shot down by flak onto a polder at Noordbeemster, about ten miles east-south-east of Alkmaar, and two of the crew were killed, while F/Sgt Norris and four others were captured. Sgt Brown and crew undertook the other sortie over Holland, Operation MARROW 34/37/POLO/SQUASH/CROQUET, and took off at 23.00 in BB317. They were fired upon by heavy flak as they raced across Vlieland at 50 feet, and shells burst above them, but they made it unscathed to the reception point, where three agents, Anton Mink, Laurens Punt and Oscar de Brey, were dropped into the hands of the waiting Germans. All three would be executed, but, they were, in fact, the last to fall directly into the enemy net, after warnings were at last heeded, that the Dutch networks had been compromised. Sgt Brown and crew were oblivious to the events on the ground, and pressed on to the next reception point to deliver stores, although one container fell out as the bomb doors were opened, and this was attributed to a faulty release mechanism.

The first departure on this night had taken place at 22.41, and had involved HR666 and the crew of F/O Ruttledge, who were assigned to Operations LABRADOR 1/BULLFROG/GOFER/PHYSICIAN 27 over Belgium. The ORB provides no information, other than to report a successful outcome. F/L Dodkin and crew undertook the second of the Belgian sorties, taking off at 22.50 in BB364 to carry out Operations MUSKRAT/VAMPIRE, the plan for which, called for the dropping blind of two agents and one package a dozen miles north-east of Antwerp, near Westmalle. The headed out over Orfordness, but on approaching the enemy coast, F/L Dodkin turned back to kill time, in the hope that the light from the moon would increase. They retraced their steps from Orfordness to the Dutch island of Tholen, which they crossed at 700 feet. A course was set for Roosendaal in southern Holland, and then the target, within three miles of which, and still in poor visibility, the two agents jumped from 800 feet. S/L Griffiths and crew undertook the third sortie to Belgium, taking off at 23.10 in BB378 on Operations LEMUR 7/8/CARACAL 4/SAMOYED 1. Again the ORB provides scant information, but records that the first three elements were successfully dealt with. The remaining two sorties were to be conducted over France, beginning with the departure at 23.05 of P/O Bown and crew in BB330 on Operations PHYSICIAN 30/FARMER 3, of which the first element only was completed. F/O Wilkinson and crew took off at 23.11 in BB309 on Operations FARMER 5/TENCH I/ROACH 37, and succeeded only in completing the third element.

There was just a single 138 Squadron sortie on the night of the 22/23rd, undertaken by F/L Austin and crew in DG253. They took off at 23.51 on Operation COCKLE 24/23/PRIVET 4, and returned at 05.12 to report a successful outcome. After a nine-day break from major operations, the bombing offensive resumed with the preparation of a new record non-1,000 force, to be unleashed for the second time in the month upon Dortmund. A massive 826 aircraft departed their stations on the evening of the 23rd, and those reaching the target destroyed almost two thousand buildings, and seriously damaged many more, including some important war industry factories. Predictably, losses were again heavy as "Happy Valley" lived up to its reputation, and the thirty-eight missing aircraft represented a new high for the campaign. 138 Squadron was also busy on this night, launching six sorties to France to bring an end to what had been a busy month of operations. F/O Gebik and crew set the ball rolling, when taking off in BB379 at 23.20 on Operations ROACH 30/BLUEFISH, which, for an undisclosed reason, they failed to complete. F/O Ruttledge and crew were in HR666, and took off at 23.42 on Operation CRAB 9, which, the ORB informs us, they were able to complete, and were the only successful crew on this disappointing night. F/O Wilkinson and crew set off at 00.47 in BB309 for Operation PRIVET 2, and they were followed into the air at 01.10 by the crews of S/L Griffiths and Sgt Brown in BB330 and BB317 on Operations PHYSICIAN 26 and PHYSICIAN 38 respectively. The final departure was that of F/L Dodkin and crew at 01.20 in JD154 on Operation PHYSICIAN 16.

On the 24th, W/C Batchelor concluded his short term of office as 138 Squadron's commanding officer, and was posted to Chedburgh as a group captain and station commander. Later in the war he would move to a similar post at Mildenhall, and remain in the RAF until his retirement in 1964. In 1987 he would become the chairman of the Bomber Command Association, and pass away at the age of 79 in 1994. Had S/L Robinson not failed to return from operations earlier in the month, he may, perhaps, with his previous experience as a squadron commander, have succeeded W/C Batchelor. In the event, the position passed to W/C "Dickie" Speare, another seasoned campaigner, who had served as a flight commander with 7 Squadron back in the spring of 1941, and until recently, had held a similar post with 460 Squadron RAAF.

On the night of the 25/26th, over seven hundred aircraft converged on Düsseldorf, but cloud, decoy markers and dummy fire sites conspired to throw the attack off course, and damage within the city was comparatively minor. Moderate success was achieved at Essen by a force of five hundred aircraft two nights later, in what was the penultimate major operation of the month. On the 28th, 138 Squadron's new commanding officer lost the services of two of his most experienced pilots, when F/L Austin and F/O Ruttledge were posted to the newly formed 1575 Flight for operations out of Tunisia. Their departure coincided with a massive influx of new crews, however, and the postings-in would continue into the new month. Eight Polish pilots had arrived on the 24th, F/L Matylis, F/Os Wroblewski and Krzehlik, F/Sgts Bakanacz, Engel and Jonski and Sgts Bober and Rzewuski, and they were followed on the 27th by S/L Pitt, and on the 29th by P/O Sancewicz. On the night of the 29/30th, over seven hundred aircraft set out for Barmen, which, with its twin Elberfeld, forms the conurbation known as Wuppertal. It was one of those occasions, when all facets of the plan came together in perfect and terrible harmony. Almost four thousand houses were destroyed, along with hundreds of industrial premises, and a further nineteen hundred buildings were classed as seriously damaged. The death toll was set at around 3,400, by far the highest to date at a German urban target, and with 80% of the town's built-up area reduced to rubble, most of the survivors were homeless. Some of these might have been cheered by the news, that thirty-three of their tormentors would not be returning home, and that the Command's last three operations had cost a total of eighty-three bombers. It had been a costly month also for 138 Squadron, in which four crews and five aircraft had been lost from seventy-two sorties.

June 1943

The first week and a half of June was a strangely quiet period, and for once, the moon squadrons opened their month's account ahead of the bomber brigade. The departure of 2 Group at the end of May, to form the nucleus of the 2nd Tactical Air Force, meant that Bomber Command was now an entirely strategic force operating mostly four-engine types. It was expanding steadily, with many squadrons adding a C Flight, which, in due course, would be hived off to form new squadrons. SOE/SIS also had an increasing work load, and June would prove to be even busier for 138 Squadron than May. The crew of F/O Hart arrived on the 4th, and those of F/L Milne on the 5th and F/O Goszczynski on the 7th, as the increase in squadron strength continued.

Polish pilot F/O Goszczynski was assigned to 138 Squadron in early June 1943 and later flew with the crew of navigator F/O Krywda (PISM via PH).

The squadron began its new phase of operational activity on the night of the 10/11th, when mounting seven sorties to France and two to Holland, the former getting away first, beginning with the departure at 22.15 of F/O Downes and crew in BB330. They were assigned to Operations ROACH28/29, and, on their return to Tempsford at 04.50, they were able to confirm a successful outcome. F/O Wilkinson and crew got away at 22.45 in HR666 to undertake Operations PRIVET 2/ARTIST 4, but their efforts were thwarted by the absence of a reception committee. BB317 contained the crew of F/L Hooper, who took off at 22.55 on Operation ROACH 47/48/PHYSICIAN 54. Having successfully delivered five containers at the last-mentioned drop site, engine problems forced the abandonment of the rest of the sortie, and the remaining ten containers had to be jettisoned. JD171 took off at 22.57 with the crew of F/O Malinowski on board, whose brief, according to the ORB, was to attempt Operations PHYSICIAN 38/52. According to Freddie Clark, they were engaged on Operation ROACH 54/40/BLUEFISH, in which endeavour they were unsuccessful, and cited enemy opposition as the cause of their failure. Another recently-arrived crew, that of P/O Kalkus, took off at 23.01 in BB379 on Operations SCIENTIST 34/ARTIST 6, and, again through the lack of a reception committee at the first drop site, they were able to complete the second element only. Sgt Brown and crew took off in DG253 at 23.03 on Operations ROACH 43/PHYSICIAN 53, and completed the second element before landing safely at 04.05. The departures continued thick and fast with the take-off of DT726 at 23.05, with P/O Bown at the controls. He and his crew were bound for Operations ROACH 41/50, but they succeeded in completing only the second element. Operations TURNIP 11/MARROW 38 were handed to S/L Griffiths and crew, who set off for Holland at 23.20 in JD180, and returned at 03.10 to report a successful outcome. Last away on this night, at 23.40, was JD156, containing the crew of F/L Dodkin, who were to attempt Operation MARROW 40/41. They landed safely exactly four hours later, having completed only the first element.

On the night of the 11/12th, it was the weather, rather than the lack of reception committees that thwarted all seven sorties, and only P/O Bown and crew achieved any degree of success, when completing only the second element of their brief, Operations ROACH 23/JUGGLER 2 in DT726 between 22.55 and 04.40. The details of the other sorties are as follows; F/O Zbucki in JD179 on Operations ROACH 47/48, 22.50 to 02.15. F/O Malinowski in JD171 on Operations ROACH 54/40/BLUEFISH, 22.52 to 05.00. F/O Wilkinson in HR666 on Operations ROACH 35/PHYSICIAN 46, 22.57 to 02.06. Sgt Brown in BB364 on Operations ROACH 24/PHYSICIAN 48, 23.00 to 02.30. F/O Downes in BB330 on Operations PHYSICIAN 16/26, 23.03 to 03.25. F/L Dodkin in JD156 on Operations FARMER 3/OTHELLO/LABRADOR 2, 23.05 to 02.05. The weather conditions did not prevent the main event of the night, a raid by almost eight hundred aircraft on Düsseldorf, from being a major success. Despite an errant Oboe marker, which lured away a proportion of the bombing, sufficient hit the centre of the city to cause a massive area of fire, and knock out production at dozens of war industry factories. Almost thirteen hundred people were killed, and eight ships were sunk or damaged in the inland port. The thirty-eight missing bombers equalled the Command's highest losses of the campaign to date, and to these were added five aircraft lost from a simultaneous 8 Group attack on Münster, which was conducted as a mass H2S trial.

A moderately effective attack on Bochum followed on the night of the 12/13th, when 138 Squadron launch three sorties to France. F/L Hooper and crew took off first, at 23.10, in JD154, to carry out Operations PHYSICIAN 60/42/WATCHMAKER, and returned at 03.10 to report a successful outing. S/L Griffiths and crew took off at 23.18 in JD180 on Operations COCKLE 26/40, but were able to complete only the first element. BB379 lifted off the ground at 23.27 with the crew of P/O Kalkus on board, and when they returned from Operation COCKLE 28, they were able to report a successful sortie. Tempsford resounded to the roar of Merlin engines on the following night, the 13/14th, as a flurry of activity either side of 23.00 saw ten Halifaxes take off, mostly for France, and with mixed fortunes. JD171 was the first away at 22.45, with the crew of F/O Malinowski on board. They were to undertake Operations ROACH 47/48/53, which they were able to complete in a sortie lasting six hours and ten minutes. F/O Wilkinson and crew took off at 22.50 in HR666 to carry out Operations SCIENTIST 22/26, but their efforts were in vain. JD180 climbed away from Tempsford at 22.52, bearing S/L Griffiths and crew on Operations DONKEYMAN 5/ROACH 40/BLUEFISH, of which they completed only the first element. On board JD179 with F/O Zbucki and crew, was the first American OSS agent to be dropped into France. They took off at 22.56, and headed for the Tours area to conduct Operations SACRISTAN/CARDINAL/SCIENTIST 39/BUTLER I, and completed all elements. Agent, E F Floege, was forty-five years old, and had been born in Chicago, but ran a French bus company in Angers. He was dropped with a sabotage instructor, "Olivier", who would make his way to Lille. Although eventually captured, Floege would escape and survive the war. Departures continued at Tempsford with the take-off for France and Belgium, at 22.58, of P/O Kalkus and crew in JD171, who were bound for Operations

OTHELLO/ROACH 38/FARMER 3. They returned after five hours and fifteen minutes to report completing the first element only. At 23.03, F/O Downes lifted BB334 off the runway to head for France on Operation SCIENTIST 29. Their sortie involved the longest round-trip of the night, lasting a minute under nine hours, but despite the effort invested, they had to report an unsuccessful outcome. F/L Hooper and crew took off for Belgium at 23.05 in JD154, although this aircraft is also recorded in the ORB as the mount of Sgt Brown and crew. They were to attempt Operation LABRADOR 2/PHYSICIAN 58, but managed to complete only the first element. This was the final sortie of F/L Hooper's current tour, and, after a short rest, he would take up a posting with 161 Squadron as a Lysander pilot. Sgt Brown and crew took off at 23.10, perhaps in JD154, briefed to carry out Operations COCKLE 34/39, but were unsuccessful. F/Sgt Armstrong and crew were undertaking their maiden SOE sortie, Operation COCKLE 37, when taking off at 23.30 in, it is believed, BB378. The ORB cites aircraft "D" 628, which did not exist, and BB378 was the owner of D at the time. Sadly, they were unsuccessful on this occasion, for which, no explanation is provided. The final take-off on this night was that of F/L Dodkin and crew in JD156 at 23.55. They were assigned to Operations PHYSICIAN 44/ROACH 24, in which endeavour they were successful.

A predominantly Lancaster force pounded the Ruhr city of Oberhausen on the night of the 14/15th, while 138 Squadron dispatched six sorties to France late in the evening. F/O Zbucki and crew began proceedings with a take-off at 22.55 in JD179 to carry out Operations JUGGLER 4/ROACH 23, but they returned at 05.05 to report failing to complete the drop. F/O Malinowski and crew were next away in JD155 at 22.57 to undertake Operations ROACH 46/DONKEYMAN I, which they were able to complete in a round-trip of just under four and a quarter hours. *(The ORB records both JD155 and JD171 as bearing the code letter "P". JD155 was coded "M", but as both aircraft were operating on this night, it can not be certain which crew was on board.)* F/L Dodkin and crew took off at 23.15 in JD156 on Operations PHYSICIAN 58/ROACH 44, which they failed to complete. Four minutes after their departure, JD171 took off with F/O Wilkinson at the controls, and he and his crew successfully fulfilled their brief for Operations PHYSICIAN 48/46. At 23.20, Sgt Brown and crew took off in DG253 to attempt Operations ROACH 30/PHYSICIAN 56, and completed the second element only. Finally, at 00.09, F/Sgt Armstrong and crew set off on Operations PHYSICIAN 45/61, flying in BB378, and they returned four hours and ten minutes later to report a successful outcome.

The main force stayed at home on the night of the 15/16th, while 138 Squadron launched three sorties to France in a brief flurry of activity either side of 23.00. F/O Downes and crew were first away at 22.58 in BB378, and carrying two Canadians, Lieutenants Frank Pikersgill and John Macalister, to drop into the Cher Valley, north of Valencay under Operations ARCHDEACON/PLUMBER/PHYSICIAN 55/56. The two men were to set up a sub-circuit, but they would be arrested after five days on the ground. S/L Griffiths and crew took off in HR666 at 23.00 to undertake, and, ultimately, complete, Operations SCIENTIST 22/26, which, based on the ten-hour flight time, must have been deep in southern France, perhaps in the previously-visited Lons-le-Saunier region. P/O Kalkus and crew were the last to depart Tempsford, at 23.04 in DT726 on Operation SCIENTIST 30, in which endeavor, despite a round-trip of more than ten hours, they were unsuccessful.

138 Squadron ground crews spent the 16th preparing seven Halifaxes for operations to France that night, and two new crews were posted in, those of Sgt James and F/Sgt Sherwood. Cologne would be the main target for a bombing contingent of 212 aircraft from 1, 5 and 8 Groups, sixteen of which were to employ H2S as a blind bombing device, rather than Oboe. The recently-arrived S/L Pitt and crew took off at 22.56 in JD156 to start the ball rolling, but their maiden SOE sortie, Operations PUBLICAN 1/PHYSICIAN 51, were not to be rewarded with success. BB379 took to the air at 23.00 with the crew of P/O Zbucki on board, bound for Operations BUTLER 2/SCIENTIST 43, which they were able to complete as briefed. F/Os Downes and Wilkinson are both logged as taking off at 23.06 in BB330 and JD180 on Operations PHYSICIAN 72/MISTRAL 1 and PHYSICIAN 75/71 respectively, and both returned to report successful outcomes. Having taken off at 23.09, engine problems curtailed the efforts of F/O Malinowski and crew in JD171, forcing them to abort Operations ROACH 51/30. Sgt Brown and crew had Operations DONKEYMAN 8/PHYSICIAN 60 as their task, as they took off in DG253 at 23.10, and their efforts were blessed with success. F/Sgt Armstrong and crew were last away, at 23.20, in BB378, to attempt Operations PHYSICIAN 46/43, of which only the first element was completed.

France was the destination for all six 138 Squadron crews on the night of the 17/18th, the long hours of daylight concentrating take-off times at around 23.00. P/O Kalkus and crew began to roll at 22.59 in BB379, heading for their drop site for Operations SCIENTIST 61/PARSON. Their brief was to deliver an agent, Francois Vallee, to the Rennes area of north-western France. Vallee was already a seasoned campaigner, who had been awarded the Military Cross for his SOE work in Tunisia. Sgt Brown and crew took off a minute later in BB364 on Operations PUBLICAN 1/ROACH 56/BUTTERFISH/BLOATER, but, for an undisclosed reason, their efforts failed. F/O Malinowski and crew took off at 23.04 in JD155 to attempt Operations ROACH 51/30, and were successful only with regard to the first element. At 23.05, JD180 took to the air with the crew of S/L Griffiths on board, bound for Operations JUGGLER 1/PERCH 42/BLUEFISH, of which the first element only was successful. F/Sgt Armstrong and crew got away at 23.08 in BB378 to carry out Operations PHYSICIAN 66/DONKEYMAN 9, but returned at 04.20 to report an unsuccessful outcome. F/L Dodkin and crew completed the departures at 23.15 in JD156. Their brief was to undertake Operation PHYSICIAN 43, and they returned after just three and a half hours to claim success.

A training crash on the morning of the 19th wrote off veteran Halifax W1229, which was under the captaincy of W/O Klosowski at the time. He had F/O Krzehlik and F/Sgt Rzewuski beside him under instruction as the Halifax landed at Tempsford at 10.35 in a strong cross wind, which caused it to bounce as it touched down. The undercarriage collapsed, but all on board were able to walk away. The major activity on this night was an attack by almost three hundred Halifaxes and Stirlings from 3, 4, 6 and 8 Groups on the Schneider armaments works at Le Creusot in France. This had been the target for a massed daylight raid by 5 Group Lancasters in the previous October, and belonged to the very same Jacques Schneider, who had put up the famous and coveted Schneider Trophy, which Britain had won outright with the Mitchell-designed Supermarine S6B more than a decade earlier. The plan of attack called for the main force crews to identify the target for themselves in the light of Pathfinder flares, but this was something to which they were not accustomed, and the factory complex escaped a telling blow.

Eight 138 Squadron Halifaxes had been made ready for operations, six with destinations in France, and two to deliver supplies to Holland. Those bound for France took off first, beginning with F/O Lewicki and crew on their maiden SOE sortie at 22.49 in JD155. They had been assigned to Operations SCIENTIST 65/67, which, despite having to dodge flak at the French coast, they were able to complete. F/O Zankowski and crew were also embarking on their maiden SOE sortie as they departed Tempsford in BB379 at 22.50 to attempt Operations SCIENTIST 42/69, but their efforts would not be blessed with a successful outcome. Two departures were logged at 22.55, those of S/L Pitt and crew in JD172, and F/L Milne and crew, the third debutants on this night, in JD154. They were assigned to Operations WAITER and SCIENTIST 44/62 respectively, and while the former was successful, the latter was not. F/O Downes and crew were in HR666, which lifted off the ground at 23.04 on Operation SCIENTIST 9, and returned almost nine hours later to report a successful outcome. F/Sgt Armstrong and crew got away at 23.05 in DT726 on Operations SCIENTIST 56/15, and completed only the second element. BB309 led the way to Holland at 23.29 with F/O Wilkinson at the controls. Operation LEEK 8/CATARRH 12 took them just three hours and fifty-four minutes to complete from take-off to landing. F/L Dodkin and crew were in BB364, and they took off at 23.35 on Operations LETTUCE 11/TURNIP 11/SOTURN I, only to have the weather thwart their efforts.

On the following night, sixty Lancasters from 5 Group carried out a moderately successful attack on the old Zeppelin works at Friedrichshafen, which had now been turned over to the production of Würzburg radar sets. The target was deep in southern Germany close to the Swiss border, and the outward flight down the length of France provided cover for the Tempsford units to carry out their work over that country. 138 Squadron made ready ten Halifaxes for yet another night of major activity, and sent the first one, JD171, racing down the runway at 22.49 with the crew of F/O Zankowski (navigator) on board. They were to attempt Operations TRAINER 8/PHYSICIAN 76, and returned almost six hours later to confirm a successful sortie. Two departures are recorded for 22.50, those of BB378 and BB316, which had the crews of F/O Wilkinson and F/L Milne on board, undertaking Operations PUBLICAN I/ROACH 56/BUTTERFISH/BLOATER and PHYSICIAN 79/73/MISTRAL 2 respectively. The former failed to complete their drop, probably through adverse weather conditions, which blighted some regions of France with ten-tenths low cloud and rain, but the latter was able to report a successful outcome. F/O Lewicki and crew took off at 22.54 in JD155 on Operations ROACH 35/38/39, and returned almost six hours later to admit defeat. P/O Kalkus and crew were next away at 22.56 in BB379, to carry out Operations ROACH 40/41/42/BLUEFISH/DAGGER, which they completed in a round-trip of five and a half hours duration. W/C Speare chose this night for his first sortie since taking command, and departed Tempsford at 22.57 in JD180 to attempt Operations PHYSICIAN 50/70. He landed at 03.27 to report a successful outcome, after dropping a total of fifteen containers onto his assigned reception points. The two take-offs logged at 23.00 were those of F/O Malinowski and F/L Dodkin in DT726 and BB334, on Operations SCIENTIST 71 and SCIENTIST 66/68 respectively. The former sortie, which took nine and a half hours to complete, is recorded in the ORB as unsuccessful, while a Polish source states otherwise. The latter is described as successful. DG253 took to the air at 23.05 with the crew of Sgt Brown on board, but their efforts to complete Operation SCIENTIST 58 went unrewarded. F/O Zbucki and crew completed the departures at 23.06, when taking off in

HR666 on Operation SCIENTIST 48, and, despite spending almost ten hours aloft, they also had to report a gallant failure.

The Ruhr offensive resumed on the night of the 21/22nd with the first of a hectic round of four major operations in the space of five nights. More than seven hundred aircraft took off for Krefeld, and 619 of these bombed within three miles of the city centre aiming point. These districts became engulfed in a raging fire, and 47% of the entire built-up area was destroyed, this amounting to over five and a half thousand houses. More than a thousand people lost their lives, and 72,000 others were rendered homeless. The attack took place in moonlight, and this assisted the night fighter crews in finding their quarry. Forty-four bombers failed to return, and although this was not the highest loss to date in a single night, it was a new record for a single target. The moon squadrons were also out and about on this night, once more over France, for which 138 Squadron made ready three Halifaxes. S/L Griffiths and crew led the way, with a departure at 23.00 in JD180, bound for Operations PUBLICAN I/ROACH 56/BUTTERFISH, the first element of which only was completed. According to the ORB, F/O Downes and crew took off next, at 23.04, in DT542, NF-Q, an aircraft which had come to grief on take-off at Malta's Luqa airfield back in December. The ORB entry is probably an error, and the likelihood is, that the scribe, in seeking an NF-Q, checked back in the records and picked DT542 rather than the current Q, JD269. Operations PRIVET 2/SCIENTIST 40 were successfully carried out, and the Halifax returned safely after a trip of almost six hours. P/O Kalkus and crew were in JD179, and took off at 23.07 on Operations PHYSICIAN 58/68, of which the first element only was completed.

On the following morning, W/O Klosowski, with F/O Krzehlik and F/O Matylis under instruction, returned from a training flight in DT727 to attempt a three-engine landing. The Halifax swung off the runway, and came to a halt embedded in a hangar, injuring two members of the crew. This was W/O Klosowski's second landing crash in four days, although his hands were probably not on the controls on either occasion. He was, in fact, filling in as an instructor, after finishing his second tour, and was awaiting the start of his third. That night, over five hundred aircraft were involved in a devastating raid on the Ruhr city of Mülheim, in which over eleven hundred houses were destroyed, and a further twelve thousand were damaged to some extent. Industrial and public buildings were also severely afflicted, and it was later assessed, that this attack wiped out 64% of the town's built-up area. On the debit side, it was another night of heavy losses for the Command, this time amounting to thirty-five aircraft.

Twelve sorties were mounted by 138 Squadron on this night, ten of them to France and one each to Belgium and Holland. The ORB entries are once more barely legible, and the following is the best that can be made of them. The first to depart Tempsford was BB334 at 22.34 with the crew of F/L Dodkin, who had been briefed for Operations SCIENTIST 37/36. They returned after a flight of four minutes under ten hours, suggesting that the drop site, which was successfully serviced, lay deep in southern France. F/O Malinowski and crew were the next away at 22.39 in JD171 on Operation TOMCOD I, which also had a successful outcome. Sgt James and crew took off a minute later in BB330 to undertake their maiden SOE sortie, Operation STATIONER ?, which they failed to complete. Two departures are logged at 22.45, those of DT726 and HR666, with the crews of F/O Zankowski and F/L Lewicki on Operations SCIENTIST 71 and SCIENTIST 58 respectively, and both were completed successfully during round-trips of more than eight hours. At 22.50, it was the turn of F/O Hart and crew to begin their maiden SOE sortie in JD154 on Operations PHYSICIAN 51/77. Sadly, it was not destined to be a successful debut, but the cause of their failure is not disclosed. S/L Pitt and crew were assigned to Operations ROACH 54/TOE A/BLUEBELL, and took off at 22.59, it is believed, in JD172, returning at 04.35 to report a successful outcome. BB378 took off at 23.00, carrying P/O Bown and crew on Operations ROACH 2?/40/41, but engine failure forced them to return home after two and a half hours in the air. BB309 took to the air at 23.02 with the crew of F/O Wilkinson on board, bound for Belgium to carry out Operations MOUFLON/CARACAL 5/GIBBON 4, which, according to the ORB, was successfully accomplished, while Freddie Clark states that it failed through adverse weather conditions. The two departures logged at 23.05 involved the crews of Sgt Brown and F/O Zbucki in BB364 and JD179 respectively, who were assigned to Operations PHYSICIAN 67/ROACH 55 and DONKEYMAN 9/PHYSICIAN 59. Neither sortie achieved its aims, the former for an undisclosed reason, and the latter because of navigation instrument failure. F/O Downes and crew were last away on this night of hectic activity, taking off at 23.54 in DT543 to carry out Operations LETTUCE 11/TURNIP 11 over Holland. The attempt was not successful, for which the weather was responsible.

The moon period ended on the night of the 23/24th, when the main force stayed at home, and 138 Squadron sent three aircraft each to France and Holland. F/L Milne and crew started the ball rolling at 23.32, as they took off, possibly in DG316, for Operation SCIENTIST 28 over France. The landing time of 08.50 suggests that it was a deep penetration flight, which was concluded successfully. F/O Zbucki and crew took off at 23.57 to undertake Operation SCIENTIST 46, an eight-hour round trip, with a time on target of 02.47. Unfortunately, an engine problem forced them to turn back when an hour out, when they must have been somewhere near the French coast. The ORB records JD179 NF-Z as the Halifax, but JD179 was coded F, and a Polish source claims that it was DG543 NF-G. BB364 took off at 23.59 with Sgt Brown and crew on board, and headed for France to conduct Operation SCIENTIST 48, only to turn back early on with engine problems. A Polish source has F/O Kalkus and crew departing Tempsford at midnight in BB379, with F/Sgt Zabicki in the pilot's seat. F/O Kalkus was the son of G/C Kalkus, RAF, who was the Polish commanding officer of 18 O.T.U, which was responsible for training Polish airmen. They were bound for Holland on Operations TURNIP 2/LETTUCE 2, and were on the way home when hit by flak and finished off by a night fighter. The Halifax crashed about five miles beyond the northern suburbs of Amsterdam, killing the pilot, crew captain and two others, and delivering the survivors into enemy hands. S/L Griffiths and crew were in JD180, and took off at 00.20 to carry out Operations LEMONTREE/PARSNIP 6, an SIS drop first attempted on the night of the 10/11th, and which had failed twice more since. The first element involved the delivery of an agent and his packages blind, and the second, the dropping of seven containers and four boxes of chocolate. All proceeded according to plan, but it was Giskes who benefitted from the supplies, and, no doubt, shared in the chocolate. BB309 was the mount of F/O Wilkinson and crew, as they brought the current phase of operations to a conclusion with a take-off at 00.35 on Operation LEEK 9 over Holland. Sadly, compass failure caused the sortie to be abandoned, and they were back on the ground in three hours and ten minutes. During the course of the month, the squadron dispatched over ninety sorties, many of them successfully concluded, and lost a single crew.

Above left: Navigator F/O Kalkus, captain of crew killed during special operation to Holland on 23/24 June 1943. Above right: F/Sgt Zabicki, 1st pilot of navigator F/O Kalkus's crew. (PISM via PH)

On the 24/25th, after their night's rest, over six hundred Pathfinder and main force aircraft descended upon Wuppertal, to try to visit upon Elberfeld the devastation experienced by its twin Barmen a month earlier. In this they were successful. More than three thousand houses and 171 industrial premises were reduced to rubble, and it was later estimated, that only 6% of the town's built-up area remained intact. Eighteen hundred people were killed on the ground, but a further thirty-four aircraft were lost as the defenders fought back. The run of successes was brought to an end on the following night, when the notoriously elusive oil town of Gelsenkirchen escaped all but minor damage. In an echo of the past, bombs were sprayed all over the Ruhr, and thirty aircraft and crews represented a high price to pay for the failure.

June was brought to an end with the first of a three raid series against Cologne spanning the turn of the month. Mounted on the night of the 28/29th, the operation was beset with difficulties, which included cloud cover over the target, the consequent use of unreliable skymarkers, failure of equipment in half of the Oboe Mosquito force, and a long delay in opening the attack. Despite these annoyances, Cologne suffered one of the most devastating attacks of the entire war, in which 6,400 buildings were destroyed and fifteen thousand others were damaged. More than 4,300 people lost their lives, while the Command sustained a slightly reduced loss of twenty-five aircraft. Unknown to the shaken residents of the Rhineland Capital, their ordeal had only just begun.

July 1943

With the moon not rising for almost two weeks, 138 Squadron's first sortie of the month was attempted during the dark period on the night of the 1/2nd. Sgt Brown and crew took off at 22.50 in BB378 to attempt Operation TOMCOD 5, but found the conditions over France to be unsuitable, too dark, in fact, and the sortie was abandoned. The campaign against Cologne continued at the hands of more than six hundred aircraft on the night of the 3/4th, when a further 2,200 houses were reduced to ruins along with twenty industrial buildings. The series was concluded by an all-Lancaster force on the night of the 8/9th, after which, the city authorities were able to establish, that eleven thousand buildings had been destroyed during the three raids, five and a half thousand people had lost their lives, and a further 350,000 were without homes.

By the time that clandestine operations resumed, on the night of the 12/13th, the Ruhr offensive had effectively run its course. A second attempt on Gelsenkirchen on the 9/10th had gone the way of the first, and two other operations to the region would not take place until the final week of July. Harris could look back over the past few months with genuine satisfaction at the performance of his squadrons. Much of Germany's industrial heartland now lay in ruins, forcing it to disperse its industry, and use up some of its enormous manufacturing slack. In addition to this, massive resources were being invested in home defence, rather than on the eastern front, where they were most urgently required. It is true, that the Command's losses had been grievously high, but the factories were more than keeping pace with the rate of attrition, and eager new crews were flooding in from the training schools in the Dominions and America to fill the gaps.

The crews of F/O Perrins and Sgt Hodges had been posted in on the 10th, and they would undergo a period of familiarization. According to Freddie Clark, twelve sorties were attempted by 138 Squadron on this first night of the new phase of operations, eleven of them to France, and one to Belgium. The ORB records only nine of them, each with a destination in France. First off the ground at 22.44 was BB309 with the crew of the newly-promoted F/L Wilkinson, who had been assigned to Operations ROACH 56/63, neither of which was completed. P/O Bown and crew took off at 22.50 in DT726, and failed also with their attempt at Operations ROACH57/111. F/O Hart and crew had been briefed for Operations BUTLER 4/SCIENTIST 73, and took off at 23.00 in JD154, returning at 04.15 to report completing the first element only. 23.02 brought the take-off of HR666 with F/O Downes and crew on board, whose brief was to attempt Operations PUBLICAN 3/ROACH 89, in which endeavour they were unsuccessful. BB334 was next away at 23.05, carrying the crew of F/L Zbucki on Operations ROACH 126/MUSICIAN 4, which they failed to complete, and having spent only three hours and thirty minutes in the air, it seems likely that the weather, or, perhaps, a technical issue, was responsible for curtailing their efforts. F/O Zankowski and crew took off in BB317 at 23.12 to carry out Operations ROACH 99/SCIENTIST 86, and they, too, failed to complete. The ORB records S/L Pitt's destination for Operations CLAUDIUS, POINTER, GIBBON 5, LABRADOR 3 and CARACAL 6, as France, while Freddie Clark writes that it was Belgium, but the weather rendered the sortie ineffective anyway. We are not privy to the take-off time of JD155, and know only that it crashed at 00.30 at St-Paul-sur-Risle, about twenty miles south-east of le Havre. F/L Lewicki was the crew captain, with F/Sgt Jonski at the controls, and all on board lost their lives while outbound to the drop site for Operations ROACH 94/92.

The newly-promoted F/L Malinowski took off with his crew in JD171 at 00.35, to undertake Operations ROACH 86/121, of which only the second element was completed. It had been a disappointing night, that had seen only four locations serviced as planned for the loss of a valued crew. There was much other activity over France on this night, as almost three hundred 1, 5 and 8 Group Lancasters made their way to and from Turin, and this would obviously have alerted the defences.

The night of the 13/14th brought a devastating raid on Aachen, which left almost three thousand buildings totally ruined. It was also another night of feverish activity for 138 Squadron, which saw the launch of eleven of its Halifaxes on supply drops to France. Proceedings began at 22.38 with the departure of F/O Downes and crew in HR666 on Operations ROACH 77/78, which they were able to complete. Three aircraft were logged as taking off at 22.45, JD179, BB309 and JD156, with the crews of F/L Zbucki, F/L Wilkinson and Sgt Brown on Operations SCIENTIST 54/56, ROACH 61/134 and ROACH 127/85 respectively, and all were successfully carried out. JD269 took off at 22.53 with F/L Milne at the controls bound for Operations ROACH 95/109, and the run of successes continued. DT726 was the next to take to the air, at 22.55, with P/O Bown and crew on board, heading for Operations ROACH 30/44, which, for an undisclosed reason, they were unable to complete. F/O Freyer and crew took off on their maiden SOE sortie at 23.03 in JD171 to attempt Operations TOMCOD 30/15, and managed to complete the first element. Sgt James and crew were on their second SOE sortie, having failed on their first, and took off at 23.05 in BB330, no doubt eager to gain their first success. Their brief was to attempt Operation SCIENTIST 79, and when they landed in the breaking dawn at 04.35, they were able to report a successful outcome. F/O Hart and crew took off at 23.08 in JD154 to carry out Operation SCIENTIST 48, but their sortie was one of the night's few failures. S/L Griffiths and crew brought the departures to a conclusion, when taking off at 23.12 in JD180 to attempt Operations TOMCOD 32/39, of which the first element only was completed. A Polish source has F/O Zankowski and crew also involved on this night in JD312, and assigned to Operations ROACH 54/56, for which a logbook entry provides testimony. It had been a successful night for the squadron, in which sixty-eight containers had been delivered.

There were just three 138 Squadron aircraft to make ready on the 14th for French targets that night, and W/C Speare led the way, when taking off at 22.45 in JD269 on Operations ROACH 69/TOMCOD 5, of which he completed the first element only. F/O Malinowski and crew followed in their commanding officer's wake at 22.48 in JD171, to attempt Operations SCIENTIST 72/TOMCOD 31, and returned at 04.50 to report a successful outcome. F/Sgt Armstrong and crew took off at 23.02 in BB378 on Operations SCIENTIST 73/ROACH 120, and managed to complete the second element. The following night, the 15/16th, brought a squadron record of sixteen sorties, and such is the volume of activity from this point, that it is necessary to condense the account into a more diarized form, with additional information where available. In chronological order, the sorties for this night, all of which were initially to France, were as follows; F/L Wilkinson in JD180 on Operation SCIENTIST 50, 22.25 to 05.00, successful. F/O Downes in HR666 on Operation SCIENTIST 57, 22.28 to 04.10, successful. F/O Freyer in JD179 on Operations SCIENTIST 84/32, 22.30 to 04.40, unsuccessful. F/O Zankowski in JD312 on Operation SCIENTIST 104, 22.32 to 05.34, unsuccessful. W/O Scott in BB334 on Operations ROACH 79/80, 22.35 to 01.35, unsuccessful. F/O Hart in JD154 on

Operations ROACH 88/112, 22.38 to 04.38, successful. F/O Perrins in JD156 on Operation SCIENTIST 78, 22.41 to 04.42, unsuccessful. F/L Milne and crew took off at 22.43 in JD269 on Operations ROACH 138/126/HERD 9, the first two elements of which were supply drops over France. After successfully delivering fifteen containers, they flew on to Germany, to a location about five miles north-west of Mülheim an der Mosel, close to the border with Luxembourg, where an agent was dropped blind. The operational plan had called for the drop to coincide with a bombing raid over western Germany, but it was actually an all-Halifax attack on the Peugeot motor works at Montbeliard, near the Franco/Swiss frontier, that provided the cover, after which, a safe return was made to land at 04.45. F/O Krywda in JD171 on Operations SCIENTIST 91/92, 22.44 to 04.30, unsuccessful. F/Sgt Sherwood in BB317 on Operations ROACH 82/SACRISTAN I, 22.45 to 04.55, unsuccessful. P/O Bown and crew took off at 22.50 in DT726 on Operations CLAUDIUS/POINTER/MUSICIAN 4/OTHELLO 1, the first two elements of which were in France, and the others in Belgium. Two agents and two packages were dropped, but no reception committee appeared at OTHELLO, and that element remained uncompleted. F/Sgt Armstrong in BB309 on Operations SCIENTIST 76/83, 22.55 to 05.15, second element only successful. S/L Pitt in JD172 on Operations ROACH 124/84, 22.55 to 04.00, unsuccessful. Sgt James in BB330? on Operations ROACH 95/SALESMAN 5, 23.01 to 03.33, second element only completed. Sgt Brown in DG253 on Operations ROACH 83/55, 23.03 to 05.00, successful. Sgt Hodges in BB378 on Operations BRICKLAYER 1/BUTLER 3, 23.05 to 04.05, first element only successful.

The unprecedented workload on the ground crews continued on the 16th, when another fourteen Halifaxes were prepared for operations to France that night. The number of sorties being launched matched that of a front-line bomber squadron, although, there were no long trains of bombs to load in the summer heat. The night's Order of Battle was as follows; F/L Milne in JD269 on Operations SCIENTIST 41/44, 22.38 to 05.36, unsuccessful. F/L Wilkinson in BB309 on Operations TOMCOD 27/28, 22.45 to 06.30, successful. F/O Freyer in JD312 on Operations TOMCOD 18/ROACH 73? 22.45 to 05.30, successful. F/O Hart in JD154 on Operations ROACH 64/PUBLICAN 3, 22.45 to 06.00, unsuccessful. P/O Bown in DT726 on Operations ROACH 119/59, 22.46 to 06.20, second element only completed. F/O Downes in HR666 on Operations ROACH 52/63, 22.47 to 06.20, successful. Sgt James in BB330 on Operations ROACH 57/111, 22.48 to 06.50, unsuccessful. Sgt Brown in DG253 on Operations ROACH 104/87, 22.50 to 07.45, successful. F/O Perrins in JD156 on Operations ROACH 107/72, 22.50 to 06.25, successful. W/O Scott in JD172 on Operation PRIVET 5, 22.59 to 07.12, unsuccessful. F/O Krywda in JD319 on Operations TOMCOD 12/17, 23.00 to 06.24, successful. Sgt Hodges in BB317 on Operations ROACH 62/SCIENTIST 86, 23.04 to 05.00 (Mildenhall), unsuccessful. F/O Malinowski in JD171 on Operations SCIENTIST 42/88, 23.31 to 05.30 (Mildenhall), successful. S/L Griffiths in JD180 on Operations ACROBAT 5/ROACH 115, 23.37 to 06.23, successful.

The pace slackened somewhat on the night of the 17/18th, when just three sorties were dispatched to France. F/L Zbucki and crew took off in JD319 at 22.45 to attempt Operations TOMCOD 5/10, and they returned at 05.15 to confirm a successful outcome. F/Sgt Sherwood and crew followed at 22.50 in BB334 on Operation DONKEYMAN 10, which was also concluded successfully during a flight lasting four hours and fifty minutes. F/O Zankowski and crew were last away at 23.05 in JD312 on Operations ROACH 105/122, and completed the first element only. A return to a maximum effort on the night of the 22/23rd brought thirteen sorties to France and two to Denmark, but the weather would have a say in their outcome. F/O Malinowski and crew took off for Denmark at 21.28 in JD171 on Operations TABLEMARGERINE/TABLEGOSSIP 4/5/TABLESANDWICH, and succeeded in dropping an agent and two packages at the last-mentioned, and something at TABLEGOSSIP 5, but were prevented by the weather conditions from completing the other elements. F/O Zankowski and crew departed Tempsford at 21.41 in JD312, also bound for Denmark to carry out Operation TABLEJAM 1, and delivered six containers before returning to land at Syerston at 04.26, where they were joined by the Malinowski crew twenty-eight minutes later.

The crews bound for France stayed on the ground, and it was a further forty minutes, before they were led away at 22.20 by F/L Wilkinson and P/O Bown and their crews in JD180 and DT726 respectively, having been briefed for Operations COVEY and PENNYFARTHING. The former was completed, but the latter not, and both Halifaxes landed at Tangmere on return, as would the remainder of those operating out of Tempsford. The other sorties were as follows; F/L Milne in DG253 on Operations ACROBAT 2/MESSENGER, 22.23 to 05.30, unsuccessful. F/O Freyer in HR666 on Operations BOOMERANG/ROACH 7, 22.27 to 05.40, two agents successfully dropped. Sgt James in BB334 on Operations SACRISTAN/CORISTOR, 22.30 to 05.05, unsuccessful. F/Sgt Sherwood in BB330 on Operations SCIENTIST 84/32, 22.36 to 04.25, unsuccessful. F/Sgt Armstrong in BB378 on Operation DONKEYMAN 15, 22.38 to 05.25, successful. F/O Perrins in JD156 on Operation SCIENTIST 103, 22.40 to 04.02, unsuccessful. F/O Downes in JD179 on Operations ROACH 60/GURNET/REVOLVER/ROACH 64, 22.57 to 02.40 unsuccessful. S/L Pitt in JD172 on Operations STATIONER 18/DEAN/TOMCOD 15/SCIENTIST 74, 23.00 to 06.00, third element only successful. F/O Hart and crew took off in JD269 at 23.00 to undertake Operations ROACH 62/PUBLICAN 2/BEVY, but failed to make contact with a reception committee at either of the first two drop sites. They continued on to the third pinpoint, a dozen or so miles south-south-west of Melun, on the edge of the Forest of Fontainbleu, some fifty miles south of Paris. The operations order allowed the crew captain leeway in selecting the precise location within a five-mile radius, and, if none were identified, to bring the "full load" home. The agents, Dutchman Guido Zembsch-Schreve and his wireless operator, Anglo-Frenchman, J M C Planel, were to set up a reseau, Pierre/Jacques, and were dropped as planned with their packages, landing in a field of uncut corn on the edge of the forest. Zembsch-Schreve would be arrested in April 1944, and, unknowingly cross paths with PoW Freddie Clark in Paris in May. Afterwards, he was to spend time in Ravensbrück and Buchenwald concentration camps, as well as Camp Dora, the forced labour facility in the Harz Mountains, devoted to the underground construction of the V-2. Happily, he would survive the war, and one day meet up with Freddie Clark in London. The two final sorties on this night were; F/O Krywda in JD319 on Operations SCIENTIST 76/96, 23.07 to 04.47, first element only successful. W/O Scott in BB309 on Operation DONKEYMAN 18, 23.25 to 05.00, unsuccessful.

Since Aachen, Germany had been left unmolested by Harris's hordes. During this period, however, he had been planning a follow-up to the Ruhr offensive, to be unleashed against one of Germany's premier cities. The intention of Operation Gomorrah was to erase the objective from the map in a short, sharp series of attacks until the job was done, and it was estimated, that ten thousand tons of bombs would be required. Having been spared by the weather from hosting the first one thousand bomber raid in May 1942, Hamburg now suited Harris's criteria perfectly. As Germany's Second City, it possessed the necessary political status, and was an important centre of war industry, particularly in the area of U-Boot construction. As far as operational considerations were concerned, the city was accessible from the sea, without the need to fly deep into German airspace, and was close enough to the bomber stations to allow a large force to approach and withdraw within the few hours of darkness afforded by mid summer. Finally, beyond the range of Oboe, which had proved so decisive at the Ruhr, Hamburg boasted the wide River Elbe through its centre, to provide a strong H2S signature for the navigators high above.

The final week of July had become the traditional time to attack Hamburg, and so it was now, and as the crews prepared on the afternoon of the 24th, for the first operation of what would become a four-raid series, a new device was being loaded into their aircraft. Window had actually been devised a year earlier, but its use had been vetoed in case the enemy copied it for use against Britain. Ironically, the German scientists had already developed their own version known as Düppel, which had also been withheld for the same reason. It consisted of aluminium-backed strips of paper packed in bundles, which, when released into the air stream, floated slowly to earth in giant, reflective clouds. This swamped the enemy radar system with false returns, making it impossible for night fighter, searchlight and flak crews to identify and lock on to a genuine target. Windowing would begin at a predetermined point over the North Sea on the way out, and continue throughout the raid until a second point was reached on the way home.

A force of 791 aircraft stood ready for take-off in the late evening of the 24th, and the majority experienced a relatively uneventful outward flight. A number of aircraft were shot down during this stage of the operation, however, but each was massively off course, probably returning early with technical difficulties, and was consequently outside of the protection of the bomber stream. The efficacy of Window was immediately apparent to the crews on their arrival in the Hamburg defence zone, where the usually efficient co-ordination between the searchlights and flak batteries was absent. The markers were a little scattered, but most fell close enough to the city centre to provide a strong reference point for the main force crews, and over the next fifty minutes, almost 2,300 tons of bombs were delivered. The bombing began near the aiming point, but a pronounced creep-back developed, which cut a swathe of destruction from the city centre along the line of approach across the north-western districts, and out into open country, where a proportion of the effort was wasted. Never-the-less, it was a highly destructive attack, in which fifteen hundred people lost their lives, and this was the highest death toll at a target beyond the range of Oboe.

An added bonus for the Command was the loss of a very modest twelve aircraft, for which much of the credit belonged to Window. At a stroke, the device had rendered the entire enemy defensive system impotent for the time being. An advantage was rarely held for long, though, before a counter-measure was found, and this would eventually see the balance swing back in the enemy's favour. While the above operation was in progress, fourteen 138 Squadron Halifaxes took advantage of any diversion it caused, to slip into France. The details are as follows; F/O Zankowski in JD312 on Operations SCIENTIST 90/89, 23.02 to 05.38, unsuccessful. F/O Krywda in DG253 on Operations SCIENTIST 81/45, 23.10 to 08.58, successful. P/O Bown in DT726 on Operations SCIENTIST 69/87, 23.10 to 07.05 (St Eval), unsuccessful. F/O Downes in HR666 on Operations SCIENTIST 109, 23.17 to 04.53, unsuccessful. S/L Griffiths in JD180 on Operations TRAINER 18/10, 23.18 to 09.10, successful. F/Sgt Armstrong in BB378 on Operations SCIENTIST 93/59, 23.20 to 04.35, unsuccessful. F/L Milne in JD269 on Operations STATIONER 89/DEAN/SCIENTIST 74, 23.28 to 05.37, third element only completed. F/O Perrins in JD156 on Operation SCIENTIST 103, 23.42 to 05.07, unsuccessful. F/O Freyer in JD171 on Operation SCIENTIST 78, 23.45 to 05.20, successful. W/O Scott in JD319 on Operation SCIENTIST 48, 23.48 to 05.10, successful. F/Sgt Sherwood in BB317 on Operations SCIENTIST 77/96, 23.53 to 06.10, unsuccessful. Sgt James in BB334 on Operation SCIENTIST 63, 23.55 to 03.40, successful. Sgt Hodges in BB309 on Operations SCIENTIST 52/100, 00.05 to 06.05, unsuccessful. F/O Hart and crew took off at 23.59 in JD172 to carry out Operations PARSON 1/DEACON/DRIVER/SCIENTIST 50. The purpose of the first element was to drop two agents, H H Gaillot and his wireless operator, Georges Clement, into the PARSON circuit operating in the Rennes area. Gaillot was a Belgian interior decorator, approaching fifty years of age, and, along with his colleague, would fall into enemy hands when the Germans closed down the circuit. All elements of this operation were successfully completed, and a safe return made to Tempsford at 05.10.

On the following night Harris decided to switch his attention to Essen, to take advantage of the body blow dealt to the enemy's defences by Window. The result was another highly accurate and concentrated assault on this city, during which, the Krupp complex sustained its heaviest damage of the war, and over 2,800 houses and apartment blocks were destroyed. The night of the 26/27th was quiet, indeed, even for the moon squadrons, and 138 Squadron dispatched just a single sortie, which, according to the ORB, was to France. W/C Speare and crew took off in DG253 at 21.54, and successfully carried out Operations TABLEMARGERINE and TABLEGOSSIP 4/5, the code names for which are associated with drops over Denmark. Whether it is the destination or the code names which are incorrect, is unknown. F/Sgt Hayter and crew were posted in on the 27th, and were joined on the following day by Sgt Trotter and crew. After the night's rest, 787 aircraft took off in the late evening of the 27th to return to Hamburg for round two of Operation Gomorrah. What followed their arrival over the city was both unprecedented and unforeseeable, and was the result of a lethal combination of circumstances.

A period of unusually hot and dry weather had left tinderbox conditions in parts of the city, and the initial spark to ignite the situation came with the Pathfinder markers. These fell two miles to the east of the planned city centre aiming point, but with unaccustomed concentration into the densely populated working class residential districts of Hamm, Hammerbrook and Borgfeld. The main force crews followed up with uncharacteristic accuracy and scarcely any creep-back, and delivered most of their 2,300 tons of bombs into this relatively compact area. The individual fires joined together to form one giant conflagration, which sucked in oxygen from surrounding areas at hurricane velocity to feed its voracious appetite. Such was the ferocity of this meteorological phenomenon, that trees were uprooted and flung bodily into the flames, along with debris and people, and the temperatures at the heart of the fire exceeded one thousand degrees Celcius. The inferno only began to subside once all the combustible material had been consumed, and by this time, there was no one left within the firestorm area to rescue. It would actually be weeks before many of the burned-out buildings had cooled sufficiently to allow access to basements, where some of the more gruesome finds would be made, and an accurate assessment of casualties could begin. An estimated forty thousand people died on this one night alone, and on the following morning, the first of an eventual 1.2 million inhabitants began to file out of the tortured city.

Another night's rest preceded the third Hamburg raid, for which 777 aircraft took off on the evening of the 29th. Early returns had reduced the numbers to a fraction over seven hundred by the time the target was reached, but these carried another 2,300 tons of bombs to deliver onto the city centre. The Pathfinders were again two miles east of the aiming point with their markers, which fell a little to the south of the firestorm area. The main force approached the markers on a north-south heading, and a creep-back developed as some crews bombed the first markers or fires they encountered. This took the bombing across the firestorm devastation of two nights earlier, before it fell onto other residential districts beyond, where a new area of fire was created, although of lesser proportions. The defences were beginning to recover from the shock of Window, however, and, as they did so, the bomber losses began to rise. Twenty-eight aircraft failed to return on this night, on top of the seventeen missing from the firestorm raid. 138 Squadron dispatched just two sorties to France, F/L Wilkin and crew taking off at 22.27 in JD269 to undertake Operation WHEELWRIGHT 2, and F/O Zankowski and crew at 22.36 in JD319 on Operation TOMCOD 33, and both returned to confirm successful outcomes.

On the following night, the 30/31st, a relatively modest force of under three hundred Halifaxes, Stirlings and Lancasters in roughly equal numbers, devastated the previously unmolested Ruhr town of Remscheid. Over three thousand houses were destroyed, 83% of the built-up area was reduced to rubble, and eleven hundred inhabitants lost their lives. This operation brought down the final curtain on the Ruhr offensive, but, because of its oil-producing plants, it was a region that would never be left in peace, and a new and even more terrifying campaign against it would begin in the autumn of 1944.

August 1943

Operation Gomorrah was concluded on the night of the 2/3rd of August, when 740 aircraft departed their stations and headed into violent electrical storms on the route to northern Germany. This persuaded many crews to abandon their sorties, and either jettison their bombs over the sea or drop them on alternative targets. Some crews pressed on to Hamburg, but the bombing was scattered in the absence of target indicators, and little further damage was inflicted upon the city. There were no further operations during the first week of August, during which period F/Sgt Cole and crew were added to 138 Squadron strength, and they were followed by a Polish crew with two pilots, F/Sgt Koziel and Sgt Szewdowski. The second week began for the main force with the first of a series of raids on the major cities of Italy, which was now teetering on the brink of capitulation. Bomber Command's involvement was designed to help nudge it over, and elements of 1, 5 and 8 Groups began the process on the night of the 7/8th with attacks on Genoa, Milan and Turin.

The moon rose on the following night, and this was the signal for the moon squadrons to emerge once more. 138 Squadron undertook three supply drops to France on this night, each of them successfully. F/L Wilkinson and crew took off at 21.47 in BB309 on Operation SCIENTIST 130, F/O Hart and crew departed at 21.55 in JD156 to take care of Operation WHEELWRIGHT 12, and F/O Zankowski and crew were last away at 22.05 in JD312 on Operations TOMCOD 34/ROACH 142. On the 9/10th over 450 aircraft took off for the southern German city of Mannheim, situated on the eastern bank of the Rhine. A highly effective attack destroyed thirteen hundred buildings, and caused a loss of production at forty-two factories, in return for the modest loss of nine aircraft. Twenty-four hours later it was the turn of Nuremberg to suffer its most effective raid to date at the hands of around six hundred aircraft. Considerable damage resulted in central and southern districts, where preserved medieval houses were destroyed, and a large area of fire developed. While this operation was in progress, two 138 Squadron aircraft sneaked into Denmark on supply drops. F/O Freyer and crew took off at 21.00 in JD362 to carry out Operations TABLEJAM 6 and 7, and they were followed into the air at 22.10 by F/O Krywda and crew in JD319 bound for Operations TABLEJAM 2 and 3. The five sorties thus far during the new month had resulted in the dropping of sixty-nine containers.

There was no main force activity to mask clandestine operations on the night of the 11/12th, when 138 Squadron sent nine aircraft to France and three to Belgium. Among the latter was the crew of F/O Hart, who took off at 21.53 in JD269 to attempt Operations TYBALT/HILLCAT/MANDRILL 1/BULLFROG 1. They crossed the French coast at Pointe-du-Haut-Banc at 100 feet, before heading for Guise and then Givet on the Franco/Belgian border. From there a DR run was carried out eastwards to the first pinpoint, where, despite heavy rain and low cloud, two agents were dropped blind from 700 feet. Two containers were delivered to the next pinpoint, and five containers and two packages went down at the third one near Saint-Hubert. Sgt Brown and crew were outbound for France in JD179 to deliver eight containers and three packages under Operation DICK 22, and seven containers under Operation TRAINER 12, when engine problems developed, forcing them to dump the cargo and return early. The other sorties on this night were as follows; F/Sgt James in HR666 on Operation WHEELWRIGHT 13, 21.47 to 03.05, successful. F/L Perrins in JD156 on

Operations TOM 3/1, 21.56 to 02.31, second element only completed. F/L Wilkinson in BB330 on Operations CARACAL 6/SAMOYEDE 1/LABRADOR 3, 21.57 to 03.45, third element only completed. F/Sgt Armstrong in BB378 on Operations SPRUCE 17/18, 21.59 to 04.40, unsuccessful. W/O Scott in BB334 on Operations SCIENTIST 86/131, 22.00 to 04.48, unsuccessful. F/O Zankowski in JD312 on Operations SPRUCE 21/20, 22.05 to 06.43, unsuccessful. S/L Pitt in JD172 on Operations SCIENTIST 88/84, 22.09 to 04.14, successful. W/C Speare in JD180 on Operations GREYHOUND/WOODCHUCK/MISTREL 4/BUTLER 5, 22.11 to 04.31, elements one, two and four successful. F/O Wasilewski in JD171 on Operation SCIENTIST 137, 22.13 to 04.20, successful. P/O Bown in DT726 on Operations MUSKRAT 1/2, 22.20 to 01.45, successful.

The Italian campaign continued at Milan and Turin on the night of the 12/13th, a night on which 138 Squadron dispatched a creditable fifteen sorties, a figure last achieved on the night of the 22/23rd of July. All were to France, but only four were completed as planned, and one aircraft failed to return. According to a personal account given to Ken Merrick, and recounted by Freddie Clark, Canadian, W/O Scott, and his crew were the last to depart Tempsford on this night, at 22.30, and crossed the French coast at Cabourg at 1,500 feet, before setting course for the target area and descending to 1,100 feet. They were flying in BB334, and attempting to clear up Operations SPRUCE 21/20, one of the previous night's failed operations, when light flak set the port-outer engine on fire. At the same time, a ME110 night fighter attacked, and the Halifax's rear gunner returned fire before being killed. W/O Scott carried out a crash-landing at Ecorcei, some fifty miles south-east of Caen, during which action, another crew member lost his life, and then, together with the dispatcher, he evaded capture, returning home via Gibraltar in early October. It was later established, that F/Sgt Foster, the rear gunner, had shot down the night fighter responsible for his death. This account is different from the one given by W/O Scott and Sgt Trusty to MI9 in November 1943, which does not mention the night fighter, and describes the Halifax flying at tree-top level when hit, and burning furiously on the ground. Scott also did not mention to Merrick, that his face had been scorched.

The details of the other sorties on this night are as follows. F/L Perrins in JD156 on Operations TRAINER 26/12, 21.42 to 05.25, first element only completed. F/Sgt James and crew were in BB330 on Operations SCULLION A/BOB 6/TRAINER 21, and took off at 21.44. They dropped an OSS agent, American, Lt Demand, at the first pinpoint, and eight containers at the second, but were thwarted at the third by the lack of a reception committee. They landed safely at 05.55. F/O Freyer in JD362 on Operations TRAINER 15/25, 21.45 to 06.00 successful. F/Sgt Sherwood in BB317 on Operations TRAINER 22/20, 21.45 to 04.59, unsuccessful. S/L Griffiths in JD180 on Operations WHEELWRIGHT 25/16, 21.50 to 05.25, first element only completed. S/L Pitt in JD172 on Operations TRAINER 13/SPRUCE 18, 21.55 to 06.15, successful. F/O Krywda in JD319 on Operations TRAINER 17/SPRUCE 25, 21.55 to 05.47, first element only completed. F/L Milne in JD269 on Operations WHEELWRIGHT 14/15, 21.56 to 04.44, successful. F/Sgt Hodges in JD172 on Operation PIMENTO 29, 22.00 to 00.15, successful. F/L Wilkinson in BB309 on Operations BOB 4/13, 22.04 to 06.10, unsuccessful. F/Sgt Armstrong in BB378 on Operation PIMENTO 30, 22.08 to 05.18, successful. F/O Hart in JD171 on Operation SCIENTIST 73, 22.08 to 05.08, successful. P/O Bown in DT726 on Operations TRAINER 9/STATIONER 8, 22.10 to 05.10, successful. F/Sgt Hayter, (maiden SOE sortie) in HR666 on Operation SCIENTIST 177, 22.26 to 05.33, unsuccessful.

Bomber Command's only operational sorties on the night of the 13/14th were those launched from Tempsford. Eight of these were by 138 Squadron to France, one to deliver an agent, and the others cargo. F/Sgt Hodges and crew started the ball rolling in BB309 at 21.23, when taking off on Operations WHEELWRIGHT 21/24, of which only the first element was completed. F/O Zankowski and crew were next away in JD312 at 21.32 on Operations SPRUCE 17/JOCKEY 6, and they completed the second element only. F/O Freyer and crew departed Tempsford at 21.43 in JD362 on Operations PIMENTO 33/34, and landed at 06.45 to report a successful outcome. F/O Krywda and crew were in JD319, and took off at 21.44 on Operations PIMENTO 32/37, which they were able to complete. F/L Wasilewski and crew were on Operation SCIENTIST 167, and took off in JD171 at 21.45 to achieve a successful outcome. F/Sgt Brown and crew were in JD156, and took off at 21.47 on Operations SPRUCE 22/CORISTOR/PIMENTO 31, which they were unable to complete. The only agent to be carried on this night, is believed to be Eric Cauchi, who was on board JD269 with F/L Milne and crew, who were undertaking Operations STATIONER 17/DEAN/SCIENTIST 171, and took off at 21.48. The drop site was south of Chateauroux, where a reception committee awaited the agent and seven packages. Freddie Clark mentions a new roller device in use in the Halifax for dispatching packages, which, apparently worked well. The final departure was that of F/Sgt Sherwood and crew at 21.50 in BB317 to carry out Operation SCIENTIST 105, which they completed.

On the following night, as Milan was hit again, a further twelve 138 Squadron crews ventured into French airspace. S/L Griffiths and crew took off at 21.40 in JD180 on Operation PIMENTO 12, one element of which involved the dropping of leaflets over the town of Annecy, in the foothills of the Alps, south of Geneva. It was during the execution of this, that two engines were knocked out by ground fire, and S/L Griffiths was compelled to carry out a crash-landing in the village of Meythet, as a result of which, five members of the crew and five unfortunate civilians were killed. Griffiths was semi-conscious as he emerged from the wreckage with a fractured right arm and left shoulder blade, and met up with his despatcher, Sgt Maden, who had been thrown clear. According to Griffiths' MI9 debrief on his return to England at the end of November, they were immediately apprehended by Italian soldiers, but he managed to escape during a few moments of confusion as the wrecked aircraft exploded. It is believed, that Sgt Maden was shot and killed by his captors at this point, as he made a bolt for freedom. Griffiths began walking, and was eventually taken in by French people, ultimately completing his evasion through Switzerland and Spain, and arriving home via Gibraltar.

The other sorties on this night were as follows; F/L Perrins in JD156 on Operations TRAINER 33/ACROBAT 8, 21.37 to 05.30, first element only completed. P/O Bown in DT726 on Operations PIMENTO 36/BOB 27, 21.40 to 05.40, successful. F/L Wilkinson in BB309 on Operations PIMENTO 35/38, 21.43 to 05.10, unsuccessful. F/Sgt James in HR666 on Operations TRAINER 24/BOB 22, 21.48 to 04.30, unsuccessful. P/O Brown in DG253 on Operations BOB 29/31, 21.50 to 04.55, successful. F/O Wasilewski in JD171 on Operations SCIENTIST 147 and WHEELWRIGHT 16, 21.52 to 06.00, successful. F/O Hart in JD154 on Operations WHEELWRIGHT 18/SCIENTIST 116, 21.55 to 05.55, first element only completed. F/Sgt Armstrong in BB378 on Operation BOB 28, 21.55 to 04.20, successful. F/O Zankowski in JD312 on Operation SCIENTIST 110, 22.00 to 06.05, unsuccessful. F/Sgt

Hayter in JD319 on Operation SCIENTIST 163, 22.02 to 03.43, unsuccessful. Sgt Trotter in BB317 on Operations SCIENTIST 155/HARRY 9, 22.04 to 04.15, unsuccessful.

During the course of the 16th, the crews of F/Sgt Kennedy and Sgt Copas were posted in, to join nine Polish pilots and a host of other airmen who had arrived on the 13th. The Italian campaign concluded at Turin on the night of the 16/17th, when there was also massive activity at Tempsford, as twenty-one Halifaxes were made ready for operations. 138 Squadron, alone, prepared fifteen Halifaxes for sorties over France, with departures beginning at 20.15 with the crew of F/O Zankowski. The pilot was F/O Krzehlik, who, earlier in the day, had received a telegram, informing him that his wife, Mary, who was in London, had presented him with a baby daughter. Krzehlik could not be released, however, and it must have been with greater apprehension than usual, that he taxied out for take-off. The crew was flying in JD312, NF-J, and were half an hour from their drop site to carry out Operations WHEELWRIGHT 17/24, when an engine overheated, and power had to be reduced for the remainder of the outward trip deep into south-western France. The drop proceeded according to plan, but, immediately afterwards, the engine problems became critical, and forced the pilot to put JD312 onto the ground at 23.30 near Arx, east of Roquefort. The occupants were met within minutes by a party of Frenchmen, who asked that the petrol be removed before the Halifax was set on fire. The entire crew evaded through Spain, and arrived home via Gibraltar towards the end of October.

Pilot F/O Krzehlik was captain of a Polish crew which failed to return to base on 16/17 September 1943. (PISM via PH)

F/L Milne and crew took off in JD269 at 20.40 to attempt Operations SCIENTIST 175/PETER 1/TRIREM/LOUGRE/COTRE, the first element of which required the delivery of fifteen containers to a site some twenty-five miles south of Aubusson. While crossing the coast at 4,000 feet over Pointe de la Percee at around 22.00, inaccurate light flak was seen from flak ships, and, half an hour later, while at 1,000 feet and south-east of Laval, an aircraft was observed to be engaged by ground fire, and fall in flames to crash. The identity of the victim has never been established. Having completed the first element, F/L Milne headed north-east to a drop site twenty-five miles south-east of Montlucon in central France, where three agents and five packages were delivered from 600 feet during three passes. They returned safely to Tempsford to land at 03.53. Logged as taking off at the same time as F/L Milne, S/L Pitt and crew were in JD172, and had been assigned to Operations PENNYFARTHING/SCIENTIST 125, the first element of which required the blind dropping of two OSS agents into the Clermont-Ferrand region of south-central France. Having fulfilled their brief in that regard, they flew on to a second drop site to deliver fifteen containers.

F/Sgt Armstrong and crew took off at 20.42 in BB378 to undertake Operations BOB 3/MARIOTE/AMPERE/GALLER/BOB 11, and crossed the French coast at Cabourg at 9,500 feet, before setting course for the Cote-d'Or region in the east of the country. Clear skies and

Above right: The page from the logbook of Sgt Pawlikowski, despatcher in F/O Krzehlik's crew, with the entry referring to the special operation flown on 16/17 September 1943 to France. (PH)

bright moonlight aided the dropping of three agents and six packages onto a reception point some twenty miles north of Dijon, before flying on for a further ten minutes and delivering fifteen containers at the last target. of which eleven were successful. F/Sgt James and crew were handed Operations SCULLION B/SCIENTIST 180/WHITSUN, and took off in HR666 at 21.08. The French coast was crossed at Cabourg at 6,000 feet, and a course set for Cosne, north-west of Dijon and then to a reception point north of Autun, where a six-man team of saboteurs, led by Irish Guardsman, Lt Hugh Dormer, was to be dropped. They were to attempt to destroy the nearby synthetic oil plant, an operation which had failed in April. The six men, a container and a package were safely parachuted into the arms of a reception committee, after which, F/Sgt James flew to Nevers and then north east to a point near Nogent-le-Rotrou for supply drops. *(Although the saboteurs would plant their explosives, very little damage was achieved, and all but Dormer and one other were captured. Dormer would return to his regiment, and lose his life on the 1st of August 1944 during a tank battle.)*

The details of the other sorties are as follows; F/O Krywda in JD319 on Operations TRAINER 31/30, 20.30 to 04.58, first element only completed. F/L Wasilewski in JD171 on Operations TRAINER 27/13, 20.32 to 05.08, successful. F/O Freyer in JD362 on Operations SCIENTIST 82/116, 20.35 to 04.55, unsuccessful. P/O Brown in DG253 on Operations DICK 23/BOB 44, 20.45 to 03.10, successful. F/Sgt Hodges in BB330 on Operations DICK 24/26, 20.47 to 01.45, second element only completed. P/O Bown in BB309 on Operations BOB 38/37, 20.50 to 01.26, successful. Sgt Trotter in JD154 on Operation SCIENTIST 139, 20.53 to 02.53, unsuccessful. F/L Perrins in JD156 on Operations EASTER/FARMER 7, 21.10 to 00.30, successful. F/Sgt Hayter in JD179 on Operation SCIENTIST 150, 21.51 to 04.43, unsuccessful. One other unrecorded sortie took place, which, it is believed, returned early with engine trouble. A total of fourteen agents and 184 containers were delivered by the squadron during the course of this night, and, had a reception committee been evident at two other locations, the statistics would have been even higher.

Since the start of hostilities, intelligence had been filtering through concerning German research into rocket weapons. Through the interception and decoding of signals traffic, the centre for such activity was found to be at Peenemünde, an isolated location on the island of Usedom on Germany's Baltic coast. Regular reconnaissance flights helped to build up a picture of the activity there, but Churchill's chief scientific adviser, Professor Lindemann, or Lord Cherwell as he became, steadfastly refused to give credence to rockets as weapons, and even when confronted with a photograph of a V-2 on a trailer at Peenemünde, taken by a PRU Mosquito as recently as June, he stubbornly remained unmoved. It required the urgings of Dr Jones and Duncan Sandys to persuade Churchill of the need to act, and, it was finally agreed that an operation should be mounted at the first available opportunity. This arose on the night of the 17/18th of August, for which a detailed plan was meticulously prepared. The three-phase operation was undertaken by 597 aircraft, assigned in waves to the housing estate, the assembly buildings and the experimental site, their participation controlled by a Master Bomber, G/C John Searby, the commanding officer of 83 Squadron. The final wave, made up of aircraft from 5 and 6 Groups, was mauled by night fighters arriving belatedly on the scene, and almost three-quarters of the forty missing aircraft came from these. Sufficient success was achieved to set back the development programme of the V-2 by a number of weeks, and the testing was ultimately moved eastwards into Poland, out of range of Harris's bomber force. The vulnerability of Peenemünde to air attack caused a major rethink, and it was decided to move the production of secret weapons underground. Almost immediately, construction of an underground factory began at Nordhausen, and once completed, it would be staffed by forced workers.

138 Squadron took advantage of the attention-grabbing activity over northern Germany to slip nine aircraft into France, and all but one of these operations was successfully concluded. The only failure involved F/Sgt Hayter RAAF and his crew, who were undertaking Operations BOB 43/34 in JD179, and were shot down to crash at Ercorci, close to the spot where W/O Scott had crashed five nights earlier. Six of the crew were killed on impact, and the flight engineer lingered until the following day before he, too, succumbed. P/O Bown and crew took off at 20.35 in HR666, and headed for the south of France to carry out Operations DRESSMAKER A/B. The first pinpoint was near Albi, north-east of Toulouse, where two agents were dropped blind along with a package, and, sixteen minutes later, a further two agents and a package were dropped further south near Mazamet. Their brief was to attack the tanneries at Mazamet, which, in the event, were found to be unused. The final drop site received thirteen containers, and the round-trip took eight hours and twenty minutes. The details of the other sorties on this night are as follows; F/L Perrins in JD156 on Operations TABLEJAM 5/4, 19.40 to 03.20. F/O Hart in JD154 on Operations TABLEJAM 8/9, 19.42 to 03.10. F/Sgt Hodges in BB330 on Operations SPRUCE 22/CORISTOR/SPRUCE 16, 20.40 to 02.10, last element only completed. Sgt Trotter in DG252 on Operations BOB 46/21, 20.45 to 03.37. F/L

Wilkinson in BB309 on Operations ACROBAT 8/BOB 25, 21.01 to 04.38. F/Sgt Sherwood in JD172 on Operation SCIENTIST 181, 21.02 to 04.02. F/Sgt Armstrong in BB378 on Operations TOMIC/LABRADOR 4/CARACAL 6, 21.35 to 03.29.

There was no main force activity on the 18/19th, and the only aircraft flying that night, other than those from Tempsford, were thirty O.T.U. Wellingtons leafleting over France. Eleven 138 Squadron Halifaxes also set out for France to deliver stores, but P/O Brown, who had taken off at 20.14, was soon back in the circuit, complaining of a strong smell of aviation fuel from the internal fuel tank. He overshot the landing at 20.29, and ran off the end of the runway onto scrub land, writing-off the veteran Halifax, DG253, happily, without crew casualties. The details of the remaining sorties are as follows; F/O Krywda in JD319 on Operations TRAINER 33/28, 20.22 to 05.10, unsuccessful. F/L Milne in JD269 on Operation SCIENTIST 62, 20.25 to 04.05, successful. F/O Freyer in JD362 on Operation SCIENTIST 77, 20.35 to 03.45, unsuccessful due to lack of reception. F/Sgt Cole in BB378 on Operation SCIENTIST 192, 20.45 to 02.21, successful. F/L Wasilewski in JD171 on Operation SCIENTIST 168, 20.50 to 04.32, successful. F/Sgt James in BB330 on Operation SCIENTIST 106, 20.53 to 03.28, successful. S/L Pitt in DG252 on Operations SCIENTIST 90/89, 21.50 to 05.05, successful. F/Sgt Sherwood in BB317 on Operations PARSON 1/2, 22.41 to 03.56, first element only completed. F/L Wilkinson in JN910 on Operations TOM 8/9, 22.47 to 01.57, successful. F/O Hart in JD154 on Operations TOM 6/7, 22.55 to 03.05, unsuccessful.

The night of the 19/20th brought nine more sorties to France, and one to Belgium, and all but two were successful. F/Sgt James and crew were handed the complex four-location sortie to Belgium under Operations LEAR/BUCKHOUND/SAMOYEDE 1/LABRADOR 5/GIBBON 5/CARACAL 6, which involved two agents and a dozen containers. They took off at 22.25 in JN910, and all went according to plan, although no details are available, and they returned

Halifax JD-361 NF-L with a Polish aircrew of 'C' Flight. (Z. Wysocki via PH)

safely at 03.25. Details of the other sorties on this night are as follows; F/L Perrin in JD154 on Operations PAUL 11/15, 20.33 to 05.08, successful. F/Sgt Armstrong in BB378 on Operations PAUL 12/16, 20.42 to 04.47, successful. P/O Brown in BB317 on Operations PAUL 10/13, 20.45 to 04.40, first element only completed. F/L Milne in JD269 on Operations PETER 4/JOHN 5, 21.16 to 04.50, unsuccessful. F/Sgt Hodges in BB330 on Operations DICK 22/BOB 32, 21.35 to 04.55, successful. F/O Freyer in JD362 on Operations BOB 36/40, 21.40 to 05.10, successful. F/L Wasilewski in JD171 on Operations BOB 35/39, 21.43 to 05.02, successful. Sgt Trotter in DG252 on Operations DICK 17/18, 21.47 to 04.27, successful. F/Sgt Cole in JD319 on Operations HARRY 9/DICK 30, 22.00 to 04.00, unsuccessful.

Sgt Gregory and crew were posted in on the 20th, and they would be followed over the enduing three days by F/O Bartter and crew, and new pilots, S/L Passey DFC and Sgt Olkiewicz. Meanwhile, the hectic schedule continued on the night of the 20/21st with seven sorties to France and one to Belgium. F/L Wilkinson and crew departed Tempsford at 21.59 in BB309 on Operations TRAINER 19/PETER 4, and successfully delivered two agents, fifteen containers and five packages. F/O Hart and crew took off at 22.40 in JD172 to undertake Operations SACRISTAN, JOINER and DICK 30, and dropped Andre Bouchardon, a wireless operator, to join the previously-mentioned Ernest Floegge. The former would narrowly escape capture in December, and, despite being shot, would make it back to England with Floegge in February 1944. The other sorties on this night are detailed as follows; F/O Krywda in JD171 on Operation SCIENTIST 91, 21.20 to 05.21, unsuccessful. F/Sgt Sherwood in BB317 on Operations SCIENTIST 95/92, 21.32 to 04.17, unsuccessful. P/O Bown in JN910 on Operations DICK 28/27, 22.00 to 03.16, successful. Sgt Trotter in DG252 on Operation BUTLER 67, 22.29 to 02.24, successful. F/L Perrins in JD156 on Operations TOM 3/PHILOTIS/OTHELLO I, 22.44 to 04.36, second and third elements only completed. F/Sgt Hodges in BB330 on Operations PORTER and SCIENTIST 190, 22.50 to 01.50, unsuccessful.

F/L Wasilewski and crew started the ball rolling on the night of the 22/23rd, when taking off in JD171 at 20.51 to undertake Operations PAUL 13/2. Sadly, after more than eight hours in the air, they returned to report an unsuccessful attempt. They were followed by; F/L Milne in JD172 on Operations PAUL 8/9, 21.20 to 04.40, unsuccessful. F/Sgt James in BB330 on Operations PETER 6/STATIONER 24, 21.21 to 05.05, successful. F/Sgt Sherwood in BB317 on Operations DICK 16/19, 22.18 to 05.15, second element only completed. F/O Freyer in JD362 on Operations PETER5/SCIENTIST 112, 22.25 to 05.05, second element only completed, as no reception at the first one. P/O Brown in JD156 on Operations DONKEYMAN 22/MERCEDES, 22.55 to 04.55, successful. F/O Hart in JD154 on Operations HARRY 6/MISTRAL 4, 23.11 to 04.16, successful. F/Sgt Cole in BB378 on Operation SCIENTIST 193, 23.15 to 04.55, unsuccessful. W/C Speare in JN910 on Operations DICK 20/21, 23.17 to 04.24, first element only completed. P/O Bown in BB309 on Operations DONKEYMAN 18/PUBLICAN 4, 23.25 to 05.10, first element only completed. Part of the main force returned to action on this night, when over four hundred aircraft failed to concentrate their bombs on the Ruhr town of Leverkusen, wherein lay an important I.G. Farben chemicals factory engaged in synthetic oil production, and employing slave labour.

The night of the 23/24th was momentous for the Command as a whole, as it signalled the start of the first phase of the Berlin offensive. Harris had long believed, that Berlin, as the seat and symbol of Nazi power, held the key to ultimate victory. He maintained the belief, that bombing alone could win the war, and if this could be achieved, it would remove the need for the kind of protracted and bloody land campaigns, which he had personally witnessed during the Great War. At the time it was a perfectly reasonable theory, and Harris was the first commander in history in a position to put it to the test. It is only in the light of recent conflicts, that we know with absolute certainty of the necessity to physically occupy the enemy's territory in order to gain complete submission. The Berlin campaign would be the longest and most bitterly fought battle of the war, and nothing before or after came closer to breaking the Command's spirit. 727 aircraft took off for the Capital in mid evening, and once over the target, the Pathfinders were confronted by the usual difficulties of trying to identify the city centre from the jumble of images on their H2S screens. In the event, they marked the southern outskirts of the city, and some of the main force crews approached from the south-west instead of a more southerly direction, depositing many bomb loads onto outlying communities and open country. This would be a feature of the entire campaign, but at least, on this night, considerable damage was inflicted upon the southern districts, where 2,600 buildings were destroyed or seriously damaged, and this represented the best result yet at the "Big City". On the debit side, the loss of fifty-six aircraft was a new record.

The moon period ended on this night, but not before 138 Squadron, according to Freddie Clark, crammed in another dozen sorties. The ORB records ten, which suggests, that there may have been two unrecorded early returns. The details of the ten are as follows; F/Sgt Hodges in BB330 on Operations SCIENTIST 127/135, 21.53 to 05.25, unsuccessful. Sgt Trotter in JD154 on Operation SCIENTIST 123, 22.32 to 05.12, successful. F/L Milne in JD269 on Operations SCIENTIST 113/111, 22.32 to 05.30, first element only completed. S/L Pitt in JD172 on Operation DONKEYMAN 30, 22.40 to 05.40, unsuccessful. F/O Freyer in JD362 on Operation SCIENTIST 110, 22.42 to 05.05, successful. F/O Krywda in JD171 on Operations DONKEYMAN 31/33, 22.52 to 06.08, unsuccessful. F/L Perrins in JD156 on Operation SCIENTIST 184, 00.25 to 04.32, successful. F/Sgt Cole in BB378 on Operations DICK 15/HARRY 9, 00.35 to 04.55, first element only completed. P/O Bown in BB309 on Operations DONKEYMAN 13/28, 00.38 to 04.45, unsuccessful. F/Sgt James in JN910 on Operations PORTER/SCIENTIST 190, 00.44 to 05.15, first element only completed. This concluded a mammoth effort by 138 Squadron during the month, which produced a record 124 sorties, at a cost of five aircraft and four crews, although a goodly number of the missing men were making their way back home by the scenic route. The Polish C Flight had now been allocated three Liberators, and its complement of Halifaxes was reduced accordingly.

A four-night break from operations allowed a little respite before the next major outing for the heavy squadrons, which was to Nuremberg on the night of the 27/28th. This was not a successful operation, despite accurate early marking by the Pathfinders. A creep-back developed, which could not be corrected because of communications difficulties and problems with H2S sets among the 8 Group contingent. As a result, most of the bombing hit open country, although there was a scattering across the south-eastern and eastern suburbs, and thirty-three aircraft failed to return. The twin towns of Mönchengladbach and Rheydt provided a much less distant objective for over six hundred aircraft on the night of the 30/31st, and this was the first heavy assault of the war on these frontier towns. The operation was an outstanding success, in which more than 2,300 buildings were destroyed.

An unidentified airman sits at the controls of a Halifax. The absence of apparent flying clothing suggests that he was on the ground at the time and is probably ground crew.

Twenty-four hours later came the second raid on Berlin, for which over six hundred aircraft began taking off shortly before 20.00 hours. The presence of some cloud in the target area combined with H2S equipment failures to prevent accurate marking, and the target indicators fell well to the south of the intended city centre aiming point. An extensive creep-back, extending some thirty miles back along the line of approach, further reduced the effectiveness of the bombing, and the result was a disappointing attack, which destroyed less than a hundred buildings. A ferocious defence claimed forty-seven aircraft, the bulk of them Halifaxes and Stirlings, and alarm bells began to sound at Bomber Command HQ.

September 1943

Possibly as a result of the above-mentioned losses, the current phase of the Berlin offensive ended with an all-Lancaster assault on the night of the 3/4th of September. The marking and bombing undershot to a large extent, but some bombs fell across residential districts and the Siemensstadt industrial area, where a number of war industry factories lost production. Now that Berlin was off-limits until the winter, other German cities would keep the Command busy throughout the autumn, beginning with Mannheim and Ludwigshafen on the night of the 5/6th. This highly successful attack was planned to exploit the creep-back tendency of large-scale operations. With an approach from the west, and an aiming point in the eastern half of Mannheim, the bombing would spread back along the line of approach and spill across the Rhine into Ludwigshafen on the west bank. This was precisely what happened, and it resulted in massive damage in both of the target cities. A thousand houses were destroyed in Ludwigshafen alone, and the important I.G Farben chemicals factory was severely damaged. Bomber losses were again high, however, reaching thirty-four, and the percentage losses amongst the Halifax and Stirling contingents gave further cause for concern. A raid of moderate size against Munich on the night of the 6/7th was rendered inconclusive by cloud, most crews having to bomb on estimated positions, after a timed run from a lake south-west of the city.

It was now, that the crews at Tempsford began to prepare for their next round of operations as the moon rose. F/L Wilkin had returned to the fold, and now held acting squadron leader rank. The first sorties of this new phase were to take place on the night of the 8/9th, with a number of new crews making their SOE debut. It coincided with the launching of Harris's token contribution to Operation Starkey, a plan involving all of the armed services, to mislead the enemy into believing that an invasion was imminent. Harris was not amused at being ordered to participate in what he described as play-acting, but poor weather conditions delayed bombing operations, and it was not until this night of the 8/9th, that the two coastal batteries, code-named Religion and Andante, situated respectively north and south of the small resort town of le Portel near Boulogne, could be attacked. The operation failed to make an impact on the gun emplacements, but devastated le Portel, and killed around five hundred of its inhabitants. It was also far from a perfect night for 138 Squadron, which sent eight Halifaxes to France, only for five of them to fail through the absence of reception committees. The details of these sorties are as follows; F/L Perrins in HX161 on Operations DICK 50/45, 19.40 to 01.18, unsuccessful. S/L Wilkin in JN910 on Operations DICK 59/58, 19.45 to 02.26, unsuccessful. F/O Bartter in BB309 on Operations DICK 55/53, 19.59, to 02.56, successful. Sgt Kennedy in JD156 on Operations DICK 43/44, 20.05 to 02.10, unsuccessful. Sgt Copas in BB330 on Operations DICK 51/57, 20.07 to 02.20, first element only completed. F/Sgt Cole in BB378 on Operations HARRY 13/12, 20.10 to 02.45, first element only completed. Sgt Gregory in JD269 on Operations DICK 4/BUTLER 7, 20.37 to 01.30, successful. F/Sgt Trotter in DG252 on Operations DICK 37/36, 20.41 to 02.00, successful.

The 9th was the long awaited day, when a new season of operations to Poland could be resumed, which were given the codename RIPOSTA (riposte) and six Polish crews set off for their homeland carrying agents and stores. F/L Zbucki and crew were first away, at 18.01 in HX161, to carry out Operation NEON I. On board were three passengers, six containers and a package for delivery to a drop site about five miles north-west of Wyszkow railway station. Unfortunately, they became lost because of low cloud, and had insufficient reserves of fuel to complete the operation. F/L Gebik and crew took off at 18.07 in HR666 on Operation FLAT 8, carrying six containers and six packages to drop near Wolomin railway station, a dozen miles north-east of Warsaw. The sortie was entirely successful, and the Halifax landed safely after a round-trip of twelve and a half hours duration. F/O Krywda and crew were in JD319, and took off at 18.11 to carry out Operation FLAT 2, another supply drop consisting of six containers and six packages for a drop site near Grojec. The target area, south-west of the capital, was located, and the cargo delivered as planned in another flight of twelve and a half hours. S/L Krol's crew, with W/O Klosowski at the controls of JD171, departed Tempsford at 18.15 on Operation NEON 4, and delivered three agents, six containers and a package to a reception point near Grodzisk Mazowiecki, also situated south-west of Warsaw. Among the parachutists was Elzbieta Zawacka, the only Polish woman to be dropped into the homeland. On the way back, they were twice attacked by a night fighter, which resulted in damage to the aircraft, and were fired upon by flak as they crossed Denmark, but landed safely at 07.15. F/L Kuzmicki and crew were in BB330, bound for a supply drop of six containers and six packages to a reception point in the same area, this time near Skierniewice. They took off at 18.30 on Operation FLAT 6, and had

Navigator F/L Kuzmicki, who took part in many special operations in 138 Squadron, was killed on 6 January 1944 during a supply-dropping operation to Poland flown by Polish 1586 Special Duties Flight. (PISM via PH)

reached the Baltic, when a flak ship holed a fuel tank, and they were forced to turn back. F/O Freyer and crew were last away, in BB309 at 18.40 on Operation FLAT 1, a supply drop of six containers and six packages onto a reception point near Lowicz, west of Warsaw. This was another successful sortie, with a flight duration of thirteen hours. Later on the 10th, P/O Cook DFC, DFM, AFC was posted to the squadron. For the next three nights nothing happened, no Bomber Command operations were mounted, while, on the night of the 13/14th, it was left to ten Pathfinder Mosquitos to disturb the sleep of the residents of Cologne and Duisburg.

On the following night, the 14/15th, 138 Squadron mounted a massive effort to Poland with eleven sorties, while a single Halifax was sent to France. There would have been a dozen sorties to Poland, had BB378 not lost an engine before take-off. The only other activity on this night was an operation by 617 Squadron against the Dortmund-Ems Canal, which was recalled over the North Sea, and a nuisance raid by eight Pathfinder Mosquitos at Berlin. With the shorter days came earlier starts, and F/Sgt James and crew began proceedings with a take-off in HR666 at 17.53, on what would turn out to be the blackest night yet for 138 Squadron. Operation FLAT 12A required them to deliver six containers and six packages to a reception site near Ostrow Mazowiecka, located fifty miles north-east of Warsaw. While outbound over the Great Belt, the Halifax was shot down into the sea off Korsor, and only two men, both Canadians, survived to be taken prisoner. F/O Freyer and crew took off at 17.55 on Operation NEON 7, with F/Sgt Bober at the controls of JD362. They, as in the case of all of the NEON operations, were carrying three passengers, six containers and a package, which were successfully delivered to a drop site near Garwolin, south-east of Warsaw, in a round-trip lasting twelve and three-quarter hours. F/O Krywda and crew took off at 17.56 with F/Sgt Sancewicz in the pilot's seat of JD319. They were to undertake Operation NEON 10, and, ultimately, carried out their drop at a reserve site near Lowicz, after a reception committee failed to show up at the primary. They attracted flak over Denmark on the way home, and sustained damage to the port wing, but landed safely after almost thirteen and a half hours in the air.

F/O Hart and crew took off at 17.59 in JN910 to carry out Operation FLAT 12, a supply drop at an undisclosed location. On the way home, they were shot down to crash into the Baltic off Rugenwalde, which is now known as Darlowo, and only the flight engineer escaped with his life. The next to take off were F/L Milne DFC and crew in JD269 at 18.04. They were flying Operation NEON 9, to deliver their passengers and stores to a site near Minsk Mazowiecki, to the east of the capital, but failed to arrive. It was later established, that the Halifax had been shot down over the Danish coast at 20.40, and had crashed onto a railway line a couple of miles north of Esbjerg, killing all ten occupants. JD156 took off at 18.05 with the crew of F/L Malinowski on board, for whom the pilot was W/O Hulas. The target for Operation NEON 8 was a reception site near Tluszcz, located north-east of Warsaw, and, apart from flak damage to the bomb bay fuel tank, all went according to plan during a round-trip of more than twelve hours duration. F/L Perrins and crew took off at 18.08 in HX161, bound for Operation FLAT 11, a supply drop at a reception site, which, ultimately, they were unable to locate, and the effort put into the thirteen-hour round-trip was expended in vain. BB309 was the next to depart Tempsford, at 18.09, with W/O Bakanacz at the controls, bound for a drop site near Radzymin, on the south-eastern edge of the Zegrze Reservoir, north of Warsaw. Operation NEON 6 was the last of the agent drops, and was carried out successfully during a thirteen-hour flight.

The supply drop, Operation FLAT 24, was undertaken by W/O Ziolkowski and crew, who took off at 18.15 in JN911. They were carrying six containers and six packages for delivery to a site near Kalisz, some sixty miles west of Lodz. They crossed the North Sea at low level, and met heavy flak at the Danish coast, but completed the operation as briefed and returned safely. F/L Gebik DFC and crew were in JD154, which took off at 18.23, piloted by F/L Jakusz-Gostomski DFC, who had previously served with distinction with 300 Squadron. They were undertaking Operation FLAT 22, which was using a reception site somewhere near Kalisz, and were approaching it at very low level. The Halifax hit the top of a two-storey house in Skalmierzyce village, south-west of Kalisz, and exploded, killing all on board. The last of the Poland-bound Halifaxes was JD172, which took off at 18.30 with the crew of S/L Pitt on board, whose task was to deliver supplies to a reception site at Sroda, a few miles south-east of Poznan, under Operation FLAT 23. They carried out their brief successfully, and returned safely home after a round-trip of eleven hours and forty minutes duration. The single sortie to France was given, surprisingly, to the new Polish crew of P/O Pretkiewicz, who took off in

Above left: Navigator F/L Gebik who was killed during the special operation to Poland on 14/15 September 1943. Above right: The first pilot of F/L Gebik's crew, F/L Jakusz-Gostomski. Before being posted to 138 Squadron both completed tours of operation; Jakusz-Gostomski with 300 Squadron and Gebik with 305 Squadron. (PISM via PH)

DG252 at 20.30 on Operation PARSON 3/4, which they failed to complete for an undisclosed reason. There was a somber air at Tempsford on the following morning, as the loss of four experienced SOE crews was contemplated. In return for their sacrifice, seven sorties had been successfully completed, in which twelve agents, forty-two containers and twenty-two packages had been delivered.

Part of the main force returned to action on the night of the 15/16th, when 369 crews from 3, 4, 6 and 8 Groups were briefed for an attack on the Dunlop Rubber factory at Montlucon in central France. The operation was a major success, under the cover of which, and despite the previous night's carnage, 138 Squadron sent eight crews to France. The ORB goes completely haywire at this point, with pages out of sequence and some absent. The five sorties listed for this night are as follows; P/O Bown in JN910 on Operations MONK 1/JOCKEY 7, 19.25 to 05.10, successful. P/O Brown in JD362 on Operations TRAINER 44/35, 19.35 to 03.59, successful. F/Sgt Hodges in DT726 on Operations SPRUCE 31/CORISTOR/JOHN 5, 20.21 to 02.53, successful. P/O Pretkiewicz in BB317 on Operation SPRUCE 28, 20.23 to 003.29, successful. S/L Wilkin and crew had been briefed to carry out Operations BOB 62, PIQUIER, IROQUIOS, FLAM-AN, BRUTO and BOB 58. They took off at 19.45, and dropped a team of four agents and packages onto a previously used site twenty miles north of Dijon, before flying a further eight minutes to deliver fifteen containers. Two other unrecorded sorties were also completely successful, while Operation DETECTIVE 4, flown by F/O Bartter and crew, was partially completed. One agent was dropped as planned, but two other sites lacked a reception committee. Even so, the night had seen a total of five agents dropped into hostile territory along with much-needed supplies.

With the losses from Poland still fresh in the mind, four more sorties were dispatched there on the night of the 16/17th, while five others were sent to France, under the diversion of another 3, 4, 6 and 8 Group effort. This one was directed at the important railway yards at Modane in southern France, on the main route into Italy. The location of the target in a steep valley thwarted the crews' best endeavours, however, and the operation failed. With further to travel, the 138 Squadron crews heading east took off first, beginning with F/O Freyer and crew in JN911 at 18.23. The were undertaking Operation NEON 2, and successfully delivered three passengers, six containers and a package to the reception point near Minsk Mazowiecki, before returning safely. JD156 left the ground at 18.26 on Operation FLAT 5, with the crew

Navigator F/Lt Wasilewski. (PISM via PH)

of F/Sgt Trotter RAAF on board, and headed for the reception site at Tluszcz carrying six containers and six packages. As they approached the Danish coast at 1,000 feet, the Halifax was intercepted by a night fighter and badly damaged, leaving F/Sgt Trotter with no option but to ditch. This he did some twelve miles off the Jutland peninsular, where he and three others were picked up by the enemy after two hours in the water. The remaining three crew members failed to survive either the engagement or the ditching. F/L Wasilewski and crew were in BB309, which took off at 18.29, with F/Sgt Miecznik at the controls, also bound for the drop site near Tluszcz to carry out Operation NEON 3. They were carrying two passengers, six containers and a package, which were delivered without difficulty to a clearly visible reception committee. They were on their way home at 04.00, now with second pilot, Sgt Kasprzak, in the pilot's seat, when they were attacked and severely damaged by a JU88 night fighter, which they shot down. Kasprzak attempted to pull off a crash-landing near Slaglille in Denmark's Zeeland region, but struck a farmhouse, killing four members of the crew, including F/L Wasilewski. Tragically, the farmer, Lauritz Christensen, his wife, mother and two of his seven children were also killed. Sgt Kasprzak succumbed to his injuries in hospital soon afterwards, while the rear gunner fell into enemy hands. F/Sgt Miecznik had been thrown clear on impact, and spent six weeks recovering from a broken arm and leg, before passing into Sweden, and arriving home in January 1944. F/O Krywda and crew took off at 18.30 in BB378 on Operation NEON I, carrying three agents, six containers and a package. The sortie proceeded apparently without a hitch, and the Halifax returned safely after a round-trip of twelve hours and thirty minutes.

F/Sgt Cole and crew led the way for the France-bound contingent, taking off at 19.32 in JD362 on Operations JOCKEY 4/1, and landing at 04.20 to report a successful outcome. The details of the other four sorties, all of which were successful, are as follows; S/L Passey in an unidentified aircraft on Operations PIMENTO 44/41, 19.50 to 04.00. W/C Speare in JD172 on Operations SPRUCE 25/MUSTER, 19.54 to 03.40, agent dropped on second element. Sgt Copas in BB317 on Operations TRAINER 52/49, 20.11 to 03.28. Sgt Gregory in DG252 on Operation MISTRAL 5, 20.34 to 01.18.

A series of four operations over four weeks against Hanover would begin on the night of the 22/23rd, but in the meantime, the main force stayed at home. Pathfinder Mosquitos roamed around Germany, gardeners planted their vegetables, and while the moon lasted, the Tempsford squadrons went quietly about their business. From now on, they would be joined by aircraft and crews on loan from main force squadrons, predominantly 3 Group's Stirling brigade, which was having a tough time over Germany, and would ultimately be withdrawn from the main offensive. Two 214 Squadron Stirlings flew sorties on the night of the 18/19th, but neither crew was able to identify the drop zone in the face of ground fog. The 138 Squadron ORB shows six sorties for the night of the 18/19th, but Freddie Clark suggests, that there were only three, and the remaining three belong to the night of the 19/20th. However, the ORB shows a total of eight sorties for the two nights, and, as the maiden Liberator sortie and two failures to return are well documented as occurring on the night of the 19/20th, I am assuming five for the 18/19th, one to Poland and four to France. F/O Freyer and crew took off BB378 at 17.40, bound for Poland on Operation FLAT 20. They were carrying three passengers, six containers and a package, which they successfully delivered to an undisclosed reception point, before returning to land at Acklington at 07.10. S/L Passey and crew took off in BB317 at 21.31 on Operations JOHN 15/19, but returned at 05.25 to report an unsuccessful outcome. They were followed into the air at 21.35 by HR666, in which P/O Bown and crew were heading for France to attempt Operations TRAINER 33/81. They landed at 05.35 to report a successful sortie. The recently-commissioned P/O Armstrong and his crew took off at 21.56, in BB378 to carry out Operations HORDE/WHEELWRIGHT 28, and, on their return at 06.04, they reported having completed the first element only. F/O Bailey and crew were undertaking their maiden SOE sortie, and took off last in DG252 at 22.45 on Operation STATIONER 27, which they were able to complete.

On the following night, the Polish C Flight undertook its first Liberator sortie in BZ860, which contained the crew of F/L Malinowski, for whom W/O Hulas was the pilot. They took off at 21.55, and headed for the Vichy area of France on Operations TRAINER 42/40. They identified ground features to confirm the accuracy of their navigation, but no reception committee was present at either site, and the sortie was abandoned. On the way home they were shadowed by an unidentified aircraft, which they lost in cloud, and were fired upon by inaccurate light flak when crossing the coast at Cabourg at 6,000 feet. The other two sorties on this night were to Holland, for which no take-off times are provided. S/L Wilkin DFC MC (Czech) MiD, RCAF, and his crew were attempting Operations CATARRH 14/LEEK 9, and were approaching the Frisians on the way to the drop zone, when DG252 was hit by flak and crashed into the sea without survivors. Curiously, only five names are listed as being on board, and three of them were holders of the coveted DFM. F/Sgt Sherwood and crew were in BB317, having been briefed for Operations PARSNIP 7/LETTUCE 12, and successfully delivered

Left: P/O George Berwick DFM, flight engineer for S/L Wilkin when their Halifax DG252, NF-B was shot down near the Frisian Islands (Aircrew Remembered). Right: F/O Hugh Burke (left of picture) with his friend F/Sgt George Wall and two unidentified companions. F/O Burke was with the Wilkin crew when they were lost (John Coleman via Peter Green)

fourteen containers and a package. They were hit by flak on the way home, and ditched in the North Sea, which resulted in the deaths of F/Sgt Sherwood and one other. The five survivors managed to get into the dinghy, but one was washed out and lost before rescue came at the hands of the enemy. This brought to an end a catastrophic six-night period, during which, eight aircraft and crews had been lost, and it would be a further nine months before anything like this occurred again.

During what remained of the moon period, Freddie Clark writes that five more sorties were undertaken by the squadron to France and one to Poland. The ORB provides little help, but I can find only four to France. F/O Krywda and crew were in the newly acquired Halifax LK276, and took off at 18.01 to head for their homeland on Operation NEON 5. They were carrying three passengers, six containers and a package for delivery to the familiar drop site near Minsk Mazowiecki, which they located without apparent difficulty, and returned safely after more than twelve hours aloft. F/L Zbucki and crew took off in Liberator BZ858 at 23.20, bound for France to attempt Operations STATIONER 20/11, the delivery of six containers. As they approached the French coast, the pilot, W/O Ziolkowski, became ill, and the sortie had to be abandoned. The operation was attempted again on the following night, same aircraft and crew, taking off at 23.25, but was abandoned again after a little over an hour, and a Polish source suggests that this might have been the result of instrument failure. The next sortie on the night of the 22/23rd involved LK276 and the crew of F/Sgt Cole, who took off at 23.36 to carry out Operations DETECTIVE 1/WRESTLER/STATIONER 12. The first drop site was approximately twenty miles south-east of Tours, where fifteen containers and five packages were delivered. Sixteen minutes later, they arrived at the second reception point, about ten miles south-south-west of Chateauroux, onto which WAAF, Pearl Witherington, parachuted. She would eventually become the circuit commander of WRESTLER, and remain so until the liberation of France. LL280 contained the crew of W/C Speare, and took off at 00.27 on

Operations YAPOK/OTHELLO 2/TOM 14. They managed to complete the third element only, and brought another very busy month of operations to a close. While the SOE crews were doing their stuff, over seven hundred other crews were taking part in the first of the Hanover operations. Despite clear skies over the target, the main force operation failed through a stronger-than-forecast wind, which drove the markers and bombing towards the south-eastern corner of the city. A diversionary raid by a small force of Pathfinder Lancasters and Mosquitos on Oldenburg near Bremen involved the dropping of much Window and many flares, and this possibly restricted the losses from the main raid to a sustainable twenty-six.

On the following night, Mannheim hosted its second heavy assault of the month, this one aimed at its northern districts, which had escaped relatively lightly two and a half weeks earlier. Another heavy blow was delivered, which left over nine hundred houses, twenty industrial premises and a number of public buildings in ruins. A small 8 Group diversionary raid on Darmstadt could not prevent the loss of thirty-two aircraft on this occasion. The second Hanover raid was undertaken by 678 aircraft on the night of the 27/28th, while nineteen other Lancasters and six Mosquitos carried out a feint at Brunswick, fifty miles or so further east. The bombing at Hanover was well concentrated, but inaccurately forecast winds caused it to be concentrated five miles north of the city centre, where it was wasted on outlying communities and open country. This disappointment was compounded by the loss of thirty-eight aircraft, plus another from the Brunswick contingent.

October 1943

There was a hectic start to October for the main force Lancaster squadrons, which were involved in six major operations during the first eight nights. The month's account opened at Hagen in the Ruhr on the night of the 1/2nd, when an outstandingly accurate attack based on Oboe skymarking left forty-six industrial concerns completely destroyed. On the following night, over three hundred buildings were wrecked in Munich in a partially effective raid, before the Halifaxes and Stirlings joined in at Kassel on the night of the 3/4th. Here the blind markers overshot the aiming point, and pushed the main weight of the attack into the city's western suburbs and beyond. Two aircraft factories were hit, however, and one suburb became a sea of flame. Frankfurt suffered its first really destructive raid on the night of the 4/5th at the hands of almost four hundred aircraft, which left the eastern half of the city and the inland docks extensively damaged. An area of fire raged out of control, claiming many public and commercial buildings near the city centre. This was the first night of the new moon period, and 138 Squadron began a frustrating phase of operations involving fifteen sorties in five nights, only three of which could be completed. F/O Johnson and crew were posted in on the 4th, and, that night, three sorties were recorded on the ORB. F/Sgt Cole and crew took off in BB330 at 20.00 to undertake Operation PAUL 13 over France. For whatever reason, but most probably appalling weather conditions afflicting the near Continent, the drop failed to be completed. F/L Perrins and crew departed Tempsford at 20.52 in LW281 on Operation PETER 39 over France, which they were able to complete before returning safely to land at 02.30. Another new Halifax, LW275, was provided as the transport for F/L Cook and crew, who took off at 23.14 on Operation WHEELWRIGHT 13, again over France, in which endeavor they were successful.

A two-night break for the main force preceded an all-Lancaster attack on Stuttgart on the night of the 7/8th, for which 1 Group's 101 Squadron operated its night fighter communications jamming ABC Lancasters for the first time in numbers. The operation was moderately effective, and the loss of a very modest four aircraft suggested a successful debut for the radio counter-measures (RCM) element. From this point on, a number of 101 Squadron Lancasters would be included in most major operations, even after the formation of 100 Group, which would be dedicated to the RCM role from November. With six sorties scheduled for France and one for Belgium on this night, F/Sgt Gregory and crew started the ball rolling at 18.51 in LW281, to attempt Operation BOB 68. On return at 02.02, they reported an unsuccessful outcome, which set the tone for the night's efforts. F/Sgt Cole and crew took off in LW275 at 19.05 on Operations OSRIC 1/CARACAL 7, and headed for the target area near Waterloo. Gee fixes assisted in the navigation to Hal, a town in north-western Belgium and west of the drop site, but low cloud obscured the ground, and high cloud blotted out the moonlight, preventing them from seeing a reception signal. They were coned by searchlights and fired upon by light flak as they crossed the French coast at Haut-Banc at 1,500 feet, and had to jettison the cargo, which had been set alight, but made it home to a landing at 23.56. Details for the other sorties are as follows; F/O Bailey in LW272 on Operations OSRIC 5/MANDRILL 5, 18.55 to 23.56, unsuccessful. F/Sgt Copas in BB330 on Operation TOM 3, 19.45 to 00.04, unsuccessful. F/O Pretkiewicz in JN921 on Operation TOM 17, 19.50 to 23.10, unsuccessful. F/O Blazewski in JD319 on Operation TOM 19, 19.53 to 23.30, unsuccessful. F/L Paszkiewicz in HX161 on Operation TOM 16, 20.06 to 23.35, unsuccessful.

Navigator F/Lt Paszkiewicz. (PISM via PH)

F/O Ashley and crew were posted in on the 8th, and that night, the third raid on Hanover took place. For once at this target, everything proceeded according to plan, and a devastating attack ensued after most of the bombs fell within two miles of the city centre aiming point. Almost four thousand buildings were completely destroyed, while thirty thousand others were damaged to some extent, and twelve hundred people lost their lives. During the day, 138 Squadron prepared five Halifaxes for operations, while two of the Liberators, BZ859 and BZ860 were fueled up for the long trek to Maison Blanche in Algeria. S/L Cooke and crew were the first to take-off, at 18.05 in LW276, bound for Norway to undertake Operation GREBE, but, on landing at 02.51, they reported an unsuccessful outcome. F/L Perrins and crew were engaged on Operation GREBE 1, also over Norway, and departed Tempsford at 18.43 in LW280, only to experience the same disappointment. The remaining three sorties were over France, beginning with F/L Hodges and crew, who took off in JN921 on Operation DICK 54, and also failed, as did F/Sgt Gregory and crew, who took off in LW281 at 19.45 on Operation WHEELWRIGHT 42. The only success of the night was achieved by F/O Bown and crew, who lifted off in BB378 at 19.55 on Operation SWALLOW 1, to provide further support for GUNNERSIDE, the attack on the heavy water plant at Vemork. Whether this was a supply drop or included passengers is not made clear, but they returned at 03.30 to give the "thumbs up".

The main force squadrons, particularly those with Lancasters, were now in need of respite, and there would be ten days before the next major foray. 138 Squadron, meanwhile, dispatched a single Liberator sortie to Poland on the night of the 9/10th. BZ858 contained the crew of F/L Malinowski, with W/O Hulas at the controls, and took off in the late afternoon to carry out Operation COTTAGE 7, a supply drop of six containers to a reception site located about twenty miles south of Naleczow, a hundred miles south-east of Warsaw. According to the captain's MI9 interrogation on his return to England, it became clear before the drop zone was reached, that the fuel consumption was unacceptably high. They delivered their cargo as planned, but, on the way home over the Baltic, now in broad daylight, Malinowski opted to head for Sweden, where the Liberator was abandoned to its fate some twenty miles north of Varberg. The original story, however, mentions being fired upon by an enemy warship while outbound over the Baltic, with resultant damage to the fuel tank and a severe petrol leak. Whichever account is true, the crew arrived safely on the ground, and, after a somewhat lengthy period of internment, they were released to return to England, some on the 15th of June 1944, and the remainder in September. For F/Sgt Stefan Miniakowski, one of the gunners, this was the second experience of baling out during an operation without being captured. Back in April 1942, he successfully evaded, after his 300 Squadron Wellington was shot down by a night fighter over France on the way to Cologne.

Scandinavia dominated proceedings over the next two nights, with seven sorties to Norway and one to Denmark. F/L Perrins and crew began proceedings on the evening of the 10th, when taking off at 16.33 in JN921 to attempt Operation GREBE 1. They carried out their instructions successfully, and landed at Kinloss at 01.30. They were joined there between 02.27 and 03.30 by four other crews, who had successfully completed their drops over Norway. Among them was P/O Bown and crew, who had taken off in LW276 at 17.00 to undertake Operation FEATHER, the blind delivery of seven saboteurs, led by Peter Deinboll. They were also carrying five containers and packages for a drop site to the west of Orkla, south-west of Trondheim. They reached the target area at 3,000 feet shortly after 22.00, and landed at Kinloss at 03.00. In the event, the mission to sabotage the Orkla pyrites mines, proved to be beyond the means of the team. The details of the other sorties on this night are as follows; F/O Bailey in LW281 on Operation CAPRICORN, 16.52 to 03.05, successful. F/Sgt Hodges in BB378 on Operation APOLLO, 16.55 to 03.30, successful. F/Sgt Cole in LW280 on Operation GREBE, 16.57 to 02.27, successful. On the following night, the 11/12th, S/L Cooke and crew took off at 17.56, bound for Norway in LW284 on Operation BUNDLE. They were carrying four agents and stores to be dropped blind onto a site in the Oslo area. It required two runs to deliver the seven containers and then the saboteurs, whose brief was to destroy shipping in Oslo and Fredrikstad. The sortie was successfully concluded with a landing at Kinloss at 02.00. S/L Passey and crew took off at 18.55 in LW272, bound for Denmark on Operations TABLEJAM 11/12. The second element only was completed, before a safe return was made to Kinloss at 02.25. Twenty-four agents and much-needed supplies were successfully delivered during the above sorties.

The night of the 13/14th was devoted to operations over France, for which, six Halifaxes were made ready. S/L Pitt and crew were first away at 17.00 in LW280 on Operation JOCKEY 8, which they failed to complete. F/O Blazewski and crew took off at 18.45 in JD171, with F/O Dziedzic at the controls, to carry out Operation JOCKEY 10 at a reception site some ten miles south of Avignon and five miles east of St-Remy. When fourteen minutes short of the target, and flying at 1,500 feet, they were picked up by two searchlights and fired upon by coloured tracer. They pinpointed on the River Rhone north of Arles, and made a DR run over the drop site as far as Cavaillon, where they turned to start a second run on a reciprocal course. Now at 1,000 feet, and flying in a region with a high point above that altitude, they came under fire again from both light and heavy flak from multiple directions, and, observing no signal from the ground, decided to beat a hasty retreat, eventually landing, like all of the others on this night, at Exeter. Also logged as taking off at 18.45 was the crew of F/Sgt Hodges in BB330. They were assigned to Operations TRAINER 65/DIRECTOR 63, which they failed to complete, and it was a similar story for F/L Paszkiewicz and crew in LW276, who took off at 19.34 on Operation JOCKEY 16. There were two successful sorties, however, undertaken by the crews of F/O Krywda and F/Sgt Gregory, who took off in JD319 and HX161 on Operations PIMENTO 31/35 and JOCKEY 17 respectively.

The Liberator demonstrated its massive endurance on the night of the 14/15th, when BZ860 completed a round-trip of fifteen hours and five minutes duration. It had taken off at 17.20 with the crew of S/L Krol on board, whose task was to attempt Operation COTTAGE 28. This required the delivery of six containers and six packages to a reception point in Poland, located

Halifax JD319 NF-A from Polish Flight C of 138 Squadron. (J. Cynk via R. Gretzyngier)

about five miles from Skierniewice, some thirty-five miles north-east of Lodz. According to a Polish source, the strengthening anti-aircraft defences in Denmark had forced a rethink on the route, which, on this night, passed through Swedish airspace. The operation was a success, and ended with a safe landing at Kinloss. F/O Freyer and crew were also sent to their homeland, and took off in BB378 from a forward base on the 8 Group airfield at Little Snoring in Norfolk at 18.25. They were to carry out Operation COTTAGE 44, a supply drop of six containers and six packages, which was successfully accomplished during a flight of almost twelve and a half hours. The other sortie on this night was conducted by F/O Bailey and crew to Norway, under Operations TABLEJAM 11/16. They took off, it is believed, in LW272 at 18.48, and completed only the first element, before landing at Waterbeach in Cambridgeshire at 03.10.

Three sorties were mounted by 138 Squadron on the night of the 15/16th, two to Poland and one to Norway. JD171 took off from Little Snoring at 17.57 with the crew of F/O Krywda on board, who had been briefed for Operation COTTAGE 55, a drop onto a site located about ten miles south of Kalisz in Poland. They completed the sortie, and landed at Kinloss at 06.40. LW281 took off at 18.05 to deliver containers and packages to a reception site a dozen miles from Jarocin, forty miles south-east of Poznan, under Operation COTTAGE 56. F/L Paszkiewicz and crew located the target area, but were able to drop only the packages, because of a technical failure of the container release mechanism. W/C Speare and crew were in LW284, and took off at 19.45 to carry out Operation GOLDFINCH over Norway. For an undisclosed reason, the drop was not successful, and the sortie ended with a landing at Kinloss at 02.05.

F/L Perrins used Kinloss as a forward base for what would become a twelve-hour sortie to Norway on the night of the 16/17th. He took off at 19.08 in LW280 on Operation BRUNHILD, and headed out over the Shetlands en-route for Ros Lake and Lake Torne in northern Sweden. In conditions of low cloud, three runs were made across the drop zone, which, if not actually in Sweden, was very close to it, and during the last pass, a flashing light was fleetingly observed on the ground, prompting the departure of an agent, six containers and three packages from 800 feet. The agent signalled his safe arrival on the ground, and F/L Perrins began the long trek home, apparently remaining on the Swedish side of the frontier, and passing over Vega in the south of the country some two hours after the drop. The ORB records three other sorties on this night, all to France, beginning with the departure of S/L Passey and crew at 19.30, supposedly in the Halifax that was already heading for Sweden in the hands of F/L Perrins! Their brief was to undertake Operations BOB 68/B/F, which they were able to do, and returned safely to land at 02.35. JN921 took off at 20.18 with the crew of F/Sgt Copas on board, who were to carry out Operation HARRY 19. They too were successful, and were safely back on the ground at 00.39. F/O Bartter and crew were the last away from Tempsford, at 20.30, flying in HX161 on Operation WHEELWRIGHT 32, which they failed to complete. Sgt Baker and crew had been posted in on the 17th, and they were followed by pilot, F/L Mill, on the 17th.

The night of the 17/18th brought eight sorties to France, including those flown by F/Sgt Pick and S/L Cooke. The former took off at 20.10 in JN921 on Operations SCIENTIST 115/TRAINER 29, supply drops, which failed after the bomb doors refused to open. The latter took off in JD172 at 20.16 to undertake Operation TRAINER 96, which was abandoned because of a fire developing in the aircraft, possibly caused by flak. F/Sgt Gregory and crew are recorded as being in NF-V, with the serial number 860 (a Liberator, which was NF-U). He and his crew were on Operation PAUL 21, taking off at 20.02, and returning at 03.56, to report an unsuccessful outcome. The details of the other sorties are as follows; F/O Blazewski in JD319 on Operation STATIONER 20, 19.50 to 04.15, successful. F/L Styles in LW281 on Operation PAUL 20, 20.29 to 04.00, unsuccessful. F/O Johnston in LW280 on Operation WHEELWRIGHT 42, 20.35 to 03.35, successful. Sgt Thomas in HX161 on Operation WHEELWRIGHT 31, 20.52 to 03.53, successful. P/O Brown in LW284 on Operation WHEELWRIGHT 33, 22.45 to 06.45, successful.

The final Hanover raid took place on the night of the 18/19th after a nine-night break for the heavy squadrons, and was an all-Lancaster affair. It became another failure, when cloud prevented the Pathfinders from accurately pinpointing their position, and most of the bombs found open country. 138 Squadron dispatched nine sorties, beginning at 18.50 with the departure from Foulsham of JD362 with the crew of F/O Freyer on board. They were bound for Poland on Operation OXYGEN 8, carrying three passengers, six containers and a package for delivery to a previously used drop site ten miles south-east of Lowicz. They successfully fulfilled their brief, before returning safely to the 4 Group airfield at Lissett in Yorkshire at 07.50. A second departure from Foulsham involved the crew of F/O Krywda in JD319, which was also bound for Poland on Operation OXYGEN 1, with F/O Goszczynski at the controls, and carrying an identical load for delivery to a site near Lubiec village, twenty miles north-west of Warsaw. This operation is not recorded in the ORB, as it had to be abandoned about an hour after take-off because of engine failure.

Take-offs from Tempsford on this night did not begin until much later, and, according to the ORB, all were to targets in France. F/O Bartter and crew led the way at 22.50 in LW281 on Operations DICK 51/SLING/TINKER 3/DIPLOMAT A, but were unsuccessful. F/O Bailey was recorded as being in V 860, which would appear to be BZ860 NF-U, the Polish Flight Liberator. This may be an error, as is the recorded destination of France. They took off at 23.11 to undertake Operation TYBALT 6/RIGI over Germany, right on the border with Luxembourg, but returned at 05.51 to report failing to identify the drop site, and this was the second time that the operation had been attempted. S/L Passey DFC took off in LW281 at 00.05 to undertake Operations BADMINTON/RUGGER/MUSKRAT 3 and 4, a multiple drop sortie over Belgium and Holland. According to the evasion report provided by rear Gunner, Sgt Healey, RCAF, while searching at around 400 feet for the Belgian pinpoint, they were hit by machine-gun fire from the ground. (Bill Chorley states in Bomber Command Losses, that they were attacked by a night fighter). Both starboard engines were set on fire, but S/L Passey pulled off a crash-landing between Herentals and Geel, some miles east of Antwerp, and he, six members of his crew and both agents, one Belgian and the other Dutch, Jan van Schelle, managed to evade capture, while the flight engineer was taken prisoner. The details of the other sorties on this night are as follows; F/Sgt Cole in DG286 on Operation TYBALT 3 over Belgium, 22.55 to 04.15, unsuccessful. F/O Bown in LW276 on Operations OTHELLO 2/YAPOK/TOM 29, 23.05 to 04.05, third element only completed. F/Sgt Copas in JN921 on Operations TOM 25/MANELEUS, 23.17 to 03.50, second element only completed. Sgt

The starboard side of the fuselage of Halifax JD319 NF-A with clearly-visible white-red checkerboard painted on aircraft flown by Polish crews of 138 Squadron's C Flight. (PISM via WM)

Watson in HX161 on Operation TOM 19, 23.50 to 03.20, unsuccessful.

Two nights later, another all-Lancaster force of 350 aircraft took off for the first major raid on Leipzig in eastern Germany. The weather conditions were appalling, and the results were inconclusive. 138 Squadron put up a Liberator and ten Halifaxes on this night, including another, his last, by S/L Krol and crew to Poland. They took off at 16.54 in Liberator BZ860 on Operation COTTAGE 10, to deliver six containers to unspecified sites, the first of which produced no reception committee. The cargo was dropped at the second site, after which, a safe return was made to Tempsford, where they landed at 09.20, after the longest SOE flight recorded, of sixteen hours and thirty minutes duration. The details of the other sorties on this night, all to France, are as follows; S/L Pitt in JD172 on Operations PARSON 8/BATTEN, 23.20 to 05.41, first element only completed. F/Sgt Gregory in LW284 on Operations OTHELLO 2/YAPOK/TOM 12 and 22, 23.34 to 04.25, third and fourth elements only completed. F/O Johnson in LW280 on Operation PARSON 10, 23.42 to 04.45, successful. F/L Styles in JD180 on Operations TYBALT 3/FLAMILIOUS/GUINEAPIG, 23.45 to 05.15, successful. F/L Pulczynski in JD362 on Operations HARRY 7/SCIENTIST B/VERGER, 23.51 to 04.09, unsuccessful. F/Sgt PICK in BB330 on Operations PARSON 6/7, 23.59 to 05.25, unsuccessful. Sgt Watson in DT726 on Operation FARMER 6, 00.06 to 04.00, partially successful. F/Sgt Copas in NF-V 860, another reference to this unidentified Halifax, on Operation FARMER 10, 00.12 to 03.32, successful. Sgt Thomas in HX161 on Operation FARMER 8, 00.18 to 04.00, successful. F/Sgt Hodges in JN921 on Operations DICK 41/SLING, 00.45 to 05.45, unsuccessful.

The next night, the 21/22nd, brought the final four sorties of the moon period, all of them to France, but the continuing bad weather rendered them all failures. They were; F/L Paszkiewicz in JD171 on Operation JOCKEY 15, 21.02 to 03.10. F/O Bartter in DT726 on Operation DIRECTOR 57, 21.15 to 02.33. F/Sgt Cole in JN921 on Operation TRAINER 56, 21.18 to 05.30. P/O Brown in LW280 on Operation PAUL 23, 21.30 to 03.35. On the night of the 22/23rd, and for the second time during the month, a force of over five hundred aircraft set out for Kassel in central Germany, while a small 8 Group diversion took place at Frankfurt. The main raid began with a degree of overshooting by the H2S blind markers, but the visual markers were able to correct the error, and deliver their target indicators onto the city centre aiming point. The main force bombing was highly accurate and concentrated, and the hapless city and its inhabitants became engulfed in a firestorm. Its intensity was less than that experienced at Hamburg in July, but was, never-the-less, devastating in its effects, and more than 4,300 apartment blocks were reduced to rubble or shells. Almost six and a half thousand others sustained damage to some extent, and thus, 63% of the city's entire living accommodation was rendered uninhabitable in just one night. The death toll almost certainly exceeded six thousand people, and bodies were still being recovered from the ruins many months later. The defenders fought back to claim forty-three bombers, plus one from the Frankfurt diversion, and this concluded the month's main force operations.

On the 25th, the Polish crews were gathered into the newly formed 1586 (Polish) Special Duties Flight for posting to the Mediterranean, along with the two remaining Liberators and Halifaxes JD171, JD139, JD362 and JN911, although, it is not clear if they were all transferred at the same time. The Polish crews were to continue with the work so magnificently carried out from Tempsford in support of their beleaguered homeland, but would now also cover the entire Balkan region. They assembled at Sidi Amor near Tunis on the 4th of November as part of 334 Wing, and relocated to an airfield near Brindisi on the 22nd of December.

November 1943

The CO of Polish 1586 Special Duties Flight previously commanding C Flight of 138 Squadron, S/L Krol and his crew during the visit of King George VI and Queen Elisabeth at RAF Station Tempsford on 9 November 1943. From the right: flight engineer Sgt Maslon, wireless operator W/O Ptasiewicz, air gunner/dispatcher W/O Chodyra, air gunner F/Sgt Barcz, 1st pilot W/O Klosowski, 2nd pilot F/O Korpowski and navigator S/L Krol. (PH)

The first half of November would be less frenetic as far as the main force was concerned, than the start of October had been, but a new phase of operations was soon to begin, as Harris's gaze turned once more upon Berlin. Only one major operation was mounted against a target in Germany during the first half of the month, Düsseldorf providing the main fare on the night of the 3/4th, for which almost six hundred aircraft took off. Central and southern districts suffered extensive damage, and an 8 Group diversionary attack on Cologne was also delivered with extreme accuracy without loss. 138 Squadron sent five Halifaxes to France on this night, but bad weather caused all but one of them to land at Tangmere to report failure. The newly-commissioned P/O Hodges and crew were the first away, at 19.20 in DT726, briefed to carry out Operation JOHN 13, which had a drop site deep in south-eastern France. While approaching the target area, they crashed into a mountain near Marcols-les-Eaux, some forty miles south of St Etienne, killing all but the rear gunner, Sgt Brough, who was thrown clear when his turret broke away. Among the victims was Capt Estes of the USAAF, who was gaining experience before joining the clandestine American Carpetbaggers. Sgt Brough received help at a farmhouse, and was put in touch with the organization that would arrange his journey home, where he arrived in February 1944. The details of the other sorties are as follows; F/O Bown in JN921 on Operations POSSE/JOHN 29, 19.45 to 02.45. F/O Johnson in HX161 on Operation WHEELWRIGHT 27, 20.05 to 03.26. F/Sgt Thomas in LW272 on Operation STATIONER 2, 20..30 to 03.20. F/Sgt Gregory in LW284 on Operation Peter 37, 22.13 to 04.45.

Earlier in the day, Harris had sent a memo to Churchill, in which he asserted that, he, with the assistance of the Americans, could "wreck Berlin from end to end". He went on to say that it would cost between them 400-500 aircraft, but would cost Germany the war. The Americans, of course, were committed to victory by land invasion, where the film cameras could be on hand to capture the heroics, and there was never the slightest chance of enlisting their support for an all-out air assault on Germany's Capital. Undaunted as always, Harris would go it alone, and put preparations in hand for the campaign's resumption later in the month. In the meantime, 138 Squadron attempted five more sorties on the night of the 5/6th, two to Belgium and one each to France, Denmark and Germany. The ORB lists only four, and has France as the destination for each. F/O Bailey and crew are omitted, and they probably took off first, as they had a long-range sortie ahead of them to Denmark to carry out Operations TABLEJAM 15 and 16. Freddie Clark provides the only information, which is, that they ran into flak near the reception point, and decided to turn back. S/L Cooke and crew took off in LW275

Shortly before the posting of Polish crews to Sidi Amor in Tunisia, RAF Tempsford was visited by the Chief Commander of Polish Armed Forces, General Sosnkowski., seen standing with the CO of 1586 Special Duties Flight, S/L Krol. (A. Senatorska-Wisnioch via PH)

at 19.25 to have another go at Operation TYBALT 4/RIGI, and, this time, succeeded in dropping an agent blind across the German border with Luxembourg. They proceeded then to a second site in Belgium to deliver fifteen containers, but ground mist obscured the reception site, and the drop was abandoned. F/L Perrins and crew took off at 19.55 in LW272 bound for either France or Belgium on Operation TYBALT 6, (a code name associated with Belgium) and all we know, is that they landed at 00.40 to report an unsuccessful outcome. P/O Brown and crew had been assigned to Operation TYBALT 5, and took off at 20.05 in HX161. They landed at 01.05 with a similar story to tell. The newly-commissioned P/O Cole was the last to depart Tempsford, at 20.28, bound for France in JD171 on Operation TOM 32. He crossed the French coast at Haut-Banc, and, nine minutes later, ran into searchlights and flak. He reached Doullens, and set course for Guise, from where he made a DR run to the drop site near Maubeuge, near the frontier with Belgium. One minute short of the e.t.a, searchlights came on in front of them, and three flak guns opened up. Evasive action prevented any damage, but the sortie was abandoned.

CO of Polish 1586 Special Duties Flight, S/L Krol, with his crew and ground personnel in Brindisi, May 1944. Liberator BZ860 which previously flew in 138 Squadron with code letters NF-U, was transferred together with Polish airmen to southern Italy where it took part in almost 30 further special operations. S/L Krol is standing in the centre having W/O Klosowski, one of the most acclaimed Polish bomber pilots, on his right. (PH)

This was not a highly productive period for the squadron despite mounting seventeen sorties over the next few nights. Eight Halifaxes were made ready for operations over France during the 7th, and F/L Styles and crew led them off the ground at 21.00 in LW275. They were to attempt Operation BOB 53, but landed at 03.37 to report an unsuccessful outcome. The take-off time for F/Sgt Copas and crew was not recorded, but they were in JN921, bound for Operation TOM 6, when they crashed near Liesse-Notre-Dame, about ten miles north-east of Laon, without survivors from among the eight-man crew. The details of the other sorties are as follows. Sgt Thomas in LW272 on Operation BOB 76, 21.09 to 03.25, unsuccessful. F/L Mill in JD172 on Operation PARSON 6, 21.57 to 02.45, unsuccessful. Sgt Watson in BB330 on Operation PARSON 9, 22.05 to 03.00, successful. F/O Ashley in JD171 on Operation PARSON 11, 22.06 to 03.08, unsuccessful. F/Sgt Gregory in NF-T on Operation TOM 23, 22.12 to 002.50, successful. F/O Johnson in HX161 on Operation BOB 5, 22.20 to 04.55, unsuccessful.

Nine sorties were dispatched by the squadron on the night of the 7/8th, with mixed fortunes. The details are as follows. S/L Cooke in LW275 on Operations POSSE/BOB 18, 18.35 to 01.55, unsuccessful. F/Sgt Pick in BB378 on Operation BOB 5, 19.25 to 02.20, successful. P/O Cole in BB330 on Operation BOB 53, 19.30 to 02.10, unsuccessful. F/O Ashley in HX161 on Operation BOB 76, 19.42 to 03.07, unsuccessful. Sgt Thomas in KW284 on Operation PAUL 7, 20.02 to 03.08, successful. F/O Bartter in LL119 on Operation SPRUCE 17, 20.25 to 03.50, unsuccessful. F/O Bailey in LW272 on Operation JOHN 26, 20.30 to 03.15, successful. P/O Brown in JD172 on Operation PETER 8, 20.45 to 02.35, unsuccessful. F/L Perrins in LW280 on Operations TRAINER 36/60, 21.35 to 03.55, first element only completed.

On the 9th, King George VI and Queen Elizabeth paid an official visit to Tempsford, but their departure at 18.00 hours signalled a return to "business as usual", and eight sorties were dispatched by 138 Squadron that night. Six of these were to the reception site, TRAINER 95, located at Vercors, in the high mountain region of southern France, twenty miles south-west of Grenoble. Each Halifax carried fifteen containers and eight packages, but only four were successful, which meant that the target received only sixty containers and thirty-two packages. The successful sorties were as follows; F/Sgt Gregory in LW284, 19.53 to 03.16. F/O Bartter in BB378, 19.40 to 04.40. F/O Bailey in LW272, 19.55 to 03.15. Sgt Thomas in LW280, 19.58 to 03.30. The two unsuccessful sorties were those of W/O Pick in BB330, 20.16 to 04.15, and Sgt Watson in LL114, 20.22 to 04.09. The two remaining sorties on this night were; F/O Johnson in HX161 on Operation Marc 5, 20.00 to 03.45, unsuccessful, and F/L Stiles in JD172, 20.35 to 03.25, unsuccessful.

Over the following week twenty-five sorties were undertaken, all but two of them to France, but a combination of poor weather and absent reception committees conspired to allow only eight successful drops. The night of the 10/11th brought seven sorties, the first of which, involved F/O Bartter and crew in LW275, who took off at 19.40 on Operation TRAINER 41. They encountered unforeseen wind strength, which severely affected their fuel situation, and poor visibility confirmed the futility of pressing on. The other sorties were as follows; S/L Pitt in JD172 on Operation WHEELWRIGHT 32, 19.45 to 02.35, successful. P/O Cole in BB378 on Operation TRAINER 39, 19.47 to 03.47, unsuccessful. F/L Mill in LW272 on Operation WHEELWRIGHT 41, 20.02 to 03.15, successful. F/Sgt Kennedy in LW284 on Operation MARC 5, 20.05 to 04.25, unsuccessful. F/O Ashley in LL114 on Operation PAUL 3, 20.15 to 03.55, unsuccessful. P/O Brown in LW280 on Operation TRAINER 60/67/STARTER, 20.20 to 04.10, successful. There were five sorties scheduled for the following night, the 11/12th, all to France, and it was W/O Pick and crew who started the ball rolling at 20.35 in LW280 on Operation PARSON 18. They returned at 01.37 to report an unsuccessful outcome, one of four to do so. The other unsuccessful sorties were those of F/Sgt Gregory in LW284 on Operation PARSON 12, 20.49 to 01.15, F/O Johnson in LL114 on Operation PARSON 14, 21.00 to 01.10, and S/L Cooke in LW275 on Operation Parson 17, 20.54 to 00.55. Only F/O Bailey and crew, who took off in JD272 on Operation SACRISTAN 7 at 20.45, were able to give the "thumbs-up" on their return at 01.25.

Eight Halifaxes were made ready for operations during the 12th, seven of them for trips to France, and a singleton to Denmark. With the furthest to travel to Scandinavia, F/O Bown and crew took off first, at 17.30 in BB378 to undertake Operation TABLEJAM A. They landed at 03.10 to report an unsuccessful night, and this would be a common theme, as the weather and lack of reception continued to thwart the crews' best endeavours. F/L Perrins led the France-bound contingent into the air with a take-off at 19.05 in LW272 on Operation COMPANY, one of only two to be completed. The other was by F/O Bartter and crew in LW284, which departed Tempsford at 19.42 on Operation WHEELWRIGHT 38, and landed at 03.05. The details of the remaining sorties, all of which failed, are as follows; Sgt Thomas in JD172 on Operation WHEELWRIGHT 35, 19.35 to 04.05. F/L Stiles in LW275 on Operation PAUL 5, 19.43 to 03.35. W/O Kennedy in HX161 on Operation WHEELWRIGHT 37, 19.46 to 04.00.

F/O Ashley in LL114 on Operation TRAINER 80, 19.56 to 05.26. P/O Cole in NF-F on Operation WHEELWRIGHT 44, 20.00 to 03.00.

Results failed to reflect the effort expended again on the night of the 15/16th, when five sorties were scheduled for targets in France. There was a late take-off for all, beginning with W/O Pick and crew in LL115 at 23.50 on Operations PARSON 16/SETE I. They returned at 04.57 to report fulfilling their brief. The other successful crew was that of F/L Mill, who took off in JD172 at 00.23 on Operation HARRY 9, and returned at 04.25 with good news. The details of the remaining, all unsuccessful sorties, are as follows. F/L Stiles in LW275 on Operation BOB 26, 00.55 to 06.44. F/O Bailey in HX161 on Operation BOB 53, 01.05 to 07.10. W/O Kennedy and crew took off last at 01.35 in LW280 on Operations BOB 47/SLING, and crossed the French coast at Cabourg, before adopting a course to the drop site near Villenauxe-la-Grande, some forty miles south-east of Paris. Ten-tenths cloud at the coast cleared, only to reappear in the target area, and, despite flying at only 1,500 feet, the ground was obscured, and the supply drop had to be abandoned. On the way home near Orleans, they were hit by flak, and a shell exploded in the flight engineer's compartment, wounding him, the wireless operator and the pilot. They landed safely at 06.58, and W/O Kennedy spent the remainder of the year recovering.

The crews of Sgt Murray, F/Sgt Hayman and W/O Turvil were posted to the squadron on the 17th, and, that night, three sorties were dispatched to Norway and one to Belgium. P/O Brown and crew got away first at 20.10 in BB378 on Operation FIELDFARE, a blind drop of two agents. They arrived in the target area, and spent twenty minutes searching for the pinpoint, which was obscured by snow and ice, and, when P/O Brown was certain that they were over the correct spot, the agents refused to jump, insisting that they had been too long in the area, and might have attracted attention. They landed at Riccal in Yorkshire at 06.05, before continuing on to Tempsford, where the planners were less than pleased with the agents. P/O Cole and crew took off in HX161 at 20.50 on Operation GOLDFINCH, in which endeavor they were successful, and landed safely at 04.50. S/L Cooke and crew were also successful on Operation CURLEW, having taken off at 21.09 in LW275 and returned at 04.50. Sgt Watson and crew took off at 23.55 in NF-F for the shorter trip to Belgium to carry out Operation CHESS/CURLING/FOOTBALL. They returned at 02.10 to report an unsuccessful sortie.

During the lull in main force operations over Germany, over three hundred Lancasters of 5 and 8 Groups attempted to rectify September's failure at the Modane railway yards in southern France. The operation took place on the night of the 10/11th, and enough of the bombing was sufficiently accurate to cause serious damage. On the following night, an attempt to further disrupt the railway link with Italy failed, when a predominantly Halifax force missed the marshalling yards at Cannes. On the 17th, the eve of the resumption of the battle of Berlin, eighty-three Pathfinder Lancasters took off to carry out an attack on Ludwigshafen. This was to be a blind bombing attack employing H2S, without target indicators, the purpose of which is not clear. In the event, the raid appears to have been accurate, and the I G Farben chemicals plant was among the buildings hit. Imposter controllers operating from southern England sent spurious instructions to the enemy night fighter force, persuading many of them to land early, and, as a result, only one aircraft was missing from the operation. It is possible that this operation was mounted because Mannheim and Ludwigshafen had been pencilled in for a diversionary raid on the following night to mask the Berlin attack, and consecutive raids on the same target might lend weight to the enemy belief, that it was the main one.

Harris re-joined the long and rocky road to Berlin on the night of the 18/19th, for which over four hundred Pathfinder and main force Lancasters were detailed. Meanwhile, almost four hundred Halifaxes, Stirlings and Lancasters from 3, 4, 6 and 8 Groups headed for Mannheim and Ludwigshafen in an attempt to split the defences, or at least to confuse the enemy night fighter controller. The crews found Berlin to be completely cloud-covered, and it was impossible to assess the results of the raid. It had, in fact, been only modestly effective, lacking any concentration, and only four of the 173 buildings completely destroyed were industrial. Only nine Lancasters failed to return, possibly because of the diversion, from which a further twenty-three aircraft were missing.

Round two of the Berlin offensive came on the night of the 22/23rd, when 764 aircraft took off for the Capital. The crews were again denied a sight of the massive urban sprawl below, as ten-tenths cloud continued to lie across the northern half of Germany. They were able only to speculate about the accuracy of the attack at debriefing, although the consensus was, that the marking and bombing had found the mark. What they did not know, was that they had inflicted upon Berlin its most devastating assault of the war, which left three thousand houses in ruins along with twenty-three industrial premises, in an area stretching from the city centre westwards. A number of firestorm areas were reported, and a pall of smoke rose over the city to a height of more than eighteen thousand feet. Around two thousand Berliners lost their lives, while a further 170,000 were rendered homeless. The bomber casualties amounted to twenty-six aircraft, a sustainable 3.4%, and this could be considered entirely acceptable in the context of the scale of success.

On the following night, Harris dispatched an all-Lancaster main force, and guided by the glow of fires still burning beneath the clouds, the crews were able to deliver another devastating blow upon Berlin, which destroyed over two thousand more houses and a handful of industrial premises. The death toll on the ground was around fifteen hundred people, while twenty Lancasters failed to return. The night of the 25/26th was devoted to Frankfurt, for which a predominantly Halifax force was made ready. After a week of inactivity, 138 Squadron put two Halifaxes into the air bound for France. F/O Bartter and crew took off at 20.35 in LW275 on Operations JOHN 36/GENDARME, and returned at 03.35 to report a successful outcome. BB378 landed ten minutes later with the crew of W/O Pick on board, who had also successfully completed Operations JOHN 36/PELLE FLEAU/MINE.

After a three night break for the Lancaster crews, an all-Lancaster heavy force was prepared for the fourth trip to Berlin since the campaign's resumption. Over four hundred aircraft were detailed, and they set a course over northern France accompanied by a Halifax diversionary force, which peeled off for Stuttgart when Frankfurt was reached. The skies over Berlin were clear as the Lancasters approached from the south, but the Pathfinders overshot the city centre, and marked an area well to the north-west. Fortunately for the outcome of the raid, beneath the bombers lay industrial districts, and thirty-eight war industry factories were completely destroyed. The bomber stream became scattered as it withdrew from the target area, and night fighters were able to pick up individual Lancasters during the return flight. Twenty-eight failed to return home, while a further fourteen were written off in crashes in England. 138 Squadron's final sortie on the month was dispatched on the night of the 29/30th, when P/O Brown and crew took off in BB378 at 20.20, to carry out Operation WHEELWRIGHT 39. They returned safely at 03.50 to report a successful outcome. F/L Wilding joined the squadron as a pilot on this day, and would be granted the rank of squadron leader from the 1st of December. Despite the usual commitment of effort, determination and supreme courage by the crews, a modest twenty-four sorties were completed during the month, out of sixty-seven attempted.

Halifax JD362, NF-L completed numerous sorties, surviving her time with 138 Sqn before eventually being transferred to 1586 Flight.

December 1943

December began as November had ended, with an all Lancaster main force heading back to the "Big City" on the night of the 2/3rd. The 440 strong heavy contingent was supported by eighteen Pathfinder Mosquitos to lay route markers. Wrongly forecast winds led to a scattering of the bomber stream during the outward flight, and made it difficult for the Pathfinders to pinpoint the planned aiming point. As a result, the marking spread over the southern half of the city, and much of the bombing hit the suburbs or fell into open country, although some useful damage was inflicted on industrial areas in western and eastern districts. Forty missing aircraft made it a bad night for the Command, in fact the worst against Berlin since the opening two raids of the offensive back in August.

On the following night over five hundred Lancasters and Halifaxes took off for Leipzig, a city last attacked ineffectively in foul weather conditions back in October. The force headed directly for Berlin to mislead the night fighter controller, and then, as it turned towards Leipzig, a Mosquito feint continued on to Berlin to maintain the deception. The ploy had the desired effect, and the main operation was relatively unmolested by night fighters. Accurate marking and bombing led to the most destructive attack of the war on this eastern city, in which housing and industry suffered alike. There were no major operations thereafter until mid month, and it was left to the Mosquitos of 8 Group's Light Night Striking Force to maintain the pressure on Germany, by nightly raiding one or more targets in the Ruhr.

Operations from Tempsford were scheduled to recommence on the night of the 9/10th, and earlier in the day, three unusual-looking Lancasters bearing 617 Squadron codes arrived from Coningsby to supplement the 138 Squadron effort. It was almost unthinkable, that Harris had allowed precious Lancasters to be hived off for non-bombing operations, but it is significant, that the examples in question were those modified for the Dams raid, and, therefore, lacking the standard bomb bay. ED825 had taken American Joe McCarthy and his crew to the Sorpe Dam and back, while ED906, in the hands of Maltby and crew, was credited with the destruction of the Möhne Dam. ED886 had attacked the Ennepe Dam with Townsend at the controls, and had survived a return journey across Holland in broad daylight to be the last home from Operation Chastise. As Lancasters were an unknown quantity at Tempsford, sixteen ground crew personnel accompanied the detachment. For these SOE operations to France, the Lancasters would contain the crews of F/O Weedon, F/L Bunny Clayton and W/O "Chuffy" Bull respectively. Clayton was among the first replacements for the Dams losses, while Bull and Weedon had only relatively recently volunteered to join the famous squadron, which had acquired a suicide tag following the Dortmund-Ems Canal raid in September. Bad weather intervened, however, and no operations could be mounted by 138 Squadron on this night.

On the following night, the 10/11th, a further attempt was made, and ten aircraft took off, including the three from 617 Squadron, bound for destinations in France. *(For full details of 617 Squadron's contribution to SOE operations, read Dambusters. Forging of a Legend, Chris Ward, published by Pen & Sword 2009.)* F/O Bailey and crew were the first to depart Tempsford of the 138 Squadron contingent, leaving the ground at 19.02 in NF-V, and heading for Norway for another shot at Operation FIELDFARE. They were followed into the air at 19.05 by P/O Brown and crew, who were also bound for Norway in NF-M to attempt Operation

ANVIL I. The former landed at Kinloss at 03.27, and the latter at Tempsford at 04.55, and neither had been able to fulfil their brief. F/Sgt Thomas and crew were next away, at 19.15 in LW280 on Operations SPAGHETTI/TABLEJAM 14, which was to be conducted over Denmark. They succeeded in delivering two agents, nine containers and two packages, before returning safely to land at 02.30. F/O Johnson and crew had been briefed for Operation OSRIC 13, and took off at 19.57 in JD172 to head for France, but failed to complete the drop. Also operating over Denmark were F/Sgt Watson and crew in LL276, who had taken off at 20.07 on Operation OSPREY 1. They succeeded in delivering four agents, ten containers and six packages, before returning safely to land at 02.25. BB330 took off at 20.10 with the crew of F/O Ashley on board, who were to carry out Operation TYBALT 6, presumably over Belgium, but failed to complete, and returned to land at 01.50. (The ORB tends to cite France as the destination for almost all sorties.)

F/L Bartter and crew had been briefed for Operation TABLEJAM 18/19 over Denmark, and should have taken off much earlier in the evening in BB378. Freddie Clark quotes the PRO file report made by F/L Bartter on his return to England on the 5th of January 1944, which differs from other published accounts. Take-off had been delayed by deposits of ice on the aircraft, and the rear turret was still frosted-up when the crew was ordered into the air at 21.50, after the latest permissible time for take-off had already passed. They were assured that the turret would defrost once airborne, but it remained opaque as they crossed Jutland at 300 feet, before descending to 100 feet over the sea en-route to Zealand. They approached the drop site in bright moonlight and excellent visibility, and climbed to 800 feet to allow the agent, Dr Flemming Muus, the senior SOE operative in Denmark, to jump. At that moment, the shadow of another aircraft crossed their track, and the flight engineer, observing from the astrodome, reported, that a JU88 had turned and was about to make an attack from the rear. The enemy's first pass knocked out the intercom, rendering the pilot blind for the purpose of evasive action, and the second damaged control surfaces and set fire to a wing. Bartter was forced to crash-land BB378 in a frozen field, and did so without injury to the crew or the agent, and, while still under enemy fire. The rear gunner maintained defensive fire almost until the Halifax was on the ground, and got in his final burst as the enemy aircraft banked away. In his Bomber Command Losses Vol. IV, Bill Chorley records the attacker as a ME110, rather than a JU88, and states that it was shot down with fatal consequences for its crew. The Halifax was quickly consumed by fire, and the crew split up into two groups to attempt their escape. The five NCOs made their way towards the east, and were soon captured, but the three officers headed north, receiving local assistance, and reached Stockholm, from where they were flown home. The agent also managed to retain his freedom. The crash site is identified as between Tostrup and Banderup, a dozen or so miles south of Holbaek. The problem is, that the first two locations are in mid Jutland, while the last-mentioned is on Zealand.

W/C Speare and crew ventured out alone on the night of the 11/12th, taking off in LW280 at 20.03, and heading for Norway on Operation GOLDFINCH I. They landed back at 04.22, having failed to complete the drop. S/L Pitt DFC, AFC was officially posted from the squadron on the 11th, and promoted to wing commander rank to succeed W/C Blackburn as commanding officer of 148 Squadron, another SOE unit operating out of North Africa. He would oversee the squadron's move to Italy at the end of January 1944, and carry out his fare share of operations, but his period in command would be blighted by ill health, and he would leave the squadron in August, and be awarded a DSO in October. 1666 Conversion Unit provided two new crews on the 13th, those of Sgt Williams and F/O Carroll.

Operations resumed for both the main force and the moon squadrons on the night of the 16/17th, when Berlin was selected as the objective for an all-Lancaster heavy force numbering over 480 aircraft. The enemy night fighter controller was becoming accustomed to the direct route across Holland adopted by the bombers, and was able to start infiltrating his night fighters into the stream at the Dutch coast. Combats took place all the way to the target area, and the majority of the twenty-five losses occurred during the outward flight. Complete cloud cover over Berlin necessitated the use of skymarking, but much of the bombing still fell within the city. Arriving back in home airspace, many crews, particularly those from 1, 6 and 8 Groups, still faced their sternest test of the night. Their stations were shrouded in a blanket of impenetrable low cloud, and few, if any, had sufficient reserves of fuel to divert to other areas. The minutes between midnight and 02.00 witnessed the frantic search by exhausted crews for somewhere to land, and many aircraft came to grief as they stumbled around in the murk. Some flew into the ground, while others collided with obstacles or other aircraft. A few crews opted to take to their parachutes as their fuel ran out, and they were generally the fortunate ones. Twenty-nine Lancasters were lost in these cruellest of circumstances, and around 150 airmen lost their lives when so close to home and safety.

It was a bad night also for 138 Squadron as the conditions worsened, and its returning crews were forced to join the general melee around midnight and thereafter. Six crews had set out for France earlier in the evening, but the ORB records only four, and we will deal with those first. P/O Brown and crew took off at 20.00 in NF-M to carry out Operation DETECTIVE 2, and returned at 05.00, having been diverted to Woodbridge, apparently with a fuel leak, which had prevented the drop from taking place. F/Sgt Thomas and crew got away five minutes after Brown in LW280 on Operation MARC I, and was abandoned over Essex, presumably on the way home, and, one imagines, as a result of technical difficulties or fuel shortage. It seems clear, that the low cloud obscured the ground, because the Halifax was actually over the coast rather than inland, and four members of the crew landed in the water, from where their bodies were recovered. The pilot and both gunners survived. W/O Pick and crew had also been assigned to Operation MARC I, and had taken off in LL276 at 20.20 to head for the Arcachon region on France's south-western coast. After failing to make contact with a reception committee, Pick flew eastwards for over a hundred miles in search of a second pinpoint at Figeac, but thick fog over southern France thwarted all efforts, and they landed at Chivenor at 05.45. F/O Johnson and crew took off at 20.45 in LL119 to undertake Operation WHEELWRIGHT 36, which they failed to complete. On return, and unable to find somewhere to land, they took to their parachutes over Suffolk, and arrived safely on the ground, while the Halifax ended up in the sea off Felixstowe. S/L Wilding had aborted his sortie early on, and had managed to get back to Tempsford, before poor visibility shut the airfield down. Finally, as the clock showed a few minutes short of 05.30, F/Sgt Watson let down towards Woodbridge in LL115 after almost ten hours in the air. He and his crew had been to the Carcassonne region of France to deliver a dozen containers and five packages under Operation DETECTIVE 3, and it is not known whether or not they had been successful. On final approach the Halifax struck trees and crashed at Capel Green, killing the pilot and four of his crew, and injuring three others. According to Freddie Clark, only one man survived, which suggests that two succumbed to their injuries. 161 Squadron had also experienced a terrible night, in which two Lysanders and three Halifaxes had come to grief at home, with all but one of the crashes involving fatalities.

On the 19th 138 Squadron lost one of its new crews to an unfortunate training accident. While practicing container drops over the nearby airfield at Henlow, Sgt Williams flew BB364 into a tall chimney at a brickworks, and all nine occupants died in the ensuing crash. The main force returned to action in the late afternoon of the 20th, when almost 650 Lancasters and Halifaxes took off for Frankfurt, accompanied by a small force of 1 and 8 Group Lancasters and Mosquitos bound for Mannheim as a diversion. The enemy night fighter controller was again able to plot the bomber stream's progress, and many combats took place before the target was reached. Unexpected cloud hampered the Pathfinders' attempts to mark, and decoy fires and markers on the ground lured some of the bombing away from the city. The creep-back from this fell within Frankfurt, however, and over four hundred houses were destroyed, while almost two thousand other buildings in the city and neighbouring towns sustained serious damage. It was a bad night for the bombers, though, and forty-one failed to return home, twenty-seven of them Halifaxes, which represented a 10.5% loss rate for the type.

138 Squadron prepared three Halifaxes for operations that night, each one taking off late, and heading for France. F/L Perrins and crew departed first, at 23.48 in NF-M, to undertake Operations TRAINER 61/STOCKBROKER 1 and 3, and landed at 07.05 to report completing the second element only. F/L Stiles and crew got away at 00.40 in in LL276 on Operation TRAINER 12, which they failed to complete. F/O Ashley and crew were in BB330, and took off at 01.38 on Operation SACRISTAN 10, and they, too, returned to report an unsuccessful outcome. Three nights later, over 360 Lancasters provided the majority of the effort for yet another assault on Berlin, when a Mosquito feint at Leipzig was partially successful in delaying the arrival of the night fighters. Technical problems with their H2S equipment prevented the Pathfinders from taking advantage, and the marking was scattered. Most of the bombing fell into the south-eastern corner of the city, where almost three hundred buildings were destroyed, and sixteen Lancasters failed to return home.

The last but one wartime Christmas came and went in relative peace, but business as usual resumed on the night of the 29/30th, when a force of seven hundred aircraft was made ready for the final operation of the year to Berlin. It was also to be the first of three trips to the Capital in the space of five nights spanning the turn of the year, a concentration of effort, which would bear down most heavily on the Lancaster crews. Taking off either side of 17.00 hours, the bombers took a different route on this night, passing south of the Ruhr and approaching Leipzig before swinging towards Berlin. Mosquito diversions over the Ruhr, Magdeburg and Leipzig helped to keep the night fighter controller guessing, and few night fighters made it to the target area. Again the main weight of bombs fell into the southern and south-eastern districts, while some was wasted beyond the eastern city limits, and almost four hundred buildings were destroyed in return for the loss of twenty Lancasters.

138 Squadron launched three sorties on this night, each one a mammoth pigeon drop over France. W/C Speare led the way at 17.40 in an unidentified Halifax, and crossed the coast at Dieppe at 12,000 feet, to begin a clockwise circuit, taking in Cleres, Bacqueville, Rouen,

A Polish corporal stands next to JD362, NF-L.

Bolbec, Goderville, Cany and back to Bacqueville, using Gee-fixes to establish his turning points, and spending seventeen minutes in the target area, dispensing 191 pigeons at the rate of twelve per minute. S/L Wilding took off at 17.50, and covered the Blangy, Grandvilliers, Gournay, Buchy, St-Saëns circuit further to the east, while F/O Ashley was last away at 17.56 in LW284 to service St Omer, Arras and Doullens, further still to the north-east. Freddie Clark makes the point that 12,000 feet was a somewhat lofty launching pad for pigeons in wintry conditions, and wonders how many survived to return to England. The squadron's final sortie of the year was mounted on the night of the 30/31st, by F/O Ashley and crew, who took off in LW272 at 22.07 to carry out Operation HARRY 15, in which endeavour they were successful, and landed safely back at Tempsford at 02.18. It had been a tough year all round, but generally speaking, a successful one, during which Bomber Command had developed into a weapon of awesome power. When this might was directed accurately, it could reduce cities to ruins. Standing in its way, however, were two powerful enemies, the weather and the Luftwaffe night fighter force, and during the first quarter of 1944, they would combine to test the bomber crews' resolve to the absolute limit.

January 1944

As the New Year dawned, the toll of repeated operations to Berlin, eight since the resumption of the campaign, began to tell on the crews, particularly those of the Lancaster squadrons. They had been involved in every one, while the Halifaxes had been used sparingly, and the Stirlings, after a period of sustained heavy losses, had been withdrawn from operations over Germany altogether, following the highly successful raid on the Capital on the 22/23rd of November. The effect of the campaign was also being felt by the inhabitants of Berlin, who had witnessed the destruction of 25% of the city's living accommodation, and seen evidence of the mounting death toll. There is little doubt, that they and the crews of Bomber Command shared a common wish for the New Year, that Berlin would cease to be the main focus of attention.

Before New Year's Day was done, the first Lancasters were taking off, and by the time that the 2nd of January was an hour old, over four hundred of them were heading for the Capital via an almost direct route over Holland. Not all reached their objective, twenty-nine turning back for a variety of reasons, and around sixteen others fell victim to night fighters and flak. The remainder found the city covered by cloud, and the skymarking soon deteriorated in the face of a strong wind. The bombing was spread over seventeen miles from wooded country in the south-west to districts in the east, but nowhere was significant damage inflicted. Many of the crews, who collapsed wearily into bed at breakfast time on the 2nd, found themselves back in the briefing room later in the day, incredulous and angry at the prospect of a back-to-back trip to the "Big City", and the third in five nights. At most stations it was snowing as the briefings took place, and the crewmen silently pondered the prospect of another midnight take-off, and the fact that no diversionary measures were planned.

The strain and weakening morale manifested itself as crew after crew turned back with problems of some kind. The force was depleted by sixty aircraft returning early, and while "boomerangs" were a fact of life for very genuine reasons, some of those aborting their sorties on this night would almost certainly have pressed on under different circumstances. Bombs were again scattered over all parts of the city, and damage was only marginally greater than twenty-four hours earlier, amounting to around eighty houses destroyed. Heavy losses were beginning to bleed the Pathfinders dry of quality crews, and sideways postings between the squadrons became common to maintain a leavening of experience.

138 Squadron had begun the year with commissions for F/Sgt Thomas and W/O Pick on the 1st. The main force crews were granted two nights off before the next operation, and during this lull, on the 4/5th, while eighty aircraft from 3, 5 and 8 Groups attacked two flying bomb launching sites in France, the Tempsford squadrons opened their 1944 account. As mentioned earlier, this would be the first occasion on which the activities of the moon squadrons appeared in Bomber Command records. According to Freddie Clark, 138 Squadron dispatched twelve sorties, with destinations in Norway, France and Germany, but only eleven are recorded in the ORB. The entries are written in a new hand, with slightly more information on each sortie, but few, if any, details to identify the aircraft.

The two Halifaxes bound for Norway on supply drops under Operation GOLDFINCH 3 took off first, P/O Brown and crew leading the way at 18.35 in NF-M. The eight-hour round-trip would be one of the few successes on this night, F/O Ashley and crew returning at 04.16 to report being unable to locate the reception point, after taking off at 18.58 in DG286. P/O Cole and crew took off at 19.47 to carry out Operations BOB 54/EIGER, the first element of which, was the delivery of a dozen containers fifteen miles south of Chatillon. This was concluded successfully, but the second element, the dropping of two NKVD agents into Germany, was thwarted by cloud and icing conditions, and they were brought home. P/O Pick and crew departed Tempsford at 19.55 in LL276 on Operations TRAINER 101/SQUAD 1, which was the delivery of containers to a reception point at Sancerre in central France, and the blind drop of NKVD agents across the border in Germany, north of Freiburg. In the event, ten-tenths cloud and the failure to materialize of a reception committee thwarted the first element, while snow on the ground and icing conditions in the air prevented a visual pinpoint at the second. F/Sgt Gregory and crew were assigned to Operations MESSENGER 5/MARKSMAN 13, and took off at 20.05 in LW284. They failed to find a reception for their containers and packages, and returned home at 03.50. F/L Stiles and crew were the next away, at 20.11 in LW275, bound initially for Belgium to carry out Operation TYBALT 9, a supply drop fifteen miles south-west of Givet. They found no reception, so continued on to Gerolstein, just across the frontier in Germany, and made a DR run to a pinpoint near Coblenz for Operation JUNGFRAU, the blind drop from 800 feet of an NKVD agent and his folding bicycle, thus completing an operation left outstanding since the 10th of December. F/O Johnson and crew took off at 20.22, bound for France on Operations BATCH 1/JOHN 22, but developed engine trouble an hour out, and jettisoned the cargo near Arundel, before landing safely at Tangmere with the two agents. BB378 took off at 20.30 with the crew of F/L Downes on board, whose brief was to attempt Operations JUGGLER 5/TRAINER 24. They were also carrying agents and stores, but failed to find a reception committee, and brought the lot home. Operation WHEELWRIGHT 44 was the task handed to W/O Kennedy and crew in LW272, which took off at 20.58. They were carrying containers and packages for delivery to reception points in France, and, on return at 03.57, they were able to confirm success. F/Sgt Hayman and crew were carrying a similar all-cargo load for delivery to France under Operation JOHN 50, as they took off at 21.15, but the lack of reception forced them to bring their load back. It was a similar story for Sgt Baker and crew, who departed last, at 22.34, on Operation JOHN 49, a supply drop over France.

The Lancaster crews were called to briefings on the afternoon of the 5th, to learn that their target was to be Stettin, at the eastern end of Germany's Baltic coast. Ten Pathfinder Halifaxes from 35 Squadron accompanied almost 350 Lancasters in another very late take-off, and a mosquito diversion at Berlin played its part in keeping the main operation largely free of night fighters. Over five hundred houses were completely destroyed, along with twenty industrial premises, while almost twelve hundred other buildings were seriously damaged, and eight ships were sunk in the port. There now followed a welcome eight-night break from operations for the heavy brigade, which allowed the hard-pressed squadrons an opportunity to recover from the four long-range trips in the space of eight nights.

It was business as usual at Tempsford on the night of the 6/7th though, and 138 Squadron made ready eleven Halifaxes for take-off that evening. P/O Cole and crew started the ball rolling at 20.08 in LL284, when taking-off for France, with agents and supplies for Operations JOHN 11/COLONY 1. The second element only was completed, as no reception was found at the first, but it is not known whether this involved agents or cargo. The two departures logged at

20.12 involved the crews of F/O Carroll, on their first SOE sortie, and P/O Pick, in NF-M and LW276 on Operations BOB 23 and JOHN 38 respectively. The former, a supply drop over France, was successfully completed, as was the latter, which delivered agents and stores. F/O Ashley and crew were next away at 20.15 in DG286 on Operation TRAINER 100, a supply drop over France, which failed through the lack of a reception. F/L Perrins and crew departed at 20.23 in LL187 on Operation EVEREST 1, an NKVD sortie to Austria. They crossed the French coast at Cabourg, and adopted a south-easterly route, to pass east of Lyon, before crossing the Alps to Lake Como, north of Milan. From there the route took them to a point east of Klagenfurt in southern Austria, where they swung to the north, and carried out a DR run from St-Pölten to the drop site near the Czech border. The weather had been clear thus far, but a storm developed in the target area to create difficulties, and, on arrival, an internment camp was spotted right on the pinpoint. It was decided to fly east for five miles, where the two agents were dropped from 800 feet, before a new course was set for Malta, where a safe arrival concluded the eleven-hour flight. The next departure was that of a W/C Corby and crew in LW284 at 20.40. They were undertaking Operation STATIONER 14, a container drop over France, which they completed during a seven-hour sortie. Also bound for a container drop over France were F/L Downes and crew, who took off in NF-D at 20.44, but failed to make contact with a reception committee. F/O Bailey and crew took off in JD172 at 20.45 on Operations MARKSMAN 13/5, carrying agents and supplies for a drop site in France. They returned at 04.15 to register another success for the squadron. F/Sgt Hayman and crew were in LL114, and took off at 20.54 on Operation JOHN 23, a supply drop which failed through the lack of a reception. Halifax NF-B provided the transport for Sgt Baker and crew, who took off at 20.56 on Operation PETER 16. They delivered their containers and packages to the briefed drop site in France, and returned safely. Finally, W/O Kennedy and crew got away at 20.57 in LW272 to carrying agents and stores to France on Operations JUGGLER 5/TRAINER 34. Sadly, no reception signalled its presence, and the contents of the Halifax were returned to Tempsford.

The following night brought five successful sorties out of ten dispatched. S/L Wilding and crew took off at 20.06 in JD172 to undertake Operations BOB 18/SQUAD, the first element of which involved dropping a dozen containers to a reception point in France. The second element called for an agent to be delivered to a pinpoint on the German side of the border with France, but, as he specifically asked to be dropped between Offenburg to the north and Freiburg to the south, they fixed on Kenzingen, rather than the briefed location some fourteen miles further north, and he parachuted there. The details of the other successful sorties are as follows; F/O Ashley in NF-A on Operation GOLDFINCH 3, a container drop to Norway, 18.44 to 02.37. F/L Stiles in NF-O on Operations AUTHOR 1/2, carrying an agent and stores to France, 20.03 to 03.04. Sgt Baker in NF-B on Operation JOHN 17, a supply drop to France, 20.32 to 03.35. F/O Carroll in NF-P, also on Operation JOHN 17, 20.50 to 04.04. The unsuccessful sorties were; F/Sgt Gregory in LW284 on Operation THRUSH RED 1, a supply drop to Norway, 18.23 to 04.55, lack of reception. F/O Bailey in LW272 on Operation BOB 69, a supply drop to France, 19.05 to 02.53, lack of reception. P/O Cole in LL114 on Operation JOHN 31, a supply drop to France, 20.28 to 03.50, lack of reception. F/L Downes in NF-D on Operation MARKSMAN 1, a supply drop to France, 21.07 to 04.25, pinpoint not found. P/O Kennedy and crew had set out at 20.32 for Belgium in LK743, to carry out Operations TYBALT 3/THERSITES 4, but when they rejoined the circuit almost five hours later, the three Belgian agents, Capt Verhaegen, Sgt Goffin and Sgt Michaux, were still on board. The Halifax was also carrying a dead port-outer engine, which would not feather, and this was undoubtedly a contributory factor in the subsequent crash at Tetworth Hill, near Bedford. The Halifax caught fire, and all ten occupants lost their lives.

Four sorties were attempted by 138 Squadron on the night of the 10/11th, three to Belgium and one to France. Three were supply drops, but the first to depart Tempsford, at 20.28, were P/O Cole and crew in LL114, who were carrying three agents and six packages for delivery to TYBALT 11 in Belgium, a task in which they were successful. F/O Johnson and crew were assigned to Operations ARCHDEACON 8/MUSICIAN 11, and took off in an unidentified Halifax at 20.45, bound for north-eastern France with an agent, and stores on board. No reception committee made itself known at the first drop site, which was fortuitous, as it was in German hands. However, following a DR run from Guise to a pinpoint some fifteen miles north-east of St-Quentin, the agent jumped onto another site being worked by the Germans. F/Sgt Gregory and crew were carrying containers, packages and pigeons in LW284 as they took off at 20.53 to head for Belgium on Operation TYBALT 3, but a technical issue caused nine containers to hang-up, and ruin the attempt. F/L Stiles was also dogged by gremlins after taking off at 21.00 in NF-O, and heading for Belgium to undertake Operation SAMOYEDE 2. The bomb doors refused to open as he ran towards the reception lights, and it was found that the main hydraulic pipe had been severed. Three packages were dropped, one of which hit the tailwheel, and the reception lights were extinguished before a further run could be completed.

While the SOE squadrons hid themselves in the shadows to await the next moon, the main force and Pathfinder crews gathered for briefings on the 14th. There must have been a sense of relief as the curtains were drawn back from the wall maps, revealing Brunswick rather than Berlin as the target for the night. Situated about fifty miles beyond Hanover, Brunswick had not hosted a major operation before. 498 aircraft took off, all but two of them Lancasters, and battled their way through intense night fighter activity to and from the target. By the time the survivors reached home airspace, after a dismally disappointing raid, thirty-eight of their number had been brought down, and the Pathfinders had again sustained heavy casualties to the tune of eleven aircraft. Since the turn of the year, 156 Squadron alone had lost fourteen Lancasters and crews. Another five-night lull prepared the crews for the next operation, a maximum effort to Berlin on the night of the 20/21st, for which 769 aircraft took off. Berlin was completely cloud covered, and it was impossible to make an assessment of the raid from the air. In fact, most of the bombs had fallen in an eight-mile swathe from north to south across the city's hitherto less severely damaged eastern districts, and there was much damage to housing, industry and railway installations. It was another night of heavy losses, however, and twenty-two of the missing thirty-five aircraft were Halifaxes.

The survivors prepared for the following night's effort to Magdeburg, which, like Brunswick, had never been raided in numbers before. On this night it would face the remains of a force of 648 aircraft, which departed their stations either side of 20.00 hours. A running battle between night fighter and bomber ensued all the way to the target, which was reached ahead of time by some aircraft through stronger than forecast winds. Anxious to get away from the target area as quickly as possible, some crews bombed before the Pathfinder markers went down, and the resulting fires combined with decoy markers to draw off a proportion of the main force. The Pathfinders were not able to recover the situation, and the attack lacked accuracy and concentration, falling predominantly outside of the city. A massive fifty-seven aircraft failed to return, the majority of them victims of night fighters, and this represented a new record high casualty figure. The Halifax squadrons once more sustained the heavier losses, amounting to thirty-five aircraft.

The squadrons were given a five-night rest to lick their wounds before the next round of operations began, and this was to be a three-raid assault on the Capital in an unprecedented space of just four nights. Freddie Clark and crew arrived on posting on the 27th, joining others recently posted in, including pilots F/O Walker and F/Sgt Jones. That night, an all-Lancaster heavy force of 515 aircraft took off either side of 18.00 hours, to adopt a south-easterly course across northern Holland and into Germany, before turning north-east to a point west of Berlin. They found the city to be cloud-covered, and a strong tail wind drove the markers across the city along the line of approach. Bombs fell in many parts of Berlin, although more in the southern half, but dozens of outlying communities were also afflicted. The operation was moderately successful, if expensive, thirty-three Lancasters falling victim to the defences, most of them to night fighters arriving on the scene as the raid was in progress.

This night also signalled the start of the new moon period, and six sorties were launched by 138 Squadron. P/O Pick led the way, when taking off at 19.10 in LL114 on Operation PAUL 18, a supply drop over France, which failed because of cloud. F/L Perrins and crew were next away at 19.32 in LL187, to undertake Operation DETECTIVE 6, another supply drop over France, which was successful. F/Sgt Hayman and crew took off at 19.47 in LW272, but failed to complete Operations WHEELWRIGHT 36/59 in the absence of a reception committee. P/O Cole and crew were handed Operation JOHN 25, and took off at 20.04 in LW276, carrying agents, containers and packages. They were also thwarted by cloud, and returned to land at 02.59. W/C Corby and crew took off at 20.20 in LL284 to carry out Operation PETER 24, a supply drop in northern France, which they completed. S/L Wilding and crew were last away, at 20.38, in JD172 on Operation PETER 16A. They were carrying an agent and stores, which were delivered according to instructions.

The inclusion of Halifaxes in the Berlin operation on the following night allowed a force of 677 aircraft to take off around midnight, and they were routed over Denmark to approach the target from the north-west. A hot reception awaited the bombers over the target, where single and twin engine fighters accounted for twenty-seven aircraft, despite which, the marking and bombing were accurate and concentrated, and much damage was caused within the southern half of the city. Around 180,000 people were rendered homeless on this night, and many public and administrative buildings were damaged in south-central districts. On the debit side, the bomber casualties had reached forty-six by the time the survivors landed. 138 Squadron mounted five sorties to France on this night, all of them successfully completed as follows; P/O Cole in NF-D on Operation BOB 73, carrying agents and stores, 20.10 to 02.50. F/L Perrins in NF-N on Operation PAUL 9, carrying agents and stores, 20.30 to 02.40. S/L Wilding in JD172 on Operation AUTHOR 8, carrying agents and stores, 20.32 to 03.24. F/Sgt Murray in LL114 on Operation PAUL 9, carrying stores, 20.43 to 03.31. F/L Downes in NF-B on Operation PAUL 9, carrying agents and stores, 21.05 to 03.20. While the bomber crews were rested on the night of the 29/30th, 138 Squadron dispatched four more sorties to France, and achieved 50% success as follows; W/C Corby in NF-M on Operation PAUL 18, carrying stores, 19.35 to 04.15, unsuccessful due to lack of reception. P/O Pick in LL114 on Operation PAUL 18, carrying stores, 19.54 to 03.41, unsuccessful due to lack of reception. W/C Speare in LL183 on Operation JOHN 25, carrying agents and stores, 19.59 to 03.00, successful. F/L Downes in NF-B on Operation PETER 19, carrying stores, 20.30 to 02.05, successful.

After their night's rest, 534 bombers set out again for the Capital, arriving over the city shortly after 20.00 hours. It was a predominantly Lancaster force, with eighty-two of the new Hercules-powered Mk III Halifaxes for company. The night fighters only made contact deep inside German airspace, and scored steadily until the bombers were well into the return flight south of Brunswick and Hanover, ultimately achieving a total of thirty-three, all but one of them Lancasters. On the credit side, however, Berlin had suffered a bruising raid, in which large areas of the centre and south-western quarter were engulfed in flames, and at least a thousand people lost their lives. Undoubtedly much to the relief of the bomber crews, the weather and other considerations would keep them on the ground for the next two weeks.

February 1944

The rise of the moon dictated that the Tempsford squadrons would not share in the rest period, but the night of the 3/4th brought just a single sortie by 138 Squadron. F/Sgt Murray and crew took off at 21.02 in NF-F to carry out Operation BUTLER 14, a supply drop on a site twenty miles north-west of Angers in western France. On board, and flying as second pilot to gain experience on this, his first SOE operation, was P/O Freddie Clark, who described the moonlight as so brilliant, that it almost outshone the light of the reception committee. Fifteen containers went down from 800 feet onto a German-controlled site, before leaflets were dispensed over the Laval area, forty miles to the north. Over the next two nights, 138 Squadron would enjoy a good success ratio, completing twenty-one of twenty-five sorties over France and Scandinavia without loss. Twelve Halifaxes were made ready during the 4th for operations that night over France, the details of which, are as follows; F/Sgt Baker in NF-B on Operation WHEELWRIGHT 59, carrying stores, 19.55 to 02.48, successful. F/L Perrins in LL187 on Operation TRAINER 80, carrying an agent, stores and pigeons, 20.09 to 03.10, partially successful, agent not dropped. F/L Bailey in LW272 on Operation PAUL 13, carrying stores, 20.10 to 04.05, successful. F/L Mill in JD172 on Operations PAUL 36/9, carrying stores, 20.16 to 04.22 (Tangmere), successful. W/O Gregory in LW284 on Operation PAUL 13, carrying stores, 20.27 to 05.22, unsuccessful due to lack of reception. F/Sgt Hayman in LL114 on Operation TRAINER 109, carrying stores and pigeons, 20.28 to 04.33, successful. F/L Downes in NF-A on Operation PAUL 29, carrying stores, 20.30 to 05.07, unsuccessful due to lack of reception. P/O Pick in LL276 on Operation AUTHOR 9, carrying stores, 20.30 to 03.16, successful. P/O Cole in NF-M on Operation TRAINER 80, carrying an agent and stores, 20.41 to 03.59, partially successful, agent not dropped. S/L Cooke in LW275 on Operation MARC 1, carrying an agent and stores, 20.46 to 04.04, successful. F/O Carroll in NF-F on Operation WHEELWRIGHT 37, carrying stores, 20.56 to 05.02, successful. F/O Ashley, with Freddie Clark as second pilot in NF-D on Operation AUTHOR 9, carrying stores, 21.25 to 04.40, unsuccessful due to lack of reception.

The night of the 5/6th was another busy one for 138 Squadron, which scheduled thirteen sorties to carry out drops over France, Belgium, Denmark and Norway, the details of which are as follows; F/L Bailey in LW272 on Operation GULL 1 over Norway, carrying stores, 18.42 to 04.27, successful. W/O Gregory in LL114 on Operation SANDPIPER 2 over Norway, carrying stores, 18.45 to 02.16, successful. F/L Stiles in NF-O on Operation THRUSH RED, carrying stores, 18.55 to 04.07, successful apart from one container hanging-up. P/O Cole in NF-W on Operations TABLEJAM 29/28 over Denmark, carrying stores, 19.41 to 02.25, second element only completed, as no reception at first one. F/Sgt Hayman in NF-P on Operation TINKER 4 over Belgium, carrying an agent and stores, 19.45 to 02.55, partially successful, agent not dropped. F/Sgt Baker in NF-A on Operations TABLEJAM 23/22 over Denmark, carrying an agent and stores, 19.51 to 03.00, successful. F/L Downes in MA-V, borrowed from 161 Squadron, on Operations PHONO 5/TRAINER 101, carrying agents and stores, 20.10 to 02.17, unsuccessful through lack of reception. F/O Ashley in NF-B on Operations NEWSAGENT 2/APACHE 2 over France, carrying agents and stores, 20.25 to 04.05, successful. F/L Perrins in an unidentified Halifax on Operations PIMENTO 54/JOHN 52 over France, carrying an agent and stores, 20.29 to 03.43, successful. S/L Wilding in NF-J on Operations TABLEJAM 31/30 over Denmark, carrying an agent and stores, 20.39 to 03.16, second element only completed as there was no reception at the first one. P/O Pick in LW284 on Operations BATCH 1/JOHN 52 over France, carrying agents and stores, 20.50 to 03.50, successful. F/O Carroll in LL114 on Operations PETER 17A/HIDE 1 over France, carrying stores, 21.10 to 02.37, successful. F/Sgt Murray in NF-M on Operations SPIRITUALIST 1/PETER 50 over France, carrying agents, stores and pigeons, 22.20 to 04.39, first element only completed, as there was no reception at the second one.

Just four of the squadron's Halifaxes were involved in operations over southern France on the night of the 7/8th, but for two of them there was to be no return. S/L Cooke, the A Flight commander, took off with his crew in LW275 at 19.30 on Operation JOCKEY 5, and set course for Marseilles in southern France. While flying above cloud, a fire broke out in the starboard-inner engine, which had to be shut down, and it proved impossible to maintain altitude. As the Halifax sank through the cloud, it began to ice up, and this decided its fate. It was abandoned near Mantaille, some one hundred miles short of the planned destination, and all crew members arrived safely on the ground to evade capture, and they were back in England by May. We do not know the take-off time for F/O Carroll and crew, who were undertaking Operation JOHN 35 over France in LL114. The Halifax crashed at Autrans, ten miles west of Grenoble, and there were no survivors. F/O Carroll, who was on his fifth SOE operation, had trained in South Africa with Freddie Clark, and they were good friends, who had enjoyed a drink together two nights earlier. F/L Downes and crew took off at 22.52 in NF-D to carry out Operations DACRE 1/HARRY 18 over France, carrying an agent and stores, which were delivered to their drop sites as briefed. W/C Speare and crew departed Tempsford at 23.02 in NF-J, bound also for France on Operation HARRY 17. They were carrying an agent and stores, which remained on board after the reception committee failed to make itself known.

Three new crews were posted in from 31 Base at Stradishall on the 8th, those of F/Sgt Towers, F/O McMullen RAAF and F/Sgt Williamson RAAF. That night, 617 Squadron carried out an operation of great significance against the Gnome & Rhone aero-engine factory at Limoges. The marking was carried out by W/C Cheshire in a Lancaster at very low level, after making a number of passes across the site to warn the workers. Eleven other squadron aircraft then bombed the target with great accuracy from medium level, and the operation was an outstanding success, demonstrating as it did the potential of the low-level visual marking method. These were the only heavy bombers at large on this night, but eight 138 Squadron Halifaxes were also over France, and two over Belgium, attempting to deliver agents and stores to the various organizations on the ground.

Among the former was F/O Freddie Clark, flying for the first time as crew captain. He and his crew were assigned to Operation BOB 78, a supply drop, and they took off in NF-V (P/O Thomas is also recorded as being in this aircraft) at 21.05 to head for the drop zone in the Morbihan region of north-western France. On the fourth DR run from Chattilon-en-Bazois, three bonfires sprang up ahead, and the drop was carried out from 600 feet through a snow shower. F/L Mill and crew took off at 21.00 in JD172 on Operations IAGO 1/MONTAND 1/ARCHDEACON 10 over Belgium and France. The first element involved the dropping of two agents blind on the French side of the border, and then three more near Arquennes, south of Brussels. The third element was a supply drop onto what was a German-controlled site, but, fortunately, the weather prevented it from taking place. The Germans were not to go empty-handed, however, as F/Sgt Baker and crew delivered fifteen containers to them at the ARCHDEACON 11 site. They had taken off in NF-B at 20.40 to undertake that and FLAVIUS 2, and had already successfully dropped two agents blind into Belgium from around 650 feet, after carrying out a DR run from Guise. P/O Thomas and crew were in NF-V?, and took off at 20.58 on Operations PHONO 5/TRAINER 101, to deliver two French agents, Alexandre and Ledoux, one Canadian, Deniset, and an American wireless operator, Byerly, into the hands of the Gestapo, along with eight containers. The PHONO reseau had been in enemy hands for five months, and none of those falling into the net on this night, survived the war. P/O Thomas also dropped seven containers at the other site, which had not been compromised. The details of the other sorties are as follows; P/O Pick in NF-A on Operation FOOTMAN 1, carrying stores, 19.45 to 04.19, unsuccessful due to lack of reception. F/Sgt Murray in NF-L on Operations TRAINER 80A/TRAINER 131, carrying agents and stores, 20.00 to 03.20, second element only completed. W/O Gregory in LL276 on Operation WHEELWRIGHT 36A, carrying stores, 20.15 to 03.30, successful. F/Sgt Hayman in NF-M on Operations PAUL 29/APACHE 3, with PAUL 9A as an alternative, carrying stores, 20.50 to 05.45, alternative successful. F/O Ashley in NF-D on Operation TOM 40A (PARDARIUS), carrying stores, 21.10 to 01.25, unsuccessful due to adverse weather. F/L Perrins in LL187 on Operation PETER 16B, carrying agents and stores, 21.22 to 02.54, successful. The magnificent efforts of the squadron on this night had resulted in the dropping of eighteen agents and 102 containers, mostly to deserving recipients.

After a night's rest, four 138 Squadron Halifaxes set out for France on the evening of the 10th, beginning with NF-M, which took off at 20.25 with the crew of F/O Johnson on board. They had been briefed for Operations APACHE 3/FOOTMAN 3, the delivery of agents and stores, but were unable to complete because of adverse weather conditions. F/Sgt Murray and crew were the next to get away at 20.27 in LL192, bound for Operations STATIONER 32/WHEELWRIGHT 36B. They were carrying agents stores and pigeons, which had to be returned to base after an escape hatch flew open and curtailed the sortie. F/L Mill and crew took off at 20.30 in LL287 carrying agents, stores and pigeons on Operations STATIONER 31/WHEELWRIGHT 37, which they concluded successfully before returning safely at 05.30. Last off the ground, also with an agent and stores to deliver, were F/O Walker and crew in LL251, who were unable to locate their briefed pinpoint and returned with their load. The following night brought a further four sorties, and again, all were to destinations in France. F/O Ashley and crew took off first, at 20.37 in NF-B, to carry out Operation PAUL 34, a supply drop, which they completed as briefed. A minute after their departure, NF-L lifted off with P/O Pick at the controls, and agents and stores on board for delivery under Operations STATIONER 32/WHEELWRIGHT 36B. This was also completed successfully, and a safe return made at 03.46. More than an hour had elapsed at Tempsford, before S/L Wilding and crew took off at 21.45 in NF-J on Operations FOOTMAN 3/APACHE 3. On board were agents, stores and pigeons, but adverse weather conditions prevented the drops from taking place, and they landed at Tangmere at 04.45. F/Sgt Jones and crew waited on the ground for a further two hours, before taking off in LL187 at 23.56 on Operation TRAINER 140, a supply drop, which they completed as briefed.

There was an early briefing for crews on every main force and Pathfinder station on the 15th, as preparations were put in hand for the penultimate raid of the war by RAF heavy bombers on Berlin. It was to be a mighty effort, involving the largest non-1,000 force to date of 891 aircraft, and it would be the first time, that over five hundred Lancasters and three hundred Halifaxes had operated to a single target. Together with the extensive diversionary operations, which included Mosquito attacks on enemy night fighter airfields in Holland, mining in Kiel Bay and a small 8 Group Lancaster raid on Frankfurt-an-Oder to the east of Berlin, more than a thousand aircraft were to be in action. The main operation began with a few aircraft taking off before 17.00, but the vast bulk of the giant armada got away between 17.00 and 18.00, swinging north over Denmark, before setting an almost southerly course to the target. The night fighter controller observed the progress of the bomber stream, but held his response back until it crossed Denmark's Baltic coast a little north of Flensburg. The now familiar running battle ensued all the way to the target, and around twenty aircraft in the rear half of the stream were brought down.

Berlin was, therefore, spared these bomb loads, and those of the seventy-five early returns, but even so, almost eight hundred aircraft remained, and they carried in their bomb bays a record 2,640 tons of bombs. Much of this was deposited squarely in the central and south-western districts of the city, causing almost twelve hundred medium and large fires, destroying a thousand houses and hundreds of temporary wooden barracks. Many important war industry factories were also hit, but as happened on all of the Berlin operations, scores of outlying communities found themselves in the firing line, and many bombs were wasted in this way. The bombers withdrew to the south and headed for northern Holland, making their way to the North Sea via the Ijsselmeer. Forty-three aircraft failed to make it home.

The night of the 15/16th was also one of high activity at Tempsford, where thirteen 138 Squadron Halifaxes departed for France over a period of more than two hours. First away, at 21.10, was the crew of F/L Bailey in NF-V on Operations CLOWN 1/JOHN 54/CANDYTUFT/BONHEUR. They were carrying an agent and stores, but continuing adverse weather conditions prevented their delivery, and they had to be brought home. The details of the remaining sorties on this night are as follows; F/O Clark in LL252 on Operation TRAINER 120, carrying stores, 22.00 to 06.20, unsuccessful due to adverse weather. F/Sgt Murray in LL192 on Operation JOHN 21A, carrying stores, 22.02 to 04.55, successful. F/L Mill in LL287 on Operation MONK 7, carrying stores, 22.09 to 05.43, unsuccessful due to adverse weather. F/Sgt Jones in NF-Q on Operation TRAINER 120, carrying stores, 22.14 to 06.32, unsuccessful due to lack of reception. F/O Johnson in NF-M on Operation TRAINER 120, carrying stores, 22.26 to 05.30, unsuccessful due to adverse weather. P/O Thomas in NF-J on Operation JOHN 21A, carrying stores, 22.30 to 05.05, successful. F/Sgt Baker in NF-B on Operation JOHN 29, carrying stores, 22.33 to 05.49, unsuccessful due to adverse weather. F/O Ashley in NF-D on Operation JOHN 29, carrying stores, 22.36 to 06.40, unsuccessful due to adverse weather. F/L Stiles in NF-L on Operation MONGREL 5, carrying stores, 22.53 to 06.45, successful. F/O Walker in LL251 on Operation MONGREL 5, carrying stores, 23.04 to 06.06, successful. F/Sgt Hayman in LL289 on Operation Paul 29, carrying stores, 23.14 to 05.53, unsuccessful due to icing conditions and engine failure. W/O Gregory in LW284 on Operation MONGREL 5, carrying stores, 23.22 to 07.10, unsuccessful due to adverse weather.

A further six Halifaxes had by now been added to the squadron's strength, and the SOE cause was further bolstered by the Stirling squadrons of 3 Group, which, having been withdrawn from the battle over Germany, could now play a major role in SOE operations. They would continue to do so until the group converted to Lancasters later in the year. There was also a major contribution from 38 Group operating out of its own stations. The highly-experienced S/L Russell was posted in from 1654 Conversion Unit on the 18th to fill the vacancy for A Flight commander. He had commanded 5 Group's 50 Squadron between October 1942 and August 1943, and, like the earlier-mentioned W/C Robinson, he had dropped a rank in order to remain on operations. Unlike Robinson, however, he would regain his wing commander status, when handed command of 138 Squadron at the start of May. Posted in on the same day were the crews of F/O Kingsley RCAF, Sgt Mackay RCAF and W/O Yardley.

The survivors from Berlin were allowed three nights off before the next operation, which was to Leipzig on the night of the 19/20th, for which a late take-off was planned around midnight. Extensive diversionary operations were again laid on, but the enemy night fighter controller reserved most of his strength to meet the main raid as it crossed the Dutch coast. The two forces remained in contact all the way into eastern Germany, where some aircraft arrived early through stronger than forecast winds. They were forced to orbit in the target area until the Pathfinder markers went down, and around twenty of them fell victim to the local flak batteries, while four others were lost through collisions. The attack was inconclusive in the face of complete cloud cover and skymarking, but what was not in question was the scale of the mauling inflicted on the Command. When all of the returning aircraft had been accounted for, there was a massive shortfall of seventy-eight, by far the heaviest casualty rate to date. The Halifax loss rate was over 13% of those dispatched, and Harris immediately withdrew the Merlin powered Mk II and V variants from future operations over Germany.

Despite the horrendous losses, and the withdrawal of the older Halifaxes, almost six hundred aircraft were made ready on the following night for the first of three heavy raids over a three week period on Stuttgart. For once, the night fighter controller was deceived by the diversionary measures, and the bomber stream remained largely unmolested during its time over enemy territory. Despite cloud cover and scattered bombing, much damage was caused in the city's central districts, and also to areas in the north-west and north-east. A modest nine aircraft failed to return, and in an attempt to maintain such acceptable statistics, a new tactic was tried out for the next two operations. It was decided to split the bomber force into two distinct waves, separating them by two hours, in the hope that the enemy night fighters would be caught on the ground refuelling and re-arming as the second wave passed through.

The system was tried first during an operation to the ball bearing town of Schweinfurt on the night of the 24/25th. The first wave, comprising 392 aircraft, took off between 18.00 and 19.00 hours, and the second wave of 342 aircraft between 20.00 and 21.00 hours. Both phases of the attack suffered from undershooting, and the operation was a failure in that respect. However, the second wave lost 50% fewer aircraft than the first in an overall casualty figure of thirty-three, and this suggested some merit in the system. Tempsford mounted six Halifax sorties to France on this night, three by each squadron. F/L Mill started the 138 Squadron ball rolling at 20.05, when lifting LL187 off the runway to attempt Operation JOHN 35, a supply drop, which he completed successfully, before landing at 02.40. W/O Gregory and crew were assigned to Operation JOHN 33, another supply drop, and took off in NF-J at 20.19. They were unable to locate the reception point, and brought their load home to land at 03.44. F/L Stiles and crew took off at 21.00 in NF-D on Operation PETER 16, which they were able to complete, and landed safely at 02.33. Shortly before 08.30 on the 25th, a 138 Squadron Halifax apparently took off to carry out a sea search in the hope of finding downed bomber crews from the Schweinfurt raid, and returned a little over three hours later. This is not recorded in the ORB, and the result of the search is not known.

That night, the experiment continued at Augsburg, the beautiful and historic city in southern Germany, which had been the scene of the epic daylight raid by 44 and 97 Squadron Lancasters in April 1942, for which W/C Nettleton had been awarded the Victoria Cross. It was Augsburg's misfortune to be the victim of one of those relatively rare occasions, when all facets of the bombing plan came together in perfect harmony. The unusually concentrated marking and bombing, with scarcely any creep-back, devastated the old centre of the city, obliterating forever centuries of cultural history. Over 2,900 houses were destroyed, five thousand others were damaged to some extent, and up to ninety thousand people were rendered homeless. During the second phase of the attack, however, some of the bombing did eventually spread into the industrial areas in the north and east. The loss of twenty-one aircraft confirmed the viability of splitting the bomber force, and it would be a tactic employed on numerous occasions in the future, particularly during the final six months of the war. Earlier in the day, BB330 was apparently involved in a minor accident at Tempsford, and was subsequently declared a write-off.

138 Squadron stayed at home while the Augsburg raid was in progress, and remained off operations for the next three nights, when the leap year provided an additional night to fly in February. 138 Squadron took advantage of this bonus opportunity, and dispatched eleven Halifaxes on the evening of the 29th. The ORB records them as having destinations in France, however, four of them were to locations in Belgium. The details of these sorties are as follows; P/O Cole in LL284 on Operations TYBALT 12/OTHELLO 2 over Belgium, carrying stores, 20.22 to 00.40, unsuccessful due to adverse weather. P/O Pick in NF-L on Operation OSRIC 21 over Belgium, carrying stores, 20.25 to 01.35, unsuccessful due to lack of reception. F/O Walker in LL279 on Operation WHEELRIGHT 55, carrying stores, 20.27 to 03.20, unsuccessful due to lack of reception. W/O Gregory in LL251 on Operation OSRIC 22 over Belgium, carrying stores, 20.33 to 01.41, unsuccessful due to lack of reception. P/O Thomas in NF-J on Operations WHEELWRIGHT 60/27A, carrying stores, 20.45 to 03.07, unsuccessful due to lack of reception. F/L Downes in NF-D on Operations MUSICIAN 7/ARCHDEACON 6A, carrying agents and stores, 20.55 to 01.05, unsuccessful due to adverse weather. F/Sgt Baker in NF-B on Operation DICK 54, carrying stores, 20.57 to 02.40, unsuccessful due to lack of reception. F/L Ashley in LL276 on Operation HARRY 15B, carrying agents and stores, 21.09 to 02.07, successful. F/O Clark in LL192 on Operation HARRY 24, carrying stores, 21.26 to 01.13, successful. F/Sgt Hayman in LL187 on Operation OSRIC 2 over Belgium, carrying stores, 21.42 to 02.03, unsuccessful due to the weather. F/L Johnson took off in NF-M at 21.17 on Operation BUTLER 12, carrying two agents, eight containers and seven packages. They crossed the French coast at Pointe de la Percee, before carrying out a forty-minute DR run to the target, and meeting flak at Bayeux on the way. The stores and agents, J T Detal, a Belgian, and P F Dulcos, floated down onto the German controlled site, and neither would survive their capture and imprisonment.

March 1944

The dawning of March brought the final month of the long and increasingly bitter winter campaign. Thereafter would come a new offensive to prepare the way for the invasion of Fortress Europe. Matters, though, were already well in hand in this regard, and the first salvoes of Bomber Command's contribution, the Transportation Plan, would be fired before the new month was a week old. In the meantime, the second raid of the series on Stuttgart was mounted on the night of the 1/2nd by a force of 557 aircraft, made up predominantly of Lancasters, with 129 Mk III Halifaxes in support. Dense cloud on the route to the target prevented night fighters from making contact with the bomber stream, but also hampered the Pathfinders in their marking. Cloud also prevented an assessment of the raid by the crews, but it was a successful attack, concluded for the remarkably low loss of just four aircraft, and for most of the main force Lancaster squadrons, this would be the last operational activity for two weeks.

138 Squadron flew seven sorties on this night, but only two of them were completed. The details are as follows; F/L Ashley in LL192 on Operation STATIONER 34, carrying stores, 19.50 to 03.30, successful. F/L Stiles in NF-D on Operation DICK 68, carrying stores, 19.55 to 02.03, unsuccessful due to adverse weather. F/L Bailey in NF-V on Operation BOB 75, carrying stores, 20.00 to 01.52, successful. P/O Thomas in LL279 on Operation DICK 24, carrying stores and pigeons, 20.07 to 02.15, unsuccessful due to lack of reception. S/L Wilding in LL307 on Operations APACHE 3/TRAINER 117, carrying an agent and stores, 20.24 to 04.38, unsuccessful due to adverse weather. F/Sgt Jones in LL308 on Operation HARRY 27, carrying stores, 20.45 to 00.03, unsuccessful due to lack of reception. F/L Mill in LL287 on Operations STATIONER 37/DATCHWORTH 1, carrying agents and stores, 20.50 to 02.36, unsuccessful due to adverse weather.

On the following night, while Halifaxes bombed an aircraft factory near Paris, 617 Squadron attended to a similar plant at Albert, in north-eastern France. F/L Downs and crew were one of eleven from 138 Squadron on duty on this night, also over France, and took off at 20.51 in NF-D to carry out Operations MUSICIAN 12/TOM 5, the first element of which happened to be a German controlled site. They made a DR run from Guise to the drop site, where three agents and six packages were delivered. The crew reported a strong smell of cordite invading the aircraft, and a large amount of smoke coming from the town of Albert, confirming that 617 Squadron had done its job effectively. They continued on to the second drop site, some twenty miles north-east of Albert, but no one was waiting on the ground to receive the stores. The three agents, and three others delivered by a 161 Squadron crew, all died in captivity. The other sorties to France by 138 Squadron crews on this night resulted in four agents and stores being delivered into the proper hands. The details of the other sorties are as follows; P/O Pick in NF-L on Operation BOB 136, carrying two agents and stores for delivery to the Sezanne area, east of Paris, 19.36 to 02.28, successful. P/O Cole in LL284 on Operations STATIONER 31/WHEELWRIGHT 81, carrying agents and stores, 20.14 to 04.28. Two agents, Roger Landes and A L J Sirois, were dropped into the Aiguillon area, south-east of Bordeaux. Landes would organize and arm two thousand men by D-Day. The second element could not be completed for an unspecified reason. F/Sgt Baker in LL364 on Operation BOB 117, carrying stores, 20.20 to 03.16, successful. F/Sgt Jones in LL308 on Operation BOB 107, carrying stores, 20.36 to 03.11, unsuccessful due to lack of reception. F/Sgt Hayman in NF-M on

Operation BOB 76, carrying stores, 20.40 to 02.43, successful. F/O Walker in LL251 on Operation MUSICIAN 11A, carrying stores and pigeons, 20.45 to 00.45, unsuccessful due to lack of reception. W/O Gregory in LL279 on Operation BOB 150, carrying stores, 20.46 to 03.12, unsuccessful due to lack of reception. F/L Perrins in LL187 on Operations DATCHWORTH 1/STATIONER 34, carrying agents and stores, 20.50 to 02.53, second element only completed, after adverse weather thwarted the first. F/O Clark in LL272 on Operation BOB 55, carrying fifteen containers and six packages for delivery to the Dijon area, 20.51 to 03.00, successful. On the way home, the starboard-outer engine was damaged by flak from Orleans marshalling yards. F/O Kingsley in LL276 on Operation BOB 108, carrying stores, 20.54 to 03.40, unsuccessful due to adverse weather.

A massive seventeen operations were attempted by the squadron on the night of the 3/4th, twelve over France and five over Belgium, but the weather and a lack of reception would render more than half of them ineffective. Flying only their second SOE operation since joining the squadron from Stradishall in February, F/O Kingsley and crew ran into difficulties of some kind, while carrying out Operation JOHN 23 over northern France in LL279. The Halifax crashed near Bernay, some thirty miles south-east of Caen, killing all but the two gunners, who fell into enemy hands. The details of the other sorties are as follows; F/O Clark in LL272 on Operation BOB 17, carrying stores, 18.54 to 02.36, unsuccessful due to lack of reception. F/L Mill in LL287 on Operation STOCKBROKER 5, carrying stores, 19.29 to 02.50, successful. F/Sgt Murray in an unidentified Halifax on Operation BOB 142, load not specified, 19.34 to 03.04, unsuccessful, target not located. F/Sgt Mackay in LL187 on Operation JOHN 55, carrying stores, 19.34 to 03.47, unsuccessful due to lack of reception. F/L Stiles in NF-D on Operation JOHN 68, carrying stores, 20.06 to 02.56, successful. P/O Cole in LL284 on Operations JOHN 22/BATCH 1, carrying agents and stores, 20.10 to 03.25, successful. F/O Walker in LL251 on Operations PETER 22/DATCHWORTH 1, carrying agents and stores, 20.18 to 03.13, successful. F/L Ashley in LL276 on Operation JOHN 56, carrying stores, 20.22 to 03.06, successful. F/O McMullen in LL192 on Operation BOB 133, unspecified load, 20.40 to 00.14, unsuccessful, early return due to fuel leak. P/O Pick in LL280 on Operation OSRIC 14 over Belgium, carrying stores, 20.55 to 01.56, successful. W/C Corby in LL308 on Operation ACOLYTE 6, carrying agents and stores, 20.58 to 03.10, successful. F/Sgt Baker in LL364 on Operation TYBALT 4 over Belgium, carrying stores and pigeons, 21.22 to 02.10, unsuccessful due to adverse weather. P/O Thomas in NF-M on Operation OSRIC 21 over Belgium, carrying stores, 22.30 to 02.50, successful. F/L Bailey in NF-V on Operations PANDARUS/OSRIC 7 over Belgium, carrying agents, stores and pigeons, 22.32 to 03.52, first element only completed. F/Sgt Hayman in LL289 on Operation TYBALT 28 over Belgium, carrying stores and pigeons, 22.56 to 03.41, unsuccessful due to adverse weather. S/L Wilding in LL307 on Operation JOHN 68, carrying stores, 23.27 to 06.27, unsuccessful due to lack of reception.

Over the next three nights, according to Freddie Clark, thirty-four sorties were attempted by 138 Squadron, at the rate of twelve, twelve and ten. The ORB, however, records only nine sorties on the night of the 5/6th, although two others are identified by Clark's account, leaving a discrepancy of just one. Most of the activity was to be over France, with a few also over Belgium, but the weather and the absence of receptions would lead to a success rate of less than 50%. The details for the night of the 4/5th are as follows. S/L Russell in LL280 on

Operation BOB 142 (maiden SOE sortie), carrying stores, 19.40 to 03.22, successful. F/L Mill in LL287 on Operation BOB 17, carrying stores, 19.41 to 03.38, successful. F/L Perrins in LL187 on Operation JOCKEY 21, carrying stores, 19.51 to 04.11, successful. F/Sgt Jones in LL289 on Operation JOHN 48, carrying stores, 20.16 to 04.45, unsuccessful due to adverse weather. F/L Stiles in LL251 on Operation DIPLOMAT 1, carrying agents and stores, 20.18 to 02.41, successful. F/L Bailey in NF-V on Operation PAUL 9, carrying agents and stores, 20.18 to 01.25, unsuccessful due to lack of reception. F/L Downes in NF-D on Operations APACHE 3/PETER 57, carrying agents and stores, 20.35 to 00.35, unsuccessful due to adverse weather. Sgt Mackay in LL252 on Operation JOHN 55, carrying stores, 20.53 to 02.50, unsuccessful for unspecified reason. P/O Thomas in LL284 on Operation PAUL 9, carrying stores, 20.55 to 05.00, unsuccessful due to lack of reception. F/L Johnson in NF-M on Operation JOCKEY 21, carrying stores, 21.15 to 01.10, unsuccessful after failing to locate drop site.

The night of the 5/6th was characterized by unusually active enemy defences in the Pas-de-Calais region, which predominantly afflicted aircraft entering France over the Haut-Banc coast. The main concentration of searchlights, flak and night fighters was in the Hesdin/Frevent area, close to the location of an enemy airfield at Nuncq. F/L Ashley and crew took off at 21.01 in LL280 on Operation TOM 35, carrying containers and packages. The Halifax was hit many times by flak at a point between Abbeville and Arras, forcing the sortie to be abandoned, and was then harried by searchlights and flak for ten minutes as it raced for the coast at 500 feet. Four sorties to Belgium also attracted the enemy's attention as they passed through this area on the way to their drop sites. Two of them are those omitted from the ORB. F/Sgt Baker and F/Sgt Ratcliffe were engaged on Operations TYBALT 28 and TYBALT 29 respectively, and both referred to blue searchlights, which seemed to pass them on from one beam to the next in a chain. F/Sgt Baker's Halifax was hit by flak at 500 feet in the Frevent area, probably on the way home, after failing to raise a reception committee at his drop site. F/Sgt Ratcliffe reported searchlights and flak from ten miles inland as far as Guise, and was unable to identify his target in the Sedan area because of poor visibility and snow on the ground. F/L Johnson and crew took off in NF-M at 20.25, carrying containers, packages and pigeons to deliver to TYBALT 18, but no reception awaited them, possibly because of the snowy conditions, and they turned for home. They were also illuminated as they passed through the Frevent area at 100 feet, but managed to avoid being hit by the light flak. S/L Wilding and crew were assigned to Operations CAWDOR/TYBALT 12, and took off at 20.40 in LL307 bound for Belgium. They, too, reported intense searchlight and flak activity as they passed through the same area at 200 feet on their way to Givet, on the French side of the border, from where a DR run was to be carried out. Three agents dropped blind onto the first pinpoint, along with their packages, before they headed for the second drop site, where fifteen containers and three packages were released. On the way home, when at 8,000 feet south-west of Arras, they were attacked from the starboard side by a ME410, which caused substantial damage to the Halifax and wounded the despatcher. The rear gunner responded with two hundred rounds, making no claims, and they arrived on the ground at Tangmere at 01.25. The details of the night's remaining sorties are as follows; F/Sgt Hayman in LL289 on Operation BOB 133, carrying stores, 19.10 to 02.40, successful. P/O Cole in LL284 on Operation TRAINER 68, carrying agents and stores, 20.00 to 04.07, successful. P/O Pick in LL276 on Operations APACHE 3/PAUL 34, carrying agents and stores, 20.02 to 05.30, successful. F/Sgt Williamson in NF-V on Operation BUTLER 3B, carrying stores, 20.41 to 02.10, unsuccessful due to lack of reception. F/L Downes in NF-D on Operation OSRIC 22 over Belgium, carrying stores, 21.05 to 01.46, unsuccessful due to lack of reception. F/O Walker in LL251 on Operations MONGREL 12/FOOTMAN 14, carrying agents and stores, 21.15 to 06.05, first element only completed, as no reception at the second one.

It was at this point, that Halifaxes of 4 and 6 Groups, including the Mk II and Vs, took the main role in opening the Transportation Plan. This called for the systematic dismantling by bombing of the French and Belgian railway networks, to prevent their use by the Germans to bring up forces to face the coming invasion. Halifaxes opened the proceedings at Trappes marshalling yards on the night of the 6/7th, after the marking had been carried out by Oboe Mosquitos. A successful operation left track, rolling stock and installations severely damaged. 138 Squadron put up ten aircraft under cover of this activity, and again saw only a modest number completed as planned. The details are as follows; F/O McMullen in NF-L on Operation DICK 77, carrying stores, 19.48 to 04.05 (Tangmere), unsuccessful due to lack of reception. F/Sgt Williamson in LL308 on Operation DICK 32, carrying stores, 20.14 to 00.25, unsuccessful due to navigational difficulties. F/O Clark in LL252 on Operation DICK 54, carrying stores and pigeons, 20.15 to 01.47, unsuccessful due to lack of reception. W/C Speare in LL192 on Operation JOHN 14 carrying stores, 20.19 to 03.20 (Tuddenham), successful. F/Sgt Jones in LL289 on Operation JOHN 59, carrying stores, 20.24 to 04.12 (Tangmere), successful. S/L Russell in LL276 on Operation JOHN 47, carrying stores, 20.27 to 04.09, successful. Sgt Mackay in LL287 on Operation DICK 62, carrying stores, 20.45 to 01.47, unsuccessful due to lack of reception. F/L Bailey in NF-V on Operation JOHN 59, carrying stores, 20.50 to 03.20, successful. P/O Thomas in NF-M on Operation JOHN 16, carrying stores, 20.57 to 03.48 (Tangmere), unsuccessful due to adverse weather. F/L Mill in LL187 on Operation GOLDFINCH 4 over Norway, carrying stores, 21.53 to 05.50 (Downham Market), successful.

The following night brought a similarly successful attack on the railway yards at le Mans by a force consisting predominantly of Halifaxes, while 138 Squadron dispatched eleven Halifaxes to France. F/L Stiles and crew were the only ones to carry agents as well as containers, packages and pigeons, and took off in LL252 at 20.25 to undertake Operation PAUL 54. The drop site was near Angouleme, and, employing the "Rebecca/Eureka" transponder radio navigation system, they were able to pick up the drop site beacon when thirty-four miles away. On the first run at 700 feet, they delivered three agents, including the Mayer brothers, along with fifteen containers and three packages, and a further three packages were dropped on the second run. The details of the remaining sorties are as follows; F/L Perrins in NF-Y on Operation FIELDFARE over Norway, carrying three agents, stores and pigeons. 18.54 to 02.40 (Kinloss), successful. F/Sgt Hayman in LL289 on Operation CHAFFINCH 5 over Norway, carrying stores, 19.23 to 03.31, successful. F/L Downes in NF-L on Operation LAPPING 1 over Norway, carrying stores, 19.26 to 05.10 (Kinloss), unsuccessful due to ten-tenths cloud. P/O Cole in NF-V on Operations DAG/MANI over Norway, carrying three agents and stores, 19.29 to 05.40, successful. S/L Wilding in LL287 on Operation PUFFIN 2A over Norway, carrying stores, 19.35 to 03.47, successful. P/O Pick in LL276 on Operation PAUL 30 over France, carrying stores, 19.38 to 03.10, successful. F/O Walker in LL251 on Operation PAUL 33 over France, carrying stores, 20.10 to 04.40, unsuccessful due to lack of reception. F/L

Stiles in LL252 on Operation PAUL 54 over France, carrying agents, stores and pigeons, 20.25 to 03.15, successful. W/O Gregory in LL308 on Operation PAUL 56 over France, carrying stores and pigeons, 20.32 to 03.43, successful. F/L Johnson in NF-M on Operation PAUL 54 over France, carrying agents, stores and pigeons, 20.34 to 03.36, unsuccessful due to failure to locate target. F/L Ashley in LL192 on Operation HARRY 27 over France, carrying stores, 21.05 to 00.40, unsuccessful due to the reception committee being disturbed.

On the night of the 10/11th 5 Group sent a hundred Lancasters to attack four factories in France, including the Michelin works at Clermont-Ferrand. All four raids were declared successful, and they possibly distracted the defences from the presence over the alpine region, south of Geneva in Maquis country, of thirteen 138 Squadron Halifaxes, all undertaking Operation UNION 3. Each crew was assigned to a specific location for a cargo drop, but if unable to locate it, the stores were to be delivered to any other reception point displaying a light. Take-off began at 20.06, and continued until 21.24, each crew adopting a route out via Dijon, Lake Bourget and Moutiers, although low cloud and snow on the ground made pinpointing a challenge. A Rebecca signal was picked up at Moutiers, and, in the distance, Mont Blanc glistened in the moonlight. Fire beacons could be seen through gaps in the cloud, and drops were carried out from around 5,000 feet. Mountain peaks in the region, rising to well above that altitude, made it a hazardous location to be in at night, and all were pleased to be on their way home. The details of each sortie are as follows; P/O Pick in LL192, 20.06 to 03.17, unsuccessful due to lack of reception. S/L Russell in LL276, 20.23 to 03.34, successful. F/L Ashley in LL284, 20.25 to 04.26, successful. F/O Clark in LL252, 20.30 to 04.31, successful. F/L Downes in NF-D, 20.46 to 04.00, successful. F/L Bailey in NF-V, 20.47 to 04.12, successful. F/Sgt Hayman in LL289, 20.51 to 04.08, successful. F/O McMullen in NF-L, 20.56 to 04.55, successful. F/L Mill in LL287, 21.00 to 05.00, success doubtful. F/L Johnson in LL251, 21.03 to 03.43, successful. F/O Walker in LL183 (161Sqn), 21.05 to 04.40, successful. P/O Thomas, in unspecified aircraft, 21.10 to 04.55, successful. W/O Gregory in LL187, 21.24 to 04.38, successful. A total of 165 containers and sixty-six packages were delivered, and only two crews failed to complete a drop onto an illuminated pinpoint.

A second attack by 4 and 6 Groups on the le Mans railway yards took place on the night of the 13/14th, and this time fifteen locomotives and eight hundred wagons were destroyed, while collateral damage was inflicted upon two nearby factories. Eight 138 Squadron crews were in action over France on this night, along with others from 161, but results amounted to a one in five success rate. The details of each sortie are as follows; F/L Ashley in LL192 on Operation DICK 73, carrying stores, 23.05 to 06.10, successful. F/Sgt Jones in LL287 on Operation DICK 71, carrying stores and pigeons, 23.10 to 05.13, unsuccessful due to lack of reception. F/Sgt Williamson in LL276 ? on Operation TRAINER 173, carrying stores and pigeons, 23.26 to 06.14, unsuccessful due to lack of reception. F/L Johnson in NF-M on Operation DICK 73, carrying stores and pigeons, 23.28 to 05.58, unsuccessful due to lack of reception. F/O Clarke in LL252 on Operation DICK 71, carrying stores, 23.30 to 05.36, unsuccessful due to lack of reception. W/O Yardley in LL276 ? on Operation STATIONER 44, carrying stores and pigeons, 23.32 to 04.29, successful. F/Sgt Mackay in NF-V on Operation TRAINER 168, carrying stores, 23.35 to 05.16, unsuccessful due to lack of reception. F/O McMullen in NF-L on Operation TRAINER 190, carrying stores and pigeons, 23.42 to 05.19, unsuccessful due to lack of reception. W/O Godfrey RCAF and crew arrived on posting on the 14th, and, that night, just two 138 Squadron crews were operating, both assigned to supply drops over Norway. P/O Cole and crew were first away, and took off in LL284 at 20.04 on Operation GULL 5. They were not able to locate the drop site, probably because of snow on the ground, and they returned with their cargo to land at 05.07. F/L Perrins and crew took off in LL251 at 20.39 to undertake Operation PHEASANT 2, and returned safely at 04.25 to report a successful outcome. F/Sgt Lawrence RAAF and crew arrived from 6 Group's 424 Squadron RCAF on the 15th.

The Command returned to the fray in numbers on the night of the 15/16th, when 863 aircraft, the second largest non-1,000 force to date, took off to return to Stuttgart. The route along the length of France, almost to the Swiss border, delayed the inevitable contact with night fighters, but they caught up shortly before the target was reached, and began to take a heavy toll. Strong winds played a part in a disappointing marking performance, and although some bombs hit central districts, the majority fell short and into open country. The disappointment was compounded by the heavy loss of thirty-seven aircraft. 138 Squadron had six Halifaxes aloft, all departing after midnight, four of them to Holland, but of all the night's sorties from Tempsford, less than half would be completed. The details of the 138 Squadron sorties are as follows; F/L Stiles in LL276 on Operation BOB 73 over France, carrying agents and stores, 00.24 to 06.12, successful. F/L Downes in NF-D on Operation OSRIC 24 over Holland, carrying stores and pigeons, 01.21 to 03.44, unsuccessful due to adverse weather. W/O Gregory in LL251 on Operation OSRIC 7 over Holland, carrying stores and pigeons, 01.22 to 04.52, successful. F/O Pick in NF-L on Operation OSRIC 27 over Holland, carrying agents and stores, 01.27 to 04.10, unsuccessful due to adverse weather. F/Sgt Baker in LL284 on Operation OSRIC 30 over Holland, carrying stores and pigeons, 01.30 to 03.40, unsuccessful due to adverse weather. F/L Mill in NF-M on Operation TOM 44 over France, carrying stores, 02.20 to 06.38, successful. Later on the 16th, the squadron welcomed F/O Coldridge RCAF and crew on posting.

Another massive force, this time of 846 aircraft, set out during the early evening of the 18th for the first of two raids in four nights on Frankfurt. Part of the enemy night fighter response was drawn to the north to face a mining diversion, but the remainder made contact with the bomber stream as it bore down upon the target. Accurate Pathfinder marking preceded a concentrated attack, which fell mainly into central, western and eastern districts, destroying or seriously damaging over six thousand buildings. Although housing accounted for most of this total, industrial, commercial and public buildings also figured prominently, and the loss of twenty-two aircraft was a relatively modest price to pay for the scale of the success. Six 138 Squadron aircraft also ventured out on this night to destinations in France, beginning at 20.15 with the departure of F/O Thomas and crew in NF-M on Operation PAUL 9A. They crossed the French coast at Pointe de la Percee, and observed a dozen night fighter flares being dropped ahead to illuminate another aircraft. They picked up the "Rebecca" signal over sixty miles out, and reported large fires and explosions in the Bergerac area, where, unknown to them, 617 Squadron was hammering an explosives factory. Three agents were delivered according to instructions, along with containers and packages, and a safe return made at 05.24. F/Sgt Hayman and crew were next away at 20.17 in NF-Z, bound also for Operation PAUL 9A to deliver stores, which they accomplished as briefed, before landing back at Tempsford at 03.09. F/Sgt Jones and crew took off in NF-V at 20.22 as the third assigned to Operation PAUL 9A, and they, too, were successful in delivering stores. F/L Downes and crew departed at 20.25 in

LL284 on Operation WHEELWRIGHT 64A, which required the dropping of agents and stores. While flying at 3,000 feet, they picked up the "Rebecca" signal twenty-five miles out, and also reported the glow from Bergerac as they headed towards it from a hundred miles away. The drop site was somewhere near Marmande, south-east of Bordeaux, where the two agents, WAAF Yvonne Baseden, a wireless operator, who would survive Ravensbrück concentration camp, and Baron Gonzagues de St-Genies, parachuted, along with containers and packages. F/O Clark and crew took off at 20.33 in LL252 on Operation WHEELWRIGHT 61A, a supply drop, which they completed. On return at 02.56, they added to the testimony of the commotion at Bergerac, where the smoke had reached 5,000 feet. The final departure was that of F/O Pick and crew in LL192 at 20.44, who had been assigned to Operation PETER 54. No reception committee made itself known at the drop site, and this was the only failure of the night.

PETER 54 was rescheduled for the night of the 20/21st, when three sorties would also be dispatched on Operation MARKSMAN 22, and two on JOHN 59A. F/O Pick and crew started the ball rolling in NF-L, with a take-off at 20.04 on JOHN 59A. They delivered their stores as briefed, as did F/O Clark and crew in LL252 at the same target, after taking off at 20.49. S/L Wilding and crew re-flew the PETER 54, sortie between 20.21 and 02.36, but were defeated by adverse weather conditions. F/Sgt Hayman and crew took off in LL276 at 20.25, carrying the agents for MARKSMAN 22, and stores, while F/Sgt Jones and F/L Walker followed up at 20.38 and 21.00 in NF-V and NF-M respectively carrying only containers and packages. All returned safely after successfully carrying out their briefs. W/O Palmer RCAF and crew arrived on posting on the 21st.

More than eight hundred aircraft again took off for Frankfurt on the evening of the 22nd, and produced an even more devastating raid than the one of four nights earlier. Although all parts of the city were afflicted, the western districts received the greatest concentration of bombs. Half of the city was left without water, gas and electricity for an extended period, and the old Frankfurt, which had developed from the middle ages, was obliterated. Despite the failure of the bulk of the night fighter force to make contact, thirty-three aircraft failed to return, and one must assume that the flak batteries enjoyed a successful night. 138 Squadron put up five Halifaxes on this night, all to France, the details of which are as follows; F/O Pick in NF-L on Operation JOHN 75, carrying agents and stores, 19.35 to 03.57, successful. F/L Walker in NF-V on Operation JOHN 70, carrying stores, 20.00 to 02.59, successful. F/Sgt Jones in LL276 on Operation JOHN 75, carrying stores, 20.12 to 04.24, unsuccessful after failing to locate the drop site. F/Sgt Hayman in LL289 on Operation WHEELWRIGHT 60A, carrying stores, 20.16 to 02.55, successful. S/L Wilding in LL287 on Operation PETER 47A, 20.49 to 02.45, carrying stores, successful.

The time had now arrived for Harris to launch the final assault of the campaign on Berlin. It would be the nineteenth since he began back in August, and the sixteenth since the resumption in November. It would also be the final raid of the war by RAF heavy bombers on the Capital. The force of 811 aircraft for this momentous occasion departed their respective stations either side of 19.00 hours, and encountered a wind of unprecedented strength from the north, which scattered the bomber stream, and drove aircraft continually south of their intended track. The windfinder system, designed to provide the crews with accurate information on wind speed and direction, broke down in the face of the first recorded example of a "jetstream", and this resulted in the bomber force losing cohesion. This denied the attack any meaningful chance of concentration, and, as so frequently happened at Berlin, many bomb loads were wasted on over a hundred outlying communities. Sufficient housing was destroyed to leave twenty thousand people homeless, but industry escaped reasonably lightly. The bomber stream became even more dispersed on the return flight, and many aircraft were driven by the wind into the flak zones around Leipzig and the Ruhr. An estimated two thirds of the seventy-two shot down bombers were credited to them.

138 Squadron launched six sorties on this night, all to France, the details of which are as follows; F/Sgt Murray in LL276 on Operation PETER 38, carrying stores, 19.59 to 02.45, unsuccessful after failing to locate drop site. F/L Downes in NF-D on Operation FOOTMAN 15, carrying agents and stores, 20.05 to 03.06 (Dunkerswell, Devon), successful. F/O Thomas in NF-V on Operation PETER 45, carrying stores, 20.07 to 03.16 (Dunkerswell), successful. F/Sgt Jones in LL289 on Operation JOHN 73, carrying stores, 20.09 to 02.59 (Dunkerswell), successful. F/L Wilkinson in LL284 on Operation 73, carrying stores, 20.48 to 03.25, successful. F/L Walker in NF-M on Operation PETER 52, carrying stores, 21.18 to 04.18, successful.

The Berlin offensive may now be over, but the winter campaign still had a week to run, and two further major operations for the crews to negotiate. The first of these was directed at Essen on the night of the 26/27th, and probably caught the defenders by surprise. Within range of Oboe, which had proved the decisive factor in the Ruhr offensive a year earlier, the city wilted under another highly effective attack, which destroyed over seventeen hundred houses, and seriously damaged almost fifty industrial buildings for the modest loss of nine aircraft. 138 Squadron dispatched just two sorties on this night, both stores drops to destinations in France. F/L Wilkinson and F/O Clark took off in LL289 and LL276 at 20.00 and 20.24 on Operations JOHN 76 and JOHN 71 respectively, and both returned safely to report successful outcomes.

The final operation of the winter offensive was to be against Nuremberg, the birthplace of Nazism, a city, which had sustained heavy damage during countless operations, but had, perhaps, thus far escaped the worst ravages of a Bomber Command assault. The controversy surrounding this operation began with the disputed route, which, together with an inaccurate weather forecast, and the presence of another "jetstream" wind, conspired to hand the 795-strong force on a plate to the waiting Luftwaffe night fighters. The carnage began over Charlerois in Belgium, and continued all the way to the target, the burning wreckage of RAF bombers on the ground sign-posting the way. Eighty-two aircraft fell during the outward flight and around the target area, and together with the fifty-two early returns, this dramatically reduced the numbers available to attack the target city. Other absentees were around 120 crews, most of whom had probably been unaware of their true position when turning towards Nuremberg. At the appointed time, they found themselves over a built-up area, which, on seeing a number of Pathfinder markers, they took to be the target. It was, in fact, Schweinfurt, some fifty miles to the north-west, and it was only on their return, that the majority discovered their error. The ninety-five failures to return represented the greatest disaster to afflict the Command in the entire war, and others were written off in crashes at home, or with battle damage too severe to repair.

Under the cover of this operation, 138 Squadron committed five aircraft to sorties over Belgium. We do not know what time F/L Mill and his crew took off in LL287 to undertake Operation OSRIC 27. We do know, however, that they were hit by flak over the Scheldt, when heading for the drop zone just south of Antwerp. The Halifax was crippled, and had to be ditched in a river across the border in Holland, just west of Hansweert. Three crew members and both Belgian agents, Lts Deprez and Giroulle, lost their lives as the aircraft filled with water, but F/L Mill evaded capture, and the four other survivors, including the recently arrived W/O Godfrey, who was flying as second pilot to gain experience, were taken prisoner. W/O Gregory and crew took off at 20.58 in LL306 on Operations TYBALT 22/BALTHASAR 1, and ran into the same "hotspot" that had accounted for F/L Mill. Gregory dived from 300 to 50 feet to avoid searchlights and three light flak guns, and reached his first drop site near Spiere to deliver twelve containers. Thirty-seven minutes later he dropped three agents, three containers and two packages near Peruwelz, close to the frontier with France, before returning safely home. S/L Russell and crew took off in LL280 at 21.08 on Operation TYBALT 11, a stores drop consisting of fifteen containers. They were also fired upon from the same location, but the rear gunner shot out two of the three searchlights from 400 feet, and the flak stopped. They returned at 00.45 to report a successful outcome. P/O Baker and crew took off in LL276 on Operation OSRIC 32, a supply drop, which they failed to complete through the lack of a reception. F/L Ashley and crew were last away in LL192 on Operation OSRIC 7, another supply drop, which also failed, after the reception committee failed to show up.

The following night brought little activity as the Command licked its wounds, but almost thirty aircraft were out and about over occupied territory in support of various resistance organisations. Freddie Clark writes, that fourteen sorties were mounted by 138 Squadron, including his own. However, the ORB records fourteen, plus the fact that Clark and crew were missing as a result of Operations on this night, which makes fifteen, twelve to France and three to Denmark. F/O Freddie Clark and crew, who had arrived on the squadron at the end of January, were briefed for two drop zones in France, one of them on behalf of SIS. They took off at 21.00 in LL252 to carry out Operation ORAGE, the SIS drop of six containers and two packages, and PETER 5, which was to receive nine containers and six packages. The Americans had banned all air traffic around the usual entry point into France at Cabourg, forcing a new route to be adopted, for which, information on flak concentrations was not available. The first drop was at PETER 5, located south-west of Tours, where no reception committee was evident. This was not a problem, as it could be visited again on the way home after making the drop at ORAGE, near Chateauroux, where a triangle of fires was observed, but no response from the ground to the signal flashed from the Halifax. Strict instructions to drop only if the correct response was received, persuaded Clark to fly off, and return twice more, but still there was no signal from the ground. Rather than risk compromising the site through engine noise, it was decided to return to PETER 5, which remained unresponsive. Turning for home, Clark thought he saw a torch beam, and went to investigate, which took the Halifax over the airfield at St-Symphorien, Tours. They were picked up by a searchlight, and fired upon when at 300 feet, and the port-inner engine caught fire. The extinguisher failed to dampen the flames, and then the port wheel flopped down to put the aircraft into an unrecoverable, sinking turn to port. Clark put LL252 down a few miles beyond the airfield, as a result of which, the navigator and a gunner lost their lives, while the remainder were taken into captivity.

The details of the other sorties on this night are as follows. P/O Pick in NF-L on Operation GIRTH 1 over Denmark, carrying stores, 17.54 to 03.47, successful. F/L Stiles in LL284 on Operations BETA/HAMMOND over France, carrying stores, 18.56 to 04.20 (Acklington), successful. F/L Johnson in NF-M on Operation THRUSH RED over France, carrying agents and stores, 19.05 to 03.10 (Acklington), successful. S/L Wilding in LL307 on Operation TABLEJAM 23 over Denmark, carrying agents and stores, 19.09 to 02.07, successful. F/Sgt Jones in LL187 on Operation GREBE RED 3 over Denmark, carrying stores, 19.11 to 03.56 (Acklington), successful. F/L Walker in LL251 on Operations SOLDAT/FEMME/HOMME over France, carrying stores, 19.45 to 01.45 (Tangmere), successful. F/L Bailey in NF-V on Operation DONKEYMAN 38 over France, carrying stores, 19.47 to 01.02, unsuccessful due to compass trouble, unable to locate drop site. F/Sgt Williamson in LL305 on Operation DICK 45 over France, carrying agents and stores, 20.27 to 01.17, successful. F/L Downes in NF-D on Operation STATIONER 33 over France, carrying stores, 20.47 to 02.40 (Ford), unsuccessful due to lack of reception. F/L Wilkinson , also recorded as being in NF-D, on Operation PHONO 16 over France, carrying stores, 20.50 to 00.43, successful. W/O Yardley in NF-C on Operation STATIONER 50 over France, carrying stores, 20.58 to 02.00, unsuccessful due to lack of reception. F/Sgt Hayman in LL289 on Operations PETER 38/SYRINGA/RHODODENDRON over France, carrying agents and stores, 21.27 to 03.23 (Tangmere), first and third elements only completed. F/Sgt Mackay in LL306 on Operations MAREE/PETER 58 over France, carrying stores, 21.42 to 02.45, unsuccessful due to failure to locate drop site. F/O McMullen in LL192 on Operation STATIONER 49 over France, carrying stores, 00.01 to 04.10 (Tangmere), successful. Of the Norwegian sorties, two were completed, one delivered stores to an SIS location but brought the agent home, and one failed. During the course of the month, twenty-seven crews carried out a magnificent 153 sorties, dropping thirty agents and delivering 1,216 containers and 488 packages, along with 581 packs of leaflets and 651 pigeons.

April 1944

That which now faced the bombing brigade was in marked contrast to what had been endured over the winter. The frequent deep penetration forays into Germany on dark, often dirty nights, were to be replaced by mostly shorter range hops to France and Belgium in improving weather conditions. An added bonus, was that these targets, unlike Berlin, Frankfurt, Nuremberg, Schweinfurt, Augsburg, Leipzig and Stuttgart, would fall within the range of Oboe. The main fly in the ointment, as far as the crews were concerned, was a decision from on high, which decreed that most such operations were worthy of counting as just one third of a sortie towards the completion of a tour. Until this flawed and ridiculous policy was rescinded, mutterings of discontent would pervade the bomber stations. The view from the top, that operations against French and Belgian targets would be a "piece of cake" would not be borne out, and they would require of the crews a greater commitment to accuracy, to avoid, as far as possible, friendly civilian casualties.

Now that the entire Command was available to concentrate on the Transportation Plan, it would proceed apace, and despite the prohibitive losses of the winter, the bomber force was in remarkably fine fettle to face its new challenge. Harris was now in the enviable position of being able to achieve that, which had eluded his predecessor, namely to attack multiple targets simultaneously with forces large enough to make an impact. He could assign targets to individual groups, to groups in tandem, or to the Command as a whole, as dictated by operational requirements, and whilst pre-invasion considerations dominated, Harris was never going to entirely shelve his favoured policy of city-busting.

The first week of April brought no dramatic events, as the main force remained at home. 138 Squadron, however, began the new month with four sorties on the night of the 1/2nd, three of them to Denmark and one to France. F/L Ashley and crew took off first at 18.45 in LL308, bound for Operation Girth 1, a supply drop over Denmark, which they concluded successfully. F/Sgt Murray and crew got away at 19.42 in NF-C on Operations TABLEJAM 43/45, another supply drop over Denmark, of which only the first element was completed. W/O Gregory and crew were in LL307, and took off for the south of France at 19.52 to carry out a supply drop under Operation BIT, which was also successfully completed. Finally, F/L Bailey and crew took off in NF-V at 19.56 on Operations TABLEJAM 49/48, and they were able to deliver their cargo as briefed to round off an effective night of operations.

Of great significance on the night of the 5/6th, was an operation by 144 Lancasters and a single Mosquito of 5 Group against an aircraft factory at Toulouse. The outcome of the raid would confirm the effectiveness or otherwise of low level visual marking. The Mosquito was piloted by W/C Cheshire of 617 Squadron, and it was the first use of the type in this role. The operation was an outstanding success, and proved to be the defining moment of the war for 5 Group. Within two weeks it would have its own target marking force, transferred over from the Pathfinders, and would, thereafter, operate independently from the rest of the bomber force. 138 Squadron prepared a dozen Halifaxes for operations on this night, all but one to France, the details of which are as follows; F/L Stiles in LL284 on Operations JOHN 60/DIRECTEUR, carrying stores, 19.07 to 04.17 (Chivenor), successful. F/Sgt Jones in LL187 on Operation TOM 56, carrying stores and pigeons, 20.45 to 02.56 (Exeter), successful. F/L Johnson in NF-

M on Operation TYBALT 18 over Belgium, carrying stores, 20.49 to 05.03 (Davidstowe), unsuccessful due to adverse weather. F/Sgt Hayman in LL289 on Operation TOM 42, carrying stores and pigeons, 20.55 to 02.26 (Dunkerswell), unsuccessful due to lack of reception. F/L Ashley in LL192 on Operations SCANDALE/PUBLIQUE, carrying stores, 21.10 to 05.39 (Davidstowe), first element only completed, no reception at second one. F/L Walker in LL251 on Operation DITCHER 37, a drop site near Monceau-les-Mines in east-central France, where an agent and six packages were delivered, and JOHN 34, in the same area, which received fifteen containers, 21.30 to 04.35 (Chivenor), successful. F/L Downes in NF-D on Operation DICK 45, a drop site near Chauray in western France, where four agents, fifteen containers and six packages were delivered successfully from 600 feet, 21.37 to 03.10 (Exeter). F/Sgt Williamson in NF-V on Operation STATIONER 60, carrying stores, 22.07 to 03.45 (Exeter), successful. F/Sgt Mackay in LL306 on Operations PRIMULA/STATIONER 60, carrying stores and pigeons, 22.15 to 05.30 (Davidstowe), successful. W/O Yardley in LL276 on Operations DICK 45/MEADOWSWEET, carrying fifteen containers for the first element and packages for the second, 22.15 to 03.26 (Exeter), successful. P/O Baker in LL280 on Operation TRAINER 221, carrying stores, 22.30 to 02.12 (Dunkerswell), successful. F/O McMullen in NF-L on Operations STATIONER 55/MAREE, carrying stores, 22.37 to 05.18 (Davidstowe), first element only completed, due to incorrect reception layout at the second one.

The new bomber offensive began in earnest on the night of the 9/10th, when two operations were mounted against railway targets in France. 239 aircraft from 3, 4, 6 and 8 Groups attacked the Lille-Delivrance goods station to excellent effect, destroying in the process over two thousand items of rolling stock, and extensively damaging track and buildings. The success of the operation was marred only by the heavy casualties inflicted on French civilians in adjacent residential districts. Around five thousand houses were destroyed or damaged, and 456 people were killed. This was a problem, which would never be addressed satisfactorily, and the night's other operation at the Villeneuve-St-Georges railway yards in Paris, conducted by elements from all the Groups, also resulted in civilian deaths, although on a much smaller scale.

138 Squadron dispatched sixteen sorties to France on this night, but more than half failed through a lack of reception. The details are as follows; F/L Ashley in LL192 on Operation WHEELWRIGHT 90, carrying stores and pigeons, 20.52 to 05.45, unsuccessful due to lack of reception. F/Sgt Mackay in NF-K on Operations PIMENTO 78/AUBRETIA, carrying stores, 21.02 to 04.40, second element only completed, as no reception at first one. W/O Gregory in LL306 on Operation STATIONER 43, carrying stores, 21.02 to 04.52, unsuccessful due to lack of reception. He reported being fired upon from a road by six machine guns when at 2,000 feet, and picking up a number of holes in the tail. P/O Baker in LL280 on Operation WHEELWRIGHT 51, carrying stores, 21.07 to 04.49, successful. W/O Yardley in NF-D on Operations TRIMOUILLE/WHEELWRIGHT 73, carrying stores, 21.08 to 00.41, unsuccessful due to early return with wireless failure. F/Sgt Hayman in LL289 on Operation STATIONER 44, carrying stores, 21.11 to 04.03, successful. F/L Pick in LL276 on Operation TOM 35, carrying stores and pigeons, 21.13 to 05.48 (Waterbeach), unsuccessful due to lack of reception. F/Sgt Jones in LL187 on Operation STATIONER 36, carrying stores, 21.16 to 03.56, unsuccessful due to lack of reception. F/Sgt Williamson in NF-V on Operation PIMENTO 78, carrying stores, 21.31 to 05.00, unsuccessful due to lack of reception. S/L Wilding in LL307 on Operations DARWEN 1/STATIONER 33, carrying stores, 22.02 to

03.49, first element only completed, as no reception at second one. W/O Palmer in LL251 on Operation STATIONER 52, carrying stores and pigeons, 22.07 to 03.30, successful, apart from one container hanging-up. F/Sgt Lawrence in NF-C on Operation STATIONER 53, carrying stores and pigeons, 22.08 to 03.25, unsuccessful due to lack of reception. F/L Thomas in LL308 on Operation TOM 51, carrying stores and pigeons, 22.50 to 05.40 (Waterbeach), successful. F/O McMullen in NF-L on Operation DICK 7, carrying stores and pigeons, 23.12 to 06.30 (Waterbeach), unsuccessful due to lack of reception. F/L Stiles in LL284 on Operation HARRY 28, carrying agents and stores, 00.20 to ?, successful. F/L Johnson in NF-L on Operation SCIENTIST 52, carrying stores, 00.28 to 04.10, unsuccessful due to lack of reception.

On the following night, the 10/11th, while the main force attacked four railway yards in France and one in Belgium, 138 Squadron dispatched a dozen sorties, nine of them to France and three to Belgium. F/Sgt Hayman and crew were the first to depart Tempsford, at 21.00 in LL306 to carry out Operation JOHN 38 over the Condrieu region of south-eastern France. They were carrying four agents and fifteen containers, which were successfully delivered from 700 feet into the hilly terrain below. On return at 04.34, Hayman reported witnessing the destruction by flak of an aircraft flying at 4,000 feet in the Belleme area, thirty miles north-east of le Mans, and this was almost certainly LK738 of 161 Squadron. The details of the other sorties are as follows; S/L Russell in LL280 on Operations LILLY/PERFECTURE/MARIN over France, carrying stores, 21.01 to 04.58, successful. An unidentified crew in LL289 on Operations MINISTRE/EXECUTION/PUBLIQUE over France, carrying stores, 21.18 to 05.25, first element only completed, as no reception at the second and third ones. F/L Pick in LL276 on Operation OSRIC 26 over Belgium, carrying agents, stores and pigeons, 21.23 to 05.33, successful. W/O Yardley in NF-C on Operations TRIMOUVILLE/WHEELWRIGHT 73 over France, carrying stores, 21.29 to 03.50, second element only completed, as no reception at the first one. F/Sgt Williamson in NF-V on Operation PETER 52 over France, carrying stores, 21.33 to 05.08, successful. F/L Walker in LL251 on Operations GALLERY 2/OSRIC 52 over Belgium, carrying agents and stores, 22.05 to 05.44, successful. F/L Ashley in LL192 on Operation OSRIC 35 over Belgium, carrying stores and pigeons, 22.05 to 05.54, unsuccessful due to lack of reception. F/Sgt Jones and crew were in an undecipherable Halifax, which took off at 22.11 on Operations OUREGAN/PETER 52, to be carried out over the Chateauroux region of France. They were carrying six SIS agents for the former, and stores for the latter, and on their return at 05.14, they were able to report a successful outcome. F/L Johnson in NF-M on Operations JOHN 56 and STOCKBROKER 3 over France, carrying an agent and stores, 22.50 to 01.21, unsuccessful due to early return. F/L Bailey in Stirling NF-X on Operation DONKEYMAN 38 over France, carrying stores, 23.02 to 04.44, unsuccessful due to lack of reception. P/O Baker in LL307 on Operations WALT/PETER 52 over France, carrying stores, 23.12 to 06.16, second element only completed, as no reception at the first one.

While elements of the main force went to Aachen on the night of the 11/12th, and devastated central and southern districts, the hectic SOE schedule continued with a further eleven sorties by 138 Squadron, ten of which were to destinations in France. The single departure for Holland/Belgium took place at 23.00, and involved S/L Wilding and crew in LL307 on Operations OSRIC 31/FLAVIUS, which resulted in the successful delivery of agents and stores, and a safe return at 04.30. The details of the sorties to France are as follows; F/O

McMullen in LL276? on Operation LACKAY 2, carrying stores, 21.21 to 05.17, unsuccessful due to lack of reception. F/Sgt Mackay, also in LL276? on Operation JOHN 6, carrying stores, 21.30 to 04.43, unsuccessful due to lack of reception. F/Sgt Murray in NF-C on Operation JOHN 4, carrying stores, 21.35 to 05.13, successful. F/L Wilkinson in LL280 on Operations STOCKBROKER 3/JOHN 12, carrying agents and stores, 21.37 to 05.20, successful. F/L Thomas and crew took off at 22.18, possibly in LL419, NF-V, on Operations BOB 165/ARCHDEACON 3B, carrying five agents for the former, in the Conde area of central France, and twelve containers for the latter, a German-controlled site in the Vervins area, close to the Belgian frontier. Both drops were completed successfully, and a safe return made at 05.27. W/C Corby in LL306 on Operations PIMENTO 46/MAQUIS, carrying agents, stores and pigeons, 22.21 to 05.03, second element only completed, first not attempted. F/Sgt Lawrence in LL192 on Operation STATIONER 53, carrying stores and pigeons, 22.42 to 03.36, successful. F/L Bailey in Stirling NF-X on Operation PIMENTO 7, carrying stores and pigeons, 22.53 to 05.49, unsuccessful due to lack of reception. F/L Johnson in NF-M on Operations STATIONER 41/SCIENTIST 69, carrying agents, stores and pigeons, 23.10 to 04 28, first element only completed as no reception at the second one. W/O Palmer in NF-V? on Operation STATIONER 50, carrying stores, 23.12 to 04.58, unsuccessful due to lack of reception.

There were no main force operations during the following week, and the moon period ended for 138 Squadron with six cargo sorties to Belgium on the night of the 12/13th. F/Sgt Hayman and crew took off first at 01.19 in LL289 to undertake Operation OSRIC 2. They crossed the Dutch coast at 100 feet at Tholen on the eastern Scheldt, the route in for all of the night's sorties, before making their way to the drop site near Colfontaine, south-west of Mons, where the reception committee failed to show up. F/L Pick was next away, at 01.24 in NF-C on Operation OSRIC 37, and crossed the coast at 200 feet, turning then onto a course for a drop site a dozen miles west of Charleroi, where fifteen containers were delivered. F/Sgt Jones and crew were in LL307, and took off at 01.35 on Operation OSRIC 35, to cross the coast at a dangerous 500 feet, but getting away with it to complete the drop. W/O Yardley and crew were in NF-L on Operation OSRIC 22, and took off at 01.44. On reaching the Scheldt Estuary, they were confused by the low spring tide, and, unable to positively identify their position, they turned back. F/O Baker and crew took off at 01.48 in LL364 on Operation OSRIC 40, and were confronted by two searchlights at Tholen, whose defenders were now thoroughly alerted, but came through to complete the drop. F/Sgt Williamson and crew brought up the rear, taking off at 02.02 in LL419 for Operation OSRIC 30. They approached Tholen at 600 feet, but hit the deck while still over the sea, and turned south towards Wichelen, east of Ghent, from where the DR run was successfully completed.

On the 14th, Bomber Command became officially subject to the dictates of the Supreme Headquarters Allied Expeditionary Force (SHAEF) under General Dwight Eisenhower for the pre- and post-invasion campaigns, and would remain thus shackled until the Allied armies were sweeping towards the German frontier at the end of the summer. 138 Squadron welcomed the crew of F/O J A Kidd on the 15th, and that of his twin brother, F/O G D Kidd, on the 18th, the day on which F/Sgt Hayman was commissioned, and F/L Wilkinson was posted across the airfield to join 161 Squadron. The Kidds were twenty years old, and were posted in from 6 Group's 431 Squadron RCAF. Bombing operations resumed on the night of the 18/19th, with attacks on four railway targets, while a large mining effort took place in northern waters. 5 Group operated with its own full marker force for the first time on the night of the 20/21st, in a two phase operation against the railway yards at La Chapelle just north of Paris, while elements from the other Groups carried out a devastating assault on Cologne. This night heralded a new moon period, and 138 Squadron celebrated the fact by beginning a spell of largely successful cargo drops to locations in France. Just two sorties were dispatched on this night, and both were successful. F/L Ashley and crew took off at 21.34 in LL419 to undertake Operation Dick 51, carrying an agent and stores, while F/Sgt Williamson and crew departed at 22.27 in NF-V to complete a cargo drop under Operation BUTLER 21A. The night of the 21/22nd was relatively quiet, but 138 Squadron prepared five Halifaxes for Operations over France, one with an agent on board, and the others for supply drops only. The details are as follows; P/O Baker in NF-L on Operation JOHN 25, carrying an agent and stores, 21.21 to 04.48, successful. W/O Gregory in Ll276 on Operation JOHN 61, carrying stores, 21.22 to 04.31, successful. F/L Stiles in LL284 on Operation JOHN 88, carrying stores 21.30 to 04.20, unsuccessful. F/L Bailey in LL187 on Operation JOHN 71, carrying stores, 21.32 to 04.25, successful. F/L Johnson in NF-M on Operation WHEELWRIGHT 98A, carrying stores, 21.44 to 04.29, successful. 5 Group unsuccessfully tested its low-level marking system at a German urban target, Brunswick, on the night of the 22/23rd, while the rest of the main force attacked Düsseldorf and inflicted massive damage. During the course of the 23rd, 138 Squadron made ready six Halifaxes for supply drops over France, and it fell to W/O Gregory and crew to start the ball rolling, with a take-off at 21.18 in LL306 on Operation JOHN 113. The drop was carried out successfully, as were all, the details of which are as follows; F/L Ashley in LL364 on Operation JOHN 70, 21.21 to 04.49. F/O McMullen in NF-K on Operation WHEELWRIGHT 60B, 21.35 to 03.50. F/L Bailey in LL419 on Operation JOHN 32, 21.43 to 03.17. S/L Russell in LL280 on Operation JOHN 93, 21.45 to 05.02. F/Sgt Williamson in LL187 on Operation WHEELWRIGHT 60B, 21.51 to 04.51.

Karlsruhe provided the main force target on the night of the 24/25th, while the Independent Air Force (5 Group) went to Munich for a second attempt at using its marking method at a heavily defended target in the Reich. 138 Squadron, meanwhile, loaded four Halifaxes with stores for delivery to destinations in France, although F/L Ashley and crew had an agent on board LL364 as well, as they took off at 21.40 on Operation JOHN 67. They landed at 04.35, having completed the drop as briefed, and set the trend for the remaining three, F/L Stiles in LL284 on Operation PETER 11, 21.23 to 05.18, F/Sgt Williamson in LL308 on Operation JOHN 82, 21.42 to 05.32, and F/O McMullen in LL280 on Operation WHEELWRIGHT 99, 21.49 to 04.18. The night of the 26/27th was one of heavy activity, involving three major operations at widely dispersed targets. Almost five hundred aircraft, drawn from all but 5 Group, attacked Essen to good effect, while Halifaxes and Mosquitos of 4, 6 and 8 Groups continued the railway campaign with a successful assault on the yards at Villeneuve-St-Georges, and 5 Group went to Schweinfurt. 138 Squadron was active over France with seven Halifaxes, all of them successfully dropping stores, details as follows; F/Sgt Lawrence in LL364 on Operation JOHN 90, 21.33 to 04.58. F/L Pick in NF-C on Operation JOHN 75, 21.37 to 05.52. F/L Thomas in LL306 on Operation PETER 45, 21.52 to 06.07. F/L Johnson in NF-M on Operation PETER 79, 21.55 to 05.48. S/L Wilding in LL307 on Operation PETER 52, 21.58 to 04.52. F/L Walker in LL251 on Operation PETER 79, 22.01 to 05.39. W/O Palmer in LL308 on Operation JOHN 66, 22.05 to 05.24.

F/Sgt George Williamson RAAF and his crew, lost on the night of 27/28th April 1944 when their Halifax LL356, NF-U crashed into the North Sea off Terschelling. The only body recovered was that of F/Sgt Williamson. Standing l-r: Sgt George Croad, flight engineer; F/Sgt James Smythe RCAF, air gunner; Sgt Hubert Benbow, WOP/AG; W/O Arthur Barnes RCAF, bomb aimer. Sitting, l-r: F/Sgt George Williamson, pilot; F/Sgt Herbert Dootson, navigator; F/Sgt Eric Clayworth RAAF, air gunner. (W/Cdr John Williamson via Aircrew Remembered).

5 Group remained at home on the night of the 27/28th, while the rest of the Command attacked the highly industrialized town of Friedrichshafen deep in southern Germany, and two railway yards in France. 138 Squadron put up a maximum effort of fifteen sorties on this night, but two-thirds of them were destined to fail, and one crew was lost. We are not told what time LL356 took off with the crew of F/Sgt Williamson RAAF and crew, we know only that they were heading for Belgium to carry out Operation OSRIC 59, a supply drop. Many were routed out over the Scheldt Estuary on this night, but the body of the pilot was washed ashore on Terschelling some months later, which suggests that they were following a more northerly track, perhaps between Den Helder and Texel, where the tidal race is particularly strong, and carries floating objects north. The Halifax was doubtless caught by coastal flak or a flak ship, which sent it crashing into the sea, taking the rest of the crew down with it. This incident set the tone for a night of disappointing results amounting to ten failures and one aircraft returning on three engines. The details are as follows; (From this point on, aircraft code letters alone will be used, unless there is no doubt about the serial number.) P/O Baker in NF-C on Operation Director 55 over France, carrying stores, 21.29 to 04.45, unsuccessful due to lack of reception. F/L Pick in NF-B on Operation STATIONER 37 over France, carrying stores, 21.34 to 03.00, unsuccessful due to lack of reception. F/L Bailey in NF-V on Operation ACTOR 3 over France, carrying stores, 21.41 to 05.15, unsuccessful due to lack of reception. F/L Walker in NF-N on Operation JOHN 72 over France, carrying stores, 21.44 to 04.28, successful. F/L Stiles in NF-E on Operation STATIONER 35 over France, carrying stores, 21.50 to 04.55, unsuccessful due to lack of reception. W/O Lawrence in NF-O on Operation DITCHER 34 over France,

carrying stores, 21.53 to 05.35, unsuccessful due to lack of reception. F/Sgt Murray in NF-D on Operation STATIONER 42 over France, carrying stores, 22.03 to 05.20, unsuccessful due to lack of reception. P/O Hayman in NF-P on Operation MONGREL 26 over France, carrying stores, 22.07 to 05.26, successful. S/L Wilding in NF-J on Operation JOHN 72, carrying stores, 22.07 to 04.40, unsuccessful due to lack of reception. F/L Ashley in NF-K on Operation STATIONER 44 over France, carrying stores, 22.09 to 05.17, unsuccessful due to uncertainty over reception. W/O Palmer in NF-Q on Operation MINISTER 2 over France, carrying stores, 22.15 to 04.45, successful. F/L Thomas in NF-R on Operation OSRIC 37 over Belgium, carrying stores and pigeons, 23.05 to 03.25, successful. F/O McMullen in NF-L on Operation OSRIC 32 over Belgium, carrying stores and pigeons, 23.32 to 02.31, unsuccessful, after being hit by flak from three ships in the Oosterschelde when at 100 feet, and returning early with a dead engine. F/L Johnson in NF-M on Operation OSRIC 2 over Belgium, carrying stores and pigeons, 23.35 to 02.08, unsuccessful due to adverse weather.

A small 5 Group force attempted to bomb an explosives works at St-Medard-en-Jalles on the night of the 28/29th, while another headed for an airframe factory near Oslo. 138 Squadron used the latter as cover for nine sorties to Norway, including that of S/L Russell and crew, who took off at 20.49 in NF-O on the SIS Operation MAKIR, with agents Oluf Olsen and Lars Larsen on board. A DR run was carried out from Lake Eikeren in good visibility, but, on arrival at the drop site, no reception committee was waiting. S/L Russell flew away towards Oslo, where he and his crew could see the 5 Group attack taking place, before returning to the drop site after half an hour. There was still no sign of any activity on the ground, and the attempt was abandoned. The details of the other sorties are as follows; F/L Ashley in NF-A on Operation POMMEL 1, carrying agents and stores, 20.35 to 05.23, successful. P/O Hayman in NF-Q on Operation BIT 5, carrying stores, 20.38 to 04.55, successful. P/O Baker in NF-B on Operations HUMNAH 1/2, carrying stores, 20.50 to 00.08, unsuccessful due to early return with fuel-feed problems. F/L Stiles in NF-E on Operation STIRRUP 1, carrying stores, 20.52 to 04.11, successful. P/O Jones in NF-R on Operation BIT 5, carrying stores, 20.55 to 05.15, successful. F/L Bailey in NF-V on Operation SADDLE 4, carrying stores, 21.13 to 05.10, unsuccessful due to lack of reception. F/O Coldridge in NF-K on Operation SADDLE 2, carrying stores, 21.14 to 05.08, successful. F/O McMullen in NF-C on Operation OSPREY 2, carrying stores, 22.13 to 05.18, unsuccessful due to adverse weather.

Twenty-four hours later, 5 Group returned to France with two small forces, unknowingly providing cover for six Halifaxes from 138 Squadron. Five of them were assigned to Operation STATIONER 70, a supply drop, but the weather conditions would prevent all but one from delivering its cargo. The details are as follows; P/O Baker in NF-B, 21.43 to 04.58, successful. F/L Thomas in NF-R, 21.48 to 05.02, unsuccessful due to adverse weather. F/Sgt Murray in NF-D, 22.00 to 04.46, unsuccessful due to adverse weather. W/O Palmer in NF-Q, 22.10 to 05.50, unsuccessful due to lack of reception. F/O Coldridge in NF-M, 22.35 to 05.28, unsuccessful due to adverse weather. F/Sgt Lawrence and crew took off at 22.04 in NF-C on Operation MARKSMAN 27, a stores drop, but they, too, fell victim to the weather conditions, and returned at 04.56 to report a disappointing outcome.

There was a marked improvement on the last night of the month, however, when nine out of thirteen sorties to France proceeded as planned. A single sortie to Belgium was also undertaken by F/O Hayman and crew, who were first off the ground at 21.38 in NF-P on Operation OSRIC 26. They successfully delivered three agents, fifteen containers and four packages, before returning safely at 05.43. The details of the supply drops to France are as follows; F/L Johnson in NF-N on Operation STOCKBROKER 7, 21.38 to 05.48, unsuccessful due to lack of reception. F/O McMullen in NF-A on Operation PIMENTO 53, 21.39 to 04.50, successful. F/Sgt Murray in NF-F on Operation WHEELWRIGHT 124, 21.43 to 04.30, successful. F/Sgt Lawrence in NF-K on Operations BOB 178/CORYOESIS, 21.45 to 04.45, successful. P/O Jones in NF-H on Operation DIRECTOR 55, 21.47 to 02.28, unsuccessful due to early return with engine trouble. F/L Bailey in NF-Y? on Operation PIMENTO 67, 21.47 to 04.50, unsuccessful due to lack of reception. W/O Palmer in NF-Q on Operation TRAINER 201, 21.50 to 05.50, unsuccessful due to lack of reception. F/O J Kidd in NF-D on Operation MASON 1, 21.54 to 06.27, no outcome recorded. F/L Stiles in NF-E on Operations TAMBOUR/CORDON, 21.55 to 05.40, unsuccessful due to lack of reception. F/O G Kidd in NF-C on Operation MASON 1, 21.59 to 05.35, successful. F/L Thomas in NF-J on Operation WHEELWRIGHT 100, 22.00 to 04.32, successful. S/L Russell in NF-O on Operation ACTOR 1, 22.03 to 05.11, successful. P/O Baker in NF-V? on Operation WHEELWRIGHT 101, 22.05 to 04.23, successful. Among awards during the month was a well-deserved DFC for F/L Bailey.

May 1944

May began with the Command mounting six small-to-medium-scale raids on the night of the 1/2nd, against railway installations and factories in France and Belgium. The new month brought a change in command for 138 Squadron, as W/C Speare concluded his lengthy tour in the hot seat, and was replaced by the newly re-promoted W/C Russell, the A Flight commander. Sadly, the latter's period of tenure, in contrast to that of his predecessor, would be brief indeed. Three new Canadian crews were posted in from 6 Group on the 1st, those of F/O Gallagher, P/O Lyne and W/O McFarlane. W/C Russell presided over his first operations that night, when six of ten sorties were bound for France and the others to Belgium. Among the latter was S/L Wilding, who was briefed also for a drop in Germany, and took off with his crew, agents and stores at 21.52 in NF-J on Operations OSRIC 2/DENVER 1, only to be defeated at both locations by adverse weather conditions. F/L Johnson and crew were assigned to Operation OSRIC 51, a supply drop over Belgium, and took off in NF-M at 21.58. They found the drop site, but were thwarted by the absence of a reception committee, and to abandon the attempt. F/L Bailey and crew took off for Belgium in NF-V at 22.05 for a supply drop under Operation OSRIC 42, but suffered instrument failure, and had to turn back. W/C Russell was also bound for Belgium, when taking off in NF-O at 22.09 for a supply drop under Operation OSRIC 43. He and his crew returned at 04.11, and were able to report the only successful sortie of the night to Belgium.

Three of the crews bound for supply drops over France were assigned to Operation TOM 45, and F/L Walker and crew were the first of the trio to depart Tempsford, doing so at 22.11 in NF-N, to be followed by F/O McMullen in NF-A at 22.15 and F/O Coldridge and crew in NF-R a minute later. They flew south to a pinpoint on the Loire, before turning north-east to their respective drop sites east and south-east of Paris, where F/L Walker delivered fifteen containers. F/O McMullen reported observing an aircraft fall in flames and crash, but avoided all enemy contact, and delivered his stores as planned. F/O Coldridge was making a second run on his drop site at 2,000 feet, when at least ten light flak guns and numerous machine guns opened up from a Luftwaffe aerodrome at Coulommiers, causing damage to the fuselage and both port engines. He dived down to 200 feet to escape, before climbing again, and discovering that his fuel tanks were holed and bleeding petrol. There was no option but to turn back, and a safe landing took place at Tempsford at 05.30. The details of the other sorties are as follows; P/O Jones in NF-Q on Operation DIRECTOR 55, carrying stores, 22.03 to 05.27, successful. F/L Stiles in NF-C on Operations CORDON/TAMBOUR, carrying stores, 22.20 to 05.25, unsuccessful due to lack of reception. P/O Hayman in NF-P on Operations GRISOU/STATIONER 36, carrying stores, 22.27 to 04.58, successful.

The night of the 3/4th turned into a disaster for 1 and 5 Groups, and controversy surrounding the causes abounds even today. The supposedly straight-forward operation against a panzer training camp and motor transport depot at Mailly-le-Camp, in north-eastern France, was dogged by communications problems, and the consequent delay in calling in the main force crews to bomb, presented enemy night fighters with a golden opportunity. This they did not squander, and forty-two Lancasters were shot down, two-thirds of them from 1 Group. Despite this, the bombing was highly concentrated and accurate, hitting 161 buildings, and destroying more than a hundred vehicles, including thirty-seven tanks, which would now not be available to respond to the invasion. While all this was in progress, fourteen 138 Squadron aircraft slipped into France to deliver cargo, and ten of these operations were completed as planned. The details are as follows; F/Sgt Mackay in NF-Y on Operation TRAINER 207, 21.47 to 05.06, unsuccessful due to adverse weather. F/O J Kidd in NF-A on Operation MASON 2, 21.54 to 04.50, successful. F/O G Kidd in NF-P on Operation MASON 2, 21.55 to 05.20, successful. P/O Baker in NF-B on Operation TRAINER 201, 21.58 to 05.25, unsuccessful due to lack of reception. F/L Johnson in NF-M on Operation TRAINER 207, 21.58 to 04.52, unsuccessful, unable to locate drop site. P/O Jones in NF-H on Operation PAUL 76, 22.01 to 05.00, successful. F/L Thomas in NF-T on Operation PAUL 60, 22.02 to 04.46, unsuccessful due to lack of reception. F/L Walker in NF-N on Operation PAUL 60, 22.06 to 04.34, unsuccessful due to lack of reception. F/Sgt Murray in NF-F on Operation FIREMAN 1, 22.10 to 04.10, successful. F/O McMullen in NF-O on Operation DIGGER 1, 22.19 to 04.17, successful. F/Sgt Lawrence in NF-C on Operation VENTRILOQUIST 5, 22.53 to 03.30, successful. W/O Yardley in NF-D on Operation VENTRILOQUIST 5, 22.55 to 03.40, successful. W/O Palmer in NF-O? on Operation VENTRILOQUIST 4, 23.00 to 03.55, successful. F/O Coldridge in NF-K on Operation HISTORIAN 2, 23.42 to 06.00, unsuccessful due to lack of reception.

With the invasion now only a month away, most of the effort from Tempsford during the coming period would be directed at France, and this was the destination for all but eight of the sorties mounted by 138 Squadron up to the end of the moon period. Sixteen 138 Squadron Halifaxes lined up for take-off late on the evening of the 5th, all of them carrying stores, some with pigeons also, to deliver to targets in France, and only two of the sorties would be outright failures. The details are as follows; F/Sgt Lawrence in NF-C on Operation CLERGYMAN 2, 21.52 to 03.43, successful. P/O Hayman in NF-P on Operations RUMEUR/BLANCHISSEUSE, 21.57 to 05.35, successful. F/Sgt MACKAY in NF-J on Operation PERCY 1, 22.00 to 04.20, successful. F/Sgt Murray in NF-F on Operation BOB 57, 22.05 to 05.30, unsuccessful due to lack of reception. P/O Baker in NF-B on Operation PRIEST 1, 22.10 to 04.49, successful. F/L Stiles in NF-E on Operation PERCY 1, 22.10 to 04.10, successful. P/O Jones in NF-H on Operation PRIEST 1, 22.14 to 05.20, successful. W/O Yardley in NF-D on Operation PERCY 1, 22.15 to 04.35, successful. F/L Johnson in NF-M on Operation PAUL 75, 22.19 to 05.56, unsuccessful due to lack of reception. F/O McMullen in NF-S on Operation PERCY 1, 22.23 to 04.50, successful. W/O Palmer in NF-Q on Operation PERCY 1, 22.25 to 05.02, successful. F/L Walker in NF-N on Operation PERCY 7, 22.35 to 03.48, successful. F/O G Kidd in NF-Y on Operation PERCY 7, 22.39 to 04.21, successful. F/O Coldridge in NF-K on Operation HISTORIAN 2, 22.48 to 04.47, successful. F/O J Kidd in NF-A on Operation PERCY 7, 22.49 to 04.13, successful. W/C Russell in NF-O on Operations BERBERUS/PRUNUS/JOHN 24, 00.52 to 05.42, second and third elements successful, first element unsuccessful due to lack of reception.

The twelve sorties dispatched on the night of the 6/7th were divided equally between France and Norway, and it was the latter that got away from Tempsford first. W/O Yardley and crew were in NF-D, and departed at 20.30 on Operation RUMP 1, carrying stores, which they delivered as briefed, before returning safely at 04.55. This set a trend for the northern drops, all but one of which was successful. The details are as follows; S/L Wilding in NF-S on Operation POMMEL 1, carrying stores, 20.47 to 04.29, successful. F/O G Kidd in NF-V on Operation SADDLE 2, carrying stores, 21.13 to 05.17, unsuccessful due to lack of reception.

P/O Hayman in NF-P on Operation OTTO 2, carrying two agents and eight containers, 21.22 to 04.10, successful. W/O Palmer in NF-Q on Operation OSPREY 2 carrying stores, 21.23 to 04.10, successful. F/O J Kidd in NF-A on Operation SADDLE 4, carrying stores, 21.26 to 04.15, successful. The crews assigned to drops over France would experience mixed fortunes, due to the non-appearance of reception committees. P/O Baker and crew took off first, at 21.53 in NF-B on Operations MESSENGER 10/DIRECTOR 54. Their brief was to deliver an agent and stores, which they managed to do, and returned to land at 05.09. P/O Jones and crew were in NF-H, and took off at 22.01 to deliver fifteen containers and eight packages to PIMENTO 67, in the Macon region of east-central France. On arrival, Jones had a choice of three receptions, all flashing "R", and chose the one closest to the briefed map reference, after which, the other lights were extinguished. On the way home he saw explosions and smoke from Tours, and an aircraft fall in flames, but there is no record of any Bomber Command activity in the area or of any losses. F/L Stiles and crew took off in NF-F at 22.02 on Operation DONALD 51, but found no reception and brought their stores back. F/O Walker and crew took off in NF-N at 22.30 to undertake Operations CASHOT/VENTRILOQUIST 6, and completed only the second element, after no reception was found to be waiting at the first drop site. It was a similar story for F/O Coldridge and crew, who had taken off in NF-K at 22.35 to undertake Operations HISTORIAN 1/CHRISTIS 2. They were fired upon by a machine gun on a railway east of Vire, when on their way down to the Cher region of central France at 2,000 feet, but the rear gunner silenced it. The first stores drop was completed according to brief, but the second lacked a reception committee. F/Sgt Lawrence and crew took to the air at 22.40 on NF-M, bound for a stores drop under Operations VENTRILOQUIST 2/HALIFAX, but again, no reception turned up, and the attempt was abandoned. F/O Wallace RCAF and crew became the latest recruits, as they arrived from 3 Group on the 7th.

The night of the 7/8th brought six more sorties to France and two to Denmark, but also great sadness as two crews failed to return. Five small-scale bombing operations were in progress over France on this night, as W/C Russell headed for his target, CITRONELLE 1. He and his crew had taken off sometime around 22.00 in LL280, NF-O, and encountered one of the night fighters stirred up by the activity. They were shot down some twenty-five miles west-north-west of le Mans, and all on board were killed. W/C Russell was a pre-war veteran, and consequently much older than most operational airmen, and was the holder of a DFC and Bar. On his arrival at Tempsford, Russell had asked Freddie Clark to collect his crew for him from 1654 HCU at Wigsley. Only one member was not wearing the ribbon of a DFC, DFM or both. His was not the only loss of the night. Australian, F/O McMullen, had been Freddie Clark's closest friend on the squadron, and took off in LL192 to head for Denmark to carry out Operation TABLEJAM 46. The Halifax crashed into the Kattegat between Denmark and Sweden, taking with it the entire crew, the bodies of only three eventually being recovered for burial. The details of the night's other sorties are as follows; F/Sgt Murray in an unidentified Halifax on Operation TRAINER 207 over France, carrying stores, 21.52 to 05.40, unsuccessful due to lack of reception. F/L Thomas in NF-S on Operation TRAINER 207 over France, carrying stores, 21.57 to 05.04, successful. P/O Baker, probably in NF-B on Operation ACTOR 2 over France, carrying stores, 21.54 to 05.25, successful, one container hung-up. W/O McFarlane in NF-E on Operation GONDOLIER 4 over France, carrying stores, 21.59 to 04.23, successful. F/Sgt Mackay in NF-N on Operation TABLEJAM 50 over Denmark, carrying stores, 22.04 to 04.22, successful. F/O Gallagher in NF-D on Operation GONDOLIER 4 over

France, carrying stores, 22.09 to 04.55, unsuccessful due to lack of reception. F/L Johnson in NF-M on Operations CORPUS 2/HARRY 43 over France, carrying stores, 23.22 to 03.58, successful.

Freddie Clark writes of eleven sorties being dispatched on the night of the 8/9th, all of them supply drops to France, and all but one successful. The ORB records only ten sorties, as follows; F/Sgt Lawrence in NF-C on Operation JOHN 117, 21.50 to 04.44, successful. F/O G Kidd in NF-J on Operation JOHN 117, 22.04 to 05.14, successful. W/O Yardley in NF-F on Operation JOHN 67, 22.04 to 04.45, successful. F/O J Kidd in NF-M on Operation JOHN 117, 22.05 to 05.28, successful. W/O Palmer in NF-Q on Operation PERCY 5, 22.06 to 04.50, successful. P/O Lyne in NF-A on Operation HYPATICA/JOHN 102, 22.14 to 05.20, unsuccessful due to lack of reception. F/O Coldridge in NF-Y on Operation PERCY 5, 22.25 to 04.39, successful. F/L Walker in NF-N on Operation DONALD 38, 22.31 to 04.35, successful. P/O Jones and crew were in NF-H, and took off on Operations MUSICIAN 7/ARCHDEACON 8 at 22.42, carrying stores. They made a DR run from Guise on each site in bright moonlight, and delivered eight containers and six packages onto the second element, which was under German control. As far as the crew was concerned, it was a successful sortie, and reported it thus on return at 04.07. P/O Hayman and crew took off at 22.45 in NF-S, and headed for the Cambrai region to drop fifteen containers and six packages onto ARCHDEACON 14, another German-controlled site. W/C Burnett, a Canadian in the RAF, was installed as 138 Squadron's new commanding officer later on the 9th. He was another officer with vast operational experience behind him, having begun the war as a Hampden pilot with 49 Squadron at Scampton. When he was rested from operations, he became an instructor at an operational training unit at Finningley, but was then posted in July 1941 to the newly formed Canadian 408 (Goose) Squadron, to take up a flight commander post. Returning from Hamburg on the night of the 15/16th of January 1942, Burnett's Hampden crashed in Yorkshire, killing his crew of three and seriously injuring him. Following a lengthy spell in hospital, he was posted to HQ 3 Group in May 1943 as a staff officer. There he remained until his appointment to command 138 Squadron.

Now, just a matter of weeks before the Normandy landings, main force operations began to be directed against gun batteries along the French coast. The success of this greatest military undertaking of all time depended upon the enemy's belief, that the main assault would come in the Pas-de-Calais. Consequently, most attacks by the Command on gun emplacements involved targets in this region of the coast, in order to maintain the deception. Only at the last minute were the defences on the Normandy approaches bombed. Seven batteries were targeted by over four hundred aircraft on the night of the 9/10th, while 5 Group sent small forces against two factories in France. 138 Squadron launched fourteen sorties on this night, twelve of them to targets in France, and two to Belgium. Five crews were assigned to a supply drop under Operation PERCY 3, the location for which, was in the Brive-la-Gaillarde region of western France, south of Limoges, for which the crews of W/O McFarlane, F/O Gallagher, W/O Yardley, F/Sgt Lawrence, and F/O Coldridge took off in NF-Y, NF-V, NF-D, NF-C and MA-W at 22.00, 22.09, 22.10, 22.14 and 22.42 respectively. The first four reached the target, and dropped their stores as briefed, but F/O Coldridge RCAF and crew were forced to take to their parachutes while outbound, leaving the 161 Squadron Halifax to crash at Rochechouart, about twenty miles west of Limoges and some seventy miles short of their destination. They all arrived on the ground intact, and all but the rear gunner evaded capture, the pilot and one other making their way back to England via Paris, Madrid and Gibraltar. Three others remained with the Maquis for three months, before also being flown home. The details of the remaining sorties on this night are as follows; F/O J Kidd in NF-A on Operation JOHN 121 over France, carrying stores, 21.56 to 04.29, successful. F/Sgt Mackay in NF-J on Operation OSRIC 51 over Belgium, carrying stores, 21.57 to 04.13, unsuccessful due to lack of reception. F/O G Kidd in NF-F on Operation JOHN 121 over France, carrying stores, 21.58 to 04.54, successful. F/L Stiles in NF-E on Operation PERCY 9 over France, carrying stores, 22.08 to 04.45, successful. P/O Hayman in NF-S on Operation DONALD 80 over France, carrying stores, 22.24 to 04.20, successful. P/O Lyne in NF-Z on Operation GONDOLIER 4 over France, carrying stores, 22.26 to 05.29, unsuccessful due to lack of reception. P/O Jones in NF-H on Operation DONALD 52 over France, carrying an agent and stores, 22.28 to 05.00, unsuccessful due to lack of reception. W/O Palmer in NF-Q on Operation TYBALT 12 over Belgium, carrying stores, 23.00 to 05.23, unsuccessful due to lack of reception. F/L Johnson in NF-M on Operations VENTRILOQUIST 2/ANTHRACITE over France, carrying stores, second element only completed, as no reception at the first one.

Eight sorties to France were undertaken by the squadron on the night of the 10/11th, while five railway yards were pounded by elements from the main force. All but one were supply drops, the exception being that flown by F/L Walker and crew in NF-N, which was last away at 23.16, to undertake Operation MINISTER 4. The drop site was located south-east of Montereau-Fault-Yonne, some fifty miles south-east of Paris, an area under scrutiny by the Germans. Rebecca and S-Phone contact was made with the reception committee, who refused to accept the containers, and asked for the agent and his luggage only to be dropped. As F/L Walker circled, he was asked to hurry, and J de Ganay, a saboteur, who would gain great success in disrupting canal and railway traffic, dropped away from 600 feet. The details of the other sorties on this night are as follows; P/O Baker in NF-E on Operation JOHN 96, 22.07 to 05.05, successful. W/O McFarlane in NF-V or Y on Operation PERCY 4, 22.23 to 05.16, successful. F/Sgt Mackay in NF-H on Operation PERCY 4, 22.29 to 05.44, successful. F/O Gallagher in NF-D on Operation PERCY 4, 22.32 to 05.15, unsuccessful due to lack of reception. F/Sgt Murray in NF-C on Operation GONDOLIER 4, 22.35 to 04.49, unsuccessful due to lack of reception. F/L Thomas in NF-S on Operation PERCY 4, 22.38 to 04.46, successful. F/L Johnson in NF-M on Operation PERCY 4, 22.44 to 05.10, successful. Later on the 11th, the crews of F/Sgt Paterson, F/Sgt Strathern and F/O Levy, all of the RNZAF, were posted in from 3 Group, presumably from 75 (NZ) Squadron at Mepal.

On the night of the 11/12th, a force of 190 Lancasters from 5 Group encountered haze during an attempt to bomb a military camp at Bourg-Leopold in Belgium. Halfway through the attack, the Master Bomber called a halt to proceedings because of the danger to nearby civilians. Other Groups, meanwhile, maintained the pressure on railway yards and coastal defences. After four operations in nine nights, most of the Command's main force squadrons stayed at home for the following week, and it was left to the Mosquitos of 8 Group to roam far and wide over Germany and the occupied countries. Training was constantly in progress at Tempsford of course, and LK736, a Halifax with a rogue reputation, was one of those in use on the 17th. Freddie Clark had operated in it on a number of occasions, and found it almost incapable of maintaining height on four engines. Shortly after taking-off in the hands of F/Sgt Strathern, an engine fire forced a crash-landing near Great Barford, five miles east-north-east of Bedford, as the result of which, the bomb-aimer was killed. The 15th saw the arrival from 11 O.T.U of S/L Geoff Rothwell, a veteran of many operations with 218 Squadron. That night, the squadron sent five Halifaxes to France to carry out supply drops. The details are as follows; F/O G Kidd in NF-C on Operation PAUL 9E, 22.08 to 04.38, successful. F/L Walker in NF-M on Operation ACTOR 6, 22.10 to 04.46, unsuccessful due to lack of reception. F/Sgt Murray in NF-E on Operation JOHN 127, 22.10 to 04.55, successful. F/O J Kidd in NF-D on Operation PAUL 9E, 22.13 to 04.40, successful. W/O Palmer in NF-Q on Operation WHEELWRIGHT 36, 22.20 to 05.10, successful. On the 17th, W/O Gregory was posted to 14 O.T.U at the end of his tour, while, on the 18th, F/O Pleasance and F/O Witham and their crews arrived from 31 Base, and F/O Ashley was officially posted out to 3 Lancaster Finishing School (3LFS).

When heavy operations resumed on the night of the 19/20th, eight separate attacks were carried out against railway installations, gun batteries and a radar station. A year and one week after the last major assault on Duisburg, Bomber Command returned to the Ruhr city on the night of the 21/22nd. Over five hundred Lancasters from 1, 3, 5 and 8 Groups were accompanied by twenty-two Mosquitos, and despite cloud cover, Oboe allowed an accurate attack to be delivered. 350 buildings were completely destroyed, and many hundreds of others sustained serious damage. The Ruhr, however, remained fiercely protected, and, in an echo of the past, twenty-nine Lancasters failed to return. On the following night, Dortmund also hosted its first heavy raid since the Ruhr campaign, and sustained heavy damage at the hands of 1, 3, 6 and 8 Groups. 5 Group, meanwhile, returned to Brunswick, where, in the face of unexpected cloud and communications difficulties between the Master Bomber and the main force, they dropped most of the bombs into the surrounding countryside. Later on the 23rd, DG286 came to grief during "circuits and bumps" training in the hands of F/L Perrins and his student, F/O Pleasance. A tyre burst at 90 mph during a take-off, but the occupants emerged from the wreckage unscathed, and with a great story to tell.

The new moon period began on the night of the 23/24th, when 138 Squadron dispatched three Halifaxes to France. W/O Palmer and crew took off first at 22.17 in NF-J on Operation JOHN 14, a supply drop. They landed at 04.55 to report a successful outcome. S/L Wilding and crew departed Tempsford at 22.24 in NF-S, to undertake Operation DITCHER 40, the delivery of five agents into the central Digoin region, in which endeavour they were successful. F/Sgt Lawrence and crew maintained the night's 100% record of success, when completing Operation VENTRILOQUIST 7 in NF-Q between 22.37 and 03.30. The night of the 27/28th brought over eleven hundred sorties by main force elements against a variety of targets, the largest force attending to the military camp at Bourg-Leopold, which had escaped serious damage during the abandoned 5 Group assault two weeks earlier. This time it succumbed to accurate bombing by a predominantly Halifax force, and severe damage resulted. 138 Squadron carried out four sorties on this night, all to France, three of them supply drops and one with agents also on board. The latter was the responsibility of F/L Thomas and crew, who took off in NF-J at 22.39 to undertake Operations VENTRILOQUIST 5 and 8. Rebecca assisted their arrival in the Chateauneuf area, where three agents and six packages were delivered onto the first site, before twelve containers were dropped onto the second reception point, despite the lights being extinguished during two of the three runs. The recently-commissioned P/O Yardley and his crew had taken off in an unidentified Halifax a minute ahead of F/L Thomas, briefed to deliver stores to PERCY 7, in the Indre region of central France. After completing a DR run from le Blanc, ten packages were dropped with some difficulty, after they became jammed, and it was only after landing at 04.03, that the fifteen containers were found to have hung-up. F/Sgt Mackay and crew had better luck with Operation JOHN 96, for which they took off in another unidentified Halifax at 22.34, and landed back with positive news at 04.56. F/L G Kidd and crew were last away on this night, at 22.47, in NF-F on Operation PERCY 7, which they completed, before returning safely to land at 04.06.

After a period of relatively small-scale activity, Tempsford was galvanized on the 28th to prepare for sixteen sorties that night, all but one by 138 Squadron, and all to drop sites in France to deliver supplies. What was not known, was that seven of the sites, DELEGATE 2, 3, 4 and 5, and BUTLER 20, 21 and 24, were being operated by the Germans, and each would receive fifteen containers. Proceedings began at 22.28 with the departure of NF-B and NF-F with the crews of P/O Baker and W/O Murray, both assigned to Operation STATIONER 121. The former returned at 03.40 to report a successful outcome, but the latter failed to raise a reception committee, and brought the cargo home to land at 04.54. The compromised drop sites were all in north-western France, in the general area of Rennes, and the crews assigned to these reception points crossed the coast west of Saint-Malo, before making DR runs on their respective targets. DELEGATE 2, 3, 4 and 5 were handed to F/L Johnson, P/O Jones, F/L Stiles and F/L Walker in NF-M, NF-H, NF-E and NF-N respectively, who departed Tempsford between 22.57 and 23.15. All returned safely between 03.13 and 04.00, to report receiving the correct signals from the ground, and delivering their cargo as briefed. BUTLER 20 and 24 were to be serviced by S/L Brogan in NF-R and S/L Wilding in NF-S respectively, with a 161 Squadron crew taking care of BUTLER 21. The 138 squadron pair took off either side of 23.00, and returned shortly before 03.30 to report a successful outcome, after also receiving the correct signals from the reception committee. The details of the remaining sorties are as follows; W/O McFarlane in NF-T on Operation STATIONER 119, 22.34 to 04.39, unsuccessful after drop site not located. P/O Yardley in NF-D on Operation STATIONER 120, 22.41 to 03.50, successful. F/L G Kidd in NF-K on Operation STATIONER 120, 22.47 to 04.20, successful. P/O Lyne in NF-O on Operation STATIONER 104, 22.50 to 04.13, successful. F/L Thomas in NF-J on Operation DONKEYMAN 54, 23.00 to 03.06, unsuccessful due to lack of reception. F/Sgt Lawrence in NF-L on Operation DONKEYMAN 53, 23.12 to 02.52, unsuccessful due to lack of reception. F/O Gallagher in NF-V on Operation VENTRILOQUIST 12, 23.20 to 04.45, unsuccessful due to lack of reception.

There was a sad end to the month for 138 Squadron as a result of operations to Belgium on the night of the 31st. Six Halifaxes were made ready for the night's work, all of which were supply drops, and, in keeping with the ORB's standard procedure, aircraft failing to return were not recorded. We do not, therefore, know what time LL276 NF-F and LL419 NF-V took off on Operations OSRIC 74 and OSRIC 78 with the crews of W/O Murray and F/O Gallagher respectively, only that both fell victim to night fighter attacks over Holland. The former was intercepted, it is believed, by a ME110, which set the port wing on fire, and caused it to crash at Halsteren in southern Holland, shortly after crossing Tholen. W/O Murray died with four of his crew, while three others became PoWs. There were no survivors at all from the eight-man crew of F/O Gallagher, a New Yorker serving in the RCAF. Freddie Clark writes that the Halifax came down on Tholen, possibly at Klippelstraat on the northern edge, while Bill

Chorley records that it was lost without trace. This proved to be just the start of an horrendous period of losses for 138 Squadron over an eight-night stretch. The details of the remaining sorties on this night are as follows; P/O Hayman in NF-P on Operation OSRIC 76, 23.07 to 02.53, successful. P/O Baker in NF-B on an unspecified operation, 23.16 to 02.59, successful. F/Sgt Mackay in NF-S on Operation TYBALT 11, 23.22 to 03.10, successful. P/O Lyne in NF-O on Operation OSRIC 79, 23.30 to 02.50, unsuccessful due to lack of reception.

Excellent detail of the engine installation on a Halifax.

June 1944

The first week of the new month was dominated by preparations for the impending invasion, and was characterized by unsettled weather. Fifty-eight 5 Group Lancasters were out on the night of the 1/2nd to attack a railway junction at Saumur, while a hundred Halifaxes from 4 Group tried in vain to hit a radio listening station at Ferme-d'Urville. 138 Squadron welcomed F/O Ford and crew from 31 Base, while the ground crews prepared sixteen Halifaxes for that night's work. All would be operating over France, and all but one would be transporting stores, but F/Sgt Lawrence had four agents on board NF-C, as he and his crew took off at 22.47 to undertake Operation STATIONER 108. They delivered three agents as briefed, but brought one home for an undisclosed reason, along with a container that had hung up. Three crews were assigned to Operation PERCY 7, those of P/O Hayman, P/O Yardley and F/O Lyne. We do not know at what time P/O Hayman and crew took off in NF-P, but F/O Lyne got away at 22.45 in NF-Y, and P/O Yardley at 23.02 in NF-D. Both of the last-mentioned carried out a DR run from le Blanc, one reporting seeing another Halifax in the area, and the other reporting parachutes on the ground south of the reception lights. LL289 did not return, having crashed in flames in the area of Longue-Jumelles, some forty miles west of Tours. P/O Hayman RAAF and four others were killed, but the two gunners survived, one of them sustaining injuries sufficient to result in his repatriation early in September. The Hayman crew were experienced and valued servants of the SOE cause, and their contribution would be missed.

The details of the other sorties on this night are as follows; F/L Thomas in NF-J on Operation STATIONER 112, 22.23 to 04.05, successful. W/O McFarlane in NF-R on Operations PUDEUR/STATIONER 119, 22.33 to 04.15, successful. F/L Johnson in NF-M on Operation STATIONER 109, 22.40 to 05.10, successful. F/L G Kidd in NF-A on Operation STATIONER 122, 22.48 to 05.24, successful. F/L Stiles in NF-E on Operation GONDOLIER 5, 22.50 to 05.05, successful. F/Sgt Mackay in NF-S on Operation STATIONER 119, 22.54 to 04.23, successful. F/Sgt Paterson in NF-B on Operation STATIONER 41, 22.55 to 05.40, unsuccessful due to lack of reception. P/O Jones in NF-H on Operation TRAINER 257, 23.00 to 05.07, successful. S/L Rothwell in NF-O on Operation VENTRILOQUIST 15, 23.02 to 05.42, unsuccessful due to lack of reception. P/O Levy in NF-K on Operation VENTRILOQUIST 15, 23.09 to 05.37, unsuccessful due to lack of reception. W/O Palmer in NF-Q on Operation STATIONER 122, 23.09 to 05.26, successful. P/O Strathern on NF-L on Operation TRAINER 256, 23.11 to 04.50, successful.

Main force operations on the night of the 2/3rd took in a railway yard at Trappes, a radar jamming station and four coastal batteries in the Pas-de-Calais. 138 Squadron briefed three crews for sorties to Belgium, and twelve for France, where a lack of reception would render two-thirds of them unsuccessful. As events turned out, the Belgian contingent would be dogged by misfortune. F/L Stiles and crew took off in LL284 NF-E to carry out a stores drop under Operation TYBALT 29. As they climbed away at 100 feet, the port-inner engine failed, causing the Halifax to crash-land at Sandy in Bedfordshire, three miles south of the airfield, where it caught fire. Five members of the crew sustained a range of injuries, none life-threatening, but F/L Stiles DFC emerged unscathed, to be declared tour-expired on fifty-nine operations. F/L Thomas and crew were in LL307, NF-J, and were heading for their Belgian rendezvous via the Scheldt Estuary and the coast of southern Holland, to deliver three agents and stores under

Operations RODERIGO 1/OSRIC 77. Sadly, they crashed onto the western end of the island of Tholen, killing all seven crewmen and two of the agents, Sgt Filot and Sgt Stroobants. The sole survivor, Sgt Masereel, was taken prisoner, and survived his captivity. F/L Johnson and crew took off at 22.35 in NF-M on Operations PLAYBILL 4/TYBALT 12, and made a DR run from the lake north of Chimay to drop two agents and three containers. They had twelve containers and two packages to deliver to TYBALT, after which, they returned home to land at 04.12. The details of the supply drops to France are as follows; S/L Brogan in NF-S on Operation BOB 182, 22.29 to 04.40, unsuccessful due to a failing to locate the drop site. W/O Palmer in NF-Q on Operation BOB 183, 22.42 to 04.55, unsuccessful due to lack of reception. W/O McFarlane in NF-R on Operation PERCY 8, 22.44 to 04.34, unsuccessful due to lack of reception. P/O Strathern in NF-A on Operation TRAINER 26, 22.50 to 04.52, successful. F/Sgt Lawrence in NF-C on Operation DONALD 4, 22.52 to 03.30, unsuccessful due to lack of reception. F/L Walker in NF-M on Operation Carver 1, 22.53 to 04.50, successful. P/O Baker in NF-B on Operation PERCY 8, 22.57 to 04.15, successful. F/O Levy in NF-K on Operation TRAINER 258, 22.59 to 04.57, unsuccessful due to lack of reception. F/Sgt Paterson in NF-O on Operation STATIONER 44, 23.00 to 04.59, unsuccessful due to lack of reception. P/O Jones in NF-H on Operations GIOTTO/BEGGAR 2, 23.06 to 04.01, second element only completed, as lack of reception at the first one. F/L G Kidd in NF-L on Operation DONALD 68, 23.09 to 04.19, successful. P/O Yardley in NF-D on Operation DONALD 2, 23.52 to 04.05, unsuccessful due to lack of reception.

After losing five aircraft and crews in three nights, the squadron stood down on the 3rd, while, that night, elements of the main force continued the deception raids on coastal batteries in the Pas-de-Calais. 138 Squadron returned to operations on the night of the 4/5th, with twelve sorties to France, nine of them cargo drops, and two with agents to deliver as well. We are not privy to the details of F/Sgt Mackay's SIS sortie, Operation ORANGE, with regard to his load, and must rely on Freddie Clark to inform us, that he suffered an engine failure immediately after take-off, but landed safely after completing a circuit. Not all of the remaining sorties would be completed as planned, but at least there would be no empty 138 Squadron dispersals to ponder at Tempsford on the following morning. The details are as follows; S/L Rothwell in NF-O on Operation DONALD 22, 22.35 to 04.40, successful. P/O Baker in NF-E on Operation STATIONER 112, 22.38 to 04.35, successful. F/L Johnson in NF-M on Operation STATIONER 111, 22.39 to 04.26, successful. F/O Levy in NF-K on Operation DONALD 19, 22.45 to 04.50, successful. W/O McFarlane in NF-R on Operation VENTRILOQUIST 15, carrying agents and stores, 22.47 to 04.44, unsuccessful due to lack of reception. F/Sgt Paterson in NF-C on Operation VENTRILOQUIST 5, 22.58 to 05.32, unsuccessful due to lack of reception, hit by flak homebound, lost an engine at the English coast, and landed fully laden on three. P/O Jones in NF-H on Operation ROUSPETEUR, 22.59 to 04.34, successful. P/O Palmer in NF-N on Operation STATIONER 110, , 23.00 to 05.35, successful. P/O Strathern in NF-A on Operation TRAINER 257, 23.00 to 04.48, successful. P/O Lyne in NF-L on Operation DONALD 9, 23.10 to 04.22, successful. F/L Walker in NF-N? on Operation DONALD 6, 23.16 to 04.44, unsuccessful, drop site not located.

More than twelve hundred aircraft were aloft on D-Day Eve, the 5/6th, most of them bound for one of ten coastal batteries overlooking the beaches onto which the invasion force was about to land. There were no direct references to the invasion at briefings, but crews were ordered to observe strict flight levels, and were prohibited from jettisoning bombs over the sea. Aircraft were taking off throughout the night, and some of those returning at low level in dawn's early light, were rewarded, through gaps in the cloud, with a sight of the giant invasion armada, as it ploughed its way sedately across the Channel below. Among the many deception and diversionary operations carried out that night were Operations Taxable and Glimmer, involving Lancasters and Stirlings from 617 and 218 Squadrons respectively. These crews were required to undertake hours of precision flying, dropping Window to simulate an invasion fleet approaching the Pas-de-Calais. Meanwhile, the Tempsford squadrons had their own role to play, in company with Stirlings from 3 Group's 90 and 149 Squadrons. Their brief was to drop dummy parachutists, made of hessian filled with straw, and dubbed "gingerbread men". They were about thirty inches tall, with explosive devices to simulate gun fire, and forty could be fitted into each Halifax. These were to be delivered to areas away from the landing grounds to give the impression of an airborne assault. The 138 Squadron participants took off either side of 23.30, and were; P/O Yardley in NF-D, P/O Baker in NF-E, and F/Sgt Lawrence in NF-O, each of whom was assigned to Operation TITANIC 1 Task 1, which involved the delivery of the dummies, while W/O Palmer in NF-R, P/O Lyne in NF-A and F/L G Kidd in NF-H carried out Operation TITANIC 1 Task 2, the dropping of Window to confuse the enemy radar. F/L Johnson and crew were in NF-M on Operation TITANIC 4, and carried genuine parachutists in the form of two three-man teams of an officer and two other ranks of the 1st SAS Regiment, to drop at the southern end of the Cherbourg Peninsular, north-east of St-Lo. Despite a cloud base down as low as 1,000 feet, Gee-fixes enabled them to pinpoint their position, and deliver the men from 800 feet, to create pandemonium with Very pistols and gramophone-generated noises among the dummies as part of the FORTITUDE deception plan. The other crews also used Gee to identify their operating areas a few miles inland from the beaches, and while these operations were ongoing, ABC Lancasters of 101 Squadron patrolled known night fighter routes to jam enemy communications.

D-Day Night brought another thousand aircraft into action, this time against road and railway communications in or near towns on the approaches to the beachhead. 138 Squadron prepared nine Halifaxes for operations over France, two with agents on board as well as stores. F/Sgt Lawrence and crew carried two agents and stores as they took off in NF-A at 23.15 on Operations DONALD 6/ASPHODEL. They carried out a DR run from Clermont-Ferrand in south-central France, and dropped the agents along with twelve containers, before heading for the second element, an SIS drop site, where a reception committee failed to show. The details of the other sorties on this night are as follows; P/O Yardley's take-off time in NF-D on Operation DAVIDSTON 1 is not recorded, but his was the other crew carrying agents and stores, landing at 04.06, after an unsuccessful sortie due to adverse weather. W/O McFarlane in NF-H on Operation ORANGE, 22.59 to 03.47, successful. F/Sgt Mackay in NF-S on Operations PERIWINKLE/WALT 3, 23.09 to 04.19, unsuccessful due to lack of reception. F/L G Kidd in NF-L on Operation BEAUNE, 23.11 to 03.43, successful. F/Sgt Paterson in NF-E on Operation HERMIT 3, 23.12 to 03.50, successful. F/L Walker in NF-P on Operation HISTORIAN 9, 23.19 to 03.37, successful. F/O Levy in NF-K on Operation HERMIT 2, 23.21 to 03.59, successful. S/L Rothwell in NF-O on Operation HERMIT 3, 23.22 to 03.10, successful.

It was similar fare on the following night, which brought attacks on four railway targets by over three hundred Halifaxes and Lancasters, while elements of 1, 5 and 8 Groups went for a six-way road junction in the Foret de Cerisy, between Bayeux and St-Lo. As on the previous night, 138 Squadron prepared nine Halifaxes for drops over France, on what would turn out to be its blackest night yet. As usual, details of sorties for missing aircraft are omitted, making it impossible to record the night's events in sequence. S/L Brogan began his take-off run at 23.15 in LL390 NF-S, to carry out Operation HISTORIAN 10, but veered off the runway, and collided with a concrete pillbox, ripping off the port undercarriage and causing other irreparable damage. Fortunately, the occupants emerged from the wreckage unscathed, and Brogan would continue with his tour. *He would be given command of 161 Squadron in late February 1945, only to lose his life on operations less than two weeks later.* P/O Lyne RCAF and crew were also briefed for Operation HISTORIAN 10, and were on board NF-O, which took off after S/L Brogan, and headed for the Blois/Orleans region of north-western France. Set on fire by flak while outbound, and almost at the drop site, LL416 crashed, killing all but gunner Sgt Hinds, who parachuted into a wooded area, and was hidden by French patriots until being liberated by American troops on the 17th of September. LL466 NF-T contained the crew of F/Sgt Mackay RCAF, who had been briefed to undertake Operation DONALD 26, and all were killed when the Halifax crashed and exploded near Doudeville, shortly after crossing the French coast over Saint-Valery-en-Caux. Close by was found the wreckage of LL306 NF-R, containing the bodies of F/L Jones RAAF and his crew, who had been flying an SIS sortie, Operations PERIWINKLE/WALT 3. The fact that all of the pilots and many of the crew members were from Canada and Australia, highlights the enormous contribution and sacrifice made by these great friends of Britain. A sortie by F/L Johnson and crew is not recorded in the ORB, but Freddie Clark writes that they were outbound on Operation HISTORIAN 8, when engine problems forced an early return. The details of the night's other sorties are as follows; P/O Baker in an unidentified Halifax on Operations DARWEN 1/PERCY 13, carrying agents and stores, 23.03 to 04.21, second element only completed, as no reception at the first. F/Sgt Paterson in NF-D on Operation HISTORIAN 12, 23.13 to 03.41, successful. W/O Palmer in NF-L on Operation BEGGAR 5, 23.35 to 02.51, unsuccessful due to lack of reception. F/O Levy in NF-P on Operation HISTORIAN 12, 23.38 to 03.58, successful. F/O Strathern in NF-F on Operation HISTORIAN 3, 23.38 to 04.01, unsuccessful due to lack of reception.

The assault on enemy railway communications continued on the night of the 8/9th at five locations, and 617 Squadron successfully delivered the first of the Barnes Wallis designed 12,000lb Tallboy deep penetration bombs onto the Saumur railway tunnel. A new campaign began on the night of the 12/13th, which would be prosecuted right through to the end of the war. With Germany now firmly on the back foot, a concentrated effort was to be made by both Bomber Command and the American 8th Air force against its synthetic oil industry. Three hundred Lancasters and Mosquitos of 1, 3 and 8 Groups carried out a stunningly accurate attack on the Nordstern refinery at Gelsenkirchen, hitting it with fifteen hundred bombs, and halting all production for a number of weeks. This deprived the German war effort of a thousand tons of vital aviation fuel for each day of the stoppage. While this was in progress, over six hundred aircraft drawn from 4, 5, 6 and 8 Groups bombed six communications targets leading to the Normandy front. On the 10th, F/L Stiles was posted out to take up duties at the Air Ministry, and F/Sgt Moffatt RNZAF and crew arrived from 31 Base. They were joined on the 12th from the same source by F/Sgt Prowse and crew.

Two 138 Squadron cargo drops on the night of the 13/14th began a concerted nine-night effort from Tempsford, during which, an attempt would be made to service sixty one drop sites. Of these, thirty nine would deliver arms to bolster the resources of the French resistance organizations. P/O Strathern and crew took off at 22.45 in NF-L on Operation HERBERT 3, and were followed fourteen minutes later by F/Sgt Paterson and crew in NF-F on Operation HUBERT 4. They returned safely at 03.24 and 03.18 respectively, each to report a successful outcome. Five sorties were mounted on the following night, beginning with W/O McFarlane and crew, who took off in NF-M at 22.49 on Operation FREELANCE 3. F/Sgt Paterson and crew followed at 22.59 in NF-L, also on Operation FREELANCE 3, but would be the night's only failure due to a lack of reception. The next two departures involved crews briefed to carry out Operation FREELANCE 2. P/O Strathern and P/O Yardley took off at 23.00 and 23.02 in NF-A and NF-D respectively, and returned home at 04.56 and 04.33. S/L Rothwell and crew were in NF-F, and departed Tempsford at 23.04 to deliver two agents and stores to PETER 38, which he accomplished after making a DR run from the River Loire.

Earlier in the evening, the first daylight operations by Bomber Command since the departure of 2 Group a year earlier, were conducted against le Havre on the evening of the 14th. The port was home to fast, light naval craft, which posed a threat to Allied shipping serving the beachhead. The two-phase operation was opened by a 617 Squadron attack on the concrete pens with Tallboys, closely followed by a predominantly 1 Group force. 3 Group completed the assault at dusk, and few if any marine craft escaped the carnage unscathed. While this was in progress, elements of 4, 5 and 8 Groups were concentrating their efforts against enemy troop and transport positions at Aunay-sur-Odon and Evrecy. The evening of the 15th was devoted to the bombing of Boulogne in a repeat of the previous night's operation against le Havre. This operation, by elements of 1, 4, 5, 6 and 8 Groups was equally effective, although the town itself suffered its worst experience of the war.

A second new campaign opened on the night of the 16/17th, this one against flying bomb launching and storage sites. 1, 4, 5, 6 and 8 Groups committed four hundred aircraft between them to attacks on four targets in the Pas-de-Calais, and each was effectively dealt with without loss. Meanwhile, a second force continued the oil offensive at Sterkrade/Holten in the Ruhr, but failed to inflict more than slight damage in the face of complete cloud cover. 138 Squadron launched five more supply drops to France on this night, the details of which are as follows; F/O Witham in NF-H on Operation HARRY 21, 22.22 to 03.41, successful. P/O Strathern in an unidentified Halifax on Operation HUBERT 6, 22.25 to 03.51, successful. W/O McFarlane in NF-P on Operation HUBERT 4, 22.27 to 03.45, unsuccessful due to lack of reception. F/Sgt Paterson in an unidentified Halifax on Operation HARRY 21, 22.29 to 03.58, successful. W/C Burnett, on his maiden SOE sortie, in NF-W on Operation HARRY 21.?? to 04.16, successful.

While railway installations and flying bomb sites occupied over four hundred main force and Pathfinder aircraft on the night of the 17/18th, 138 Squadron sent seven Halifaxes to France, four to deliver stores, all under Operation HUBERT 7, and three to drop agents under Operation HISTORIAN 2. *(The squadron scribe often failed to record the identity of aircraft during this phase.)* The cargo contingent got away first, beginning with S/L Brogan and crew at 22.34, followed at 22.42 by F/O Witham in NF-K, at 22.46 by F/Sgt Paterson, and at 22.47

by P/O Strathern in NF-E, but, sadly, all failed due to a lack of reception. W/O MacFarlane and crew took off in NF-O at 23.18, and successfully deposited four agents and stores onto the reception site, despite the poor quality of the Morse-code signal from the ground. F/L Johnson and crew departed at 23.20 in NF-M, and, like the others, carried out a DR run from Chateauneuf-sur-Loire, west of Orleans, whereupon, his agents refused to jump when presented with an incorrect signal letter. P/O Yardley and crew were airborne in NF-D at 23.26, also with four agents and stores to deliver, and they were equally unimpressed by what came from the ground, but opted to jump anyway. On the way home, these crews observed a line of stationary searchlights on the English coast from Rochester in Kent to Beachy Head, and what looked like six pilotless aircraft heading north at 10,000 feet pursued by flak. The scourge of the V-1 had begun.

Seven supply drops to France were attempted by the squadron on the night of the 21/22nd, and all but one were successful. The odd one out was conducted by P/O Levy and crew, who took off in NF-B at 23.33 on Operation HISTORIAN 12, but failed to make contact with a reception committee. The details of the other sorties are as follows; F/L J Kidd in NF-A on Operation DONALD 34, 23.16 to 05.10. F/L Johnson in NF-P on Operation FIREMAN 11, 23.19 to 05.25. F/L G Kidd in NF-F on Operation DONALD 34, 23.27 to 05.30. P/O Palmer in NF-H on Operation DONALD 34, 23.30 to 04.16. F/Sgt Lawrence in NF-D on Operation HISTORIAN 16, 23.30 to 05.38. F/L Walker in NF-N on Operation FIREMAN 11, 23.50 to 05.45. W/O MacFarlane and crew, meanwhile, had taken off in NF-O at 23.13 to undertake Operation HISTORIAN 12, carrying six agents and stores, which were delivered as briefed to complete a relatively successful night. 5 Group's main force squadrons were also back in action on this night, embarking on their first involvement in the oil campaign. Two targets were selected, Wesseling near Cologne, and Scholven/Buer in the Ruhr, and each was to be marked from low level by 627 Squadron Mosquitos. The Wesseling force was badly mauled by night fighters, and, by the time that the survivors reached home, thirty-seven Lancasters had fallen victim.

The night of the 22/23rd brought a further seven supply drops to France, all but one of them, again, successful. The details are as follows; P/O Pleasance in NF-H on Operation PETER 38, 23.11 to 05.45 (Defford), unsuccessful due to lack of reception. W/O McFarlane in NF-U on Operation STATIONER 139, 23.15 to 05.26 (Pershore). P/O Palmer in NF-M on Operation STATIONER 139, 23.16 to 05.07 (Pershore). F/L Walker in NF-N on Operation STATIONER 140, 23.17 to 05.10 (Pershore). F/Sgt Lawrence in NF-F on Operation STATIONER 139, 23.20 to 05.15 (Pershore). F/O Levy in NF-A on Operation STATIONER 140, 23.22 to 06.06 (Pershore). F/L G Kidd in NF-A on Operation STATIONER 140, 23.33 to 06.02 (Pershore). An influx of fresh blood from 11 Base on the 23rd swelled the 138 Squadron ranks, as P/O Aitken, P/O Strathey RCAF, F/Sgt Hardie RAAF, F/O O'Bern, F/O Sephton and Sgt Ouellette RCAF and their crews arrived for training.

Over seven hundred aircraft took part in operations against seven flying bomb sites on the night of the 24/25th, and these, along with railways, provided the objectives for most of the main force operations for the remainder of the month. 138 Squadron dispatched six Halifaxes to France on supply drops, the details of which are as follows; P/O Palmer in NF-U on Operation STATIONER 114, 23.05 to 04.15, successful. W/C Burnett in NF-W on an unspecified

Above left: P/O Len MacFarlane RCAF receives his DFC from a senior Canadian officer. For the majority of his time with 138 Sqn, MacFarlane was a Warrant Officer. He and his crew survived their tour of ops with the unit. Above right: Len Macfarlane in training, whilst a sergeant pilot. Below: The MacFarlane crew whilst at OTU, believed to be at Ossington. At this time, the crew was flying Wellingtons. It is believed that the whole crew, at this time, was from Canada. Left to right: W/O Len MacFarlane (pilot), Buck Buchan (MU gunner), Joe Walker (rear gunner), Harry Knox (WOP/AG), Jack Galbraith (navigator), Frank Tripp (bomb aimer). They would later be joined by a flight engineer when they moved on to heavy bombers (photo: Jan MacFarlane via Peter Green).

operation, 23.09 to 05.07, unsuccessful due to lack of reception. F/L J Kidd in NF-A on Operation FIREMAN 11, 23.11 to 04.37, successful. F/L G Kidd in NF-F on Operation FIREMAN 11, 23.25 to 04.33, successful. F/Sgt Lawrence on NF-C on Operation STATIONER 114, 23.26 to 04.56, successful. F/O Levy in NF-E on Operation HERMIT 8, 23.31 to 05.00, unsuccessful due to lack of reception. A further eight supply drops to France kept the squadron busy on the night of the 27/28th, when more than a thousand other aircraft were engaged in operations, mostly against flying bomb sites and railways. The details of the SOE sorties are as follows; F/L G Kidd in NF-L on Operation STATIONER 147, 22.22 to 04.41, successful. F/L J Kidd in NF-A on Operation STATIONER 147, 22.23 to 04.52, unsuccessful due to lack of reception. F/L Walker in NF-N on Operation Actor 15, 22.29 to 04.45, unsuccessful due to lack of reception. P/O Palmer in NF-J on Operation ACTOR 15, 22.30 to 04.50, unsuccessful due to lack of reception. W/O McFarlane in NF-U on Operation HERMIT 2, 22.45 to 04.23, successful. S/L Brogan in NF-W on Operation HUGH 22.57 to 04.55, successful. F/Sgt Lawrence in NF-F on Operation HERMIT 2, 23.16 to 04.38, successful. F/L Yardley in NF-E on Operation HERMIT 2, 23.18 to 04.32, successful.

The twelve sorties on the night of the 29/30th, were divided between two target areas, HUBERT 12, located north of Nantes in western France, which was to receive eight loads of containers and packages, and FREDERICK 2, the location of which is a mystery, which was due four loads. All aircraft would also be carrying pigeons. The weather conditions were unhelpful in both areas, and the receptions disorganized, which led to a disappointing performance all round. At HUBERT there was four-tenths cloud with a base at 3,000 feet, but the main problem was the poor layout of signal lights on the ground, and aircraft milled about at low level searching for their pinpoints. The details of the HUBERT contingent are as follows; F/L G Kidd in NF-L, 22.16 to 03.56, unsuccessful due to lack of reception. F/L J Kidd in NF-A, 22.24 to 03.49, successful. W/O McFarlane in NF-U, 22.38 to 04.13, unsuccessful due to lack of reception. F/L Yardley in NF-F, 22.45 to 04.01, unsuccessful due to lack of reception. F/L Walker in NF-N, 23.03 to 02.40, successful. F/L Levy in NF-K, 23.07 to 04.47, unsuccessful due to lack of reception. P/O Strathern in NF-E, 23.17 to 04.37, successful. P/O Palmer in NF-J, 00.03 to 04.50, unsuccessful due to lack of reception. There was ten-tenths cloud at FREDERICK, where a lake to the north of the target area provided a reference for those breaking through the cloud at between 400 to 1,200 feet, and a large bonfire was also visible. The details are as follows; F/Sgt Paterson in NF-C, 21.14 to 03.52, successful. F/O Witham in NF-B, 22.48 to 02.43, unsuccessful due to adverse weather. F/O Wallace in NF-Q, 22.59 to 03.14, successful. P/O Carley in NF-W, 23.05 to 03.07, unsuccessful due to adverse weather. June had been a sobering month for 138 Squadron, in which five crews had failed to return. Fortunately, the replacement crews had been under training, and would be ready to step into the breach in time for July's schedule.

July 1944

July and August were to be Bomber Command's most hectic months of the year, as the side-by-side campaigns against communications, oil and flying bomb sites all demanded attention. To this was about to be added tactical support for the ground forces as they broke out of the beachhead into Normandy. 138 Squadron would fly exclusively to France during July, mostly delivering much needed cargo to the various organisations, which were now not simply resisting, but were actively participating in the liberation of their homeland. Flying bomb sites dominated the first week's proceedings for the bombers, while 138 Squadron made ready fifteen Halifaxes on the 3rd for a busy night of cargo drops, with one aircraft carrying an agent also. Pleasingly, F/L Jaffé was now the squadron adjutant, and he took advantage of a new ORB page format to provide clear and concise information.

The main focus during the early part of the month was on the departments of Loire-et-Cher, HERMIT, Loiret, HISTORIAN and Nievre, GONDOLIER, a cluster of SOE lines south of Paris in north-central France. The details of this night's activities are as follows; P/O Strathern in NF-E on Operation SCIENTIST 104, 22.22 to 03.43, successful. F/Sgt Paterson in NF-B on Operation GONDOLIER 16, 22.38 to 05.12, successful. F/O Wallace in NF-W on Operations HERMIT 12/FANION, 22.44 to 04.11, unsuccessful due to lack of reception. S/L Rothwell in NF-F on Operations DONKEYMAN 64/BENZ, 22.47 to 04.17, successful. W/O McFarlane in NF-U on Operations GRATTOIR/RAPPORTEUR, 22.50 to 05.08, successful. F/L Levy in NF-K on Operation GONDOLIER 16, 22.53 to 05.52, successful. F/L Yardley in NF-D on Operation PERCY 15, 22.57 to 05.21, unsuccessful due to lack of reception. P/O Palmer in NF-J on Operation GONDOLIER 15, 23.00 to 04.20, unsuccessful due to adverse weather. F/O Witham in NF-O on Operation DONALD 34, 23.04 to 05.29, unsuccessful due to adverse weather. F/L J Kidd in NF-A on Operation PERCY 15, 23.06 to 05.16, unsuccessful due to lack of reception. F/O Ford in NF-P on Operation HERMIT 12, 23.11 to 04.23, successful. F/L G Kidd in NF-L on Operation PARAPLUIE, carrying agents and stores, 23.12 to 06.01, unsuccessful due to lack of reception. P/O Lawrence in NF-C on Operation HERMIT 12, 23.18 to 03.54, successful. F/O Pleasance in NF-H on Operation HERMIT 12, 23.27 to 04.06, successful. P/O Carley in NF-Q on Operation HERMIT 12, 23.51 to 04.30, successful.

Eleven Halifaxes were made ready on the 4th for cargo drops that night, while seven hundred other aircraft took care of business elsewhere, principally at a V-Weapon store in caves at St-Leu-d'Esserent, north of Paris, and railways at Orleans and Villeneuve-St-Georges. The details of the 138 Squadron effort are as follows. P/O Strathern in in NF-E on Operations HISTORIAN 19/DRAPEAN, 22..23 to 04.13, first element only completed, no reception at the second one. P/O Wallace in NF-S on Operation DONALD 2, 22.40 to 03.51, successful. S/L Brogan in NF-W on Operations CHALUTIER/CAEN, 22.47 to 05.00, successful. F/Sgt Moffatt in NF-O on Operation HISTORIAN 23, 22.55 to 04.34, successful. F/O Carley in NF-X on Operation DONALD 22, 22.57 to 04.19, successful. F/Sgt Paterson in NF-B on Operations HISTORIAN 19/FANION, 23.00 to 04.37, successful. F/O Pleasance in NF-R on Operation GONDOLIER 15, 23.01 to 04.52, unsuccessful due to lack of reception. F/O Ford in NF-P on Operation DONALD 34, 23.08 to 04.50, successful. F/L Yardley in NF-D on Operations TOM 76/RESTINGA 3, 23.09 to 03.47, successful. F/L Walker in NF-N on

Operations VALISE/ASPHODEL, 23.10 to 04.00, first element completed, second element partially completed. P/O Lawrence in NF-F on Operation TOM 76, 23.16 to 03.42, successful.

Eight of the ten sorties mounted on the night of the 5/6th were cargo drops, but W/C Burnett had four agents on board in addition to his stores, and F/L Levy an unspecified number. The details of the night's work are as follows; F/L Walker in NF-N on Operation ROVER 6, 22.15 to 05.00, successful. W/O McFarlane in NF-U on Operations MUSETTE/HISTORIAN 14, 22.44 to 04.25, successful. F/L Levy in NF-B on Operation PARAPLUIE, 22.46 to 04.23, successful. W/C Burnett in NF-W on Operation DONALD 19, 22.52 to 04.28, successful. P/O Palmer in NF-J on Operation TOM 73, 22.55 to 03.45, unsuccessful due to lack of reception. F/O Witham in NF-O on Operation DICK 99, 22.57 to 04.37, unsuccessful due to lack of reception. S/L Rothwell in NF-F on Operation HISTORIAN 14, 23.02 to 04.05, successful. F/L G Kidd in NF-L on Operation TOM 73, 23.02 to 04.31, unsuccessful due to lack of reception. F/L J Kidd in NF-A on Operations DRAPEAN/HISTORIAN 14, 23.04 to 04.20, successful. F/Sgt Prowse in NF-H on Operation STATIONER 160, 23.11 to 04.10, partially successful.

The first major operations in support of the ground forces took place around Caen on the evening of the 7th. Later that night, while around two hundred 5 Group aircraft returned to the flying bomb storage site in caves at St-Leu-d'Esserent, 138 Squadron mounted fifteen sorties. Although the ORB makes no mention of the fact, F/L J Kidd was carrying seven passengers along with his containers and packages. He and his crew took off at 22.44 in NF-L on Operation SCIENTIST 103, passing over the beachhead on a southerly heading, before making a DR run eastwards to the drop site near Mayenne, some fifty miles south of Caen, where the jump took place from 700 feet. P/O Palmer and crew took off at 22.42 in NF-J on Operation DIPLOMAT 4, with three agents on board, and they were delivered with their large and heavy packages during the course of three runs across the drop site in a thunderstorm. F/O Carley took off at 22.18 in NF-H to carry out Operation SCIENTIST 104, but was recalled, and landed back at Tempsford at 23.50. The details of the other sorties on this night, all cargo drops, are as follows; F/O Witham in NF-O on Operation STATIONER 156, 21.57 to 04.50, successful. F/L Yardley in NF-F on Operation ROVER 9, 22.00 to 04.55, unsuccessful due to incorrect reception. P/O Lawrence in NF-E on Operation PERCY 16, 22.05 to 05.18, unsuccessful due to incorrect reception. F/Sgt Prowse in NF-Q on Operation STATIONER 157, 22.07 to 05.05, successful. W/O McFarlane in NF-U on Operation PERCY 16, 22.10 to 05.23, unsuccessful due to lack of reception. F/O Ford in NF-S on Operation SCIENTIST 103, 22.15 to 03.56, successful. F/O Wallace in NF-R on Operation SCIENTIST 103, 22.20 to 03.31, successful. F/Sgt Moffatt in NF-X on Operation STATIONER 157, 22.29 to 05.29, successful. F/O Strathy in NF-N on Operation HISTORIAN 21, 22.45 to 05.07, successful. Sgt Ouellette in NF-B on Operation HISTORIAN 21, 22.50 to 04.48, successful. F/O Sephton in NF-K on Operation DONALD 20, 23.00 to 04.53, unsuccessful due to lack of reception. F/O O'Bern in NF-P on Operation DICK 99, 23.03 to 05.00, successful.

The night of the 8/9th was curiously quiet as the heavy squadrons stayed at home, but 138 Squadron sent five crews to France to deliver supplies. The details are; P/O Lawrence in NF-X on Operation IAN 2, 22.00 to 05.04, unsuccessful due to lack of reception. F/O Witham in NF-S on Operation IAN 2, 22.19 to 05.10, unsuccessful due to lack of reception. P/O Strathy in NF-W on Operation FREDERICK 4, 23.00 to 03.02, successful. Sgt Ouellette in NF-E on Operation FREDERICK 4, 23.11 to 03.13, successful. F/O Sephton in NF-K on Operation FREDERICK 4, 23.26 to 03.26, successful.

Fifteen sorties were planned for the night of the 9/10th, when the main force again stayed at home, although almost 350 aircraft from 3, 4, 6 and 8 Groups had been out earlier in the day attacking V-Weapon sites. Four of the 138 Squadron crews were to fly "shuttle" sorties, to targets in France, before heading for Blida in Algeria. W/C Burnett and F/L Walker were assigned to Operation DITCHER 47, to drop supplies, and P/O Palmer and F/L Yardley to JOHN 60 with stores and agents, and they took off in NF-B, NF-N, NF-H and NF-D respectively between 23.00 and 23.14. The drop sites were in eastern France, in the Alpine region close to the Swiss frontier, and W/C Burnett encountered low cloud and rain as he searched for his pinpoint . He found the reception laid out in a small valley, which made the delivery difficult, but he was able to let his stores go. An additional problem was a second "Eureka" signal being superimposed over his, and F/L Walker experienced similar problems with his "Rebecca" signals, and failed to locate his drop site. The other two crews pinpointed on Doubs, and carried out DR runs from there, P/O Palmer dropping two agents and F/L Yardley three, before setting course for North Africa, which was reached after a flight of around seven hours. All four Halifaxes arrived safely to be prepared for further drops on the way home on the night of the 11/12th. The details of the other stores drops to France on this night are as follows; F/L G Kidd in NF-L on Operations BICYCLETTE/VELO, 22.17 to 04.43, unsuccessful due to adverse weather. F/Sgt Prowse in NF-S on Operation FREDERICK 3, 22.50 to 03.25, successful. W/O McFarlane in NF-U on Operation SCIENTIST 108, 22.54 to 04.08, successful. F/O Aitken in NF-K on Operation FREDERICK 3, 23.01 to 03.55, successful. F/Sgt Moffattt in NF-X on Operation BICYCLETTE/VELO, 23.07 to 04.02, successful. F/O O'Bern in NF-P on Operation FREDERICK 3, 23.10 to 04.15, unsuccessful due to lack of reception. F/O Carley in NF-R on Operation SCIENTIST 107, 23.12 to 03.51, successful. F/L J Kidd in NF-A on Operation SCIENTIST 104, 23.16 to 04.25, successful. F/Sgt Hardie in NF-O on Operation FREDERICK 3, 23.22 to 04.21, unsuccessful due to lack of reception. P/O Strathern in NF-E on Operation SCIENTIST 108, 23.30 to 04.46, successful. F/O Pleasance in NF-J on Operation SCIENTIST 107, 23.40 to 04.12, successful.

Of nine sorties to France on the night of the 10/11th, seven were cargo drops, and two delivered agents as well as stores. F/O Sephton and crew took off at 00.26 in NF-K on Operation Scientist 107, a shallow penetration into southern Normandy to deliver Jack Hayes, whose job was to supply tactical intelligence to the American army. The sortie was successful, and Hayes would recruit thirty local volunteers to help with his task of identifying enemy dispositions. His work would last a month, and prove to be of great value to the Americans. F/O Pleasance and crew also had agents on board NF-R, as they took off at 23.13 to head for the drop site of PETER 38. There are no further details, but agents and stores were delivered according to instructions, which was confirmed on the crew's return at 04.47. The remaining sorties were supply drops, with details as follows; F/Sgt Moffatt in NF-X on Operations BICYCLETTE/VELO, 23.07 to 05.17, successful. S/L Brogan in NF-W on Operations ASPHODEL/TOM 60, 23.10 to 04.05, unsuccessful due to adverse weather. P/O Carley in NF-S on Operation PETER 38, 23.19 to 04.53, successful. Sgt Ouellette in NF-Q on Operation PERMIT 2, 23.21 to 05.00, successful. F/Sgt Paterson in NF-F on Operation PERMIT 2, 23.30 to 05.50, successful. F/Sgt Hardie in

NF-P on Operation HERMIT 2, 23.37 to 05.36, successful. F/O Witham in NF-O on Operation DONALD 20, 23.39 to 05.13, successful.

P/O Palmer and W/C Burnett took off from Blida at 20.50 and 21.04 respectively on the 11th, to carry out Operation PERCY 19 on their way home. The reception site for the stores drops was believed by Freddie Clark to be in the Eymoutiers region of central France, and both crews carried out their instructions, before landing safely at Tempsford shortly after 05.00. It is understood, that F/L Yardley remained for a time at Blida, probably while his aircraft received attention, but that F/L Walker took off with the others. An hour into the flight, LL251's port-outer engine developed problems, and had to be shut down. It was decided to turn back, but it soon became clear, even after jettisoning the cargo, that height could not be maintained in the thin, hot Mediterranean air at an airspeed of 150 mph. The lights of what turned out to be a British hospital ship were spotted in the distance, and the Halifax was ditched. The fuselage petrol tank burst, creating lethal fumes, and the automatic dinghy release failed, forcing crew members to enter the fuselage to pull the manual release. The current dragged them through the rear escape hatch, and all but the navigator, F/O Farr, were picked up by a lifeboat, before a search for him began. Sadly, he could not be found, and was presumed drowned. The survivors were put aboard the hospital ship, and landed at ORAN. They were eventually flown to Lyneham in a BOAC Liberator, arriving home on the 1st of August. The Liberator swung on landing, and was written off after colliding with a building. There were no human casualties, but F/L Walker was clearly riding his luck, and was declared tour-expired after seventy operations.

As the above crews made their way back from Blida, twelve others from the squadron were busy over France delivering stores. The details are as follows; W/O McFarlane in NF-U on Operation HISTORIAN 18, 23.02 to 04.35, unsuccessful due to lack of reception. P/O Lawrence in NF-C on Operation DONALD 93, 23.04 to 04.20, successful. F/L G Kidd in NF-L on Operation PERCY 15, 23.18 to 04.55, successful. P/O Strathern in NF-F? on Operation DICK 96, 23.18 to 04.40, successful. F/L J Kidd in NF-A on Operation PERCY 15, 23.21 to 05.00, unsuccessful due to lack of reception. F/O Strathy in NF-S on Operation PERMIT 1, 23.24 to 04.55, successful. Sgt Ouellette in NF-X on Operation PERMIT 1, 23.28 to 05.20, successful. F/O Witham in NF-J on Operation DICK 96, 23.31 to 04.44, successful. F/Sgt Paterson in NF-F on Operation HISTORIAN 37, 23.34 to 05.11, unsuccessful due to lack of reception. F/Sgt Prowse in NF-R on Operation HISTORIAN 37, 23.40 to 05.15, successful. F/O Aitken in NF-W on Operation PERMIT 1, 23.45 to 05.20, successful. F/O Sephton in NF-Q on Operation PERMIT 1, 23.49 to 06.00, successful.

Flying bomb sites and railways continued to occupy the heavy brigade during the middle part of the month. 138 Squadron continued its supply work to French targets on the night of the 15/16th, with, according to the ORB, nine sorties, one of which, piloted by S/L Rothwell, carried agents as well. Freddie Clark attributes this sortie to the night of the 17/18th, and I will, therefore, go with his more reliable testimony. The details of the eight supply drops on the night of the 15/16th are as follows; P/O Palmer in NF-U on Operation IAN 4, 22.13 to 05.20 (Mepal), unsuccessful due to lack of reception. F/L G Kidd in NF-L on Operation IAN 4, 22.22 to 05.13 (Mepal), successful. F/Sgt Paterson in NF-F on Operation STATIONER 165, 22.32 to 05.26 (Mepal), unsuccessful due to lack of reception. P/O Strathern in NF-E on Operation

STATIONER 165, 22.38 to 05.23 (Mepal), successful. F/O Pleasance in NF-S on Operation GONDOLIER 13, 22.44 to 04.36 (Chedburgh), successful. F/O Witham in NF-O on Operation GONDOLIER 13, 22.50 to 05.06 (Mepal), successful. F/L Levy in NF-K on Operation STATIONER 165, 22.52 to 05.40 (Mepal), successful. P/O Lawrence in NF-C on Operation HUGH 6, 23.15 to 05.05 (Mepal), successful.

Among seven sorties scheduled for the night of the 17/18th were three assigned to Operation GILES 2, each carrying three agents and fifteen containers. The drop site was in the Cotes-D'Armour, between Brest and St Malo, and the crews of S/L Rothwell, P/O Palmer and F/L J Kidd set off in NF-X, NF-U and NF-E at 22.30, 22.46 and 22.53 respectively, and successfully carried out their briefs. On the way home at 8,000 feet, S/L Rothwell lost his R/T and trailing aerials to a lightning strike, but arrived home safely, as did the other two, P/O Palmer complaining that he had almost collided head-on with another aircraft shortly after the drop. The details of the remaining sorties on this night, all supply drops under Operation SCIENTIST 117, are; F/O Witham in NF-O, 22.14 to 03.06, successful. F/O Pleasance in NF-R, 22.21 to 03.17, successful. F/L Levy in NF-K, 22.36 to 03.54, successful. F/L G Kidd in NF-S, 22.39 to 03.39, successful. Even before they landed, the first of more than nine hundred aircraft were already airborne, and heading towards Caen, to attack fortified villages standing in the way of the British Second Army's advance under Operation Goodwood.

The night of the 18/19th brought a return to the oil campaign by elements of the main force, with raids on the refineries at Wesseling and Scholven-Buer, both of which had escaped serious damage at the hands of 5 Group a month earlier. 138 Squadron put seven Halifaxes into the air on this night, all but S/L Brogan carrying stores alone. He had an agent to deliver to MASON 27, and stores for DICK 89, the latter the target also for F/L J Kidd and F/L Levy. F/O Pleasance, F/O Witham and F/L G Kidd were assigned to Operation SHIPWRIGHT 9, which left P/O Palmer to deal with Operation DONKEYMAN 66B on his own. F/O Pleasance and crew were the first to take off, doing so at 22.00 in LL387 NF-P, before setting course for the French coast. It is not known whether they were out or inbound at the time, but the Halifax crashed into the sea off the Normandy coast, killing all on board, and the bodies of the pilot and three others were never recovered. F/O Witham and F/L G Kidd took off at 22.05 and 22.15 in NF-O and NF-J respectively, and both completed their sorties as briefed. S/L Brogan was next away at 22.27 in NF-W, to be followed at 22.30 by F/L J Kidd in NF-B, and, at 22.37 by F/L Levy in NF-K. Within site of the drop zone, F/L Kidd's LL364 was seen by the reception committee on the ground to collide with a special duties Liberator belonging to 850 Squadron of the American 801st Bomb Group. Both aircraft plunged to earth near Marigny-l'Eglise in north-central France, taking with them their gallant crews, and there were no survivors. It was unusual for the twins to be on different operations, as the commanding officer generally accommodated their wish to be close to each other in the air. One can only imagine the sense of loss felt by the surviving twin, but he would be back in the air within days. P/O Palmer and crew took off at 22.36 in NF-U, and completed their sortie as briefed, before landing safely at 04.50.

Changes were taking place at Tempsford at this time, which were to see the departure of Halifaxes from 138 Squadron and their replacement by Stirlings. The first examples of the type actually arrived during July, but it would be the end of August before the first operational sorties were flown. Those crews approaching the end of their tour would not be included in the conversion programme, moving instead to 161 Squadron to finish on Halifaxes. This would mean the departure over the ensuing few weeks of F/Ls Kidd and Yardley, F/Os Aitken and Strathy and W/O MacFarlane, who was among the first to go, and would fly with both squadrons during the month. In fact, F/O Aitken would fly Stirlings when 161 Squadron also re-equipped, having already converted with 138 Squadron.

Flying bomb sites continued to provide the main focus for daylight operations, while railways and oil targets dominated the nights. The railway yards at Courtrai and oil plants at Bottrop and Homberg occupied elements of the main force on the night of the 20/21st, while five 138 Squadron Halifaxes delivered stores to targets in France. No doubt still reeling from the loss of his twin, F/L Kidd took off at 22.39 in NF-L on Operation PARAPLUIE, a drop on behalf of the SIS. Electrical storms were encountered, but a DR run was successfully carried out from Chateauneuf to the target, where eight passengers and fifteen containers were delivered from 650 feet. Two fighter flares were dropped as they left the target area, and evasive action was taken, and, later, while at 11,000 feet, both port engines cut, probably through icing of the carburetors, and 3,500 feet were lost before they restarted. The details of the other sorties are as follows; P/O Palmer in NF-J on Operations DONKEYMAN 66/DRAGUEUR, 22.31 to 05.05, successful. S/L Brogan in NF-W on Operation SCIENTIST 115, 22.52 to 03.32, successful. F/O Witham in NF-K on Operation SCIENTIST 115, 22.55 to 05.56, successful. F/L Levy in NF-A on Operation SCIENTIST 115, 23.17 to 03.57, successful.

The squadron mounted five sorties on two operations on the night of the 22/23rd, when the main force stayed on the ground. Operation VENTRILOQUIST 49 occupied the attention of F/L Levy, P/O Palmer and F/O Witham, who took off in NF-E, NF-W and NF-O at 22.26, 22.49 and 23.03 respectively, and returned safely to report successful outcomes. F/L Kidd and S/L Rothwell were on Operation SHIPWRIGHT 1, and departed Tempsford in NF-E and NF-F at 22.13 and 22.33 respectively, before returning shortly after 04.00, also to report completing their sorties as briefed. There had been no major operations against a German city target since Dortmund in May, while the Normandy landings and consolidation of the Allied foothold had been the overriding considerations. Now, on the night of the 23/24th, Harris launched an attack on Kiel by over six hundred aircraft, which appeared with complete surprise from behind a Mandrel RCM screen laid on by 100 Group, and inflicted heavy damage on the town and the port area, where all of the U-Boot yards were hit. 138 Squadron dispatched seven sorties on this night, F/O Wallace, P/O Strathern and F/Sgt Paterson on Operation SHIPWRIGHT 5 in NF-R, NF-A and NF-K, and F/Sgt Moffatt, P/O Aitken, F/O Ford and F/O Carley on Operation HISTORIAN 41 in NF-O, NF-X, NF-U and NF-S respectively. They took off between 22.10 and 22.53, and made their way to their reception sites, where all but F/O Carley were greeted by a reception committee, and delivered their stores as briefed.

The first of three major raids on Stuttgart, over a five night period, began on the night of the 24/25th, and involved a force of over six hundred aircraft. The central districts became heavily damaged on this night, in return for the loss of twenty-one aircraft. 138 Squadron prepared nine Halifaxes for stores drops over France, the details as follows; F/Sgt Prowse in NF-F on Operation HERMIT 18, 22.13 to 04.45, successful. P/O Strathern in NF-A on Operation SHIPWRIGHT 2, 22.17 to 04.40, unsuccessful due to lack of reception. F/Sgt Moffatt in NF-

C on Operation VENTRILOQUIST 40, 22.19 to 05.04, unsuccessful due to lack of reception. F/O Wallace in NF-U on Operation SHIPWRIGHT 1, 22.27 to 04.33, unsuccessful due to lack of reception. F/O Carley in NF-M on Operation SHIPWRIGHT 1, 22.28 to 04.13, unsuccessful due to lack of reception. P/O Aitken in NF-X on Operation VENTRILOQUIST 40, 22.29 to 05.14, successful. F/Sgt Paterson in NF-K on Operation SHIPWRIGHT 2, 22.30 to 04.54, unsuccessful due to lack of reception. P/O Strathy in NF-S on Operation HERMIT 18, 22.36 to 04.53, successful. The ORB then credits P/O Strathy with a second sortie in NF-S on Operation SHIPWRIGHT 5, 22.49 to 06.05, which was completed successfully, but clearly by a different crew in a different Halifax.

550 aircraft set out to return to Stuttgart on the following night, and delivered what would prove to be the most devastating of the three attacks. Losses were lower this time, amounting to twelve aircraft. 138 Squadron stayed at home, but made ready six Halifaxes for operations on the night of the 26/27, when only 5 Group ventured out in numbers. All of the SOE sorties were supply drops, and each was concluded successfully. The details are as follows; P/O Strathy in NF-S on Operation HERMIT 20, 21.59 to 04.26. F/O Aitken in NF-O on Operation HUGH 6, 22.01 to 04.48. F/Sgt Prowse in NF-Q on Operation HISTORIAN 13, 22.05 to 05.40. F/O Carley in NF-R on Operation HERMIT 20, 22.23 to 04.58. F/O Ford in NF-U on Operation HUGH 6, 22.25 to 05.05. F/Sgt Moffatt in NF-X on Operation HUGH 6, 23.32 to 05.56. There was no main force activity on the night of the 27/28th, when six 138 Squadron Halifaxes made their way to deliver supplies to targets in France, details as follows; F/O Wallace in NF-M on Operation PETER 52, 21.46 to 06.39, unsuccessful due to lack of reception. S/L Rothwell in NF-K on Operation PETER 52, carrying an agent as well as stores, 21.50 to 06.45, unsuccessful due to lack of reception. F/Sgt Moffatt in NF-X on Operation FIREMAN 14, 21.56 to 05.23, successful. F/O Ford in NF-U on Operation SHIPWRIGHT 5, 22.05 to 04.58, successful. F/O Aitken in NF-L on Operation FIREMAN 14, 22.22 to 06.14, successful. F/Sgt Prowse in NF-H on Operation SHIPWRIGHT 5, 22.30 to 05.20, successful.

An all Lancaster force from 1, 3, 5 and 8 Groups returned to Stuttgart on the night of the 28/29th, while elements of 1, 6 and 8 Groups targeted Hamburg. The night soon degenerated into a disaster for the Command, as night fighters intercepted the Stuttgart bound bomber stream over France in bright moonlight, and others caught the Hamburg force on the way home, bringing down thirty-nine and twenty-two aircraft respectively. In the early morning of the 30th, almost seven hundred aircraft took off to attack six German positions facing predominantly American ground forces in the Villers Bocage-Caumont area. The Master Bombers curtailed proceedings in the face of cloud cover, and only two targets were considered effectively dealt with. That night, 138 Squadron ended the month with a heavy night of activity, launching thirteen supply drops. F/L Palmer and crew were the only ones to be given two drop sites and carry passengers as well as stores, and took off at 22.19 in NF-J to carry out Operation MARTINI on behalf of the SIS. Eight men were dropped along with nine containers, before a new course was set to the second pinpoint, PERMIT 7, where a lack of a reception forced them to bring the rest of the cargo home. F/O Carley and crew took off at 22.45 in NF-M, as one of three assigned to Operation FRANCIS 12, and suffered the frustration of returning to discover that all fifteen containers had hung up, despite the bomb-release panel showing them to have dropped. The details of the other sorties are as follows; F/L Kidd in NF-L on Operation PERCY 24, 21.46 to 04.31 (Predannack), successful. F/L Levy in NF-D on Operation PERCY 24, 21.55

to 04.00 (Predannack), successful. S/L Brogan in NF-W on Operation DONKEYMAN 74, 22.03 to 05.13 (Predannack), successful. F/Sgt Moffatt in NF-X on Operation Wrestler 6, 22.10 to 02.57 (Tangmere), successful. F/O Wallace in NF-R on Operation WRESTLER 6, 22.25 to 03.30 (Ford), unsuccessful due to lack of reception. F/Sgt Paterson in NF-C on Operation PERCY 24, 22.28 to 05.17, successful. P/O Aitken in NF-A on Operation PERMIT 7, 22.35 to 03.15 (Tangmere), unsuccessful due to lack of reception. F/O Witham in NF-O on Operation FRANCIS 12, 22.36 to 02.50, unsuccessful due to lack of reception. F/Sgt Prowse in NF-H on Operation PERMIT 7, 22.40 to 03.25, unsuccessful due to lack of reception. F/O Ford in NF-U on Operation FRANCIS 12, 22.52 to 03.35, successful. F/O Strathern in NF-E on Operation PERMIT 7, 23.15 to 03.??, unsuccessful due to lack of reception. It had been a busy month for 138 Squadron, involving 173 sorties, and had cost two valuable and popular crews. In a quirky twist, having lost one F/L Kidd, another one, F/L E Kidd, a thirty-two-year-old, would join the squadron on the 20th of August.

A Flight Sergeant, astride the ubiquitous Norton 490cc motorcycle, and Corporal discuss the finer points of some documentation. Their facial expressions suggest that the photoigraph has been posed.

August 1944

The first week of August was dominated by the campaign against flying bomb sites, and over seven hundred and fifty aircraft were involved in largely unsuccessful daylight operations on the 1st. Daylight operations remained the preferred option, leaving the nights for minor operations including those on behalf of SOE. 138 Squadron's recently acquired adjutant, F/L H Jaffé, continued in his attempts to maintain a daily written record of operations, but got off to a dodgy start. Freddie Clark writes of sixteen sorties to open the squadron's August account on the night of the 4/5th, but the ORB logs seventeen, with F/L Yardley's name appearing twice on different operations in different aircraft. In fact, it seems likely that F/L Carley's sortie has been duplicated. Twelve of the night's sorties were to destinations in France, and the remainder in Denmark, and F/L Jaffé records all aircraft landing at Davidstow in Devon, which seems unlikely for those returning from Denmark. The crews bound for Denmark took off first, beginning with that of S/L Rothwell in NF-F at 21.35 on Operation TABLEJAM 13, a stores drop. F/L Yardley and crew followed at 21.50 in NF-D on Operation TABLEJAM 60, carrying agents in addition to stores. F/O Wallace was next away at 21.52 in NF-H on Operation TABLEJAM 63, another stores drop, and W/C Burnett completed the quartet, when taking off in NF-W at 21.58, also carrying stores. All completed their sorties as briefed, and landed either side of 05.00, F/O Wallace at Woodbridge in Suffolk, and the others probably there also. Of the sorties to France, F/L Palmer and crew took off in NF-J at 22.36 to carry out Operations TOM 33, and PLAYBILL 4, an SIS drop over Belgium. Both operations were completed, Freddie Clark providing the detail that a DR run to the drop site for the latter element was made from Avesnes, a few miles inland from the French coast at Berck-sur-Mer, and three agents were delivered. The details of the other sorties, all but one purely stores drops, are as follows; F/Sgt Prowse in NF-U on Operation MASON 28, 22.04 to 05.27, successful. F/Sgt Moffatt in NF-X on Operations ASPHODEL/HITCHER 5, 22.05 to 04.52, successful. F/L Levy in NF-K on Operations LABOUREUR/MESSENGER 28, 22.07 to 05.35, first element only completed, no reception at second one. F/L Kidd in NF-L on Operation SHIPWRIGHT 5, 22.12 to 04.32, successful. F/L Carley in NF-Q on Operations CULTIVATEUR/SEMEUR, 22.14 to 05.41, successful. F/O Strathern in NF-E on Operation MASON 38, 22.19 to 05.23, successful. F/O Witham in NF-O on Operation TOM 58, 22.24 to 04.03, unsuccessful due to lack of reception. F/Sgt Paterson in NF-C on Operation TOM 58, carrying agents and stores, 22.25 to 03.59, unsuccessful due to lack of reception. F/O Aitken in NF-A on Operations CARTON/SHIPWRIGHT 5, 22.30 to 04.37, successful. F/O Strathy in NF-S on Operation SHIPWRIGHT 5, 22.43 to 04.27, successful. F/O Ford in NF-N on Operation MESSENGER 28, 22.59 to 06.11, unsuccessful due to adverse weather.

After a night at home, 138 Squadron prepared fifteen Halifaxes on the 6th for operations that night over France, all but three of which were purely to deliver stores. The details of these sorties, all of which landed at Dunkerswell, are as follows; F/Sgt Prowse in NF-E on Operation WHEELWRIGHT 162, 21.21.42 to 04.23, successful. F/L Kidd in NF-F on Operation PAUL 104, carrying agents and stores, 21.48 to 04.56, successful. F/L Levy in NF-K on Operation WHEELWRIGHT 162, 21.49 to 04.46, successful. F/O Aitken in NF-S on Operation SHIPWRIGHT 25, 21.51 to 03.49, unsuccessful due to lack of reception. S/L Brogan in NF-W on Operations MECANO/SHIPWRIGHT 25, 22.01 to 06.08, first element completed, no reception at the second one. F/O Witham in NF-C on Operation PAUL 104, 22.04 to 05.20, successful. F/L Carley in NF-X on Operation WHEELWRIGHT 162, 22.11 to 04.50, successful. F/L Yardley in NF-D on Operations RAMONEUR/GREFFIER, 22.16 to 05.40, first element unsuccessful due to lack of reception, second element successful. F/Sgt Moffatt in NF-N on Operation PAUL 104, 22.18 to 05.23, successful. F/Sgt Paterson in NF-O on Operation CHARCUTIER, 22.19 to 04.02, successful. F/O Strathern in NF-R on Operations COLUMBINE/TOM 80, carrying agents and stores, 22.24 to 03.52, successful. F/L Palmer in NF-A on Operation STOCKBROKER 19, 22.26 to 05.35, unsuccessful due to lack of reception. F/O Strathy in NF-M on Operation WHEELWRIGHT 162, 22.27 to 05.03, successful. F/O Ford in NF-U on Operation TOM 54, carrying agents and stores, 22.35 to 03.28, successful. F/O Wallace in NF-J on Operation TOM 54, 22.47 to 03.09, successful.

From mid evening on the 7th, aircraft began taking off to attack five aiming points ahead of Allied ground forces in the Normandy battle area near Caen. More than a thousand heavy bombers were involved, but because of the close proximity of Allied troops, the attacks were carefully controlled by experienced Master Bombers, and only two thirds of the aircraft actually bombed. Oil depots and storage dumps provided the objectives in France for 1 and 3 Group Lancasters on the night of the 8/9th, while 138 Squadron sent in ten crews, and a further six to Belgium, all on supply drops. The first of the Belgium-bound contingent to take off was F/Sgt Paterson RNZAF and crew in LL308 NF-Q at 22.00 on Operation OSRIC 45. The Halifax was shot down to crash near Geraudot, east of Troyes in north-eastern France, killing the pilot and four of his crew. Freddie Clark tells us that the rear gunner, F/Sgt Evans RNZAF, baled out, and was given shelter in a farm. On the 12th he attended the funeral of his colleagues, and was informed by French military personnel, that one other member of the crew, F/S Searell RNZAF, had been found in a wounded state by the Luftwaffe, and shot. F/Sgt Evans would be back in England by the end of the month. This was the last Halifax V to be lost in 138 Squadron service. F/O Strathern and crew took off at 22.15 in NF-E on Operation OSRIC 76, and delivered fifteen containers as briefed. On the way home they were fired upon by an enemy aircraft, and damaged, but made it home safely. The details of the other sorties to Belgium are as follows; S/L Rothwell in NF-F on Operation TYBALT 15, 22.06 to 05.50, unsuccessful due to lack of reception. W/C Burnett in NF-W on Operation TYBALT 19, 22.14 to 05.57, unsuccessful due to lack of reception. F/O Wallace in NF-R on Operation OSRIC 23, 22.19 to 05.54, successful. F/L Kidd in NF-L on Operation CIRRONELLE 5, 23.09 to 04.34, successful. The details of the sorties to France are as follows; F/L Palmer in NF-M on Operation STOCKBROKER 19, 22.00 to 05.13, unsuccessful due to lack of reception. F/O Aitken in NF-A on Operation DONALD 22, 22.30 to 04.15, successful. F/L Yardley in NF-D on Operations RAMONEUR/DONALD 89, 22.44 to 05.49, successful. F/O Good in NF-N on Operation PRINCETON, 22.48 to 03.11, unsuccessful due to lack of reception. F/Sgt Prowse in NF-Q on Operation PRINCETON, 23.00 to 04.08, unsuccessful due to lack of reception. F/O Witham in NF-O on Operation DONALD 22, 23.04 to 04.40, successful. F/O Strathy in NF-S on Operation DONALD 22, 23.07 to 05.12, successful. F/O Carley in NF-J on Operation TOM 41, 23.24 to 04.05, successful. F/L Levy in NF-K on Operation TOM 41, 23.30 to 04.36, successful. F/Sgt Moffatt in NF-X on Operation DONALD 22, 23.50 to 05.32, successful.

The night of the 9/10th brought further operations against flying bomb and oil storage targets, while 138 Squadron dispatched thirteen cargo sorties to France, each of which successfully delivered fifteen containers and seven packages. The ORB records only twelve such sorties, detailed as follows; F/O Wallace in NF-R on Operation SHIPWRIGHT 35, 22.25 to 05.45. S/L Brogan in NF-F on Operation MARC 20, 22.56 to 05.26. F/L Palmer in NF-J on Operation MARC 20, 23.00 to 05.08. F/O Strathern in NF-N on Operation SHIPWRIGHT 35, 23.10 to 04.56. F/Sgt Prowse in NF-Q on Operation HARRY 31, 23.38 to 04.05. F/O Witham in NF-O on Operation SHIPWRIGHT 35, 23.42 to 05.32. F/O Carley in NF-W on Operation HARRY 31, 23.47 to 04.27. F/Sgt Moffatt in NF-X on Operation VENTRILOQUIST 46, 23.52 to 04.52. F/L Kidd in NF-L on Operation VENTRILOQUIST 46, 23.59 to 05.18. F/L Levy in NF-K on Operation HARRY 31, 00.01 to 04.40. F/O Strathy in NF-S on Operation HARRY 31, 00.31 to 05.08. F/O Ford in NF-G on Operation HARRY 31, 00.46 to 05.27.

The night of the 10/11th saw 138 Squadron carry out its final Halifax sorties with France as the destination. Fourteen crews took off, but F/L Levy turned back early with engine trouble. The details of the remaining sorties are as follows; F/O Carley in NF-N on Operation HECKLER 4, 21.50 to 05.33, successful. F/L Yardley in NF-D on Operation HECKLER 4, 22.01 to 05.59, successful. F/L Palmer in NF-M on Operation HECKLER 4, 22.08 to 05.08, successful. F/Sgt Moffatt in NF-A on Operation JOHN 63, 22.10 to 05.42, unsuccessful due to lack of reception. F/L Kidd in NF-L on Operation JOCKEY 33, carrying an agent and stores, 22.13 to 05.52, successful. F/O Ford in NF-Q on Operation JOHN 63, 22.21 to 05.50, successful. F/O Wallace in NF-H on Operation JOHN 63, 22.31 to 05.27, successful. F/O Strathern in NF-F on Operation JOHN 63, 22.39 to 05.55, unsuccessful due to lack of reception. S/L Brogan in NF-W on Operation SINGLET 6, 22.56 to 05.15, successful. F/Sgt Prowse in NF-R on Operation SINGLET 6, 23.16 to 05.37, successful. F/O Witham in NF-O on Operations ARABUS/HYPATICA, 23.51 to 05.10, unsuccessful due to lack of reception. F/O Strathy in NF-S on Operations VENTRILOQUIST, ARABUS and HYPATICA, 23.48 to 05.45, successful. F/O Aitken in NF-X on Operation VENTRILOQUIST 54, 00.12 to 04.55, successful. F/O Aitken would now be posted to 161 Squadron and gain promotion to flight lieutenant rank. Sadly, he would not survive the war, after failing to return from operations in March 1945. At this point 138 Squadron was stood down for two and a half weeks, while the conversion programme to Stirlings ran its course. During this period, the crews of F/Sgt Bright, on the 11th, F/L Kidd, on the 20th, P/O Nichols, on the 25th, F/O Cornwallis, on the 26th, F/O McGregor, on the 27th and P/O Corley-Smith, on the 29th, would be posted in to begin training for SOE duties.

The time was now fast approaching, when Harris could turn his attention once more upon industrial Germany. Throughout the summer the Pathfinders had been under extreme pressure, when called upon to provide aircraft for numerous simultaneous operations day after day and night after night. Only 5 Group was capable of complete autonomy, but even so, occasionally called on 8 Group to provide Oboe Mosquitos. On the night of the 12/13th Harris sent 379 Lancasters and Halifaxes to Brunswick without the presence of a single Pathfinder, to assess the ability of main force crews to identify and hit an urban target on their own, using only H2S to guide them to the mark. The experiment was not overwhelmingly encouraging, for, although the centre of the town was hit, so were other towns up to twenty miles distant. The afternoon of the 14th was devoted to large-scale support for the ground forces in the Falaise area. Eight hundred aircraft were involved in the bombing of seven aiming points ahead of the 3rd Canadian Division, each controlled by a Master Bomber and deputy. Most of the bombing was accurate, but some fell amongst Canadian troops in a quarry, killing thirteen and injuring over fifty. In preparation for his new night offensive against Germany, Harris launched a thousand aircraft on the morning of the 15th to attack nine fighter airfields in Holland and Belgium. On the night of the 16/17th, over eight hundred aircraft set out for northern Germany, 348 of their crews briefed to attack the port of Kiel. The remainder, all Lancasters, carried on eastwards to the distant Baltic port of Stettin, where a highly accurate raid ensued, in which over fifteen hundred houses and twenty-nine industrial premises were destroyed, and five ships were sunk in the harbour.

The renewed assault on Germany began again on the night of the 25/26th, when a record number of 1,311 sorties were flown on major and support operations. The main effort was by over four hundred Lancasters of 1, 3, 6 and 8 Groups, whose crews were briefed to attack the Opel motor works at Rüsselsheim, which had escaped a telling blow two weeks earlier. Although the factory was quite severely damaged on this night, production of lorries was barely affected, and fifteen Lancasters were lost. Meanwhile, 5 Group was also active over southern Germany, attempting to carry out the first major raid of the war on Darmstadt. The operation was beset with problems, but the city's reprieve would prove to be only temporary. The final operations of the flying bomb campaign took place on the 28th, as twelve sites in the Pas-de-Calais were attacked by small numbers of aircraft. Within a matter of days the region would be in Allied hands, and the V-1 threat nullified.

138 Squadron returned to action as a Stirling unit later that night with nine supply sorties to France and two to Holland. An advantage of the Stirling was its ability to carry a maximum of twenty-four containers, compared with the fifteen in a Halifax. This first night of operations in the type would not be an overwhelming success, but that was the fault of the receivers rather than the deliverers. The details of the night's work are as follows; F/L Sephton in NF-F on Operation DONKEYMAN 40, 19.50 to 03.31, unsuccessful due to lack of reception. F/L Read in NF-R on Operation LICENSEE 5, 19.52 to 02.59, successful. F/O O'Bern in NF-O on Operation DONKEYMAN 81, 19.54 to 02.25 (Exeter), successful. Sgt Ouellette in NF-H on Operation DONKEYMAN 40, 19.58 to 04.23, unsuccessful due to lack of reception. F/Sgt Banbury in NF-A on Operation LICENSEE 3, 20.01 to 03.52, unsuccessful due to lack of reception. F/O Hardie in NF-P on Operation DONKEYMAN 81, 20.09 to 03.42, unsuccessful due to lack of reception. F/Sgt Sicklemore in NF-Q on Operation LICENSEE 5, 20.11 to 03.38, successful. F/Sgt Bright in NF-C on Operation LICENSEE 5, 20.15 to 03.47, successful. F/O McGregor in NF-M on Operation LICENSEE 5, 21.34 to 04.05, successful. F/L Levy in NF-G on Operation RUMMY 1 over Holland, 21.40 to 02.06, unsuccessful due to lack of reception. F/L Strathern in NF-J on Operation GERRIT 1, 22.27 to 01.41, unsuccessful due to lack of reception.

On the following night, attacks were mounted against the ports of Stettin and Königsberg at the eastern end of Germany's Baltic coast, and much damage was inflicted upon the cities, harbor installation and shipping, and many civilians lost their lives. 138 Squadron prepared six Stirlings for this night, three each for France and Norway, and it was the latter element that got away from Tempsford first. S/L Rothwell and crew led the way in NF-F at 20.36 to carry out Operation CRUPPER 7, the first delivery from a 138 Squadron Stirling of agents. W/C Burnett and crew took off at 20.48 in NF-U to drop stores at the same site, and both returned safely at

04.29 and 05.33 respectively. F/L Strathern and crew took off at 20.53 in NF-J to undertake Operation Fjord 3, the delivery of agents and stores, also over Denmark, and they, too, were successful. The sorties to France were cargo drops under Operation WHEELWRIGHT 163, and all were completed as follows; F/L Witham in NF-A, 21.13 to 04.45. F/Sgt Moffatt in NF-C, 21.22 to 04.09, and F/O Ford in NF-M, 21.42 to 04.28.

The V-1 may now have had its teeth drawn, but the V-2's reign of terror was about to begin, and its mobile launching sites would prove to be elusive targets for the bombing brigade. This being the case, attacks on its storage sites offered the best chance of eliminating the weapon, and nine such locations in northern France were targeted on the afternoon of the 31st. That night, 138 Squadron undertook fifteen sorties, including that by F/L Wallace and crew to clear up Operation GERRIT 1, one of the failures over Holland from three nights earlier. LK131 NF-T was shot down by flak from the night fighter airfield at Gilze-Rijen, a known hotspot, where Lewis Burpee and his crew had met their end during 617 Squadron's Dams raid in May 1943. F/L Wallace RCAF and six of his crew perished in the ensuing crash, while the sole survivor, Sgt Bowker, a gunner, was taken into captivity. S/L Brogan was in the same general area, having taken off at 22.12 in NF-U on Operation KEES 1, a supply drop over Belgium. He successfully carried out his brief, and, while returning over Holland in good visibility at 500 feet, saw ground fire bring down an aircraft in the Eindhoven area. The position given rules out the likelihood, that they were witnessing the end of the Wallace crew.

For those operating over eastern France on this night, a violent storm and low cloud proved to be major problems. Among those affected was F/O Hardie and his mostly Australian crew, who had taken off in NF-P at 22.00 to undertake Operation BOB 325. While searching for the target, F/O Hardie RAAF flew LJ503 into the ground at Lombard, possibly after striking trees, and this time there were no survivors from among the eight men on board. F/L Sephton and crew were in the same area on the same operation, having taken off in NF-F at 20.43, carrying agents and stores. While flying at safety height above hilly terrain, they found themselves in ten-tenths cloud, and wisely decided to abandon the attempt and returned home to land at 03.00. The details of the other sorties, all of which were to destinations in France, are as follows; F/L Levy in NF-G on Operation BOB 263, carrying agents and stores, 20.29 to 03.41, successful. F/L Carley in NF-Q on Operation GLOVER 6, carrying agents and stores, 20.37 to 03.31, successful. F/L Read in NF-R on Operation BOB 157, 20.40 to 02.22, successful. F/L Witham in NF-A on Operation BOB 224, carrying agents and stores, 20.50 to 03.27, successful. Sgt Ouellette in NF-H on Operation BOB 157, 20.57 to 03.30, successful. F/O McGregor in NF-N on Operation BOB 263, 21.03 to 04.26, successful. F/Sgt Shaw in NF-P on Operation GLOVER 6, 21.05 to 04.17, unsuccessful due to lack of reception. F/O O'Bern in NF-O on Operation BOB 263, 21.11 to 03.35, successful. F/Sgt Bright in NF-E on Operation GONDOLIER 13, carrying agents and stores, 21.29 to 03.49, successful. F/Sgt Sicklemore in NF-M on Operation GONDOLIER 13, 21.52 to 03.46, successful. F/L E Kidd in NF-D on Operation GONDOLIER 13, 22.06 to 03.53, successful. The squadron flew 106 sorties during the month, despite losing much time to the conversion process, and, according to Freddie Clark, scattered 927 pigeons!

September 1944

As the Allied ground forces advanced, the need for port facilities became pressing to maintain a steady supply line. Much of September would be devoted to the liberation of the major French ports still in enemy hands, le Havre, Boulogne and Calais, and in preparation, over six hundred aircraft were sent to bomb six airfields in southern Holland on the afternoon of the 3rd. The assault on enemy positions around le Havre began on the 5th, and continued on the 6th, 8th 9th, 10th and 11th, although the attacks of the 8th and 9th were severely curtailed because of unfavourable weather conditions. Within hours of the final bombs falling, the garrison surrendered to British forces. 138 Squadron began its September account on the night of the 1/2nd, with just two supply drops to Holland, carried out by S/L Rothwell and W/C Burnett. The former took off at 21.50 in NF-F on Operations RUMMY 1/BOB, and successfully delivered containers and packages, before returning safely to land at 02.40. The latter was airborne at 22.00 in NF-U on Operation BERTUS 1, and also fulfilled his brief before landing at 01.30.

Two South African Air Force pilots joined the squadron from 31 Base on the 4th, Lts Haine and Nevin, and their arrival raised the number of nationalities to serve with the squadron to ten, British, Canadian, Australian, New Zealand, Polish, Czech, French, Norwegian, American, and now South African. Before war's end, a Belgian gunner would raise the number to eleven. The night of the 4/5th brought just a single 138 Squadron sortie, carried out by F/Sgt Prowse and crew, who took off in NF-B at 22.00, and returned at 04.20 after delivering stores to a drop site in France. Fourteen Stirlings were made ready on the 5th for operations over France that night, all of them supply drops, the details as follows; F/L Ford in NF-M on Operation BOB 288, 20.39 to 03.41, successful. F/Sgt Shaw in NF-D on Operation BOB 234, 20.45 to 03.30, successful. F/L Kidd in NF-L on Operation BOB 231, 20.49 to 03.10, unsuccessful due to lack of reception. F/Sgt Bright in NF-H on Operation BOB 231, 21.08 to 03.33, unsuccessful due to lack of reception. F/Sgt Banbury in NF-E on Operation BOB 234, 21.10 to 03.37, unsuccessful due to lack of reception. F/L Strathern in NF-J on Operations DITCHER 41/PLAN, 21.16 to 04.15, successful. F/L Levy in NF-G on Operation DITCHER 41, 21.25 to 04.56, successful. F/L Read in NF-R on Operation JOHN 34, 21.29 to 03.25, successful. F/Sgt Sicklemore in NF-S on Operation GONDOLIER 13, 21.31 to 03.15, successful. F/L Carley in NF-Q on Operations LACCA/ACOLYTE 9, 21.47 to 04.50, successful. F/O McGregor in NF-N on Operation GONDOLIER 13, 22.05 to 03.57, successful. F/O Nichols in NF-O on Operation GONDOLIER 13, 22.08 to 03.43, successful. F/L Sephton in NF-C on Operation JOHN 34, 22.24 to 04.26, successful. F/O O'Bern in NF-A on Operation JOHN 34, successful.

The night of the 6/7th was devoted to six successful supply drops to destinations in Denmark, involving the squadron's senior officers, details as follows; S/L Rothwell in NF-C on Operation TABLEJAM 60, 22.57 to 04.57. F/L Levy in NF-G on Operation TABLEJAM 80, 23.00 to 05.50. F/L Ford in NF-T on Operation TABLEJAM 22, 23.12 to 05.13. S/L Brogan in NF-Q on Operation TABLEJAM 76. W/C Burnett in NF-S on Operation TABLEJAM 23, 23.19 to 05.14. F/L Strathern in NF-J on Operation TABLEJAM 60, 23.21 to 04.54. It was back to France on the night of the 7/8th, when sixteen Stirlings were prepared for supply drops, all of which appear to have been successful, details as follows. Sgt Ouelette in NF-H on

Operation GONDOLIER 19, 23.16 to 05.16. F/L Kidd in NF-Y on Operation DONKEYMAN 84, 23.37 to 04.46. Lt Haine in MA-U on Operation LICENSEE 3, 23.40 to 05.05. F/Sgt Banbury in NF-J on Operation DONKEYMAN 81, 23.46 to 05.28. F/L Read in NF-R on Operation DONKEYMAN 73, 23.48 to 05.46. F/L Carley in NF-W on Operation MARC 17, 23.52 to 04.55. F/Sgt Sicklemore in NF-S on Operation GONDOLIER 19, 23.55 to 06.07. F/L Sephton in NF-C on Operation GONDOLIER 19, 23.58 to 05.56. F/Sgt Shaw in NF-D on Operation DONKEYMAN 84, 23.59 to 05.25. F/Sgt Prowse in NF-N on Operation MARC 17, 00.06 to 05.00. F/O Nichols in NF-U on Operation LICENSEE 3, 00.08 to 05.31. F/Sgt Bright in NF-G on Operation DONKEYMAN 84, 00.12 to 05.43. F/L Witham in NF-A on Operation MARC 17, 00.28 to 05.19. F/O McGregor in NF-B on Operation DONKEYMAN 73, 00.32 to 06.03. F/O Corley-Smith in NF-X on Operation LICENSEE 3, 00.45 to 05.59. F/O O'Bern in NF-M on Operation DONKEYMAN 73, 01.42 to 07.02.

On a sad note, the popular F/L Levy RNZAF was posted to 161 on the 8th, only to lose his life on the 19th of October, when just one sortie away from completing his tour. His aircraft would break up in the air near Tempsford during an air-test, and all five occupants would be killed. Of nine sorties mounted on the night of the 8/9th, eight were destined for France on supply drops, and one to Holland, the latter, Operations DRAUGHTS/BACKGAMMON, undertaken by S/L Rothwell and crew in NF-J. They took off at 00.15, and flew towards the Dutch coast underneath a heavy storm, illuminating the waves with their landing lights. The conditions quietened as they approached Vlieland, and they were able to pinpoint on the island. They successfully delivered two agents, T Biallosterski and P de Vos, onto the drop site at Spanbroek on the Den Helder peninsular, and set course for home via Vlieland. With the island in view and flying at 400 feet, the Stirling hit what S/L Rothwell believed was a balloon cable. The starboard-inner engine caught fire and shed its propeller, and the remaining engines seemed to lose power, making it impossible to maintain height. S/L Rothwell was forced to crash-land LK200 on the dunes at Cocksdorp on the northern tip of Texel, catapulting him through the roof. He and three of his crew survived to be taken prisoner, but three members of the crew lost their lives in the incident. The details of the sorties to France are as follows; Sgt Ouellette in NF-H on Operations ECOBIER?/CONSTABLE, 23.03 to 06.30, unsuccessful due to lack of reception. F/Sgt Bright in NF-C on Operation BOB 256, 23.12 to 05.53, successful. F/L Read in NF-R on Operation BOB 256, 23.28 to 05.34, successful. F/L Kidd in NF-G on Operation DONKEYMAN 85, 23.35 to 04.50, successful. Lt Haine in NF-B on Operation DICK 93, 23.40 to 05.40, successful. Lt Nevin in NF-M on Operation DICK 93, 23.53 to 05.27, successful. F/O Nichols in NF-S on Operation DONKEYMAN 85, 00.08 to 06.08, successful. F/O Corley-Smith in NF-Q on Operation DONKEYMAN 85, 00.21 to 06.22, successful.

The 10th brought a rare, and, no doubt, exciting opportunities for the squadron to indulge in daylight operations. First came a lone sortie by F/L Witham, who took off at 09.19 in NF-A to carry out Operation TITIAN, a stores drop over France on behalf of the SIS. He carried out a DR run from the French coast at le Crotoy, and delivered fifteen containers from 400 feet onto a triangle of tricolours. That afternoon, while almost a thousand aircraft were engaged in the penultimate day's attacks on enemy strong points around le Havre, 138 Squadron carried out Operation OSRIC 500. This involved sixteen aircraft in cargo drops over Belgium at dusk, delivering more than two hundred containers onto reception sites marked by bonfires lit by the Belgium White Army. All returned safely from these sorties, the details of which are as follows; W/C Burnett in NF-S, 15.03 to 20.02. S/L Brogan in NF-U, 15.04 to 19.08. F/L Sephton in NF-C, 15.22 to 19.15. Sgt Ouellette in NF-H, 15.24 to 19.17. F/Sgt Bright in NF-G, 15.26 to 19.35. F/Sgt Shaw in NF-D, 15.27 to 19.30. F/O McGregor in NF-B, 15.29 to 19.23. F/L Ford in NF-N, 15.30 to 19.27. F/L Read in NF-R, 15.32 to 19.20. F/L Carley in NF-Q, 15.33 to 19.30. Lt Nevin in NF-M, 15.35 to 19.33. F/O O'Bern in NF-O, 15.36 to 19.25. F/L Strathern in NF-W, 15.46 to 19.45. F/Sgt Sicklemore in NF-T, 15.47 to 19.43. F/L Kidd in NF-A 15.49 to 19.47. Lt Haine in NF-X, 17.12 to 21.06.

The operation was repeated on the following afternoon by fifteen crews, all of whom successfully delivered their stores without opposition, details as follows; F/O McGegor in NF-D,15.06 to 19.10. F/L Ford in NF-M, 15.08 to 19.18. F/L Kidd in NF-R, 15.14 to 19.18. Lt Nevin in NF-N, 15.16 to 19.27. F/O O'Bern in NF-O, 15.22 to 19.21. F/Sgt Shaw in NF-D, 15.24 to 19.25. F/O Corley-Smith in NF-S, 15.27 to 19.33. F/Sgt Bright in NF-G, 15.30 to 19.41. F/L Witham in NF-A, 15.31 to 19.30. F/O Cornwallis in NF-U, 15.32 to 19.36. F/Sgt Ouellette in NF-H, 15.33 to 19.48. F/L Carley in NF-Q, 15.37 to 19.32. F/O Nichols in NF-X, 15.40 to 20.03. Lt Haine in NF-W, 15.41 to 19.45. F/Sgt Banbury in NF-C, 15.41 to 19.43. As the dust settled over le Havre on that evening of the 11th, a 5 Group force of 224 Lancasters and fourteen Mosquitos returned to Darmstadt in southern Germany, and created a firestorm, which claimed the lives of over twelve thousand people, and over half of the 120,000 population was rendered homeless. It was a horrific and devastating blow, which would be repeated at small to medium sized cities across Germany with increasing frequency, as worthwhile urban targets became harder to find. On the night of the 12/13th a two-pronged attack was mounted against southern Germany. 378 Lancasters of 1, 3 and 8 Groups returned to Frankfurt for the first time since the devastating raids in March, while a predominantly 5 Group force of two hundred Lancasters targeted Stuttgart. The former resulted in severe damage to the city's western districts, at a time when a large part of its fire brigade was absent, helping to quell the fires at nearby Darmstadt. For Frankfurt, this would prove to be the last raid of the war by RAF heavy bombers. It was a similar story of destruction at Stuttgart, where the north and west-central districts were ravaged by a firestorm, and over eleven hundred people were killed.

A few days rest followed, during which lull, F/L Watson DFM arrived on posting from 1651 Conversion Unit on the 13th. He was one of a number of new recruits to join the squadron in September, after P/O Moffat RNZAF had arrived on the 1st, and F/L Wilkie RCAF on the 11th. The cargo drops to Belgium continued on the 16th, this time under Operation OSRIC 700, and again, all ten were concluded successfully, details as follows; S/L Brogan in NF-S, 14.17 to 18.20. F/L Ford in NF-H, 14.20 to 18.40. F/L Sephton in NF-F, 14.26 to 18.54. F/O McGregor in NF-B, 14.28 to 18.38. F/O Nichols in NF-R, 14.33 to 18.53. F/O Corley-Smith in NF-N, 14.39 to 18.46. F/Sgt Bright in NF-G, 14.44 to 19.04. F/Sgt Shaw in NF-D, 14.50 to 19.12. F/Sgt Banbury in NF-C, 14.59 to 18.08. F/O O'Bern in NF-O, 15.01 to 19.12.

The ill-fated Operation Market Garden began on the morning of the 17th, in the wake of attacks on enemy airfields and gun positions by elements of 1, 3 and 8 Groups during the night. By breakfast time, the first of over seven hundred aircraft had taken off for Boulogne, to deliver a total of three thousand tons of bombs onto enemy positions around the port. Shortly afterwards Allied ground forces began their advance, and captured it within a week. 138 Squadron waited until the afternoon before sending seven Stirlings to continue the supply drops to Belgium under Operation OSRIC 650, details of these successful sorties are as follows; F/O McGregor in NF-N, 13.43 to 17.50. F/O Nichols in NF-R, 13.46 to 17.46. F/O Corley-Smith in NF-S, 13.50 to 17.55. F/L Sephton in NF-F, 13.55 to 17.53. F/Sgt Bright in NF-K, 14.00 to 18.03. F/Sgt Shaw in NF-H, 14.02 to 18.10. F/Sgt Banbury in NF-C, 14.06 to 18.08. Bremerhaven wilted under its first heavy raid of the war on the night of the 18/19th, when a 5 Group force of two hundred Lancasters destroyed over 2,600 buildings, razing to the ground the central and port areas.

The squadron put up just four Stirlings for operations over Belgium in the early afternoon of the 19th, referred to in the ORB as "Special". Those involved were; S/L Brogan in NF-R, 12.46 to 15.12. W/C Burnett in NF-S, 12.47 to 15.25. F/L Watson in NF-G, 12.50 to 14.55. F/L Carley in NF-C, 12.51 to 15.17. On the following night, the 19/20th, elements of 1 and 5 Groups were briefed for an operation against the twin towns of Mönchengladbach and Rheydt, just a few miles from the frontier with Holland. The role of Master Bomber was inexplicably handed to W/C Guy Gibson VC, who was currently serving as base operations officer at 54 Base, Coningsby. Gibson was not qualified as a Master Bomber, had little up-to-date operational experience, and had only a fleeting acquaintance with the Mosquito. In the event, the operation was generally successful, but on the way home, Gibson's Mosquito crashed on the outskirts of Steenbergen in Holland, and he and his navigator were killed.

The first operations in the campaign to liberate Calais took place on the 20th and involved over six hundred aircraft. German positions were accurately bombed in clear visibility, but further attacks would be required before the port was surrendered. 138 Squadron's daylight supply drops to Belgium continued on the 21st, with eight sorties under Operation OSRIC 900. It appears that all but one landed on the Continent, and remained there overnight, for which no explanation is given. The details as provided by the ORB are as follows; F/L Watson in NF-F, 13.42 to 15.38 on the 22nd. F/L Strathern in NF-A, 13.53 to 17.30. F/Sgt Shaw in NF-G, 13.55 to 17.30 on the 22nd. F/L Read in NF-R, 13.59 to 17.34 on the 22nd. F/Sgt Ouellette in NF-C, 14.12 to 15.15 on the 22nd. F/O McGregor in NF-B, 14.16 to 14.56 on the 22nd. Lt Nevin in NF-N, 14.18 to 15.02 on the 22nd. F/Sgt Sicklemore in NF-S, 14.23 to 17.59 on the 22nd. The next assault on enemy strong points around Calais came on the 24th, but it was hampered by low cloud, and it was a similar story on the 25th, when only a third of more than eight hundred aircraft were able to bomb through breaks in the overcast. Conditions improved on the 26th, and over seven hundred aircraft concentrated their bombing on three aiming points near Calais and four gun emplacements at Cap Gris Nez. That night, with France all but liberated, 138 Squadron carried out what appeared to be its final sorties to the country, that had dominated its activities for so long. In fact, there would be further sorties to France in October and beyond. Nine Stirlings and, we are told, one Halifax, took off on Operation APPRENTICE to deliver supplies to the west-central region of le Blanc, and all were successful, the details as follows; Lt Haine in NF-E. 18.55 to 00.52. Lt Nevin in Halifax "N", 19.03 to 00.43. F/Sgt Bright in NF-G, 19.14 to 01.23. F/Sgt Shaw in NF-D, 19.22 to 00.59. F/O Woodward in NF-V, 19.37 to 01.56. F/O Temperley in NF-Y, 19.44 to 02.15. F/Sgt Banbury in NF-A, 19.48 to 01.48. F/O Corley-Smith in NF-S, 19.50 to 01.25. F/O Nichols in NF-R, 19.59 to 01.44.

From now onwards, Denmark, Norway and Holland were to be the destinations for future SOE operations. The 27th brought yet another tilt at German positions around Calais, and attacks on oil refineries at Bottrop and Sterkrade by 6 and 8 Groups. That night, 5 Group carried out the only heavy raid of the war on Kaiserslautern, and destroyed an estimated 36% of its built-up area. The final operation to free Calais took place on the 28th, and the port was captured by Canadian ground forces shortly afterwards. 138 Squadron celebrated the rising of the moon that night by sending ten Stirlings to Denmark and four to Norway. They were a mixture of SOE and SIS operations, and while only cargo was delivered to Norway, one of the sorties to Denmark involved agents. F/L Read and crew took off at 19.36 in NF-N to undertake Operations TABLEJAM 14/26 over Denmark. They reached the drop sites, and delivered a dozen containers on each from 400 feet, before turning for home. Heading out over north Jutland at 500 feet, they were attacked by a JU88 from below. F/L Read climbed for the cloud base, but they were found and attacked again at 3,500 feet ten minutes later, and lost the starboard outer engine, along with the throttle control for the starboard-inner. The flight engineer, F/O Curtis, was slightly wounded in the engagement, but remained at his post to assist his pilot in bringing LJ932 home. A crash-landing was carried out at the 1 Group station of Ludford Magna in Lincolnshire at 02.35, and the crew emerged without further injury. Both Read and Curtis were rewarded for their efforts with a DFC, and a newly promoted Squadron Leader Read would shortly take up his appointment as a flight commander with 161 Squadron.

The details of the other sorties to Denmark on this night, consisting of eighteen drop sites, are as follows; F/L Ford in NF-M on Operation TABLEJAM 95, carrying stores, 19.28 to 02.13, unsuccessful due to lack of reception. F/Sgt Ouellette in NF-H on Operations TABLEJAM 90/91, carrying stores, 19.35 to 02.22, successful. F/L O'Bern in NF-O on Operations TABLEJAM 86/82, carrying stores, 19.36 to 01.59, successful. P/O Moffatt in NF-C on Operations TABLEJAM 92/93, carrying stores, 19.40 to 02.25, successful. F/Sgt Sicklemore in NF-Q on Operations TABLEJAM 81/23, carrying stores, 19.47 to 02.08, successful. F/L Sephton in NF-F on Operations TABLEJAM 87/88, carrying stores, 19.51 to 02.10, successful. F/L Kidd in NF-D on Operations TABLEJAM 83/60, carrying stores, 19.51 to 02.19, unsuccessful due to lack of reception. F/L Witham in NF-R on Operations TABLEJAM 78/47, carrying stores, 20.03 to 02.16, first element only completed, no reception at second one. F/L Strathern in NF-K on Operations POPLAR/TABLEJAM 89, carrying agents and stores, 20.37 to 03.40, successful. A total of 191 containers were delivered to the fourteen sites with a reception committee. The details of the Norwegian supply drops are as follows; S/L Brogan in NF-U on Operation ODIN 3, 19.13 to 03.47, unsuccessful due to lack of reception. F/Sgt Bright in NF-G on Operation BIT 7, 19.30 to 03.06, unsuccessful, target not located. F/O McGregor in NF-B on Operation HALTER 2, 19.31 to 03.57, successful. W/C Burnett in NF-S on SIS Operations MAKIR 2/SIFA 3/NYOND 4, 19.59 to 04.57, successful.

The final operations of the month were carried out on the night of the 31st, eight to destinations in Norway and four to Denmark, and all were successfully completed. Ten were purely supply drops, but two were carrying agents also. The details are as follows; F/L Ford in NF-M on Operation SADDLE 8 over Norway, carrying four agents and stores, 18.53 to 02.32. F/L Watson in NF-U on Operation SADDLE 6 over Norway, carrying stores, 19.00 to 02.20. F/L Carley in NF-Q on Operation CRUPPER 8 over Norway, carrying stores, 19.04 to 03.45. F/Sgt Ouellette in NF-H on Operation SADDLE 8 over Norway, carrying stores, 19.13 to 02.53.

F/Sgt Shaw in NF-G on Operation SADDLE 4 over Norway, carrying stores, 19.16 to 02.16. F/Sgt Sicklemore in NF-S on Operation CRUPPER 9 over Norway, carrying stores, 19.30 to 04.35. F/L O'Bern in NF-O on Operation CRUPPER 9 over Norway, carrying stores, 19.09 to 03.49. F/L Sephton in NF-F on Operation CRUPPER 8 over Norway, carrying stores, 19.24 to 04.10. F/L Kidd in NF-E on Operation TABLEJAM 101 over Denmark, carrying stores, 19.36 to 02.59. F/L Witham in NF-K on Operations TABLEJAM 99/100 over Denmark, carrying five agents and stores, 19.38 to 02.06. F/O McGregor in NF-B on Operations TABLEJAM 97/98 over Denmark, carrying stores, 19.43 to 02.25. F/O Moffatt in NF-C on Operations TABLEJAM 85/19 over Denmark, carrying stores, 20.03 to 02.57.

JD319, NF-A, undertaking an engine test at her dispersal. The wheel covers and crew ladder indicate a lack of intention to actually go anywhere at this time.

October 1944

October was to be characterized by an unprecedented concentration of bombing on German cities in a second Ruhr campaign beginning at the end of the first week. Ports were still a pressing priority, however, as the need for supplies increased, in order to keep the Allied advance mobile, and Bomber Command was to play its part in weakening enemy resistance. It was to be a frustrating month for 138 Squadron, during which, bad weather would restrict it to a modest thirty sorties, twenty-one to Denmark, seven to Norway and two to France. The night of the 4/5th brought a dozen sorties, the details of which are as follows; F/L Watson in NF-R on Operation LEATHER 5 over Norway, carrying ten containers and eight packages, 18.50 to 04.35 (Kinloss), successful. S/L Brogan in NF-U on Operation FETLOCK 2 over Norway, carrying twelve containers and nine packages, 19.02 to 03.57 (Kinloss), unsuccessful due to lack of reception. F/Sgt Ouellette in NF-H on Operation GIRTH 1 over Norway, carrying twelve containers and six packages, 19.04 to 22.00, returned early due to illness of navigator. F/L Witham in NF-E on Operation MANE 2 over Norway, carrying twelve containers and twelve packages, 20.20 to 03.35, successful. W/C Burnett in NF-S on Operation STIRRUP 3 over Norway, carrying five agents, twelve containers and four packages, 20.30 to 04.31, successful. F/L Carley in NF-Q on Operation STIRRUP 3 over Norway, carrying four agents, twelve containers and five packages, 20.35 to 04.37, successful. F/L Kidd in NF-G on Operations TABLEJAM 95/102 over Denmark, carrying twenty-four containers and one package, 20.44 to 04.00, second element only completed, no reception at the first one. F/O Moffatt in NF-C on Operation MANE 2 over Norway, carrying twelve containers and six packages, 20.50 to 04.24, successful. F/L Sephton in NF-F on Operations TABLEJAM 21/71 over Denmark, carrying four agents, twelve containers and a package, 21.10 to 03.13, successful. F/L O'Bern in NF-B on Operations TABLEJAM 91/103 over Denmark, carrying twenty-four containers, 21.12 to 04.31, first element only completed, no reception at the second one. F/Sgt Banbury in NF-A on Operation TABLEJAM 83 over Denmark, carrying twelve containers, 21.13 to 04.08, successful. F/Sgt Sicklemore in NF-D on Operations TABLEJAM 76/79, carrying twenty-four containers and one package, 21.29 to 04.40, first element only completed, no reception at the second one.

On the night of the 5/6th, Saarbrücken was raided for the first time in numbers for two years, and almost six thousand houses were destroyed for the loss of just three Lancasters. This high return-low loss outcome would be repeated throughout the month and on to the end of the war, with only isolated occasions on which the defences gained the upper hand. The new Ruhr offensive opened at Dortmund on the night of the 6/7th, when over five hundred aircraft from 3, 6 and 8 Groups pounded the city, causing extensive damage to housing, industry and communications for the loss of five aircraft. 5 Group, meanwhile, was over north-western Germany, carrying out the final raid of the war on Bremen. This devastating attack left almost five thousand buildings either destroyed or seriously damaged. 138 Squadron dispatched just four sorties on this night, all supply drops to Denmark, and all successfully completed, apart from one container hanging-up. The details are as follows; F/Sgt Banbury in NF-E on Operation TABLEJAM 93, carrying twelve containers, 21.42 to 03.27. F/O McGregor in NF-S on Operations TABLEJAM 68/69, carrying twenty-two containers, 21.44 to 04.25. F/L Kidd in NF-D on Operations TABLEJAM 35/99, carrying twenty-three containers, 21.55 to 03.58.

F/O Corley-Smith in NF-Q on Operation TABLEJAM 99, carrying twelve containers, 21.58 to 03.54.

Following the failure of Operation Market Garden, the Allied right flank had become exposed to a possible danger from enemy forces approaching through the frontier towns of Cleves and Emmerich. On the afternoon of the 7th, both towns were left extensively damaged by forces of over three hundred aircraft. On the afternoon of the 10th, the squadron sent two crews to France to deliver stores under Operation MARC 25. F/O Cornwallis and crew took off at 13.42 in NF-B, and Lt Haine and crew in NF-G at 13.54, each carrying twenty-four containers and sixteen packages, and returned safely at 18.47 and 18.45 respectively to confirm successful sorties. A series of massive raids under Operation Hurricane was intended to act as a demonstration to the enemy of the overwhelming superiority of the Allied air forces ranged against it. At first light on the 14th, over one thousand aircraft took off for Duisburg, arriving overhead shortly after breakfast time, to deliver around 4,400 tons of high explosives and incendiaries. To be over the Ruhr in daylight was still a dangerous practice, and the flak defences claimed fourteen aircraft before being overwhelmed. That night, similar numbers returned to press home the point about superiority, and thus 2,018 aircraft had been dispatched against the city in less than twenty-four hours, and around nine thousand tons of bombs had been dropped for the loss of twenty-one aircraft. It was a remarkable fact, that these statistics had been achieved without support from 5 Group, which took advantage of the distraction to finally devastate Brunswick, which had escaped relatively lightly during four previous attacks in 1944. 138 Squadron was also abroad on this night, but over Denmark, for which five crews set off in mid-evening, each with twenty-four containers to deliver, details as follows; F/L Sephton in NF-F on Operation TABLEJAM 109, 20.26 to 03.25, successful. F/Sgt Ouellette in NF-D on Operation TABLEJAM 89, 20.28 to 03.21, successful. F/O McGregor in NF-U on Operation TABLEJAM 115, 20.30 to 01.39, unsuccessful, returned early due to illness of navigator. F/L Witham in NF-G on Operation TABLEJAM 116, 20.33 to 03.54, unsuccessful due to lack of reception. F/L Ford in NF-M on Operation TABLEJAM 110, 20.41 to 03.32, successful.

There were just two sorties on the night of the 15/16th, both supply drops of twenty-four containers to destinations in Denmark. F/L Witham and crew took off in NF-U at 20.17 on Operation TABLEJAM 115, and they were followed at 20.31 by F/O Moffatt and crew in NF-C on Operation TABLEJAM 116. The former was thwarted by the weather, while the latter failed to make contact with a reception committee, probably as a result of the weather conditions, and both returned with their cargo to land at Woodbridge in Suffolk at 01.57 and 03.17 respectively. F/L Read was posted to 161 Squadron on the 18th, a day of great significance for 3 Group. Just as 5 Group had, earlier in the year, it gained a degree of independence from the main force through the G-H blind bombing system, which had been under development for some time. The system could be used against area or precision targets, and was effective by both day and night. On this day, the almost virgin city of Bonn was selected as the target, so that the effectiveness of the operation could be assessed without damage from previous raids clouding the issue. 128 aircraft took off at around 08.30, and this modestly proportioned force was able to destroy seven hundred buildings, and seriously damage a further one thousand.

Switching temporarily from the Ruhr, Harris focused his attention on southern Germany on the night of the 19/20th, and sent over five hundred aircraft from 1, 3, 6 and 8 Groups to attack Stuttgart in two phases four and a half hours apart. Over a hundred miles away, meanwhile, 250 Lancasters of 5 Group were raiding Nuremberg using the Mosquito low level marking method. 138 Squadron closed its October account with five aircraft setting off for Denmark on the night of the 22/23rd. Annoyingly, for those crews involved, it turned into a frustrating waste of effort, as each crew returned to land at Kinloss with its load of twenty-four containers intact, after failing to make contact with reception committees, details as follows; P/O Bright in NF-G on Operation TABLEJAM 122, 19.31 to 03.06. F/Sgt Sicklemore in NF-O on Operation TABLEJAM 117, 19.32 to 02.44. F/L Kidd in NF-F on Operation TABLEJAM 116, 19.35 to 02.31. F/L Carley in NF-Q on Operation TABLEJAM 118, 19.36 to 02.08. F/Sgt Shaw in NF-D on Operation TABLEJAM 115, 19.41 to 02.50.

The largest Bomber Command force of the war to date, 1,055 aircraft, took off between 16.00 and 17.00 on the 23rd to deliver Operation Hurricane's message to Essen, and returned on the afternoon of the 25th with over seven hundred aircraft. The Krupp complex was among the industrial concerns badly damaged, and parts of it would remain out of action for the remainder of the war. Most of the city's surviving industry was dispersed to other parts of Germany from this point, but this would not be known in Britain, and Essen would have to endure further punishment before the end came. Cologne's turn to face the Hurricane force came first in the late afternoon of the 28th at the hands of over seven hundred aircraft. More than 2,200 apartment blocks were destroyed in districts north-east and south-west of the city centre, and much damage was inflicted upon power, railway and dockland installations. On the 30th, nine hundred aircraft returned to drop four thousand tons of mostly high explosive bombs. Massive destruction resulted, and this was followed up twenty-four hours later by almost five hundred aircraft from 1, 3, 4 and 8 Groups.

November 1944

A new squadron adjutant took over the writing-up of the squadron's activities at the start of November, and his strong legible hand was soon recording a night of heavy activity on the 1st. Eager to make up for a frustratingly unproductive October, SOE's directors planned a maximum effort of eighteen sorties for 138 Squadron, fourteen with targets in Denmark and four in Norway. The details of the night's work, which ended with most landing at Waterbeach, are as follows; F/O Cornwallis in NF-E on Operation BIT 17 over Norway, carrying eighteen containers and sixteen packages, 21.13 to 05.44, unsuccessful due to lack of reception. W/C Burnett in NF-K on Operation SADDLE 10 over Norway, carrying five agents, twelve containers and six packages, 21.36 to 05.45, successful. Lt Nevin in NF-N on Operation BIT 17 over Norway, carrying twenty-four containers and a package, 21.39 to 05.50, successful. P/O Sleven in NF-R on Operation SADDLE 10 over Norway, carrying twelve containers and sixteen packages, 21.58 to 06.03, successful. W/O Ouellette in NF-H on Operations TABLEJAM 36/139 over Denmark, carrying twenty-four containers and a package, 22.01 to 04.16, successful. F/O Moffatt in NF-C on Operations TABLEJAM 93/135 over Denmark, carrying twenty-four containers, 22.03 to 04.52, successful. F/L Strathern in NF-L on Operations TABLEJAM 111/144, over Denmark, carrying twenty-four containers and a package, 22.05 to 05.49, first element only completed, no reception at the second one. F/L Carley in NF-Q on Operation TABLEJAM 137 over Denmark, carrying twenty-four containers, 22.09 to 05.05, successful. F/Sgt Sicklemore in NF-S on Operations TABLEJAM 114/127 over Denmark, carrying twenty-four containers and a package, 22.10 to 04.26, first element only completed, no reception at the second one. F/L Ford in NF-M on Operation TABLEJAM 68 over Denmark, carrying twenty-four containers, 22.23 to 05.48, successful. P/O Shaw in NF-D on Operations TABLEJAM 41/47 over Denmark, carrying twenty-four containers and a package, 22.26 to 05.02, successful. F/L Sephton in NF-F on Operations TABLEJAM 113/126 over Denmark, carrying twenty-four containers and a package, 22.32 to 04.47, successful. P/O Banbury in NF-P on Operations TABLEJAM 26/112 over Denmark, carrying twenty-four containers and a package, 22.33 to 05.15. S/L Watson in NF-A on Operations TABLEJAM 133/132 over Denmark, carrying twenty-four containers and a package, 22.35 to 05.05, second element only completed (3 Hang-ups), no reception at first one. S/L Brogan in NF-U on Operations TABLEJAM 143/108 over Denmark, carrying 22.37 to 06.15, second element only completed, first failed due to adverse weather. F/O Nichols in NF-B on Operations TABLEJAM 78/98 over Denmark, carrying twenty-four containers and a package, 22.38 to 05.51, successful. Lt Haine in NF-T on Operations TABLEJAM 131/148 over Denmark, carrying twenty-four containers and a package, 22.40 to 04.44, successful. P/O Bright in NF-G on Operations TABLEJAM 129/134 over Denmark, carrying twenty-four containers and a package, 22.41 to 04.21, successful.

Freddie Clark writes of six 138 Squadron sorties to Denmark on the night of the 2/3rd, which were hampered by severe weather conditions. These are not recorded in the ORB, however, which leads to the conclusion that they all failed. The Hurricane force moved on to Düsseldorf on this night with almost a thousand aircraft, and they pounded the northern half of the city, leaving over five thousand houses destroyed or seriously damaged. As events were to prove, this was the final heavy raid of the war on Düsseldorf. Bochum was the target for over seven hundred aircraft from 1, 4, 6 and 8 Groups on the 4/5th, and here, too, damage was immense, amounting to more than four thousand buildings destroyed or severely afflicted, with almost a thousand people killed. Gelsenkirchen became the next Ruhr town to face a heavy Bomber Command assault, its ordeal coming by daylight on the 6th. The Nordstern synthetic oil refinery was the aiming point, and over five hundred aircraft bombed in its general area, while almost two hundred others attacked the town.

W/C Burnett concluded his tour as 138 Squadron's commanding officer on the 7th, and was posted to HQ Bomber Command as a staff officer. He was succeeded by W/C Murray, who would see the squadron through to the end of hostilities. The only operations on the night of the 7/8th were those over Norway mounted from Tempsford with an equine theme, for which 138 Squadron put up nine aircraft. S/L Watson and crew took off at 19.53 in NF-E to carry out Operation BRIDLE 7, carrying an agent, Yves Ogaard, seven containers and three packages. The drop site was twenty-eight miles east of Steinkjer, close to the Swedish frontier, and his DR run began from a lake actually on the Swedish side. The operation was entirely successful, and concluded with a safe landing at Kinloss after a round-trip of almost eleven hours. F/L Sephton and crew took off at 22.36 in NF-F to undertake Operation STIRRUP 4, carrying two agents, nineteen containers and nine packages. They pinpointed on Suldal Lake in the south-west, and made three runs across the drop site, to deliver Erling Vestre and Tor Vinje along with the stores. They returned safely to Tempsford to land at 05.49. The details of the other sorties on this night are as follow; F/L Witham in NF-A on Operation WITHERS 3, carrying twelve containers and three packages, 21.45 to 06.10 (Kinloss), successful. W/O Ouellette in NF-H on Operation BLINKERS 1, carrying sixteen containers and three packages (one container hung-up), 21.55 to 06.06, successful. F/O Moffatt in NF-C on Operation STIRRUP 2, carrying twelve containers and twelve packages, 22.44 to 06.12, successful. F/O Strathy in NF-R on Operation RUMP 3, carrying nineteen containers and two packages, 22.46 to 06.45, successful. F/O Cornwallis in NF-P on Operation HOCK 2, carrying twenty-four containers, 23.05 to 06.24, successful. F/O McGregor in NF-B on Operation HOCK 1, carrying twenty-four containers, 23.26 to 05.49, unsuccessful due to lack of reception. The eight successful sorties resulted in the delivery of three agents, 133 containers and twenty-nine packages.

The heavy brigade remained on the ground again on the night of the 8/9th, leaving the skies over enemy occupied territory to 8 Group Mosquitos and a large contingent from Tempsford. 138 Squadron prepared seventeen aircraft for destinations in Norway, on what would prove to be a bad night all round. The weather conditions were atrocious, with low cloud, icing conditions at low level and thunderstorms, and there would be no completed drops to report. The serviceability record of 138 Squadron aircraft had always been outstanding, with remarkably few early returns, but, according to Freddie Clark, starboard-inner engine problems forced two Stirlings to turn back. F/Os Strathy and Cornwallis took off at 23.24 and 23.25 in NF-S and P on Operations PELHAM 2 and CRUPPER 26 respectively, carrying containers and packages, but, are recorded in the ORB as being defeated by the weather while outbound, and returning at 02.17 and 01.18 respectively. S/L Brogan and crew departed Tempsford at 23.13 in NF-U on Operation CRUPPER 23, carrying five agents, twelve containers and six packages. The aircraft sustained a lightning strike while outbound over the sea, the flash temporarily blinding S/L Brogan and causing a sudden loss of control. Only the presence of mind of the flight engineer, F/O Wigley, prevented the Stirling from diving into the sea, and the sortie was abandoned. The cargo was jettisoned over base, before a safe landing was made at 02.16. F/O Wigley would receive a well-earned DFC for his efforts. F/L Ford and crew took off at 23.30 in NF-M on Operation CRUPPER 11, carrying agents Peter Deinboll and Arne Gjestland, along with stores. They went missing while outbound, and no trace of the aircraft, LJ993, and its occupants has ever been found. We are not told what time W/O Ouellette RCAF and crew took off in LK198 NF-H on Operation PUFFIN 2, a supply drop, but they, too, disappeared without trace, and in view of the experiences of the other crews, it seems probable that they were claimed by the weather conditions. The details of the other sorties on this night, all of which were supply drops, are as follows; F/L O'Bern on NF-O on Operation CRUPPER 25, 23.12 to 07.34, unsuccessful due to adverse weather. Lt Nevin in NF-N on Operation FLANK 3, 23.16 to 05.34, unsuccessful due to adverse weather. F/L Kidd in NF-L on Operation CRUPPER 24, 23.22 to 07.56, unsuccessful due to adverse weather. F/L Strathern in NF-K on Operations BETA 5/ODIN 3, 23.30 to 08.18, unsuccessful due to adverse weather. F/L Carley in NF-Q on Operation CRUPPER 23, 23.36 to 08.00, unsuccessful due to adverse weather. F/Sgt Banbury in NF-G on Operation Halter 3, 23.39 to 08.14, unsuccessful due to adverse weather. F/L Sephton in NF-F on Operation CRUPPER 25, 23.41 to 02.59, unsuccessful, returned early due to adverse weather. F/O Corley-Smith in NF-T on Operation PELHAM 2, 23.46 to 08.01, unsuccessful due to adverse weather. Lt Haine in NF-J on Operation CRUPPER 22, 23.52 to 07.41, unsuccessful due to adverse weather. F/O Nichols in NF-R on Operation CROP 6, 23.57 to 08.40, unsuccessful due to adverse weather. F/O McGregor in NF-B on Operation BIT 2, 00.12 to 03.34, unsuccessful, returned early due to adverse weather. P/O Sleven in NF-A on Operation BIT 2, 00.25 to 08.10, unsuccessful due to lack of reception.

There was a solitary sortie on the night of the 9/10th, undertaken by F/L Wilkie and crew to France under Operation MARC 26. He and his crew took off in NF-D at 01.57, and delivered fifteen containers and sixteen packages, before returning to land at 07.46. A number of comparatively small-scale operations took place over the ensuing week, aimed at the enemy's oil industry. This was followed on the 16th by a massive assault on the three small Rhineland towns of Heinsberg, Jülich and Düren, which lay in an arc from north to east respectively of Aachen. The attacks were to help an American advance towards enemy lines between Aachen and the Rhine, by cutting communications to the front. 1,188 Bomber Command aircraft were committed to the destruction of the towns, which took place in mid afternoon in good bombing conditions. As the bombers retreated westwards, little remained standing on the ground, and thousands of people were killed. On the evening of the 21st over thirteen hundred aircraft were committed to attacks on five main targets and numerous support and minor operations. While railway and oil installations occupied the other Groups, the "Independent Air Force" went canal-busting, targeting the Mittelland at Gravenhorst and the Dortmund-Ems at Ladbergen. 138 Squadron sent five aircraft to Denmark on this night, and had to divert them to Woodbridge on their return after fog closed Tempsford. F/O Cornwallis failed to receive the divert signal, and eventually landed at Peterhead in Scotland, with engines running on fumes. The details are as follows; F/L Sephton in NF-F on Operations TABLEJAM 154/166, carrying twenty-four containers and a package, 20.12 to 04.22, first element only completed, no reception at the second one. F/L Witham in NF-A on Operations TABLEJAM 141/152, carrying twenty-four containers and a package, 20.17 to 02.45, unsuccessful due to adverse weather. F/L Kidd in NF-L on Operations TABLEJAM 106/148, carrying twenty-four containers and a package, 20.42 to 03.11, successful. F/O McGregor in NF-B on Operation TABLEJAM 78, carrying twenty-four containers and a package, 21.17 to 04.48, successful. F/O Cornwallis in NF-P on Operations TABLEJAM 26/151, carrying twenty-four containers and a package, 22.40 to 06.02, successful.

Approaching midnight on the 26th, 270 Lancasters of 5 Group took off for Munich, to be joined in the target area by eight Mosquitos. This was the only major operation of the night, and was of little help as a diversion to eighteen aircraft from 138 Squadron heading in the opposite direction towards Scandinavia. Fourteen were bound for Denmark and the remainder for Norway, where conditions would turn out to be generally favourable, certainly in terms of visibility. This would not be the case at Tempsford, which became fogbound, forcing most crews to land at Lossiemouth. F/L Carley and crew took off in NF-Q at 18.07 on Operation CRUPPER 30, carrying five agents, twelve containers and six packages. They carried out a DR run from Enderud, some sixty miles north-west of Oslo, and easily picked up the bright reception light on a frozen lake. It took the crew fifteen minutes to prize open the ice-bound doors above the bomb bay, but having done so, they made a first pass at 700 feet to drop agents Paul Strande, Alex Hagen, Peder Holst, Erling Malm and H Munthe-Kass. During the second run at 500 feet to deliver the containers, the men were seen to be safely on the ground, and the third run completed the operation. F/O McGregor and crew took off in NF-B at 18.32 on the same operation, and also had to attack the frozen doors with a hammer to free them, before dropping eleven of the twelve containers. One container hung up, and the thirteen packages could not be delivered, and had to be brought back to a landing at Lossiemouth at 03.20.

F/L Witham DFC and crew took off at 20.00 in LK151 NF-E on Operation TABLEJAM 69 over Denmark, and headed for the drop site at Krengerup on the island of Fyn. It seems that they successfully delivered eighteen containers, and were on their way home, when attacked and shot down by a JU88 of 1/NJG.3. The Stirling crashed into the Little Belt stretch of sea just off the coast at Assens, killing F/L Witham RAAF and all others on board. F/O Sleven and crew were in the same area on Operations TABLEJAM 172/173, having departed Tempsford in NF-O at 19.35 with twenty-four containers and a package on board. On the way home, they were hit by ground fire from a mobile light flak battery, which caused damage to a fuel tank, and bomb door control cables. The bomb doors flopped open, and remained that way until the landing at Lossiemouth at 02.06. P/O Shaw and crew took off at 19.42 in NF-D on Operations TABLEJAM 26/157, carrying an agent and stores. Frozen doors again caused problems, preventing the agent from leaving the aircraft, although the stores were delivered to their respective drop sites. The agent was brought back to a landing at Kinloss, where a suspicious military policeman questioned the presence of a civilian without identification. He newly-commissioned P/O Sicklemore and his crew were assigned to Operations TABLEJAM 87/150, and took off in NF-S at 19.44, carrying twenty-four containers. Hit by machine gun fire, they were forced to abandon the sortie and return to Lossiemouth at 02.02.

The details of the other sorties on this night are as follows; F/L Strathern in NF-K on Operation AKEVITT over Norway, carrying seven containers, 18.48 to 04.20, successful. F/O Strathy in NF-U on Operation TABLEJAM 160 over Denmark, carrying twenty-one containers and a package, 19.00 to 02.20, successful. F/L Sephton in NF-F on Operation GROIN 3 over Norway, carrying fifteen containers and seven packages, 19.08 to 03.16, unsuccessful due to lack of reception. F/O Corley-Smith in NF-T on Operations TABLEJAM 127/156 over

Denmark, carrying twenty-four containers and a package, successful. F/L Wilkie in NF-Z on Operations TABLEJAM 146/147 over Denmark, carrying twenty-four containers and a package, 19.25 to 02.34, successful. S/L Watson in NF-R on Operation TABLEJAM 85 over Denmark, carrying twenty-two containers and a package, 19.32 to 02.23 (Tangmere), successful. P/O Cornwallis in NF-P on Operation TABLEJAM 162 over Denmark, carrying twelve containers and a package, 19.40 to 01.56, successful. F/L Kidd in NF-L on Operations TABLEJAM 36/112 over Denmark, carrying twenty-four containers and a package, 19.50 to 01.57. F/O Moffatt in NF-A on Operations TABLEJAM 133/163 over Denmark, carrying twenty-four containers and a package, 19.54 to 02.17, first element only completed, no reception at the second one. P/O Bright in NF-G on Operations TABLEJAM 128/161 over Denmark, carrying twenty-four containers and a package, 19.56 to 02.26, successful. Lt Haine in NF-J on Operations TABLEJAM 158/171 over Denmark, carrying twenty-four containers and a package, 20.02 to 02.27, second element only completed, no reception at the first one. Lt Nevin in NF-N on Operations TABLEJAM 138/153 over Denmark, carrying twenty-four containers and a package, 20.07 to 03.00, successful.

The weather conditions afflicting Norway on the night of the 29/30th were apparently the worst in living memory, and only two of fourteen crews reached their respective targets. S/L Watson and crew took off in NF-K at 18.37 to carry out Operation Beaver 2, an SIS drop of six containers. They returned at 04.50, having beaten the conditions to become the only successful crew of the night. The details of the other sorties are as follows; P/O Banbury in NF-A on Operation CRUPPER 24, carrying fifteen containers and six packages, 18.23 to 03.09, unsuccessful due to adverse weather. F/O Cornwallis in NF-P on Operation CRUPPER 10, carrying twelve containers and nine packages, 18.25 to 03.05, unsuccessful due to adverse weather. F/L Sephton in NF-F on Operation CRUPPER 23, carrying twelve containers and ten packages, 18.27 to 03.37, unsuccessful due to lack of reception. F/L Wilkie in NF-J on Operation PELHAM 2, carrying twelve containers and twelve packages, 18.31 to 01.44 (Kinloss), unsuccessful due to technical problems and adverse weather. F/L Strathern in NF-NF-L on Operation CRUPPER 11, carrying fourteen containers and eight packages, 18.32 to 01.18, unsuccessful due to adverse weather. F/L Kidd in NF-G on Operation CRUPPER 10, carrying twelve containers and six packages, 18.40 to 03.30, unsuccessful due to adverse weather. F/O Aitken in NF-V on Operation CRUPPER 13, carrying twelve containers and seven packages, 18.50 to 03.50, unsuccessful due to adverse weather. F/O Nichols in NF-N on Operation CRUPPER 23, carrying twelve containers and nine packages, 18.54 to 01.33, unsuccessful due to adverse weather. S/L Brogan in NF-U on Operation REINS 7, carrying three agents, twelve containers and twelve packages, 18.57 to 02.40, unsuccessful due to adverse weather. F/L Carley in NF-T on Operations SNAFFLE 3/BIT 8, carrying an agent, fifteen containers and nine packages, 19.04 to 02.30, unsuccessful due to adverse weather. F/O Moffatt in NF-D on Operation PELHAM 2, carrying twelve containers and twelve packages, 19.24 to 03.44, unsuccessful due to adverse weather. F/O Sicklemore in NF-S on Operation REINS 7, carrying twelve containers and twelve packages, 19.28 to 03.16, unsuccessful due to adverse weather. F/O McGregor in NF-R on Operation COLT 4, carrying ten containers and four packages, 19.34 to 04.16, unsuccessful due to adverse weather.

The month ended with seven sorties to Denmark on the night of the 31st, and, in contrast to two nights earlier, most were concluded successfully. The details are as follows; F/O Strathy in

NF-N on Operations TABLEJAM 163/165, carrying twenty-four containers and a package, 19.45 to 03.28, second element only completed, first one failed due to adverse weather. F/O Corley-Smith in NF-T on Operations TABLEJAM 136/168, carrying twenty-four containers and a package, 19.49 to 02.55, successful. P/O Bright in NF-G on Operations TABLEJAM 87/131, carrying twenty-four containers and a package, 20.04 to 02.27, first element only completed, no reception at second one. F/L O'Bern in NF-R on Operations TABLEJAM 21/26, carrying an agent, eighteen containers and nine packages, 20.11 to 03.31, successful. Lt Haine in NF-A on Operations TABLEJAM 148/167, carrying twenty-four containers and a package, 20.15 to 02.12, unsuccessful due to lack of reception. F/O Sleven in NF-U on Operations TABLEJAM 149/170, carrying twenty-four containers and a package, 20.15 to 02.34, successful. P/O Shaw in NF-L on Operation TABLEJAM 141, carrying twelve containers and two packages, 20.33 to 03.06 (Carnaby), unsuccessful due to flak damage. November had been a huge disappointment, despite the gallant efforts of all involved, and it had seen the demise of three more crews.

December 1944

December also began inauspiciously for 138 Squadron, when only four of seven sorties to Denmark were completed on the night of the 2/3rd. Sadly, this night's activities do not appear in my copy of the ORB. Freddie Clark writes, that the weather forced F/O Strathy to return early, and that F/L Strathern's Stirling was again struck by lightning. LK143 NF-B failed to reach the drop site for Operations TABLEJAM 169/177, and disappeared without trace with the crew of F/O Nichols. On this same night, but many miles away in Holland, a former 138/161 Squadron stalwart, W/C "Sticky" Murphy, died in the wreckage of his 23 Squadron Mosquito. He was on bomber support duties, hunting the enemy night fighters preying on almost five hundred aircraft from 1, 4, 6 and 8 Groups, as they pounded Hagen in the Ruhr. On the evening of the 4th, 5 Group sent a massive 282 Lancasters and ten Mosquitos to carry out the first and only raid of the war on Heilbronn in southern Germany. It was one of a number of seemingly insignificant, non-industrial towns to find themselves in the bomb-sights during the final six months of hostilities. Freiburg, in Germany's south-western corner, only a week earlier had been devastated by 1 and 8 Groups in a raid that had resulted in the deaths of around three thousand people. It was much worse at Heilbronn, though, where seven thousand died, and an estimated 82% of the town's built-up area was reduced to rubble in a few minutes of concentrated bombing.

It is at this point, that, for the first time, the ORB includes a full crew list for each sortie, but the entries remain handwritten, even though the rest of Bomber Command had been employing typewriters for two years or more. On the night of the 5/6th, S/L Watson and crew took off in NF-J at 00.38 on a solitary SIS sortie to Vaningen in Holland, and delivered nine containers, before returning to land at 03.41. No further SOE operations were carried out until shortly before Christmas, during which period, on the 16th, the Germans began the break-out through the Ardennes, which took the Americans completely by surprise, and became known as the Battle of the Bulge. Tempsford contributed fourteen sorties between the 23rd and 25th, nine of them by 138 Squadron, as the Allies fought back, and the Germans began to run out of steam. 138 Squadron dispatched four sorties on the evening of the 23rd, each carrying seven containers to repeat the D-Day function of dropping dummy parachutists behind enemy lines. The 138 Squadron effort was directed at locations in Germany, while 161 Squadron focused on Belgium. The details are as follows; F/L Sephton in NF-F on Operation TURMOIL (Area 1), 18.01 to 22.41, successful. F/O Strathy in NF-U on (Area 1 special), 18.07 to 22.43 (Tangmere), successful. F/O Bright in NF-G on (Area III special), 18.21 to 22.38 (Tangmere), successful. F/O Cornwallis in NF-J on (Area III special), 18.56 to 00.13, successful. On the following afternoon, Christmas Eve, five 138 Squadron Stirlings were dispatched on Operation TURMOIL 2, each carrying four containers, the details as follows; F/O Sicklemore in NF-S, 15.24 to 21.01, successful. F/L O'Bern in NF-O, 15.27 to 20.45, successful, S/L Watson in NF-K, 15.31 to 20.54, successful. F/O Moffatt in NF-C, 15.34 to 21.07, successful. F/O Corley-Smith in NF-T, 15.37 to 20.28, successful. Fog at Tempsford caused a diversion of all returning aircraft to Lyneham in Wiltshire.

The final wartime Christmas Day was celebrated peacefully on most stations, but the Boxing day festivities were curtailed for some crews from each Group, when the Command called for attacks on enemy troop positions around St Vith. The diverted aircraft and crews returned to

Tempsford on the 27th, in time to prepare for operations on the night of the 28/29th over Norway. The details of these sorties, which took place in near perfect conditions of clear skies and moonlight, are as follows; F/O Cornwallis in NF-P on Operation CRUPPER 28, carrying five agents, fourteen containers and seven packages, 18.03 to 02.22, successful. Lt Nevin in NF-J on Operation CURB 1, carrying fifteen containers and six packages, 18.08 to 03.22, successful. F/L Carley in NF-Q on Operation CURB 1, carrying two agents, fourteen containers and six packages, 18.10 to 03.15, successful. F/L Kidd in NF-L on Operation REINS 7, carrying three agents, H Stridskelv, Gunnar Bjali and Tore Fjeld, who were dropped from 750 feet, to be followed by sixteen containers and nine packages from 450 feet, 18.18 to 01.50, successful. Hit by tracer, but returned safely. F/O McGregor in NF-N on Operation CRUPPER 32, carrying three agents, thirteen containers and seven packages, 18.28 to 03.06, successful. F/O Banbury in NF-D on Operation REINS 7, carrying eighteen containers and eight packages, 18.50 to 02.59, successful. F/L Wilkie in NF-E on Operation CRUPPER 32, carrying thirteen containers and six packages, 19.11 to 03.29, successful. F/O Shaw in NF-A on Operations SABRE/VET 1, carrying two agents, sixteen containers and eight packages, 19.15 to 02.40, successful. Each crew also carried leaflets, and, because of fog at Tempsford, landed at the 100 Group station of North Creake in Norfolk.

They were back at Tempsford for midday on the 30th, to learn that fourteen crews were earmarked for Norway again that night. The details of these sorties are as follows; F/L Wilkie in NF-E on Operation CRUPPER 30, carrying fifteen containers and six packages, 21.05 to 06.12, two containers hung up, otherwise successful. F/L Carley in NF-Q on Operation HOCK 2, carrying four agents, twelve containers and fourteen packages, 21.11 to 02.58. F/L Carley considered the conditions to be unsafe for his four passengers, and brought them and the stores back home. F/L McGregor RNZAF and crew took off in NF-J at 21.14 on Operation CRUPPER 10, carrying sixteen containers and three packages. F/L Shaw and crew saw LK283 being engaged by a flak ship, and watched it explode with a terrific flash, and crash into the sea. There were, of course, no survivors. F/O Cornwallis in NF-P on Operation CRUPPER 23, carrying thirteen containers and eleven packages, 21.17 to 06.20, successful. Lt Nevin in NF-N on Operation FLANK 2, carrying fifteen containers and four packages, 21.20 to 06.39, successful. F/L Kidd in NF-L on Operation CRUPPER 13, carrying sixteen containers and two packages, 21.20 to 06.30. The packages could not be delivered because of a frozen hatch, otherwise successful. F/L Shaw in NF-D on Operation HALTER 3, carrying sixteen containers and two packages, 21.23 to 05.36, successful. S/L Brogan in NF-U on Operation PUFFIN 2, carrying five agents, eleven containers and eight packages, 21.29 to 06.30, successful. F/O Strathy in NF-K on Operation CRUPPER 10, carrying fifteen containers, one of which hung up, 21.31 to 06.39, successful. F/O Bright in NF-G on Operation CRUPPER 13, carrying seventeen containers, 21.32 to 06.52, unsuccessful due to lack of reception. F/O Corley-Smith in NF-T on Operation FLANK 2, carrying fifteen containers and four packages, 21.36 to 06.36, unsuccessful, after failing to identify the drop site. F/O Sicklemore in NF-S on Operation PUFFIN 2, carrying thirteen containers and twenty-one packages, 21.44 to 06.23, successful. S/L Watson in NF-C on Operation STIRRUP 4, carrying eighteen containers and five packages, 21.51 to 05.23, successful. F/O Sleven in NF-R on Operation CRUPPER 23, carrying twelve containers and nine packages, 22.05 to 06.55, successful. Aircraft failing to beat the Tempsford fog were diverted to the 6 Group station at East Moor.

New Year's Eve was celebrated by both Tempsford units over Norway and Denmark, 138 Squadron dispatching thirteen Stirlings, including NF-Q, which took off at 21.45 with the crew of F/L Carley, who were returning to the HOCK 2 drop site from the previous night. This time they spent twenty-six minutes over the target to allow their four agents, T.H. O Lien, Ivar Tonseth, J P Bjelland and Alfred Floisand to parachute into the snow, along with the twelve containers and fourteen packages. They returned safely at 04.55 on New Year's Day 1945. The details of the remaining sorties are as follows; Lt Haine in NF-E on Operation CROP 11 over Norway, carrying two agents, six containers and thirteen packages, 20.51 to 06.12, successful. F/L Sephton in NF-F on Operation TABLEJAM 182 over Denmark, carrying nineteen containers and two packages, 21.53 to 05.24, successful. F/L O'Bern in NF-O on Operation TABLEJAM 183 over Denmark, carrying twenty-four containers and a package, 22.03 to 04.50, successful. F/O Strathy in NF-T on Operation TABLEJAM 190, carrying twenty-four containers and a package, 22.05 to 05.15, unsuccessful due to lack of reception. F/O Sleven in NF-R on Operations TABLJAM 99/176 over Denmark, carrying eighteen containers and a package, 22.09 to 04.30, successful. F/O Banbury in NF-A on Operations TABLEJAM 181/188 over Denmark, carrying twenty-three containers and four packages, 22.10 to 05.05, successful. Lt Nevin in NF-N on Operations TABLEJAM 78/97 over Denmark, carrying twenty-four containers and a package, 22.18 to 04.42, successful. F/L Strathern in NF-K on Operation HOCK 1 over Norway, carrying fifteen containers and four packages, 22.25 to 04.07 (Peterhead), unsuccessful after sustaining damage in an engagement with a JU88, which left the rear gunner wounded. S/L Brogan in NF-U on Operation TABLEJAM 53 over Denmark, carrying twenty-four containers and a package, 22.30 to 05.15, unsuccessful due to lack of reception. F/O Cornwallis in NF-P on Operations TABLEJAM 139/192 over Denmark, carrying twenty-four containers and a package, 22.33 to 05.09, unsuccessful due to lack of reception. F/O Bright in NF-C on Operations TABLEJAM 106/189 over Denmark, carrying twenty-three containers and two packages, 22.41 to 04.53, successful. F/O Sicklemore in NF-S on Operations TABLEJAM 178/179, carrying twenty-four containers and a package, 00.14 to 06.24, successful. As the German Ardennes offensive faltered, it was clear, that the coming year would bring victory, but much remained to be done before the tenacious and courageous enemy forces finally laid down their arms.

January 1945

Over on the continent, 1945 started with a bang, as the Luftwaffe launched its ill-conceived and ultimately ill-fated Operation Bodenplatte (Baseplate). The intention, to destroy Allied aircraft on the ground at the recently liberated airfields in France, Holland and Belgium was only modestly achieved, but at an unacceptably high price of around 250 aircraft lost, with approximately 150 of the pilots being killed, wounded or taken prisoner. The major priorities for the Command in these final months of the bombing war were the continued dislocation of Germany's railway network, and the assault on her oil production. Both had been ongoing for some time, but the offensives would now gain momentum. Any city with a functioning railway or an oil-related production site was to be area bombed, and, on the night of the 2/3rd, 1, 3, 6 and 8 Groups were sent to Nuremberg. For perhaps the first time at this target, an accurate and concentrated attack was delivered, in which over 4,600 houses, most of them apartment blocks, were destroyed, along with two thousand medieval houses and four hundred industrial buildings, and more than eighteen hundred people were killed. At the same time, further to the west, a predominantly Halifax force was pounding Ludwigshafen on the west bank of the Rhine, where two of the synthetic oil producing I G Farben chemicals works were severely damaged, as were a number of railway installations.

There was a very late start for 1 and 5 Group crews on the night of the 4/5th. The latter climbed into their aircraft at midnight for a take-off time of around 01.00, to be followed an hour later by the former for what would be a controversial operation against the French town of Royan in the Gironde Estuary, where a German garrison was holding out against a siege by Free French forces making for Bordeaux. The last large-scale area raid of the war on Hanover was delivered by six hundred aircraft from 1, 4, 6 and 8 Groups on the night of the 5/6th, and the same Groups pounded Hanau and its railway yards on the 6/7th, as elements of 1 and 3 Groups did likewise at Neuss. On the following evening a 5 Group contingent joined forces with 1, 3, 6 and 8 Groups to bomb Munich for the last time.

W/C Murray participated in his first operation with 138 Squadron in the early hours of the 11th, when flying as second pilot to S/L Watson in a food drop to an isolated drop site at Naushorn, in a mountainous region of Norway. They took off from Kinloss at 05.52 in NF-E on Operation FETLOCK, carrying eight containers and five packages, and, in view of the flight taking place mostly in daylight, an extra gunner and ammunition. They arrived at the Norwegian coast at 08.12, at the same time as daylight, and sensibly assessed the risk as too great, and decided to turn back. The operation was re-flown on the following day employing two aircraft, piloted by S/L Watson and F/L Carley. The details of the former's sortie were identical, except for the earlier take-off time of 04.16. They reached the target area at 07.20, and found an excellent reception laid out in a valley. Because of the nature of the terrain, the drop was carried out in a single pass from 4,600 feet, after which, they hit the deck for the race home in broad daylight, where they arrived safely at 15.30. F/L Carley and crew took off in NF-R at 03.33, but found no reception waiting for them on arrival at the target at 07.02. They circled for a short time, but then turned for home, landing first at Linton-on-Ouse at 12.25, before setting off for Tempsford later in the afternoon. This proved to be the final sortie with 138 Squadron for S/L Watson, who was shortly to be posted to command 161 Squadron. Sadly, his tenure would be brief.

There was sporadic activity for elements of the Command around this time until the 13th, when two operations were mounted against the railway yards at Saarbrücken, firstly by 3 Group, and later by 4, 6 and 8 Groups. As the latter force was over France outbound, over two hundred 5 Group Lancasters took off for Pölitz to attack the oil refinery. On the following night, the 14/15th, 5 Group joined 1, 6 and 8 Groups for a two-phase raid on the oil refinery at Leuna near Merseburg, while smaller forces attacked a railway yard and a fuel storage depot in the west. 138 Squadron managed to launch two sorties to France on this night to blood new crews. W/O Tomlin and crew too off in NF-T at 18.10, to carry out Operation DOWNRIGHT 1 over France, carrying twenty-four containers and seven packages. The drop was carried out in very unfavourable weather conditions, which caused six containers to hang up in the wing bays, and prevented the delivery of the packages through a frozen hatch door. F/Sgt Biggs and crew took off five minutes later in NF-S on the same operation, carrying twenty-four containers and six packages, but failed to complete because of the weather and a cloud base at 550 feet. Continuing heavy snowfalls would keep the squadron on the ground for a week.

The 16/17th brought a main force area raid on Magdeburg, and heavy attacks on oil production sites at three locations. As airfield conditions improved, 138 Squadron continued its programme of introducing new crews to operations on the night of the 21/22nd, when sending three freshers to France on Operation DOWNRIGHT 1, each carrying eighteen containers and eight packages. F/Sgt Dunmal had Lt Haine beside him as he lifted NF-C into the air at 18.35, and the drop proceeded according to plan. F/Sgt Biggs and crew were in NF-Q, and took off at 18.42, while F/Sgt Sinkinson and crew departed Tempsford in NF-E at 18.52, with S/L Sephton in the right-hand seat, he having been promoted to step into the flight commander's shoes of the posted W/C Watson. Both sorties were also successful, and all three Stirlings were back home before 22.30. The only significant raids by the main force, as activity declined towards the end of the month, were against Duisburg on the night of the 22/23rd, and the Stuttgart area on the night of the 28/29th.

February 1945

January had been a loss free month for 138 Squadron, largely because so few sorties had been flown, but February would take its toll. The weather over the Continent was not helpful for bombing operations during the first week, as large areas of Germany were concealed by cloud, but 138 Squadron would produce relatively good results for a winter month. The conditions adversely affected the accuracy of a 5 Group raid on Siegen on the night of the 1/2nd, when much of the bombing fell into open country, and Mainz also escaped serious damage at the hands of 4 and 6 Group Halifaxes. At the same time, however, Ludwigshafen suffered the destruction of nine hundred houses, and its railway yards were heavily damaged. 138 Squadron sent seven aircraft to Norway on this night, but the foul conditions of low cloud, rain, turbulence and icing at 600 feet, would make life difficult for all involved. F/Sgt Tucker and crew were on their maiden operation, and took off in NF-L at 21.41 on Operation RUMP 1. The undercarriage refused to retract, and the flight engineer began the laborious task of raising it by hand with the winding handle. The effort made him ill, and, as it would take fifty minutes to get the wheels down again, it was decided to abandon the sortie. The details of the other sorties are as follows; F/O Sleven in NF-T on Operation RUMP 1, carrying fifteen containers and seven packages, 21.21 to 01.56, unsuccessful due to adverse weather. F/L Cornwallis in NF-P on Operation VET 3, carrying twenty-two containers and seven packages, 21.23 to 05.03 (Kinloss), successful. F/O Sicklemore in NF-S on Operation VET 7, carrying twenty-three containers and four packages, 21.26 to 04.49 (Oulton), unsuccessful due to lack of reception. F/O Banbury in NF-A on Operation RUMP 6, carrying sixteen containers and four packages, 21.30 to 05.08, successful. Capt Nevin in NF-N on Operation VET 7, carrying twenty-three containers and 21.37 to 05.26 (Kinloss), successful. Lt Haine in NF-F on Operation VET 3, carrying twenty-three containers and four packages, 21.58 to 02.46, unsuccessful due to adverse weather.

On the following night, 5 Group almost entirely missed Karlsruhe, while 4 and 6 Group Halifaxes failed to nail the oil refinery at Wanne-Eickel, but 1, 3, 6 and 8 Group Lancasters pounded Wiesbaden. In preparation for an advance into Germany by the British XXX Corps in the Reichswald region, the Command was ordered to bomb the frontier towns of Goch and Cleves. These formed part of the enemy defences, but both were left heavily damaged by the raids on the night of the 7/8th. On the following night, 5 Group returned to Politz to open a two-phase attack on the oil refinery. 1 Group followed up two hours later with Pathfinder support, and no further production was possible at the plant for the remainder of the war. 138 Squadron's efforts continued with seven sorties to Denmark on the night of the 9/10th. The weather rendered them all failures, and caused the squadron's first loss of the year. LK279 NF-L took off sometime after 21.00 with the seemingly ill-fated crew of F/Sgt Tucker RAAF on board. They were heading for the drop site for Operation TABLEJAM 190, but were caught in a blizzard, and all perished, when the Stirling crashed into the waters of the Little Belt, south of the Faeno Islands. The details of the other sorties are as follows; F/O Sleven in NF-N on Operation TABLEJAM 191, carrying twenty-four containers and a package, 21.05 to 03.25. F/L Cornwallis in NF-P on Operation TABLEJAM 218, carrying twenty-four containers and a package, 21.06 to 03.32. F/O Banbury in NF-A on Operation TABLEJAM 160, carrying twenty containers and three packages, 21.07 to 04.04. F/L Wilkie in NF-U on Operation TABLEJAM 127, carrying twenty-four containers and a package, 21.13 to 03.14. F/O

Sicklemore in NF-T on Operation TABLEJAM 183, carrying twenty-four containers and a package, 21.19 to 03.36. S/L Sephton in NF-F on Operation TABLEJAM 212, carrying twenty-four containers and a package, 21.21 to 03.58.

The night of the 13/14th brought the first of the Churchill inspired heavy raids on Germany's eastern cities under Operation Thunderclap. The target was the beautiful and historic city of Dresden, which had not been attacked by the Command before, but had been visited on a number of occasions by the Americans. The now familiar two-phase assault was opened by 5 Group, employing its low-level marking method. A layer of cloud stretched across the target area, and this interfered to an extent with the precision of the raid, in which 244 Lancasters delivered more than eight hundred tons of bombs. Fires gained a hold, however, and they acted as a beacon to the 529 Lancasters of 1, 3, 6 and 8 Groups following three hours behind. By the time of their arrival, the skies had cleared, and a further eighteen hundred tons of bombs rained down onto the hapless city. The result was a firestorm of gigantic proportions, certainly equalling that at Hamburg eighteen months earlier, and there was no escape for the population, which had been massively swelled by an influx of refugees from the eastern front. Estimates of the death toll have diminished over the years, and it now stands at somewhere around twenty-five thousand. The following night was devoted largely to Chemnitz, but heavy cloud helped to spare the city from a similar fate, and much of the bombing found open country. 5 Group did not take part, but was also over eastern Germany at the time, attacking the oil refinery at Rositz near Leipzig. The next night of heavy activity came on the 20/21st, when five hundred aircraft were sent against Dortmund, while others attacked oil targets and a canal.

On the following night, the 21/22nd, it was the turn of Duisburg and Worms to wilt under assaults by more than three hundred aircraft each. 138 Squadron dispatched seven sorties to Norway on this night, and a further nine to Denmark, when all of the squadron principals were in action. W/C Murray and crew were in NF-U on Operation SNAFFLE 5, and took off for Norway at 18.54. In addition to a ten man crew, which included a second pilot under training, two navigators and two air bombers, the Stirling was carrying four agents, Roger Backstom, Severre Arntzen, Aarge Larsen and Kjell Stordalen, along with eleven containers and nine packages, which were delivered to the drop site during three runs, before a safe return was made to land at 04.05. The details of the other sorties are as follows; S/L Brogan in NF-X on Operations GULTAX 4/CORONA 6 over Norway, carrying fourteen containers, 18.28 to 03.41, first element only completed, the six containers meant for the second reception fell out at the first one due to a technical fault. Lt Haine in NF-C on Operation SNAFFLE 5 over Norway, carrying thirteen containers and eleven packages, 18.51 to 03.16, successful. F/O Strathy in NF-R on Operation GIRTH 15 over Norway, carrying twelve containers and nine packages, 18.52 to 05.20, successful. F/O Sleven in NF-S on Operations TABLEJAM 213/231 over Denmark, carrying an agent, sixteen containers and a package, 18.59 to 01.50, second element only completed, agent retained due to uncertain reception. S/L Sephton in NF-F on Operation TABLEJAM 229 over Denmark, carrying seventeen containers and a package, 18.59 to 02.25, successful. F/L Wilkie in NF-Q on Operation TABLEJAM 203 over Denmark, carrying seventeen containers and a package, 19.04 to 03.03, successful. F/L Moffatt in NF-B on Operation GIRTH 15 over Norway, carrying twelve containers and seven packages, 19.06 to 05.33, unsuccessful due to adverse weather. F/O Banbury in NF-A on Operation TABLEJAM 201 over Denmark, carrying seventeen containers and a package, 19.08 to 02.07, successful. F/L Cornwallis in NF-P on Operation TABLEJAM 160 over Denmark, carrying seventeen containers and a package, 19.10 to 02.05, successful. F/L O'Bern in NF-O on Operation GIRTH 3 over Norway, carrying thirteen containers and seven packages, 19.15 to 04.45, successful. Capt Nevin in NF-N on Operation TABLEJAM 214 over Denmark, carrying seventeen containers and a package, 19.19 to 02.17, successful. F/O Corley-Smith in NF-T on Operation TABLEJAM 230 over Denmark, carrying seventeen containers and a package, 19.27 to 03.09, unsuccessful due to lack of reception. F/O Shaw in NF-D on Operation TABLEJAM 226 over Denmark, carrying seventeen containers and a package, 19.29 to 02.25, unsuccessful due to lack of reception. F/L Kidd in NF-E on Operation GIRTH 3 over Norway, carrying thirteen containers and five packages, 19.33 to 05.26, successful. F/O Bright in NF-G on Operation TABLEJAM 215 over Denmark, carrying seventeen containers and a package, 20.17 to 03.07, successful. Sadly, W/C Watson was killed in Germany on this very night, when flying as second pilot to F/L Oliver in a 161 Squadron Hudson. It would fall once more to 138 Squadron to provide a replacement commanding officer for 161 Squadron, for what was proving to be a poisoned chalice.

The squadron put up fifteen aircraft for Norway on the night of the 22/23rd, S/L Brogan carrying out his final sortie before his posting to 161 Squadron as its new commanding officer. He and his crew took off in NF-O at 19.30 to undertake Operation WITHERS 5, carrying seven containers and two packages. The drop site was found to be in an unfavourable location in a valley on the side of a hill, which dictated a minimum height of 2,000 feet. The containers were released successfully, but the packages stayed on board because of a frozen hatch. The receivers on the ground were apparently unable to locate the containers, and asked if and where they had been dropped. F/O Sleven and crew were in NF-S, and took off at 20.46 on Operation THRUSH RED 2, carrying sixteen containers and three packages. As they approached the Norwegian coast, they were attacked by a JU88 and a ME110, and took violent evasive action in the form of a corkscrew, which toppled the giro and forced them to turn for home, jettisoning the cargo on the way. The details of the other sorties are as follows; F/O Banbury in NF-R on Operation on Operation SNAFFLE 4, carrying sixteen containers and three packages, 20.24 to 05.16, successful. Lt Haine in NF-C on Operation THRUSH RED 2, carrying sixteen containers and three packages, 20.26 to 04.48, successful. F/L Moffatt in NF-B on Operation HALTER 7, carrying fifteen containers and a package, 20.34 to 04.57, successful. F/L Cornwallis in NF-P on Operation TAIL 14, carrying four agents, eleven containers and nine packages, 20.38 to 06.20, unsuccessful due to lack of reception. Capt Nevin in NF-N on Operation BIT 8, carrying thirteen containers and twelve packages, 20.40 to 06.30, successful. S/L Sephton in NF-F on Operation THRUSH RED 3, carrying two agents, twelve containers and eleven packages, 20.46 to 05.40, successful. F/O Bright in NF-G on Operation CRUPPER 37, carrying seventeen containers, 20.49 to 05.46, successful. F/L Kidd in NF-Z on Operation BIT 17, carrying sixteen containers and four packages, 20.51 to 05.10, successful. F/O Corley-Smith in NF-T on Operation TAIL 14, carrying thirteen containers and eleven packages, 20.53 to 06.49, unsuccessful due to lack of reception. F/O Shaw in NF-X on Operation CRUPPER 37, carrying fifteen containers, 20.53 to 22.37, unsuccessful due to early return with electrical failure. F/O Strathy in NF-Q on Operation THRUSH RED 3, carrying thirteen containers and eleven packages, 20.59 to 05.43, successful. F/L O'Bern in NF-U on Operation HALTER 7, carrying sixteen containers and four packages, 21.00 to 04.10, unsuccessful due to adverse weather outbound. W/O Tomlin in NF-W on Operation BIT 17, carrying fourteen containers and three packages, 21.09 to 04.32, successful.

On the night of the 23/24th, 1, 6 and 8 Groups carried out the only area bombing raid of the war on Pforzheim in southern Germany, and, in twenty-two horrifying minutes, inflicted a catastrophe upon the town and its inhabitants. A large part of the built-up area was engulfed by fire, and seventeen thousand people lost their lives, the third highest death toll at a German urban target. Five sorties are recorded in the 138 Squadron ORB for this night, and a sixth, by F/Sgt Sinkinson and crew is not mentioned because of their failure to return. They took off for Denmark in LK149 NF-D, and headed out on Operation TABLEJAM 181. They never arrived, and, based on the eventual recovery for burial of three of the crew, the Stirling went into the sea off Denmark's western coast. It was the pilot's first SOE sortie as captain. According to Freddie Clark, seven 138 Squadron crews were briefed for operations, among them that of W/O Tomlin in NF-P, which swung on take-off, without causing any damage. The ORB suggests, that he had another go at taking-off for two drop sites associated with Operation TABLEJAM 187 over Denmark, and succeeded in becoming airborne at 19.36. There were twenty-four containers and a package on board, which were brought back home after they seemed to lose their way. The details of the other sorties are; F/L Wilkie in NF-Q on Operation CURB 4 over Norway, carrying fourteen containers and eight packages, 18.21 to 03.00, successful. W/C Murray in NF-U on Operation POMMEL 19 over Norway, carrying fourteen containers and eight packages, 18.35 to 03.40, successful. F/O Shaw in NF-C on Operation CRUPPER 36 over Norway, carrying seventeen containers and a package, 18.37 to 03.20, successful. W/O Dunmall in NF-G on Operations TABLEJAM 220/107 over Denmark, carrying twenty-four containers and a package, 19.55 to 02.31, successful.

Twelve sorties were mounted by the squadron on the night of the 25/26th, nine to Norway and the remainder to Denmark. F/L Wilkie and crew took off in NF-O at 18.50 to re-run Operation WITHERS 5 over Norway, which S/L Brogan had recently found so difficult because of the terrain. Wilkie was equally unimpressed by the positioning of the reception, but managed to get down to 800 feet for the drop, and saw his load drift some five hundred yards from the lights in the wind. A message was received later from Norway in praise of the drop, but stated that they still hadn't found Brogan's containers. Capt Haine and crew had the same target to aim for, having taken off in NF-B at 18.33. They arrived forty-two minutes ahead of F/L Wilkie, and spent ten minutes over the reception site before giving up due to a lack of reception. The details of the other sorties on this night are as follows; F/L Moffatt in NF-E on Operation GROIN 8 over Norway, carrying nine containers and eight packages, 18.44 to 04.36, successful. F/Sgt Biggs in NF-Q on Operation HALTER 7 over Norway, carrying sixteen containers and three packages, 18.35 to 03.09, successful. W/O Dunmall in NF-H on Operation HALTER 7 over Norway, carrying sixteen containers and three packages, 19.05 to 03.54, successful. F/O Sleven in NF-R on Operation GIRTH 6 over Norway, carrying fourteen containers and four packages, 19.03 to 04.42, successful. F/O Bright in NF-G on Operation GIRTH 11 over Norway, carrying sixteen containers and four packages, no times given, successful. F/L Kidd in NF-S on Operations TABLEJAM 224/237 over Denmark, carrying twenty-four containers and a package, 19.50 to 02.30, successful. S/L Sephton in NF-F on Operations TABLEJAM 238/TABLEWATER 44, carrying twenty-four containers and a package, 19.53 to 02.29, successful. The ORB adds that this was the first time that containers had been dropped intentionally into water. Capt Niven in NF-N on Operation GIRTH 6 over Norway, carrying fifteen containers and seven packages, 20.05 to 03.56, unsuccessful, after failing to locate the pinpoint.

Norway and Denmark were again the destinations for 138 Squadron aircraft in poor weather conditions on the night of the 26/27th, for which the squadron made ready ten Stirlings. The details are as follows; F/O Banbury in NF-A on Operation CRUPPER 37 over Norway, carrying seventeen containers, 19.05 to 04.20, successful. F/O Shaw in NF-B on Operation THRUSH RED 2 over Norway, carrying fourteen containers and four packages, 19.30 to 04.34, successful. F/L Cornwallis in NF-P on Operation CRUPPER 37 over Norway carrying four agents, eleven containers and nine packages, 19.39. F/L Moffatt in NF-U on Operation SADDLE 14 over Norway, carrying fourteen containers and nine packages, 19.43 to 03.39, unsuccessful due to adverse weather. F/O Strathy in NF-Q on Operation TABLEJAM 234 over Denmark, carrying twenty-four containers and a package, 20 24 to 02.47, unsuccessful due to adverse weather. W/C Murray in NF-T on Operations TABLEJAM 111/187 over Denmark, carrying twenty-four containers and a package, 20.29 to 03.54, successful. F/L O'Bern in NF-S on Operation TABLEJAM 219 over Denmark, carrying twenty-four containers and a package, 20.29 to 03.46, successful. Capt Nevin in NF-N on Operations TABLEJAM 239/221 over Denmark, carrying twenty-four containers and a package, 20.30 to 03.17, successful. W/O Dunmall in NF-E on Operation TABLEJAM 126 over Denmark, carrying eighteen containers and six packages, 20.35 to 03.28, successful. F/L Kidd in NF-L on Operation TABLEJAM 123 over Denmark, carrying twenty-four containers and a package, 20.36 to 03.20, unsuccessful due to adverse weather. During the outward flight, F/O Shaw watched as an aircraft was engaged by flak, and sent crashing into the sea off the Norwegian coast. LK272 NF-P failed to return to Tempsford, and was, therefore, identified as the victim, and F/L Cornwallis and his crew were duly posted missing presumed killed. This was later confirmed, and the four agents on board also lost their lives. The crew had served with 138 Squadron for six months at the time of their deaths.

Operations to Norway on the last night of the month were rendered almost impossible by the weather, and only a handful of containers reached their destinations. One crew recorded a wind speed of a hundred mph, and many were flying on fumes as they landed, after battling against head winds. The details of the 138 Squadron sorties are as follows; P/O Bright in NF-G on Operation POMMEL 9, carrying fifteen containers and six packages, no times recorded, unsuccessful due to adverse weather. F/L O'Bern in NF-O on Operation TAIL 15, carrying fifteen containers and a package, 21.30 to 06.39, unsuccessful due to adverse weather. W/O Tomlin in NF-S on Operation POMMEL 11, carrying sixteen containers and two packages, 21.33 to 05.10, unsuccessful due to adverse weather. F/Sgt Biggs in NF-Q on Operation CRUPPER 34, carrying sixteen containers and three packages, 21.34 to 06.45, successful. F/O Sleven in NF-R on Operation POMMEL 9, carrying twelve containers and six packages, 21.36 to 04.35, unsuccessful due to adverse weather. F/O Banbury in NF-A on Operation BIT 32, carrying sixteen containers and three packages, 21.38 to 07.02, successful. Capt Haine in NF-C on Operation TAIL 15, carrying seventeen containers, 21.47 to 07.09, unsuccessful due to adverse weather. Capt Nevin in NF-U on Operation POMMEL 8, carrying seventeen containers, 21.48 to 07.16, successful. F/O Corley-Smith in NF-T on Operation POMMEL 8, carrying seventeen containers, 21.52 to 07.37, unsuccessful due to adverse weather. W/O

Dunmall in NF-F on Operation POMMEL 11, carrying seventeen containers, 21.54 to 07.10, unsuccessful due to adverse weather. F/O Wilson in NF-L on Operation CRUPPER 34, carrying sixteen containers and three packages, 21.55 to 05.17, unsuccessful due to adverse weather. F/L Shaw in NF-E on Operation BIT 32, carrying fifteen containers, 22.01 to 06.56, unsuccessful due to adverse weather.

March 1945

The end was now in sight for 138 Squadron's illustrious career in clandestine operations, and a new role beckoned. As the Nazi sphere of influence shrank by the day, the requirement for SOE and SIS operations diminished accordingly, and could no longer support two squadrons. March opened with the final raid of the war by RAF heavy bombers on Mannheim on the 1st, carried out by 1, 6 and 8 Groups. As usually happened at this target, the bombing spilled across the Rhine into Ludwigshafen, and heavy damage was caused here also. 3 Group, meanwhile, carried out an inconclusive G-H raid on the oil plant at Kamen without loss. On the following morning two forces set out to bomb Cologne for the last time, the first numbering seven hundred aircraft, which inflicted massive damage upon the already shattered city. The second attack by 3 Group had to be abandoned after only fifteen aircraft had bombed, because of a fault with the G-H station in England. It hardly mattered, and the city fell to American forces four days later.

138 Squadron opened its March account with a dozen sorties to Denmark and Norway on the night of the 2/3rd, in improved weather conditions. The details are as follows; F/O Shaw in NF-E on Operation CRUPPER 16 over Norway, carrying fourteen containers and three packages, 20.32 to 05.15, successful. F/O Corley-Smith in NF-T on Operation Tail 14 over Norway, carrying four agents, ten containers and nine packages, 20.40 to 06.05, successful. W/O Tomlin in NF-S on Operation POMMEL 11 over Norway, carrying sixteen containers and two packages, 20.40 to 04.30, successful. F/Sgt Biggs in NF-U on Operation STIRRUP 4 over Norway, carrying sixteen containers and two packages, 20.55 to 04.45, successful. W/O Dunmall in NF-C on Operation POMMEL 11 over Norway, carrying sixteen containers and three packages, 21.05 to 05.15, successful. F/L Kidd in NF-L on Operation STIRRUP 4 over Norway, carrying fifteen containers and five packages, 21.10 to 05.00, successful. Capt Nevin in NF-N on Operation TAIL 14 over Norway, carrying thirteen containers and eleven packages, 21.15 to 06.30, successful. F/O Wilkie in NF-Q on Operation SADDLE 15 over Norway, carrying two agents, seventeen containers and five packages, 21.20 to 04.20, successful. F/O Banbury in NF-A on Operation CRUPPER 16 over Norway, carrying sixteen containers and three packages, 21.30 to 06.25, successful. F/O Sleven in NF-R on Operation SADDLE 15 over Norway, carrying eighteen containers and eight packages, 21.35 to 04.35, successful. F/O Bright in NF-G on Operations SABOR 2/SADDLE 14 over Norway, carrying twenty-one containers and ten packages, 21.56 to 06.43, second element only completed, no reception at first one. W/C Murray in NF-F on Operations TABLEJAM 199/76 over Denmark, carrying a second pilot, navigator and air-bomber, as well as two agents and twenty-three containers, 22.42 to 05.43, unsuccessful due to failure to locate the targets.

The penultimate night of SOE operations involving 138 Squadron saw ten sorties depart Tempsford on the evening of the 3rd, nine bound for Norway, while W/C Murray returned to Denmark to attempt to complete Operations TABLEJAM 199/76, which had thwarted him twenty-four hours earlier. He and his nine crew members took off at 22.20 in NF-F, carrying two agents and twenty-three containers, which were successfully delivered to the drop sites, and gratefully received by those waiting on the ground. The details of the sorties to Norway are as follows; W/O Dunmall in NF-C on Operation CROP 14, carrying fifteen containers and four packages, 20.35 to 06.00, successfully delivered ten miles east of pinpoint onto the correct signal. W/O Tomlin in NF-N on Operation CURB 3, carrying seventeen containers, 20.40 to 03.20, unsuccessful due to adverse weather. P/O Banbury in NF-A on Operation CURB 3, carrying an agent, fifteen containers and a package, 20.40 to 06.20, successful. F/O Corley-Smith in NF-T on Operation TAIL 11, carrying seventeen containers, 20.45 to 05.25, successful. Capt Haine in NF-B on Operation THRUSH RED 3, carrying fifteen containers and a package, 20.45 to 06.00, successful. F/L Kidd in NF-L on Operation TAIL 15, carrying sixteen containers, 20.50 to 06.05, successful. F/Sgt Biggs in NF-U on Operation CURB 3, carrying sixteen containers and three packages, 20.55 to 04.05, unsuccessful due to adverse weather. Capt Nevin in NF-G on Operation TAIL 11, carrying seventeen containers, 21.09 to 04.49, unsuccessful due to adverse weather. F/L Wilkie in NF-Q on Operation THRUSH RED 3, carrying seventeen containers and one package, 21.10 to 05.40, successful.

The night of the 4/5th proved to be the swan song for 138 Squadron operations from Tempsford, and it became a sad occasion. Six sorties were launched to Denmark, among them that of F/O Sleven and crew, who took off in LJ999 NF-Q at 23.48 to carry out Operation TABLEJAM 241. They were carrying twenty-four containers and a package, which they delivered as briefed, and were on their way home at 150 feet, when an explosion inside the fuselage forced F/O Sleven to crash-land in shallow water in Ringkøbing Fjord, near Tippen Island, at 240 mph. Miraculously, the crew emerged unhurt from the wreck, and were able to walk onto the island of Tippen, where they were taken into captivity. Former 138 Squadron stalwart, W/C Brogan, and his crew were less fortunate, however, and all perished when their 161 Squadron Stirling crashed into the sea off Denmark. The details of the remaining sorties on this night are as follows; F/O Shaw in NF-A on Operations TABLEJAM 238/98, carrying twenty-four containers and a package, 23.40 to 06.07, successful. F/L Moffatt in NF-C on Operation TABLEJAM 212, carrying twenty-three containers and a package, 23.45 to 06.40, successful. Capt Haine in NF-B on Operations TABLEJAM 232/134, carrying eighteen containers and a package, 23.45 to 06.40, successful. F/L O'Bern in NF-N on Operations TABLEJAM 185/243, carrying twenty-four containers and a package, 23.49 to 06.09, first element only completed, no reception at the second one because of a German night exercise. F/O Bright in NF-G on Operation TABLEJAM 190, carrying twenty-four containers and a package, 23.50 to 06.30, unsuccessful due to lack of reception.

Having escaped serious damage on the night after Dresden, Chemnitz succumbed to a highly destructive raid by over seven hundred aircraft on the night of the 5/6th, while 5 Group revisited the oil refinery at Böhlen. On the following night, 5 Group went to the Baltic to attack the port of Sassnitz on the island of Rügen, a little to the north of Peenemünde, leaving the northern part of the town severely damaged, and sinking three ships. The oil refinery at Harburg, opposite Hamburg, was 5 Group's next target on the night of the 7/8th, while the eastern town of Dessau was left devastated after its first and only raid of the war at the hands of 1, 3, 6 and 8 Group Lancasters. The 138 Squadron crews approaching the end of their tours were posted to 161 Squadron, while the remainder were packed off to 1662 HCU at Blyton for conversion onto Lancasters. It had been decided, that 138 Squadron would end the war as a standard 3 Group front line bomber unit, and would be stationed at Tuddenham, near Bury St Edmunds in Suffolk, which it would share with 90 Squadron. The advance party arrived on the 9th, and the squadron was fully in residence within a day or two. The long-held NF code was now replaced with AC.

Working up to operational status would occupy almost the remainder of the month, and the squadron was sidelined, therefore, during some notable occasions. A new record was set in the late morning of the 11th, when 1,079 aircraft took off for the final raid of the war on Essen. The bombers' battle with Essen had spanned almost five years, and it was only during the last two, that the bomber had prevailed. Many gallant crews had fallen during the various campaigns, but Essen now lay totally ruined, and seven thousand of its inhabitants had lost their lives in air raids. The record was short-lived, and was surpassed a little over twenty-four hours later, when 1,108 aircraft departed their stations in the early afternoon of the 12th, to deliver the final raid of the war on Dortmund. There was still to be no let-up in the bombing of Germany, and Wuppertal was pounded by daylight on the 13th, while oil-related targets attracted the bulk of the Command's attention over the next forty-eight hours. On the 16/17th, over two hundred 5 Group Lancasters were sent to attack the historic and minimally industrial city of Würzburg in central-southern Germany. In seventeen ghastly minutes, over eleven hundred tons of bombs were dropped with great accuracy, destroying 89% of the built-up area, and killing between four and five thousand people. At the same time 1 Group was receiving a bloody nose in the last heavy raid of the war on Nuremberg.

Further attacks were unleashed on oil and communications targets over the succeeding days and nights, and 1 Group exacted revenge for the loss of twenty-four Lancasters at Nuremberg by laying waste to Hildesheim on the 22nd, when more than sixteen hundred people lost their lives. Also on this day, while 138 Squadron was still embroiled in the working up process, three of its navigators, F/L Thompson, P/O Warsh and F/Sgt Hislop, were lent to the Liberator-equipped American special duties 858 Squadron at Harrington in Northamptonshire. They would each take part in an operation to Denmark on the 26th, and although it failed through lack of reception, the Americans expressed their appreciation for the information and guidance received. The small town of Wesel had the misfortune to lie close to the area of fighting, and was believed to contain enemy troop units. Consequently, it had been a focus of the Command's attention since mid February, most of the attacks having been delivered by 3 or 8 Groups. The last one was undertaken by 5 Group with a little 8 Group support in the late evening of the 23rd. The eight attacks of varying sizes on the town had produced a pile of rubble, and it was estimated that 97% of the buildings in the main town area had been destroyed. The local authorities, in fact, claimed it to be the most completely destroyed town in the whole of Germany.

The three navigators returned from their loan period with the Americans on the 28th, the day on which briefing took place for three crews to fly the squadron's first operational sorties from Tuddenham. According to the Operations Record Book they would fly with 90 Squadron, as part of a 3 Group G-H raid on the Hermann Goering iron works at Hallendorf. In the event the operation was postponed, and rescheduled for the 29th, when an operation did take place, but it is believed, that the target was more likely the Hermann Goering benzol plant at Salzgitter near Brunswick. The 138 Squadron crews, those of F/O Liddell in NF966, F/O Horsaman in HK606 and P/O Brand in NG409, took off in quick succession at 12.33, carrying a 4,000 pounder and nine 500 pounders each. All returned safely, having bombed either with the leader or on instruments as the result of cloud. The A Flight commander, S/L Sephton, was posted out as tour expired on this day, and he was replaced by S/L Stanton from 149 Squadron.

April 1945

April would prove to be the final month of the bombing war, and it began with a 1 and 8 Group attack on what was believed to be military barracks at Nordhausen, north-east of Kassel, on the 3rd. It was, in fact, the underground secret weapons factory built after Peenemünde, and the barracks housed the forced workers. Many casualties were inflicted, and this was repeated on the following day, when 5 Group also bombed the site. The night of the 4/5th was busy in the extreme for the Command, with three major operations taking place, along with many of a support or minor nature. Elements of 3, 6 and 8 Groups were sent to attack the synthetic oil refinery at Leuna, near Merseburg in the east, and 138 Squadron provided ten of the 327 aircraft detailed. They took off in a matter of minutes from 18.45, with S/L Stanton the senior pilot on duty, and were over the target at 19,000 to 20,000 feet between 22.45 and 23.04. Six-tenths patchy cloud meant that the Master Bomber called for skymarkers, and the attack, at first, seemed to be scattered. The squadron participants delivered a total of ten cookies and seventy 500 pounders, and a number of fires and explosions were observed as they left the target area. All returned safely, from what proved to be an ineffective attack, the first crew back landing shortly before 03.00. Operations against similar targets were carried out simultaneously at Harburg and Lützkendorf by the other Groups, while 5 Group stayed at home.

3 Group stayed off the order of battle until the 9th, during which period, 5 Group was the most active. The only large-scale operation of the period was by over four hundred aircraft of 4, 6 and 8 Groups against Hamburg on the night of the 8/9th, when the shipyard areas were the intended targets, although cloud interfered with accuracy. In the mid evening of the 9th, almost six hundred aircraft took off from 1, 3 and 8 Group stations bound for Kiel, where the harbour area was to be bombed. Among the participants were eighteen Lancasters from 138 Squadron, which represented a maximum effort, and they carried a total of 180,000lbs of bombs. S/Ls Stanton and Wilkie were the senior pilots on duty as they began departing Tuddenham shortly after 19.30, and they arrived in the target area to find clear conditions. The 138 Squadron bombs were delivered from around 19,000 feet either side of 22.45 under the control of a Master Bomber, and the operation was a success. One of the town's major U-Boot construction yards was severely damaged, the pocket battleship Admiral Scheer capsized, and two other warships were damaged. Only three Lancasters were lost, but all eighteen from 138 Squadron came home, F/L Liddle and crew reporting firing a two-second burst at a BF109, which crossed their homebound path, and broke away without replying.

On the night of the 13/14th, over 480 Lancasters and Halifaxes from 3, 6 and 8 Groups departed their stations to return to Kiel. The fourteen-strong 138 Squadron contingent was led away by S/L Stanton in PP675 at 20.14, and all were safely airborne within nine minutes. They reached the target area to find a layer of eight to ten-tenths thin cloud with tops at around 8,000 feet, and delivered their cookie and twelve 500 pounders each during a twenty-minute slot from 23.30, from an altitude of 19,000 to 20,000 feet. They aimed for the target indicators as instructed by the Master Bomber, but the bombing was scattered, and the port area, the intended recipient for the attack, largely escaped serious damage.

On the following night, five hundred Lancaster crews drawn from 1, 3 and 8 Groups were briefed for an operation to Potsdam, a town on the western approaches to Berlin, and deep inside the Capital's defence zone. This would, in fact, be the first incursion by the RAF's heavy brigade into Berlin's defensive belt since the end of the Berlin campaign more than a year earlier. Sixteen 138 Squadron Lancasters lined up for take-off at Tuddenham led by W/C Murray in PP675. The other crew captains and aircraft were Capt Haines (SAAF) in NG407, F/L Ellwood in HK692, F/L Burnett in NG365, F/O Sicklemore in HK694, W/O Tomlin in PP678, F/SGT Biggs in NF966, F/O Bubb in LM275, F/O Horsaman in RF143, F/L Shaw in HK292, F/O Petfield in PA193, F/SGT Crawford in RF142, Sgt Taylor in NG409, F/L Liddell in NX571, F/O Russell in PP679 and F/O Townsend in HK615. All aircraft got away safely between 18.11 and 18.23, and the crews settled in for the long flight ahead. They arrived in the target area without incident to find clear skies, and delivered their bombs from around 20,000 feet either side of 23.00 hours. On their return the crews were able to report a concentrated attack, which caused very heavy damage, and it is reported, that around five thousand people lost their lives. One 138 Squadron crew was absent from debriefing, however, and others reported seeing two aircraft in flames over the target. One of these was a 35 Squadron aircraft, which was partially abandoned over Germany, before flying on to Allied territory, where the pilot also baled out. The other flamer was clearly 138 Squadron's RF143, which was shot down by a night fighter after being coned by searchlights, and F/O Horsaman died with all but one of his crew. It is believed, that the bomb-aimer, F/O Neve, survived, but there is no information relating to his fate once on the ground. This would prove to be the final missing 138 Squadron crew of the war, and the only one from the squadron's short spell as a standard bomber unit.

On the 18th, the island of Heligoland was subjected to a massive daylight assault by almost a thousand aircraft, including eighteen from 138 Squadron, led by W/C Murray in PP675, with S/L Wilkie in support. They took off between 10.25 and 11.05 carrying ten 1,000 pounders and four 500 pounders each, and bombed the target from 18,000 to 19,500 feet in a two and a half minute slot shortly after 13.00 hours, before returning safely to Tuddenham. They left behind them an island resembling a lunar scape. On the 19th, the squadron provided five crews for a G-H attack by forty-nine 3 Group Lancasters on a transformer station at the Munich-Pasing railway yards. F/Ls Clarine, Liddle and Burnett were the senior pilots on duty, backed up by F/Os Brand and Russell, and they were airborne by 08.14, each carrying four 1,000 pounders and ten 500 pounders. They attacked between 12.02 and 12.05 from 19,000 to 19,500 feet, and all returned safely from what appeared to be an accurate and concentrated raid. The final operation of the long running oil campaign was delivered by 3 Group against a fuel storage depot at distant Regensburg in south-eastern Germany on the 20th. One Hundred aircraft took part, of which seven were provided by 138 Squadron, and once again, W/C Murray took the lead. Taking off shortly before 10.00 hours, carrying three 1,000 pounders and ten 500 pounders each, they reached the target to bomb from 18,000 to 18,500 feet either side of 14.00, three crews on instruments and the remainder on the fall of the leader's load. All aircraft arrived safely back at Tuddenham a little after 17.00 hours, to report that the attack had fallen on the aiming point.

3 Group operated for the final time on the 22nd, as part of a heavy assault on the south-eastern suburbs of Bremen, which was to be attacked by the British XXX Corps two days hence. The 3 Group contingent included fourteen Lancasters from 138 Squadron, and they were led away

by S/L Wilkie at 15.14, each carrying a cookie and fourteen assorted 500 pounders. The 3 Group element went in first, the 138 Squadron crews bombing from 18,000 to 19,000 feet between 18.22 and 18.34, either on instruments or on the fall of the leader's bombs. The smoke and dust from their attack obliterated the aiming point, and the Master Bomber was forced to send the entire 1 and 4 Group contingents home with their bombs still on board. Four 138 Squadron Lancasters were hit by flak, but all made it home safely, F/Sgt Briggs and crew at 21.08, thus securing the honour of being the last from 138 Squadron to land from an offensive operation. The final operations by the Command's heavy squadrons took place on the 25th, and fittingly included a morning attack by Lancasters on the SS barracks at Hitler's Eaglesnest retreat at Berchtesgaden.

On the 26th, W/C Murray began a nine-day period of leave, and S/L Wilkie RCAF was left in charge of the squadron's affairs until his return. On the following day, S/L Harley Stanton was posted from his role as flight commander to take command of 115 Squadron. On the 30th the squadron sent thirteen aircraft on a supply drop to the starving residents of Rotterdam under Operation Manna, after agreement had been reached with the occupying Nazi forces. One aircraft returned damaged after being hit by food from higher up! A similar operation involving fourteen of the squadron's aircraft was mounted to the Hague on the 1st of May, and this was repeated on the 2nd and 3rd by fourteen and twelve aircraft respectively. Further sorties were flown to the Hague on the 5th, 7th and the 8th, the day on which the war with Germany officially ended. The main part of Operation Exodus, the repatriation of Allied PoWs, began on the 9th, and 138 Squadron would play its part over the ensuing days. After the war 138 Squadron remained in service until being disbanded on the 1st of September 1950. It was resurrected on the 1st of January 1955, to be the first recipient of the Valiant, the first of the V-Bombers. The squadron was again disbanded on the 1st of April 1962, and this proud number has remained on the shelf ever since.

It is impossible to estimate the contribution to victory made by resistance organisations in occupied Europe, but, whatever they achieved, and it was hugely significant, they could not have done it without the work carried out by the Moon Squadrons at Tempsford. The airmanship and professionalism of the crews, and the serviceability of the aircraft through the magnificent efforts of the ground crews, was remarkable, and stands as a shining beacon in the glorious history of wartime RAF Bomber Command.

Section Two

Motto: *'For Freedom'*
Codes: NF AC

Stations

As 419 Flight

North Weald	21.08.40. to 03.09.40.
Stapleford Tawney	03.09.40. to 09.10.40.
Stradishall	09.10.40. to 03.41.

As 1419 Flight

Stradishall	03.41. to 22.05.41.
Newmarket	22.05.41. to 25.08.41.

As 138 Squadron

Newmarket	25.08.41. to 12.41.
Stradishall	12.41. to 14.03.42.
Tempsford	14.03.42. to 09.03.45.
Tangmere (Lysander Flight)	25.08.41. to 02.42.
Tuddenham	09.03.45. to 11.46.

Aircraft

Whitley V	08.40. to 10.42.
Lysander IIIA	08.40. to 02.42.
Halifax I	10.41. to 12.42.
Halifax II	10.42. to 08.44.
Liberator	08.43. to 10.43.
Stirling	06.44. to 03.45.
Lancaster	03.45. to 09.47.

Commanding Officers

419 Flight

FLIGHT LIEUTENANT W R FARLEY	21.08.40. to 12.40.
FLIGHT LIEUTENANT F J B KEAST	12.40. to 17.02.41.
SQUADRON LEADER E V KNOWLES DFC	02.41. to 03.41.

1419 Flight

SQUADRON LEADER E V KNOWLES DFC	03.41. to 25.08.41.

138 Squadron

WING COMMANDER E V KNOWLES DFC	25.08.41. to 17.11.41.
WING COMMANDER W R FARLEY DFC	18.11.41. to 21.04.42.
WING COMMANDER R C HOCKEY DSO DFC	21.04.42. to 27.02.43.
WING COMMANDER K S BATCHELOR DFC	28.02.43. to 24.05.43.
WING COMMANDER R D SPEARE DFC	25.05.43. to 30.04.44.
WING COMMANDER W McF RUSSELL DFC*	01.05.44. to 07.05.44.
WING COMMANDER W J BURNETT DFC	09.05.44. to 07.11.44.
WING COMMANDER T B C MURRAY DSO DFC*	17.11.44. to 04.46.
SQUADRON LEADER H W WILKIE (Temp)	26.06.45. to 06.05.45.

Operational Record

419 and 1419 Flights

SORTIES AIRCRAFT LOSSES
111 1

138 Squadron

Special Duties

OPERATIONS SORTIES AIRCRAFT LOSSES % LOSSES
438 2569 70 2.7

Sorties by Aircraft Type[2]

HALIFAX	STIRLING	WHITLEY	LYSANDER	LIBERATOR	WELLINGTON
1788	503	219	64	3	1

Operational Losses by Aircraft Type

HALIFAX	STIRLING	WHITLEY	LYSANDER	LIBERATOR	WELLINGTON
62	13	12	3	1	0

Lancaster Operations

OPERATIONS SORTIES AIRCRAFT LOSSES % LOSSES
9 105 1 1.0

---

[2] *It is not possible to be absolutely accurate with the above figures, which are based on statistics provided by Freddie Clark and Martin Middlebrook/Chris Everitt.*

Section Three: Aircraft Histories

419 Flight

WHITLEY	**From August 1940 to March 1941.**
P5025	Crashed on landing at Stradishall after local flight 11.10.40.
P5029 A	To 1419Flt.
T4166	From 78Sqn. To 1419Flt.
T4264 X	FTR from SOE operation to Belgium 17/18.2.41.
Z6473	From A&AEE. To 1419Flt.
LYSANDER	**From August 1940 to March 1941.**
R2625	From 13Sqn. To 1419Flt.
R2626	From 13Sqn. To 1419Flt.
R9027	Force-landed in Scotland on return from pick-up operation to France 21.10.40.

1419 Flight

WHITLEY	**From March 1941 to August 1941.**
P5029 A	From 419Flt. To 138Sqn.
T4165	From 78Sqn. To 138Sqn.
T4166	From 419Flt. To 138Sqn.
Z6473	From 419Flt. To 1419Flt.
Z6727	Crashed in Cambridgeshire during secret equipment test 25.7.41.
Z6728	To 138Sqn.
Z9125	To 138Sqn.
LYSANDER	**From March 1941 to August 1941.**
R2625	From 419Flt. To 138Sqn.
R2626	From 419Flt. To 138Sqn.
T1508	To 138Sqn via TFU.
T1770	To 138Sqn via SDF and TFU Newmarket.

138 Squadron

WHITLEY.	**From August 1941 to October 1942.**
P5029 NF-E	From 1419Flt. Ditched off Sussex coast on return from SOE sortie to France 22/23.10.42.
T4165	From 1419Flt. Crashed while landing at Tangmere on return from SOE operation to France 10/11.4.41.
T4166 NF-B	From 1419Flt. FTR from SOE operation to Holland 27/28.3.42.
Z6473	From 1419 Flt. To 42 O.T.U.
Z6728	From 1419Flt. FTR from SOE operation to Belgium 28/29.1.42.
Z6959	From 102Sqn. To 161Sqn.
Z9125	From 1419Flt. Crashed on take-off from Stradishall when bound for SOE operation to France 10.3.42.
Z9140	From 51Sqn. Destroyed by enemy action at Luqa airfield Malta 3.1.42.
Z9146 NF-P	From 51Sqn. SOC 25.2.44.
Z9148	From 77Sqn. Returned to 77Sqn.
Z9158 NF-V	Crashed in Wiltshire on return from leaflet sortie to France 21.4.42.
Z9159 NF-D	FTR from SOE operation to France 31.10/1.11.42.
Z9223	Crashed while trying to land at Stradishall on return from a training flight 29/30.10.41.
Z9230 NF-N	From 51Sqn. FTR from SOE operation to Holland 29/30.7.42.
Z9232 NF-L	From 78Sqn. FTR from SOE operation to France 24/25.8.42.
Z9275 NF-G	From 78Sqn. To OADU and back. FTR from SOE operation to Belgium 26/27.9.42.
Z9282 NF-M	From 102Sqn. FTR from bombing operation to France 25/26.7.42.
Z9286 NF-H	
Z9287 NF-K	To PTS.
Z9288 NF-J	To 13MU.
Z9295	From 58Sqn. Destroyed by enemy action at Luqa airfield Malta 3.1.42.
Z9298	From 51Sqn. Returned to 51Sqn.
Z9385	Crashed on landing at Stradishall on return from Special Duties operation to France 28.12.41.
Z9428 NF-F/W	From 161Sqn. To 24 OTU.
BD260 NF-S	From 51Sqn. To 10 OTU.
BD504 NF-F	To Royal Aircraft Establishment.
LA763 NF-L	To 10 OTU.
LA764 NF-M	To 10 OTU.
WELLINGTON.	
P2521	From 1 GRU. To 161Sqn.
LYSANDER.	**From August 1941 to February 1942.**
R2625	From 1419Flt.

R2626	From 1419Flt. To 161Sqn.
T1508	From 1419Flt via TFU. FTR from SOE operation to France 28/29.1.42.
T1770	From 1419Flt via SDF and TFU Newmarket. To 161Sqn.
T1771	Crashed in Surrey during training 28.11.41.

HALIFAX. From October 1941 to August 1944.

L9611	From 76Sqn. Returned to 76Sqn.
L9612	From AFEE. Force-landed in Sweden on return from Special Duties operation to Poland 2.11.41.
L9613 NF-V	To 1661CU.
L9618 NF-W	From AFEE. Lost over Mediterranean while in transit to Malta 15.12.42.
R9376	From 10Sqn. Returned to 10Sqn.
V9976	From AFEE. FTR from SOE operation to Austria 20/21.4.42.
W1002 NF-Y	From AFEE. Crashed in Western Desert during transit from Malta to Gibraltar 17.12.42.
W1007 NF-U	From 78Sqn. To 1666CU.
W1012 NF-Z	From 161Sqn. FTR from SIS/SOE operation to France 19/20.2.43.
W1046	From 161Sqn. To 1666CU.
W1229 NF-A	Crashed on landing at Tempsford during training 19.6.43.
W7773 NF-S	FTR from SOE operation to Poland 29/30.10.42.
W7774 NF-T	Ditched off Norfolk coast on return from SOE operation to Poland 30.10.42.
W7775 NF-R	FTR from SOE operation to Holland 22/23.12.42.
W7776 NF-B	Force-landed in Yorkshire on return from SOE operation to Poland 1/2.10.42.
BB281 NF-O	FTR from SOE operation to Czechoslovakia 14/15.3.43.
BB309 NF-T	FTR from SOE operation to Poland 16/17.9.43.
BB313 NF-M	FTR from SOE operation to France 12/13.5.43.
BB316 NF-R	To 1662CU.
BB317 NF-N	FTR from SOE operation to Holland 19/20.9.43.
BB328 NF-U	FTR from SOE operation to France 13/14.5.43.
BB329 NF-Z	From 161Sqn. FTR from SOE operation to Holland 21/22.5.43.
BB330 NF-C	Damaged beyond repair in accident 25.2.44.
BB334 NF-X	To 405Sqn and back. FTR from SOE operation to France 12/13.8.43.
BB335	From 301FTU. To 148Sqn.
BB340 NF-D	FTR from SOE operation to France 12/13.4.43.
BB363 NF-T	FTR from SOE operation to Belgium 13/14.4.43.
BB364 NF-R	Crashed in Bedfordshire while training 19.12.43.
BB378 NF-D	FTR from SOE operation to Denmark 10/11.12.43.
BB379 NF-J	FTR from SOE operation to Holland 23/24.6.43.
DG252 NF-B	FTR from SOE operation to Holland 19/20.9.43.
DG253 NF-F	From 408Sqn. Crashed on landing at Tempsford following early return from SOE operation 18/19.8.43.

DG271 NF-C	Crashed on take-off from Tangmere for transit flight to Tempsford 4.2.43.
DG272	To 161Sqn.
DG285	To 161Sqn.
DG286 NF-A	To 161Sqn and back. Crashed on take-off from Tempsford during training 23.5.44.
DG287	To 1660CU.
DG316	To 518Sqn.
DG996	To 161Sqn.
DK119 NF-W	To 161Sqn.
DT542 NF-Q	Crashed on take-off from Luqa for transit flight to Gibraltar 17.12.42.
DT543 NF-G	SOC 20.7.44. Details unknown.
DT620 NF-T	FTR from SOE operation to Poland 14/15.3.43.
DT627 NF-P	FTR from SOE operation to Holland 11/12.5.43.
DT725 NF-J	FTR from SOE operation to France 17/18.4.43.
DT726 NF-H	FTR from SOE operation to France 3/4.11.43.
DT727 NF-K	Crashed on landing at Tempsford during training 22.6.43.
HR665 NF-L	FTR from SOE operation to Holland 24/25.3.43.
HR666 NF-E	FTR from SOE operation to Poland 14/15.9.43.
HX161 NF-M/H	To 1586Flt.
JB802 NF-S	Crashed on landing at Maison Blanche Algeria during transit 18.5.43.
JB855	To 78Sqn.
JD154 NF-V	FTR from SOE operation to Poland 14/15.9.43.
JD155 NF-M	FTR from SOE operation to France 12/13.7.43.
JD156 NF-W	FTR from SOE operation to Poland 16/17.9.43.
JD171 NF-P	To 1586Flt.
JD172 NF-S	To MAC.
JD179 NF-Z	FTR from SOE operation to France 17/18.8.43.
JD180 NF-O	FTR from SOE operation to France 14/15.8.43.
JD269 NF-Q	FTR from SOE operation to Poland 14/15.9.43.
JD312 NF-J	FTR from SOE operation to France 16/17.8.43.
JD319 NF-A	To 1586Flt.
JD362 NF-L	To 1586Flt.
JN910 NF-K	FTR from SOE operation to Poland 14/15.9.43.
JN911 NF-Z	To 1586Flt.
JN921 NF-B	FTR from SOE operation to France 6/7.11.43.
LK736	Crash-landed in Bedfordshire during training 17.5.44.
LK742	To 1667CU.
LK743 NF-J	Crashed in Bedfordshire on return from SOE operation to Belgium 7/8.1.44.
LL114 NF-P	FTR from SOE operation to France 7/8.2.44.
LL115 NF-A	Crashed while trying to land at Woodbridge on return from SOE operation to France 16/17.12.43.
LL118	From 161Sqn. To 1663CU.
LL119 NF-L	Abandoned over Sussex on return from SOE operation to France 16/17.12.43.

LL183 MA-W	On loan from 161Sqn. FTR from SOE operation to France 9/10.5.44.	
LL187 NF-H	To 1663CU.	
LL192 NF-A	FTR from SOE operation to Denmark 7/8.5.44.	
LL236		
LL249	From 161Sqn. To 1659CU.	
LL250	From 161Sqn. To 1FU.	
LL251 NF-N	From 161Sqn. Ditched in the Mediterranean during SOE operation from Blida, Algeria to France 11/12.7.44.	
LL252 NF-K	From 161Sqn. FTR from SIS/SOE operation to France 31.3/1.4.44.	
LL254	From 161Sqn. To 2 OADU.	
LL276 NF-F	FTR from SOE operation to Belgium 31.5/1.6.44.	
LL279 NF-R	FTR from SOE operation to France 3/4.3.44.	
LL280 NF-O	FTR from SOE operation to France 7/8.5.44.	
LL282	To 1FU.	
LL284 NF-E	Crash-landed in Bedfordshire when bound for SOE operation to Belgium 2/3.6.44.	
LL287 NF-S	FTR from SOE operation to Belgium 30/31.3.44.	
LL289 NF-P	From 1658CU. FTR from SOE operation to France 1/2.6.44.	
LL290	To 1667CU.	
LL306 NF-R	FTR from SIS operation to France 7/8.6.44.	
LL307 NF-J	FTR from SOE operation to Belgium 2/3.6.44.	
LL308 NF-Q	FTR from SOE operation to Belgium 8/9.8.44.	
LL354	To 2 OADU.	
LL356 NF-U	FTR from SOE operation to Belgium 27/28.4.44.	
LL359	To 301FTU.	
LL364 NF-B	From 161Sqn. FTR from SOE operation to France 18/19.7.44.	
LL380	To 1FU.	
LL381	From 161Sqn. To 2 OADU.	
LL385	To 161Sqn.	
LL387 NF-P	From 161Sqn. FTR from SOE operation to France 18/19.7.44.	
LL388	From 161Sqn. Returned to 161Sqn.	
LL390 NF-S	Crashed on take-off from Tempsford when bound for SOE operation to France 7.6.44.	
LL392	From 161Sqn. To 1FU.	
LL409	To 298Sqn.	
LL416 NF-O	FTR from SOE operation to France 7/8.6.44.	
LL419 NF-V	FTR from SOE operation to Belgium 31.5/1.6.44.	
LL465	To 161Sqn.	
LL466 NF-T	FTR from SOE operation to France 7/8.6.44.	
LL467	To 161Sqn.	
LL468	To 1FU.	
LL483	To 161Sqn.	
LL484	To 2 OADU.	
LW272 NF-E	To 1586Flt.	
LW275 NF-O	FTR from SOE operation to France 7/8.2.44.	
LW276 NF-E	To MAC.	

LW280 NF-K	Abandoned and crashed off Essex coast on return from SOE operation to France 16/17.12.43.
LW281 NF-W	FTR from SOE operation to Holland/Belgium 18/19.10.43.
LW284 NF-T	To 1586Flt.

LIBERATOR. **From August 1943 to October 1943.**

BZ858 NF-F	FTR from SOE operation to Poland 9/10.10.43.
BZ859 NF-G	To 1586Flt.
BZ860 NF-U	To 1586Flt.
BZ949	To 1586Flt.

STIRLING. **From June 1944 to March 1945.**

LJ503 NF-P	From CRD. FTR from SOE operation to France 31.8/1.9.44.
LJ932 NF-N	Crash-landed on approach to Ludford Magna on return from SOE operation to Denmark 29.9.44.
LJ990 NF-O	
LJ993 NF-M	FTR from SOE operation to Norway 8/9.11.44.
LJ999 NF-Q	FTR from SOE operation Denmark 4/5.3.45.
LK119 NF-R	To 161Sqn.
LK125 NF-S	
LK131 NF-T	FTR from SOE operation to Holland 31.8/1.9.44.
LK139 NF-A	
LK143 NF-B	FTR from SOE operation to Denmark 2/3.12.44.
LK145	
LK149 NF-D	FTR from SOE operation to Denmark 23/24. 2.45.
LK151 NF-E	FTR from SOE operation to Denmark 26/27.11.44.
LK192	
LK194	
LK198 NF-H	FTR from SOE operation to Norway 8/9.11.44.
LK200 NF-J	FTR from SOE operation to Holland 8/9.9.44.
LK204 NF-U	
LK206	To 161Sqn 5.9.44.
LK207	To 161Sqn 5.9.44.
LK208	To 161Sqn 5.9.44.
LK209	To 161Sqn 5.9.44.
LK210	To 161Sqn 5.9.44.
LK232	To 299Sqn.
LK235	To 4 OAPU.
LK272 NF-P	FTR from SOE operation to Norway 26/27.2.45.
LK274 NF-N	To 161Sqn 10.3.45.
LK278	From 161Sqn.
LK279 NF-L	FTR from SOE operation to Denmark 9/10.2.45.

LK283 NF-S	FTR from SOE operation to Norway 30/31.12.44.
LK285 NF-T	To 161Sqn 25.3.45.
LK309	
LK329	To 161Sqn 8.3.45.
PW395	To 161Sqn 6.3.45.

LANCASTER. **From March 1945.**

HK606 AC-D	From 186Sqn. To 46MU.
HK615 AC-J	From 622Sqn. To 15MU.
HK661	From 186Sqn. To 10MU.
HK682	From 186Sqn.
HK692 AC-Q	From 186Sqn.
HK694 AC-S	From 186Sqn.
HK792 AC-C	From 149Sqn. To 75Sqn.
LM275 AC-V	From 514Sqn.
LM282	From 218Sqn.
LM544	From 75Sqn. Returned to 75Sqn.
ME350	From 218Sqn.
ME751 AC-R	From 75sqn.
NF966 AC-T	From 514Sqn.
NG224	From 149Sqn. Returned to 149Sqn.
NG248	From 626Sqn.
NG365 AC-K	From XVSqn.
NG407 AC-B	From 149Sqn.
NG409 AC-P	From 149Sqn.
NX571 AC-J/X	
PA193 AC-H	From 149Sqn.
PD370	From 115Sqn.
PP675 AC-F	
PP678	
PP679 AC-L	From 90Sqn.
RF142 AC-A	From 149Sqn.
RF143 AC-O	From 149Sqn. FTR Potsdam 14/15.4.45.

HEAVIEST SINGLE LOSS.

14/15.09.43. 4 Halifaxes FTR.

Glossary

A&AEE	Aeroplane and Armaments Experimental Establishment.
AA	Anti-Aircraft fire.
AACU	Anti-Aircraft Cooperation Unit.
AAS	Air Armament School.
AASF	Advance Air Striking Force.
AAU	Aircraft Assembly Unit.
ACM	Air Chief Marshal.
ACSEA	Air Command South-East Asia.
AFDU	Air Fighting Development Unit.
AFEE	Airborne Forces Experimental Unit.
AFTDU	Airborne Forces Tactical Development Unit.
AGS	Air Gunners School.
AMDP	Air Members for Development and Production.
AOC	Air Officer Commanding.
AOS	Air Observers School.
ASRTU	Air-Sea Rescue Training Unit.
ATTDU	Air Transport Tactical Development Unit.
AVM	Air Vice-Marshal.
BAT	Beam Approach Training.
BCBS	Bomber Command Bombing School.
BCDU	Bomber Command Development Unit.
BCFU	Bomber Command Film Unit.
BCIS	Bomber Command Instructors School.
BDU	Bombing Development Unit.
BSTU	Bomber Support Training Unit.
CF	Conversion Flight.
CFS	Central Flying School.
CGS	Central Gunnery School.
C-in-C	Commander in Chief.
CNS	Central Navigation School.
CO	Commanding Officer.
CRD	Controller of Research and Development.
CU	Conversion Unit.
DGRD	Director General for Research and Development.
EAAS	Empire Air Armament School.
EANS	Empire Air Navigation School.
ECDU	Electronic Countermeasures Development Unit.
ECFS	Empire Central Flying School.
ETPS	Empire Test Pilots School.
F/L	Flight Lieutenant.
Flt	Flight.
F/O	Flying Officer.
FPP	Ferry Pilots School.

F/SGT	Flight Sergeant.
FTR	Failed to Return.
FTU	Ferry Training Unit.
G/C	Group Captain.
Gp	Group.
HCU	Heavy Conversion Unit.
HGCU	Heavy Glider Conversion Unit.
LFS	Lancaster Finishing School.
MAC	Mediterranean Air Command.
MTU	Mosquito Training Unit.
MU	Maintenance Unit.
NTU	Navigation Training Unit.
OADU	Overseas Aircraft Delivery Unit.
OAPU	Overseas Aircraft Preparation Unit.
OTU	Operational Training Unit.
P/O	Pilot Officer.
PTS	Parachute Training School.
RAE	Royal Aircraft Establishment.
SGR	School of General Reconnaissance.
Sgt	Sergeant.
SHAEF	Supreme Headquarters Allied Expeditionary Force.
SIU	Signals Intelligence Unit.
S/L	Squadron Leader.
SOC	Struck off Charge.
SOE	Special Operations Executive.
Sqn	Squadron.
TF	Training Flight.
TFU	Telecommunications Flying Unit.
W/C	Wing Commander.
Wg	Wing.
WIDU	Wireless Intelligence Development Unit.
W/O	Warrant Officer.